D0404318

Table of Contents

by
Osamu Tezuka

translation
Frederik L. Schodt

lettering and retouch
Digital Chameleon

Dark Horse Comics®

publisher
MIKE RICHARDSON

editor
CHRIS WARNER

consulting editor
TOREN SMITH for STUDIO PROTEUS

collection designers
DAVID NESTELLE and LANI SCHREIBSTEIN

English-language version produced by DARK HORSE COMICS and STUDIO PROTEUS

ASTRO BOY® VOLUME 10

The artwork of this volume has been produced as a mirror-image of the original Japanese edition to conform to English-language standards.

Published by
Dark Horse Comics, Inc.
10956 SE Main Street
Milwaukie, OR 97222

www.darkhorse.com

To find a comics shop in your area, call the Comic Shop Locator Service toll-free at 1-888-266-4226.

First edition: December 2002
ISBN: 1-56971-793-1

10 9 8 7 6 5 4 3 2 1
Printed in Canada

A NOTE TO READERS

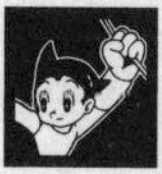

Many non-Japanese, including people from Africa and Southeast Asia, appear in Osamu Tezuka's works. Sometimes these people are depicted very differently from the way they actually are today, in a manner that exaggerates a time long past or shows them to be from extremely undeveloped lands. Some feel that such images contribute to racial discrimination, especially against people of African descent. This was never Osamu Tezuka's intent, but we believe that as long as there are people who feel insulted or demeaned by these depictions, we must not ignore their feelings.

We are against discrimination, in all its forms, and intend to continue to work for its elimination. Nonetheless, we do not believe it would be proper to revise these works. Tezuka is no longer with us, and we cannot erase what he has done, and to alter his work would only violate his rights as a creator. More importantly, stopping publication or changing the content of his work would do little to solve the problems of discrimination that exist in the world.

We are presenting Osamu Tezuka's work as it was originally created, without changes. We do this because we believe it is also important to promote the underlying themes in his work, such as love for mankind and the sanctity of life. We hope that when you, the reader, encounter this work, you will keep in mind the differences in attitudes, then and now, toward discrimination, and that this will contribute to an even greater awareness of such problems.

— Tezuka Productions and Dark Horse Comics

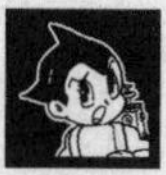

ASTRO VS. GARON

First serialized from October 1962 to February 1963 in *Shonen* magazine.

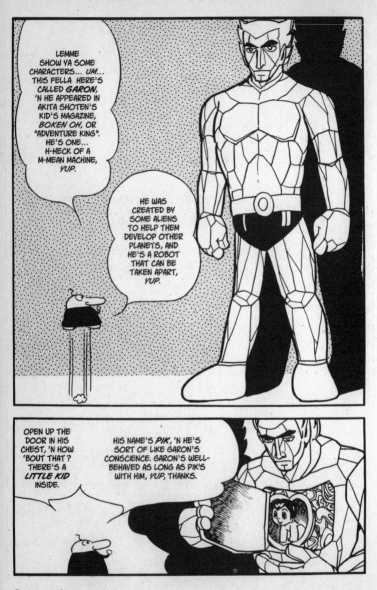

LEMME SHOW YA SOME CHARACTERS... *UM*... THIS FELLA HERE'S CALLED *GARON*, 'N HE APPEARED IN AKITA SHOTEN'S KID'S MAGAZINE, *BOKEN OH*, OR "ADVENTURE KING". HE'S ONE... H-HECK OF A M-MEAN MACHINE, *YUP*.

HE WAS CREATED BY SOME ALIENS TO HELP THEM DEVELOP OTHER PLANETS, AND HE'S A ROBOT THAT CAN BE TAKEN APART, *YUP*.

OPEN UP THE DOOR IN HIS CHEST, 'N HOW 'BOUT THAT? THERE'S A *LITTLE KID* INSIDE.

HIS NAME'S *PIK*, 'N HE'S SORT OF LIKE GARON'S CONSCIENCE. GARON'S WELL-BEHAVED AS LONG AS PIK'S WITH HIM, *YUP*, THANKS.

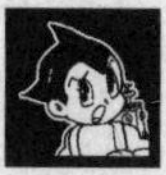

ASTRO VS. GARON

First serialized from October 1962 to February 1963 in *Shonen* magazine.

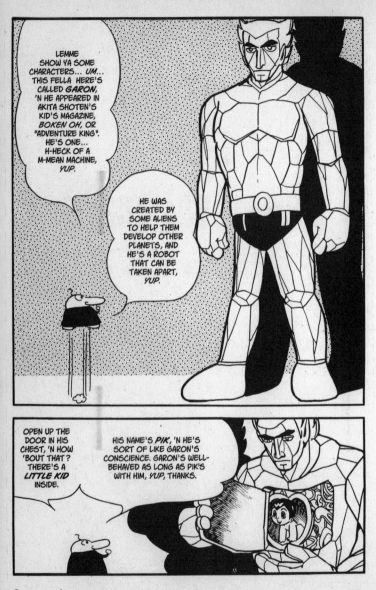

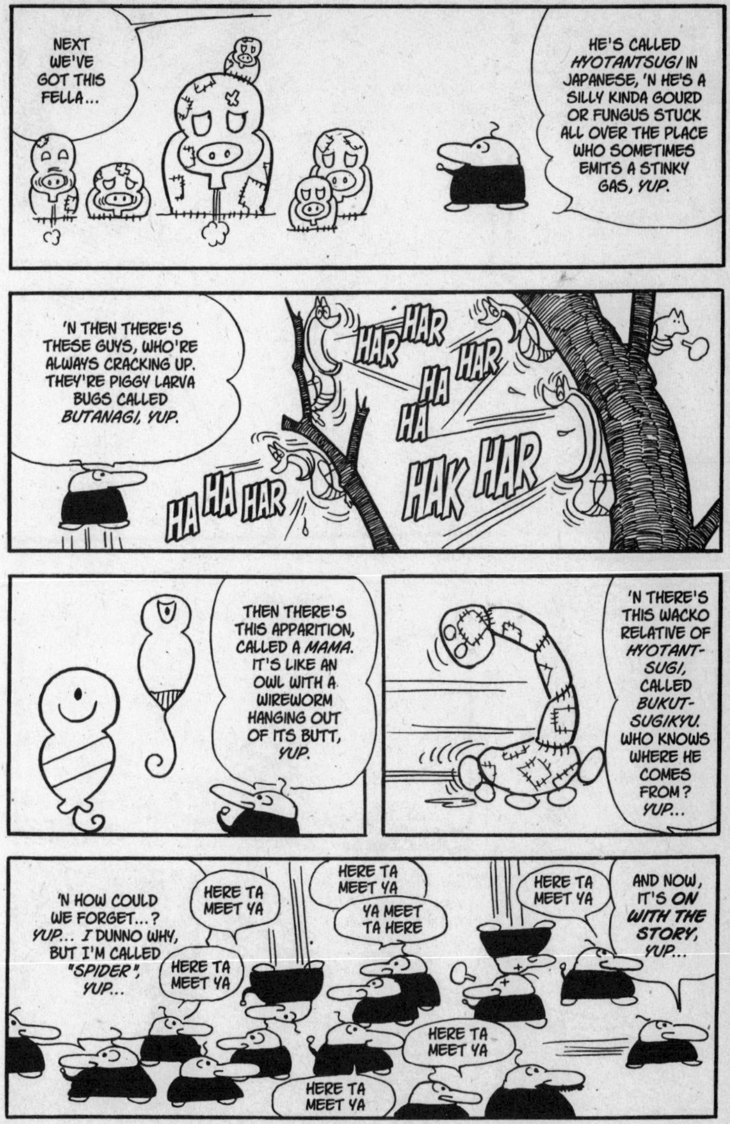
NEXT WE'VE GOT THIS FELLA...
HE'S CALLED *HYOTANTSUGI* IN JAPANESE, 'N HE'S A SILLY KINDA GOURD OR FUNGUS STUCK ALL OVER THE PLACE WHO SOMETIMES EMITS A STINKY GAS, *YUP*.
'N THEN THERE'S THESE GUYS, WHO'RE ALWAYS CRACKING UP. THEY'RE PIGGY LARVA BUGS CALLED *BUTANAGI, YUP*.
HAR HAR
HA HAR
HA
HA HA HAR
HAK HAR
THEN THERE'S THIS APPARITION, CALLED A *MAMA*. IT'S LIKE AN OWL WITH A WIREWORM HANGING OUT OF ITS BUTT, *YUP*.
'N THERE'S THIS WACKO RELATIVE OF *HYOTANT-SUGI*, CALLED *BUKUT-SUGIKYU*. WHO KNOWS WHERE HE COMES FROM? *YUP*...
'N HOW COULD WE FORGET...? *YUP*... *I* DUNNO WHY, BUT I'M CALLED *"SPIDER"*, *YUP*...
HERE TA MEET YA
HERE TA MEET YA
HERE TA MEET YA
YA MEET TA HERE
HERE TA MEET YA
HERE TA MEET YA
HERE TA MEET YA
AND NOW, IT'S *ON WITH THE STORY*, *YUP*...

10

9

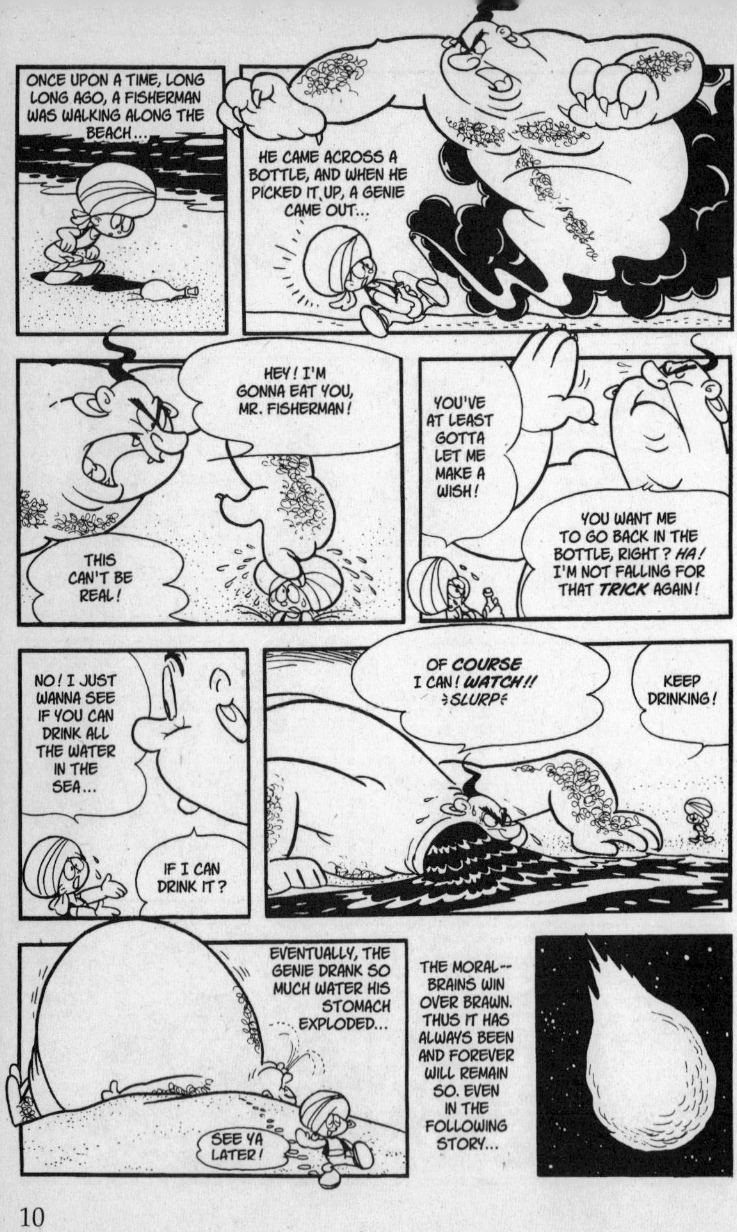

ONCE UPON A TIME, LONG LONG AGO, A FISHERMAN WAS WALKING ALONG THE BEACH...
HE CAME ACROSS A BOTTLE, AND WHEN HE PICKED IT UP, A GENIE CAME OUT...
HEY! I'M GONNA EAT YOU, MR. FISHERMAN!
THIS CAN'T BE REAL!
YOU'VE AT LEAST GOTTA LET ME MAKE A WISH!
YOU WANT ME TO GO BACK IN THE BOTTLE, RIGHT? HA! I'M NOT FALLING FOR THAT TRICK AGAIN!
NO! I JUST WANNA SEE IF YOU CAN DRINK ALL THE WATER IN THE SEA...
IF I CAN DRINK IT?
OF COURSE I CAN! WATCH!! ≷SLURP≶
KEEP DRINKING!
EVENTUALLY, THE GENIE DRANK SO MUCH WATER HIS STOMACH EXPLODED...
SEE YA LATER!
THE MORAL-- BRAINS WIN OVER BRAWN. THUS IT HAS ALWAYS BEEN AND FOREVER WILL REMAIN SO. EVEN IN THE FOLLOWING STORY...

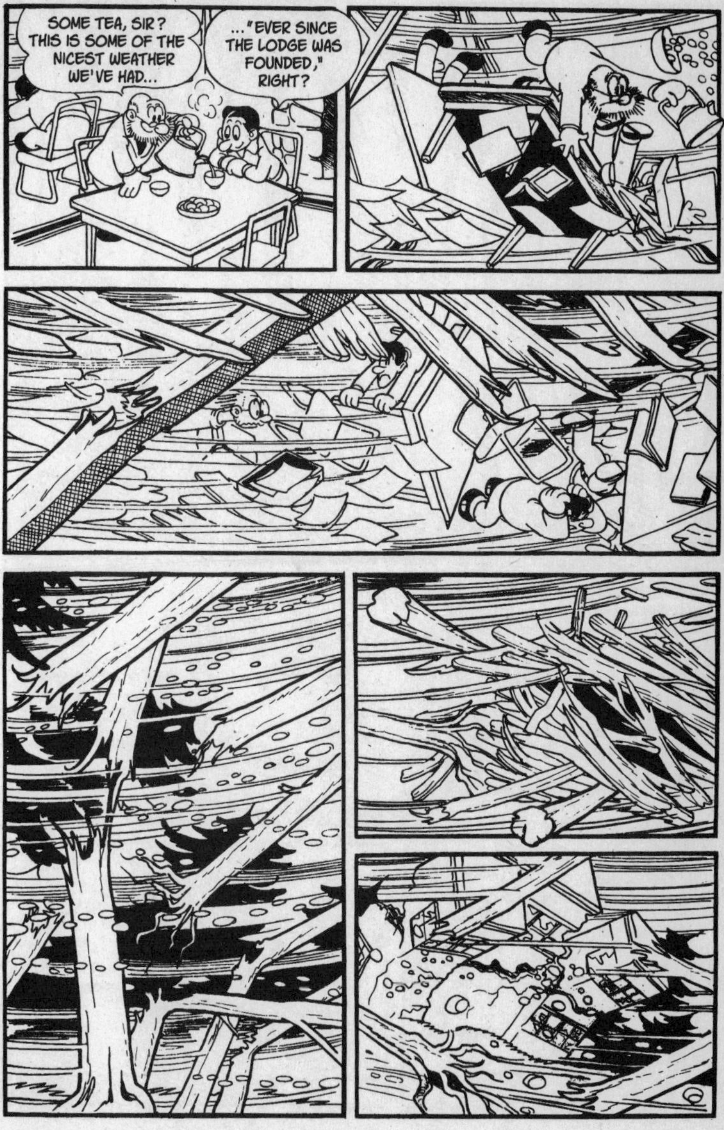
SOME TEA, SIR? THIS IS SOME OF THE NICEST WEATHER WE'VE HAD...
..."EVER SINCE THE LODGE WAS FOUNDED," RIGHT?

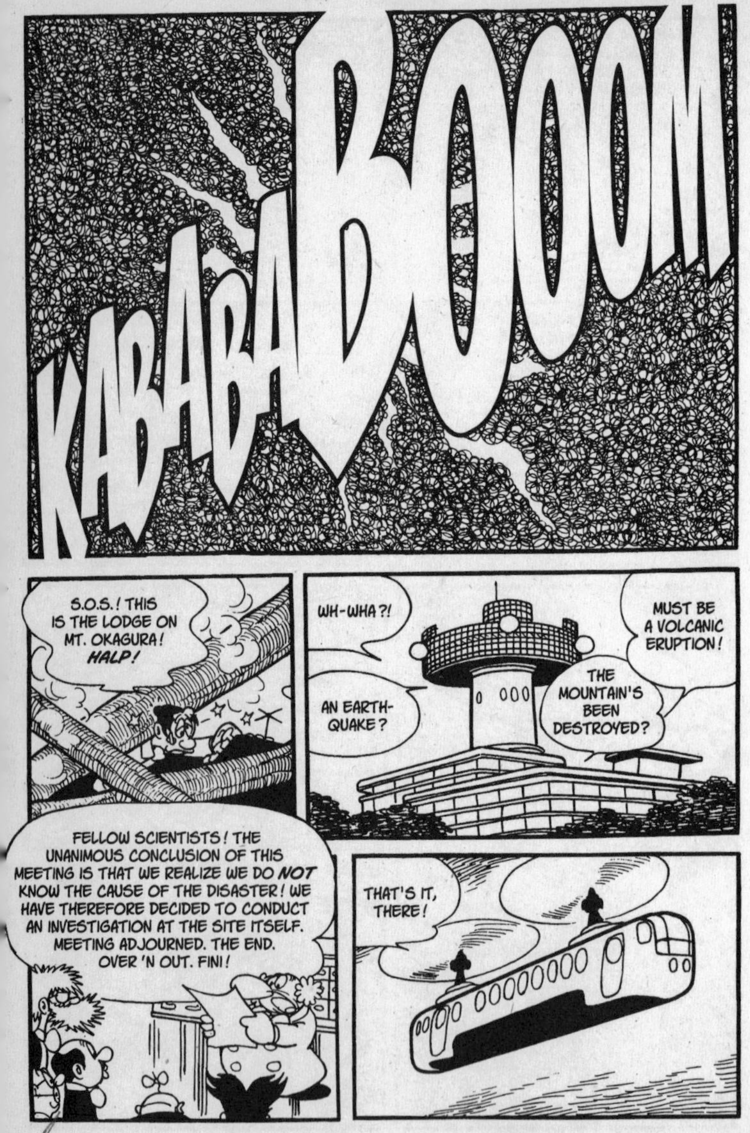

KABABABOOOM
S.O.S.! THIS IS THE LODGE ON MT. OKAGURA! ***HALP!***
WH-WHA?!
MUST BE A VOLCANIC ERUPTION!
AN EARTH-QUAKE?
THE MOUNTAIN'S BEEN DESTROYED?
FELLOW SCIENTISTS! THE UNANIMOUS CONCLUSION OF THIS MEETING IS THAT WE REALIZE WE DO ***NOT*** KNOW THE CAUSE OF THE DISASTER! WE HAVE THEREFORE DECIDED TO CONDUCT AN INVESTIGATION AT THE SITE ITSELF. MEETING ADJOURNED. THE END. OVER 'N OUT. FINI!
THAT'S IT, THERE!

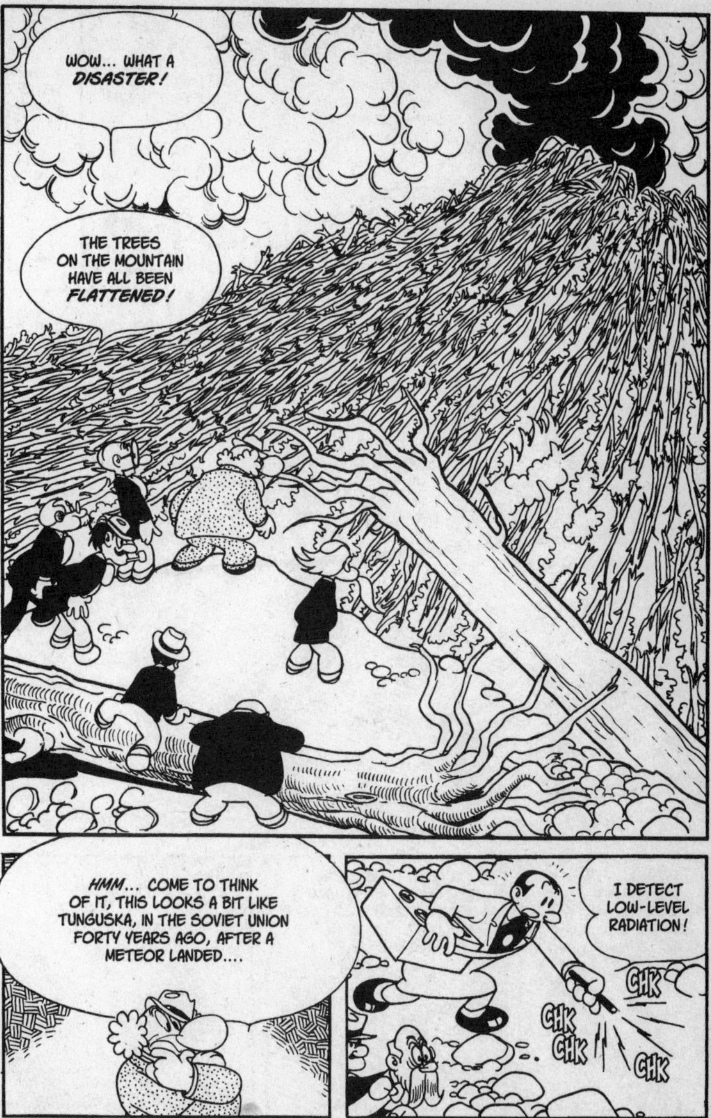
WOW... WHAT A DISASTER!
THE TREES ON THE MOUNTAIN HAVE ALL BEEN FLATTENED!
HMM... COME TO THINK OF IT, THIS LOOKS A BIT LIKE TUNGUSKA, IN THE SOVIET UNION FORTY YEARS AGO, AFTER A METEOR LANDED....
I DETECT LOW-LEVEL RADIATION!
CHK
CHK
CHK
CHK

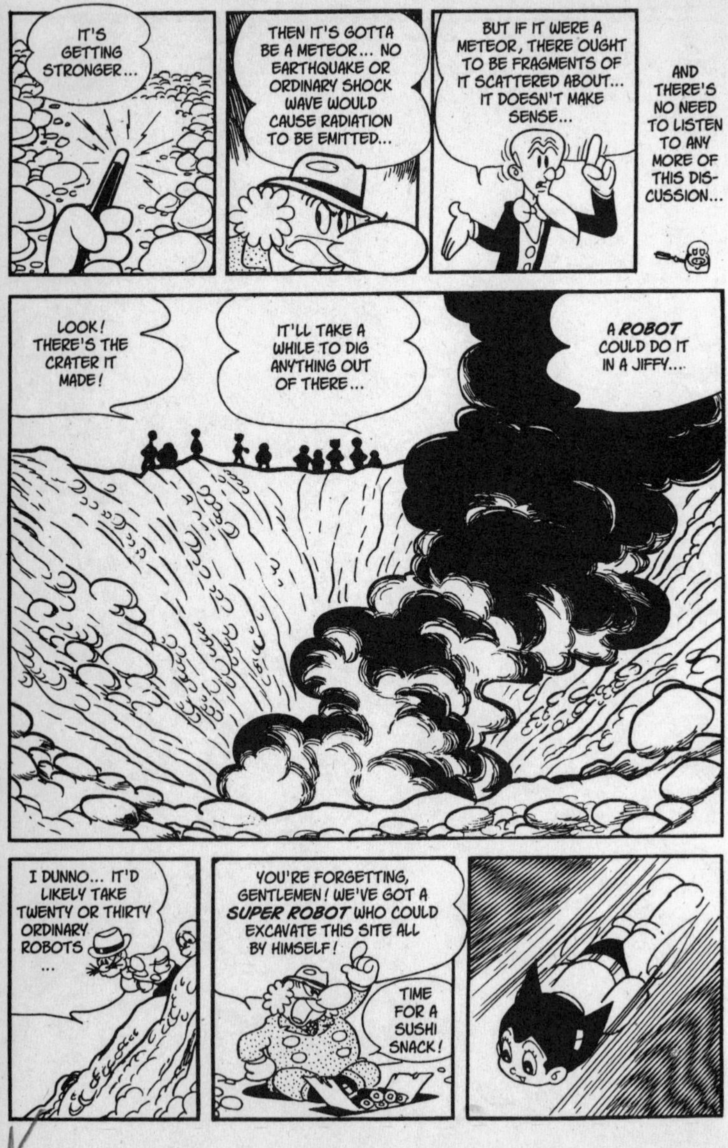
IT'S GETTING STRONGER...
THEN IT'S GOTTA BE A METEOR... NO EARTHQUAKE OR ORDINARY SHOCK WAVE WOULD CAUSE RADIATION TO BE EMITTED...
BUT IF IT WERE A METEOR, THERE OUGHT TO BE FRAGMENTS OF IT SCATTERED ABOUT... IT DOESN'T MAKE SENSE...
AND THERE'S NO NEED TO LISTEN TO ANY MORE OF THIS DIS-CUSSION...
LOOK! THERE'S THE CRATER IT MADE!
IT'LL TAKE A WHILE TO DIG ANYTHING OUT OF THERE...
A ROBOT COULD DO IT IN A JIFFY....
I DUNNO... IT'D LIKELY TAKE TWENTY OR THIRTY ORDINARY ROBOTS ...
YOU'RE FORGETTING, GENTLEMEN! WE'VE GOT A SUPER ROBOT WHO COULD EXCAVATE THIS SITE ALL BY HIMSELF!
TIME FOR A SUSHI SNACK!

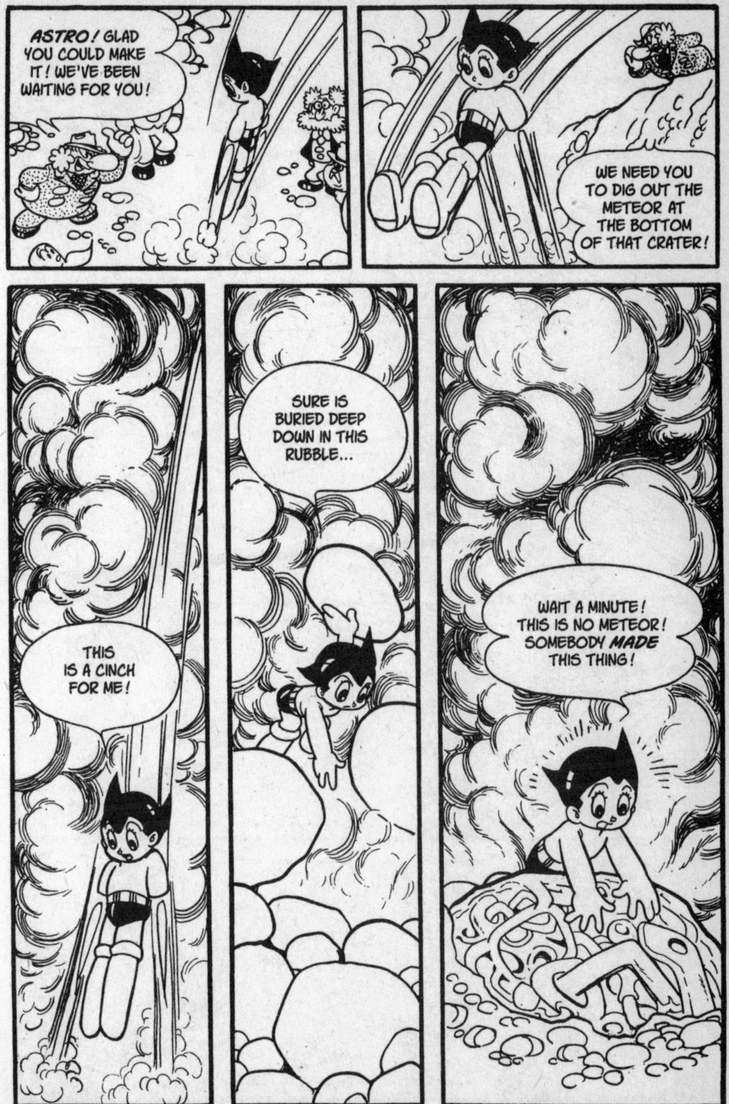
ASTRO! GLAD YOU COULD MAKE IT! WE'VE BEEN WAITING FOR YOU!
WE NEED YOU TO DIG OUT THE METEOR AT THE BOTTOM OF THAT CRATER!
THIS IS A CINCH FOR ME!
SURE IS BURIED DEEP DOWN IN THIS RUBBLE...
WAIT A MINUTE! THIS IS NO METEOR! SOMEBODY MADE THIS THING!

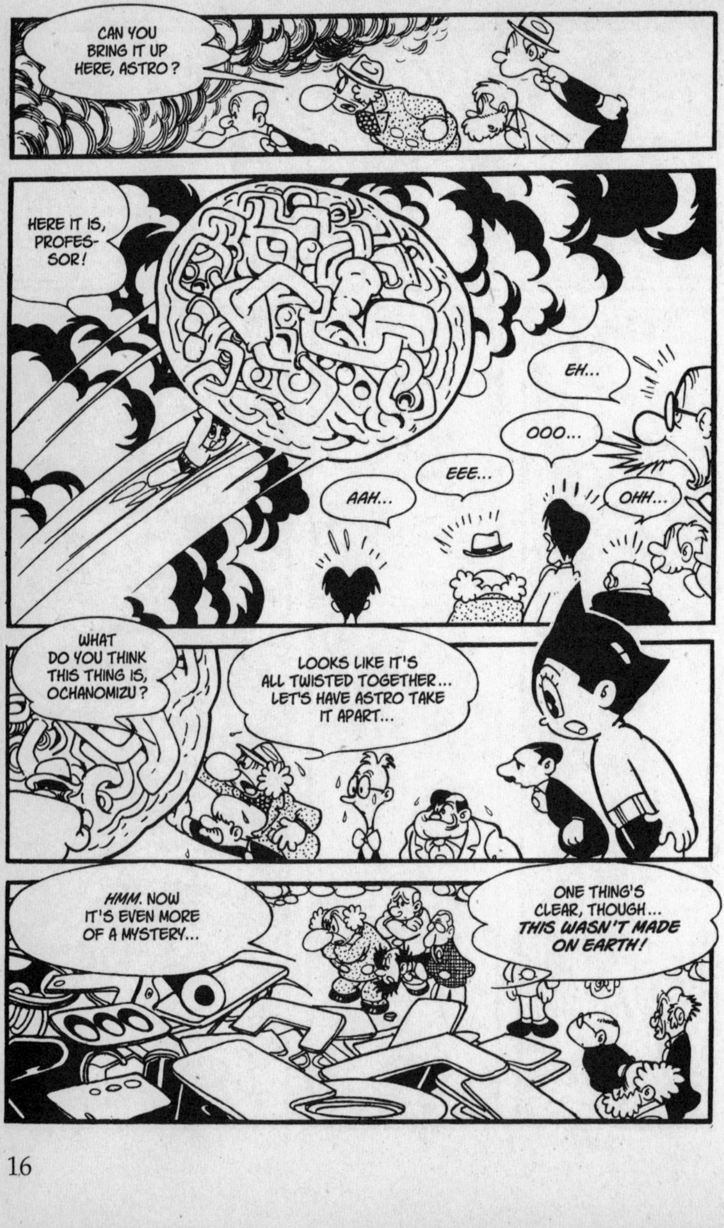
CAN YOU BRING IT UP HERE, ASTRO?
HERE IT IS, PROFES-SOR!
EH...
OOO...
EEE...
AAH...
OHH...
WHAT DO YOU THINK THIS THING IS, OCHANOMIZU?
LOOKS LIKE IT'S ALL TWISTED TOGETHER... LET'S HAVE ASTRO TAKE IT APART...
HMM. NOW IT'S EVEN MORE OF A MYSTERY...
ONE THING'S CLEAR, THOUGH... ***THIS WASN'T MADE ON EARTH!***

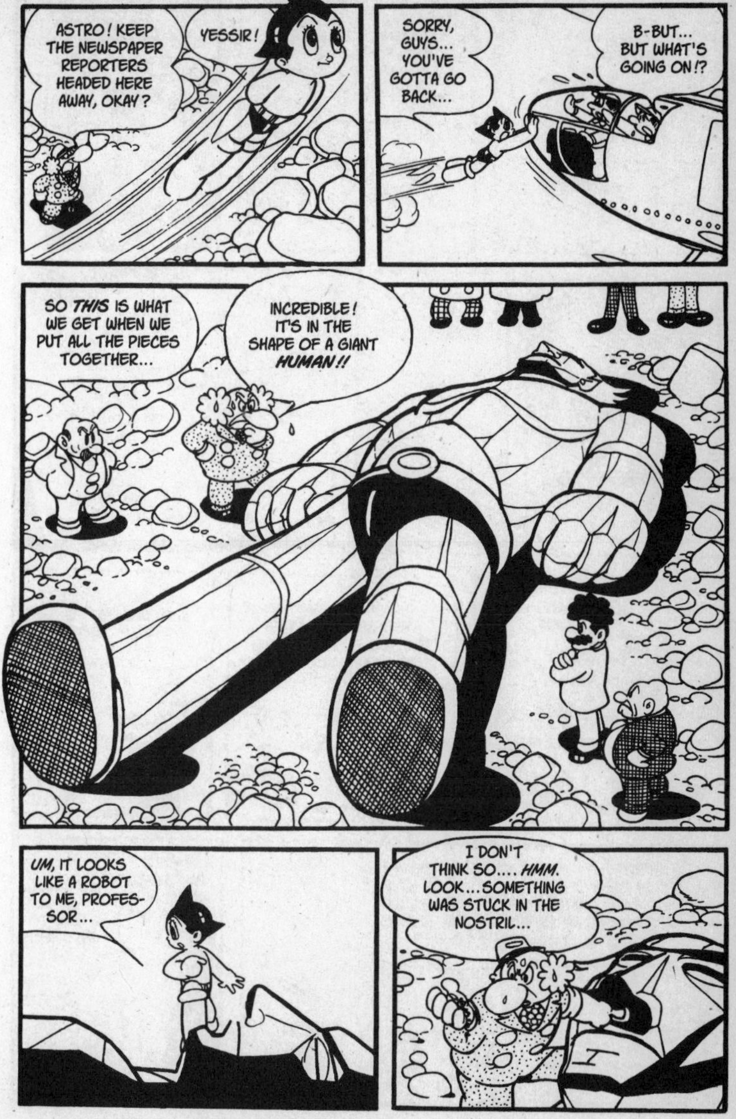
ASTRO! KEEP THE NEWSPAPER REPORTERS HEADED HERE AWAY, OKAY?
YESSIR!
SORRY, GUYS... YOU'VE GOTTA GO BACK...
B-BUT... BUT WHAT'S GOING ON!?
SO *THIS* IS WHAT WE GET WHEN WE PUT ALL THE PIECES TOGETHER...
INCREDIBLE! IT'S IN THE SHAPE OF A GIANT *HUMAN!!*
UM, IT LOOKS LIKE A ROBOT TO ME, PROFES-SOR...
I DON'T THINK SO.... *HMM.* LOOK...SOMETHING WAS STUCK IN THE NOSTRIL...

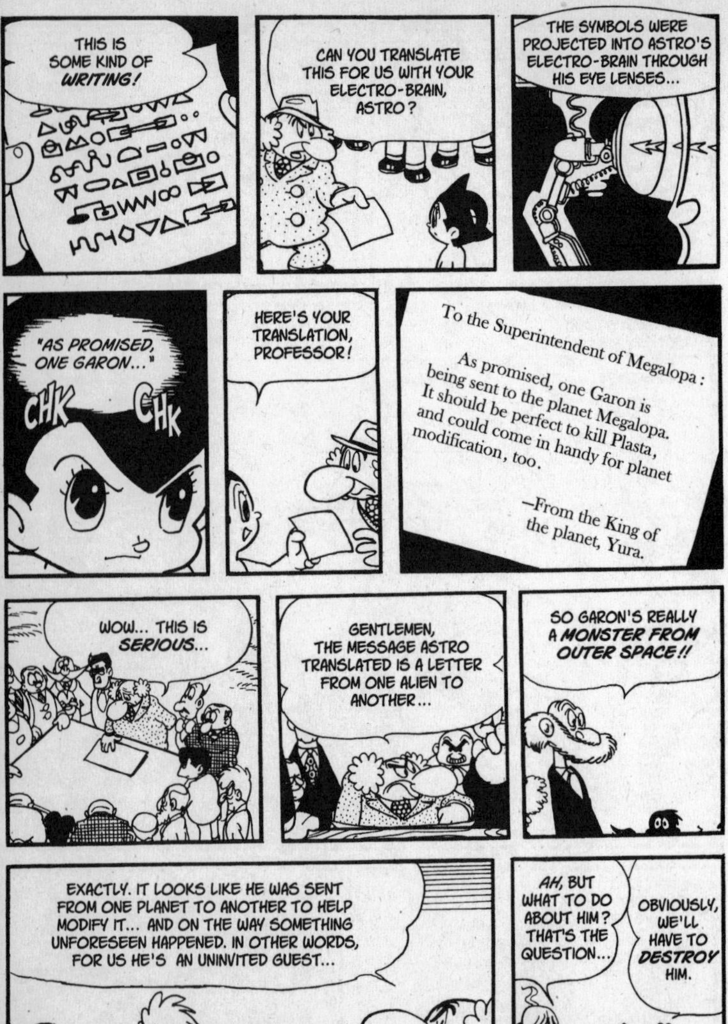
THIS IS SOME KIND OF WRITING!
CAN YOU TRANSLATE THIS FOR US WITH YOUR ELECTRO-BRAIN, ASTRO?
THE SYMBOLS WERE PROJECTED INTO ASTRO'S ELECTRO-BRAIN THROUGH HIS EYE LENSES...
"AS PROMISED, ONE GARON..."
CHK
CHK
HERE'S YOUR TRANSLATION, PROFESSOR!
To the Superintendent of Megalopa :
As promised, one Garon is being sent to the planet Megalopa. It should be perfect to kill Plasta, and could come in handy for planet modification, too.
–From the King of the planet, Yura.
WOW... THIS IS SERIOUS...
GENTLEMEN, THE MESSAGE ASTRO TRANSLATED IS A LETTER FROM ONE ALIEN TO ANOTHER...
SO GARON'S REALLY A MONSTER FROM OUTER SPACE!!
EXACTLY. IT LOOKS LIKE HE WAS SENT FROM ONE PLANET TO ANOTHER TO HELP MODIFY IT... AND ON THE WAY SOMETHING UNFORESEEN HAPPENED. IN OTHER WORDS, FOR US HE'S AN UNINVITED GUEST...
AH, BUT WHAT TO DO ABOUT HIM? THAT'S THE QUESTION...
OBVIOUSLY, WE'LL HAVE TO DESTROY HIM.

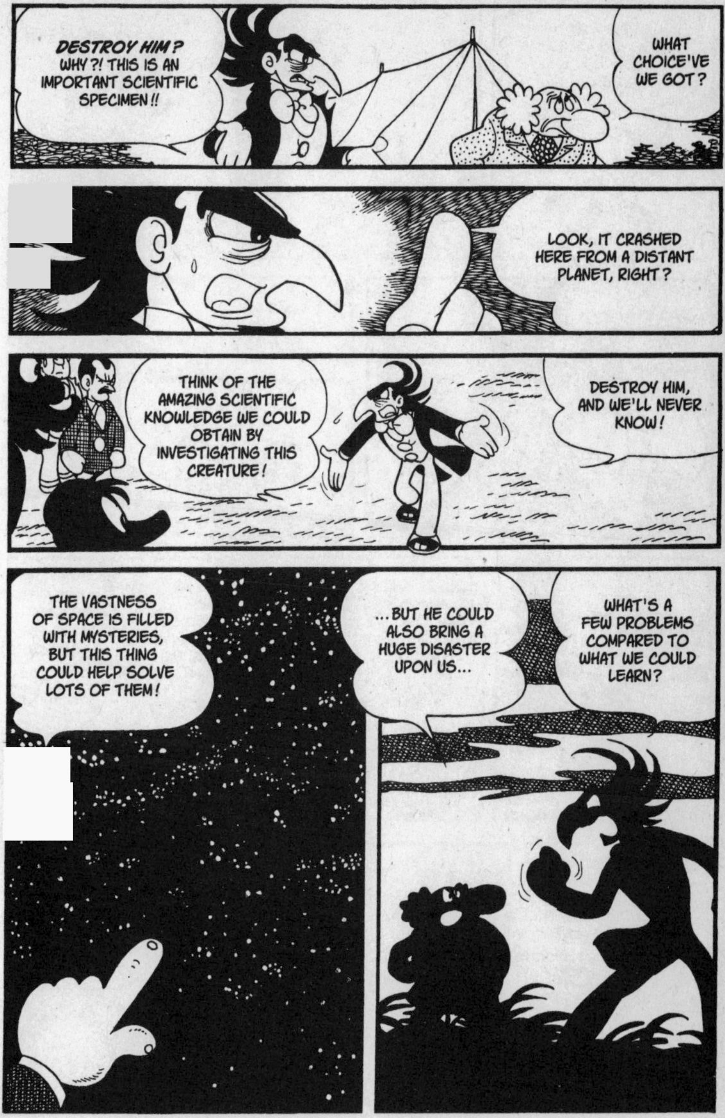
DESTROY HIM? WHY?! THIS IS AN IMPORTANT SCIENTIFIC SPECIMEN!!
WHAT CHOICE'VE WE GOT?
LOOK, IT CRASHED HERE FROM A DISTANT PLANET, RIGHT?
THINK OF THE AMAZING SCIENTIFIC KNOWLEDGE WE COULD OBTAIN BY INVESTIGATING THIS CREATURE!
DESTROY HIM, AND WE'LL NEVER KNOW!
THE VASTNESS OF SPACE IS FILLED WITH MYSTERIES, BUT THIS THING COULD HELP SOLVE LOTS OF THEM!
...BUT HE COULD ALSO BRING A HUGE DISASTER UPON US...
WHAT'S A FEW PROBLEMS COMPARED TO WHAT WE COULD LEARN?

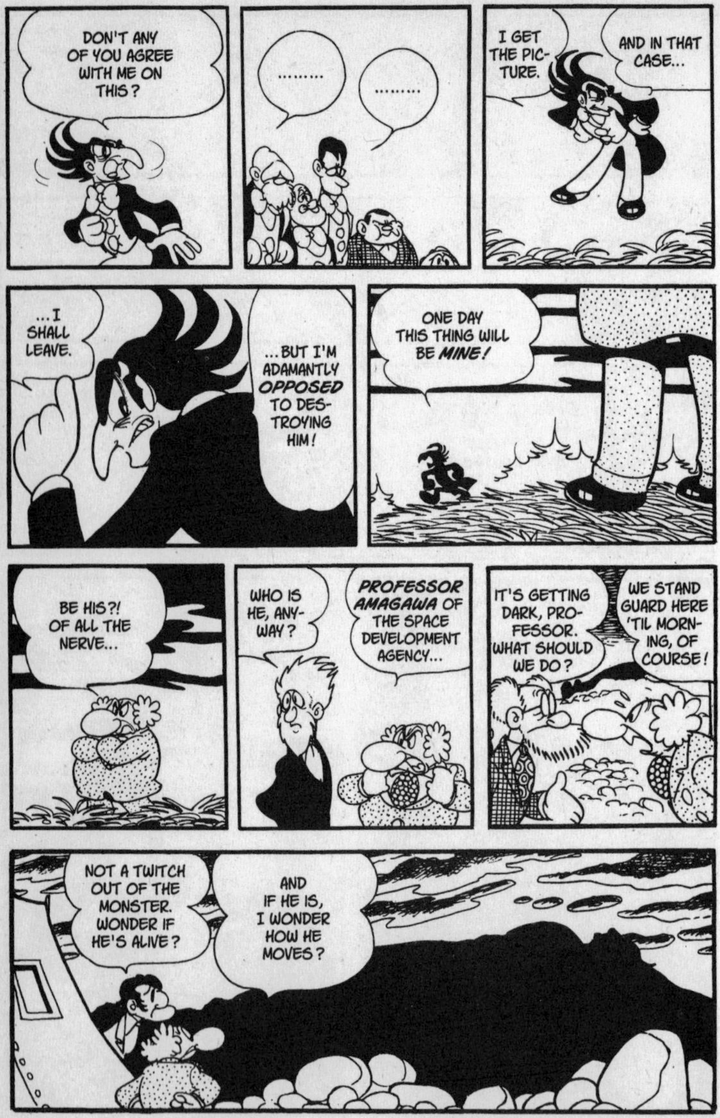
DON'T ANY OF YOU AGREE WITH ME ON THIS?
....
....
I GET THE PIC-TURE.
AND IN THAT CASE...
...I SHALL LEAVE.
...BUT I'M ADAMANTLY *OPPOSED* TO DES-TROYING HIM!
ONE DAY THIS THING WILL BE *MINE!*
BE HIS?! OF ALL THE NERVE...
WHO IS HE, ANY-WAY?
PROFESSOR AMAGAWA OF THE SPACE DEVELOPMENT AGENCY...
IT'S GETTING DARK, PRO-FESSOR. WHAT SHOULD WE DO?
WE STAND GUARD HERE 'TIL MORN-ING, OF COURSE!
NOT A TWITCH OUT OF THE MONSTER. WONDER IF HE'S ALIVE?
AND IF HE IS, I WONDER HOW HE MOVES?

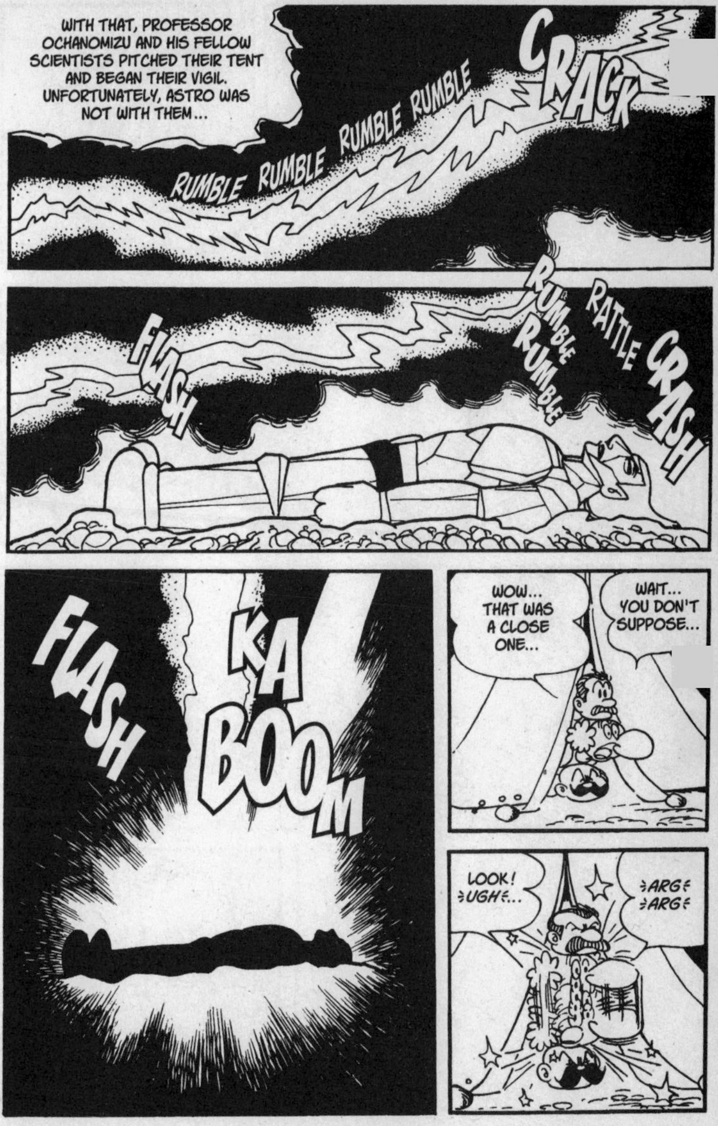
WITH THAT, PROFESSOR OCHANOMIZU AND HIS FELLOW SCIENTISTS PITCHED THEIR TENT AND BEGAN THEIR VIGIL. UNFORTUNATELY, ASTRO WAS NOT WITH THEM...
RUMBLE RUMBLE RUMBLE RUMBLE
CRACK
FLASH
RUMBLE RUMBLE
RATTLE
CRASH
FLASH
KA BOOM
WOW... THAT WAS A CLOSE ONE...
WAIT... YOU DON'T SUPPOSE...
LOOK! UGH...
ARG ARG

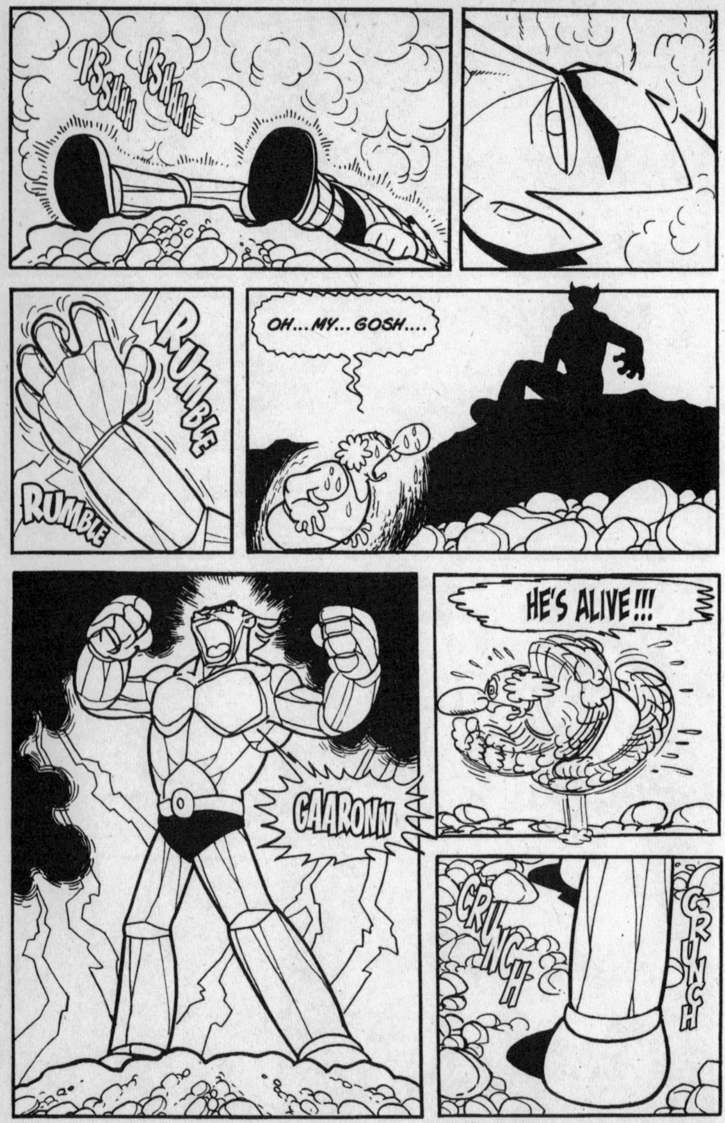
PSSHHH
PSHHHH
RUMBLE
RUMBLE
OH... MY... GOSH....
GAARONN
HE'S ALIVE!!!
CRUNCH
CRUNCH

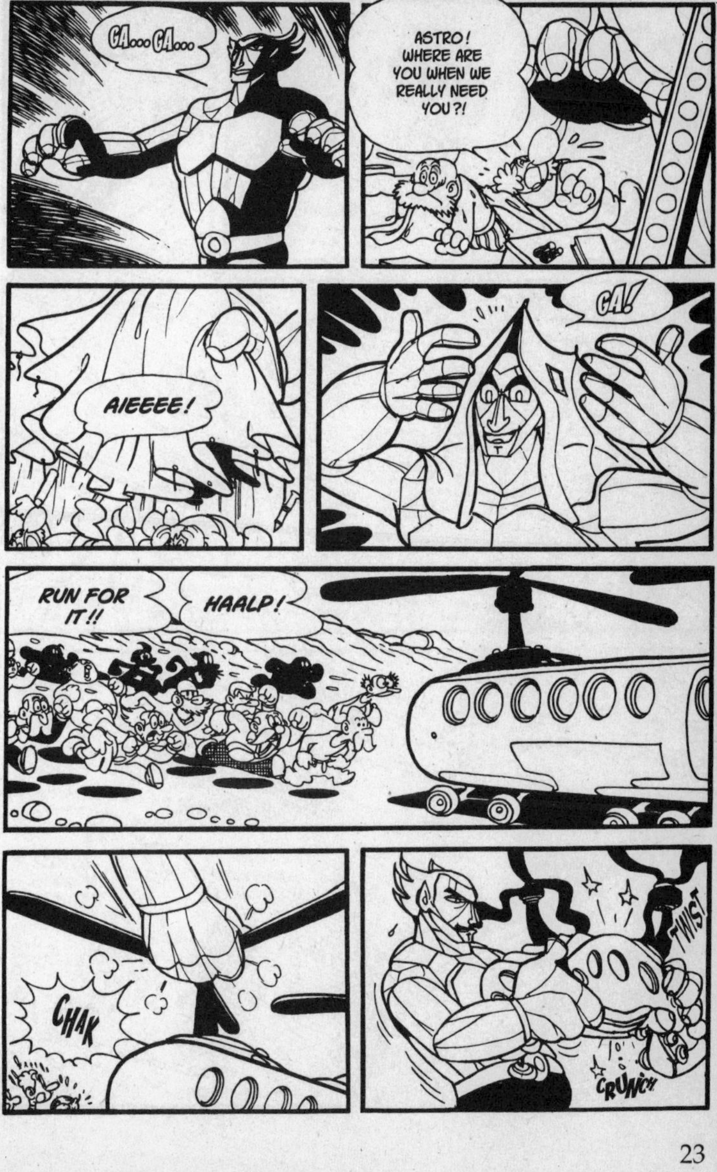
GA... GA...
ASTRO! WHERE ARE YOU WHEN WE REALLY NEED YOU?!
AIEEEE!
GA!
RUN FOR IT!!
HAALP!
CHAK
TWIST
CRUNCH

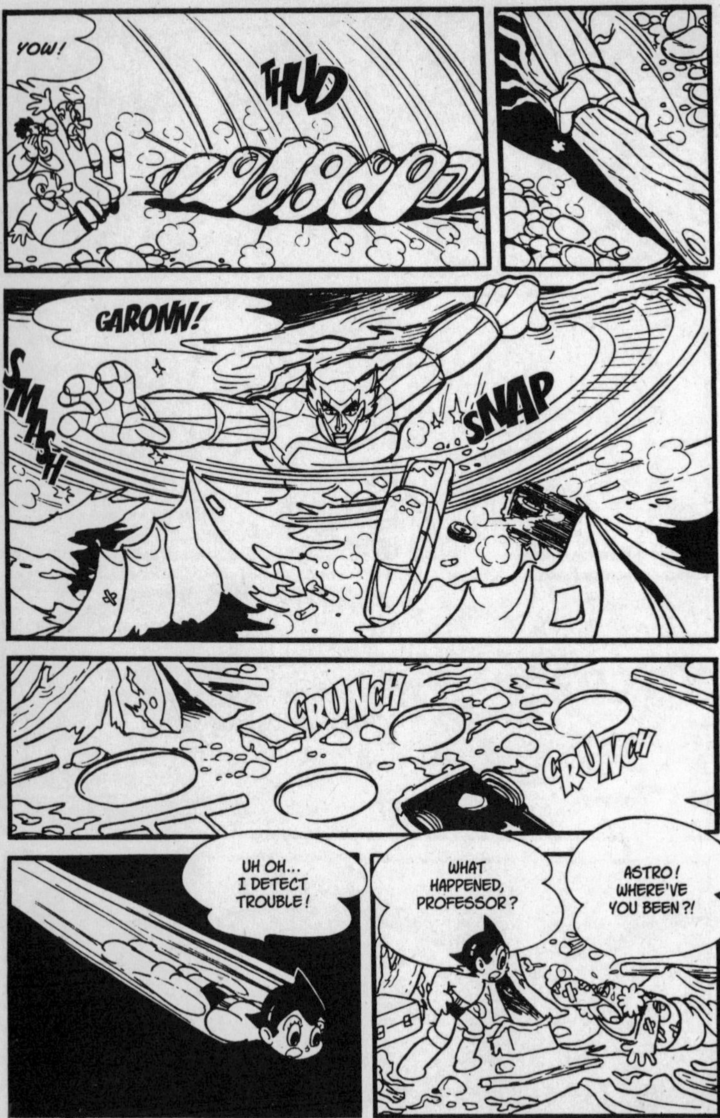
YOW!
THUD
GARONN!
SMASH
SNAP
CRUNCH
CRUNCH
UH OH... I DETECT TROUBLE!
WHAT HAPPENED, PROFESSOR?
ASTRO! WHERE'VE YOU BEEN?!

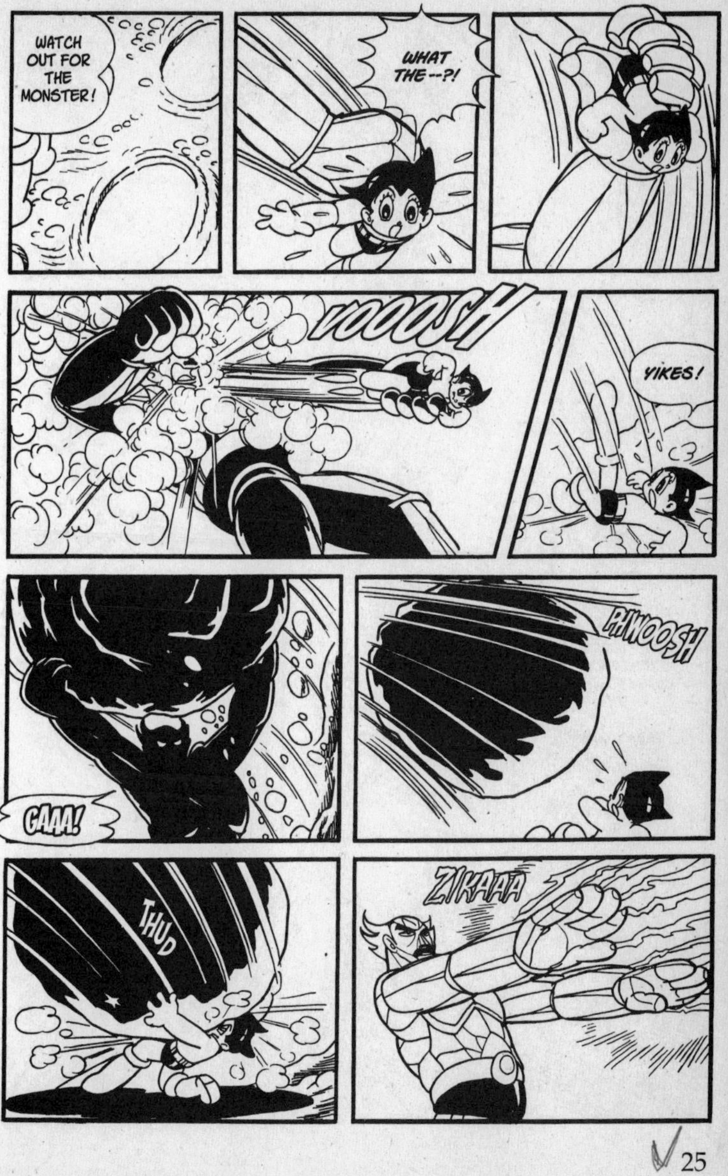
WATCH OUT FOR THE MONSTER!
WHAT THE--?!
VOOOSH
YIKES!
GAAA!
PHWOOSH
THUD
ZIKAAA

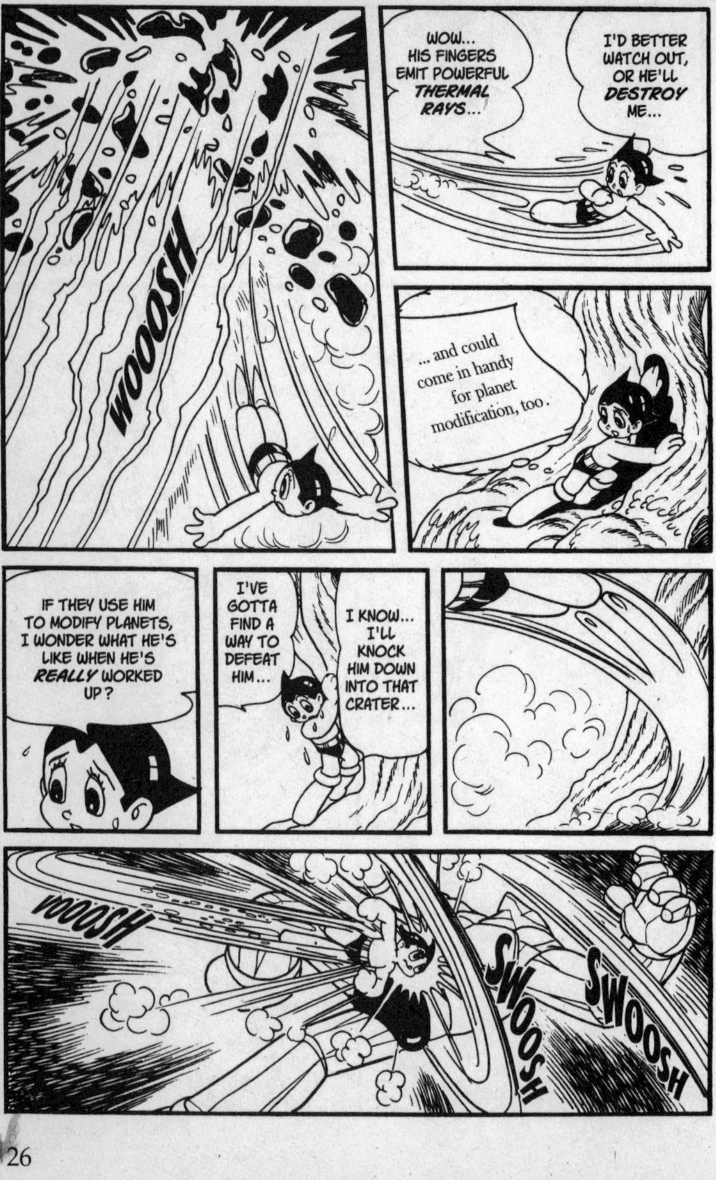
WOOOSH
WOW... HIS FINGERS EMIT POWERFUL *THERMAL RAYS*...
I'D BETTER WATCH OUT, OR HE'LL *DESTROY* ME...
... and could come in handy for planet modification, too.
IF THEY USE HIM TO MODIFY PLANETS, I WONDER WHAT HE'S LIKE WHEN HE'S *REALLY* WORKED UP?
I'VE GOTTA FIND A WAY TO DEFEAT HIM...
I KNOW... I'LL KNOCK HIM DOWN INTO THAT CRATER...
VOOOSH
SWOOSH
SWOOSH

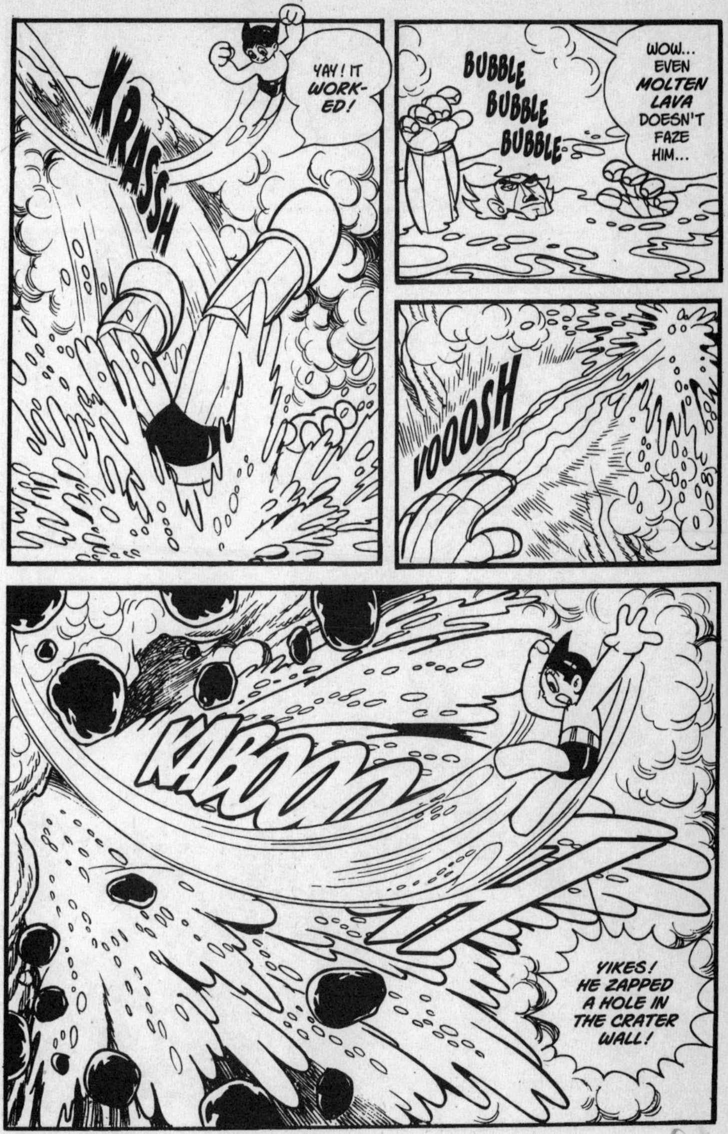
KRASSH
YAY! IT WORKED!
BUBBLE BUBBLE BUBBLE
WOW... EVEN MOLTEN LAVA DOESN'T FAZE HIM...
VOOOSH
KABOOM
YIKES! HE ZAPPED A HOLE IN THE CRATER WALL!

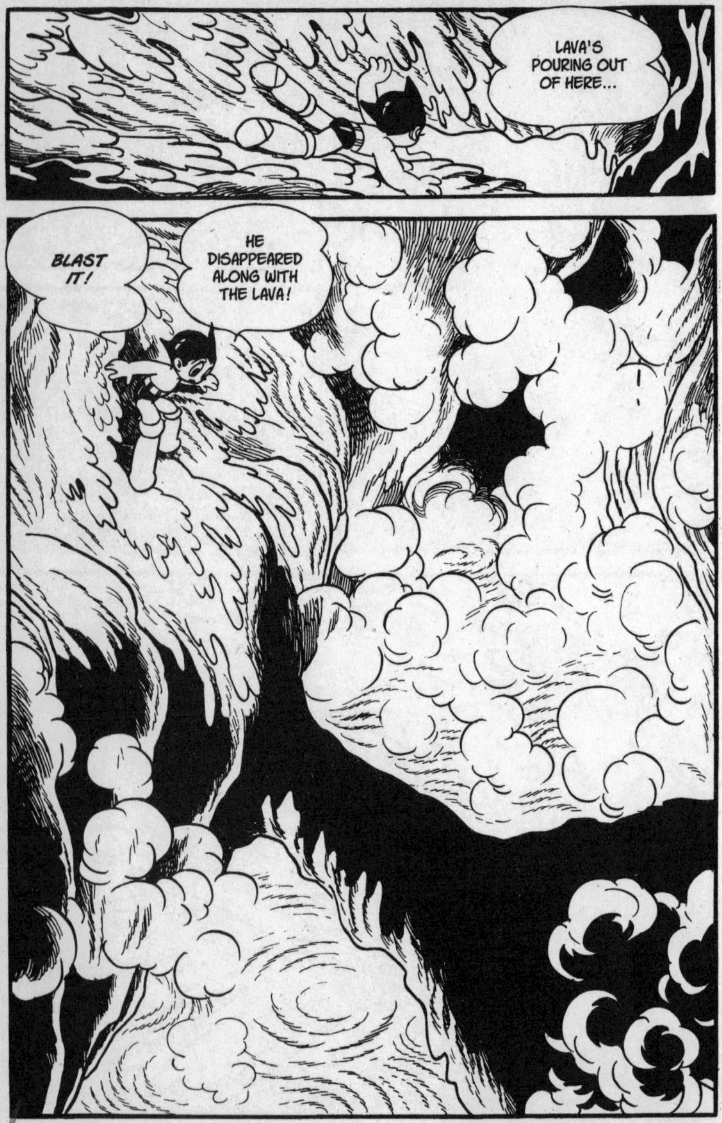
LAVA'S POURING OUT OF HERE...
BLAST IT!
HE DISAPPEARED ALONG WITH THE LAVA!

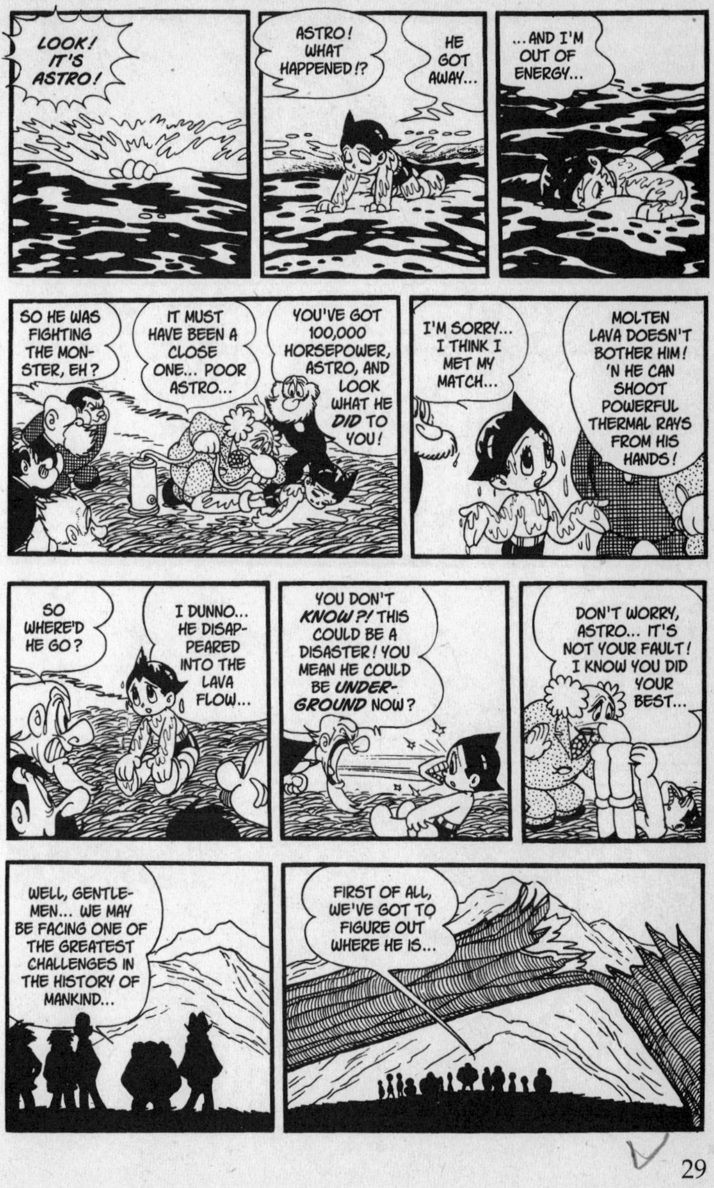
LOOK! IT'S ASTRO!
ASTRO! WHAT HAPPENED!?
HE GOT AWAY...
...AND I'M OUT OF ENERGY...
SO HE WAS FIGHTING THE MON-STER, EH?
IT MUST HAVE BEEN A CLOSE ONE... POOR ASTRO...
YOU'VE GOT 100,000 HORSEPOWER, ASTRO, AND LOOK WHAT HE DID TO YOU!
I'M SORRY... I THINK I MET MY MATCH...
MOLTEN LAVA DOESN'T BOTHER HIM! 'N HE CAN SHOOT POWERFUL THERMAL RAYS FROM HIS HANDS!
SO WHERE'D HE GO?
I DUNNO... HE DISAP-PEARED INTO THE LAVA FLOW...
YOU DON'T KNOW?! THIS COULD BE A DISASTER! YOU MEAN HE COULD BE UNDER-GROUND NOW?
DON'T WORRY, ASTRO... IT'S NOT YOUR FAULT! I KNOW YOU DID YOUR BEST...
WELL, GENTLE-MEN... WE MAY BE FACING ONE OF THE GREATEST CHALLENGES IN THE HISTORY OF MANKIND...
FIRST OF ALL, WE'VE GOT TO FIGURE OUT WHERE HE IS...

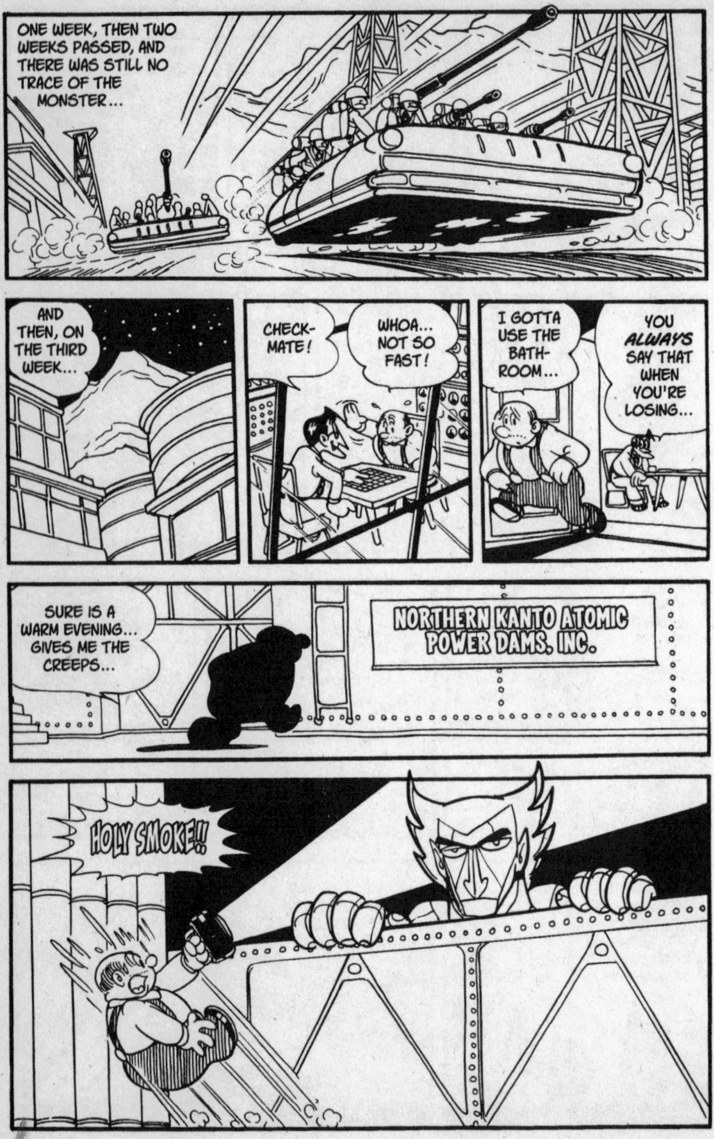
ONE WEEK, THEN TWO WEEKS PASSED, AND THERE WAS STILL NO TRACE OF THE MONSTER...
AND THEN, ON THE THIRD WEEK...
CHECK-MATE!
WHOA... NOT SO FAST!
I GOTTA USE THE BATH-ROOM...
YOU *ALWAYS* SAY THAT WHEN YOU'RE LOSING...
SURE IS A WARM EVENING... GIVES ME THE CREEPS...
NORTHERN KANTO ATOMIC POWER DAMS, INC.
HOLY SMOKE!!

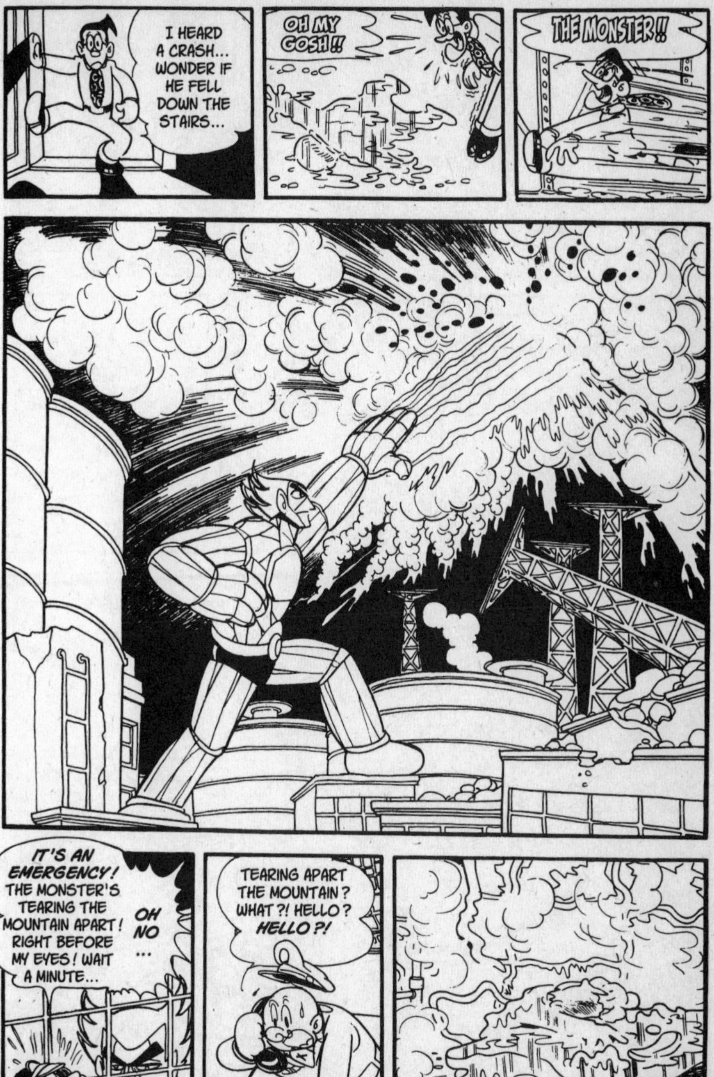
I HEARD A CRASH... WONDER IF HE FELL DOWN THE STAIRS...
OH MY GOSH!!
THE MONSTER!!
IT'S AN EMERGENCY! THE MONSTER'S TEARING THE MOUNTAIN APART! RIGHT BEFORE MY EYES! WAIT A MINUTE...
OH NO ...
TEARING APART THE MOUNTAIN? WHAT?! HELLO? HELLO?!

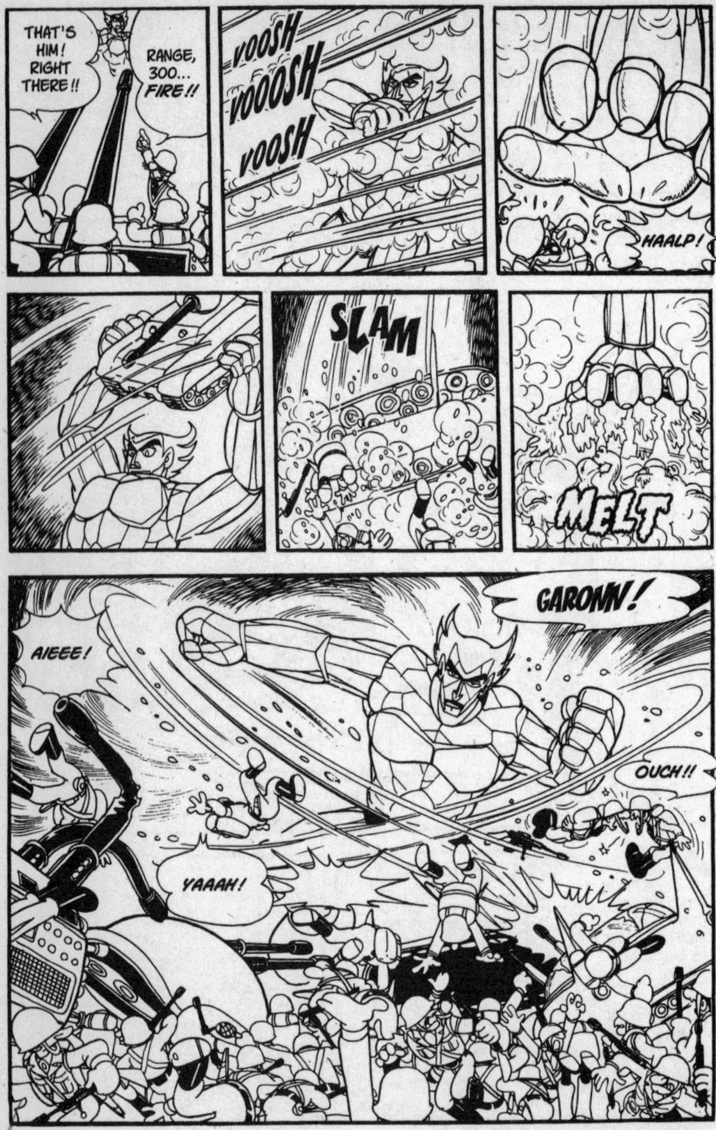
THAT'S HIM! RIGHT THERE!!
RANGE, 300... FIRE!!
VOOSH
VOOOSH
VOOSH
HAALP!
SLAM
MELT
GARONN!
AIEEE!
OUCH!!
YAAAH!

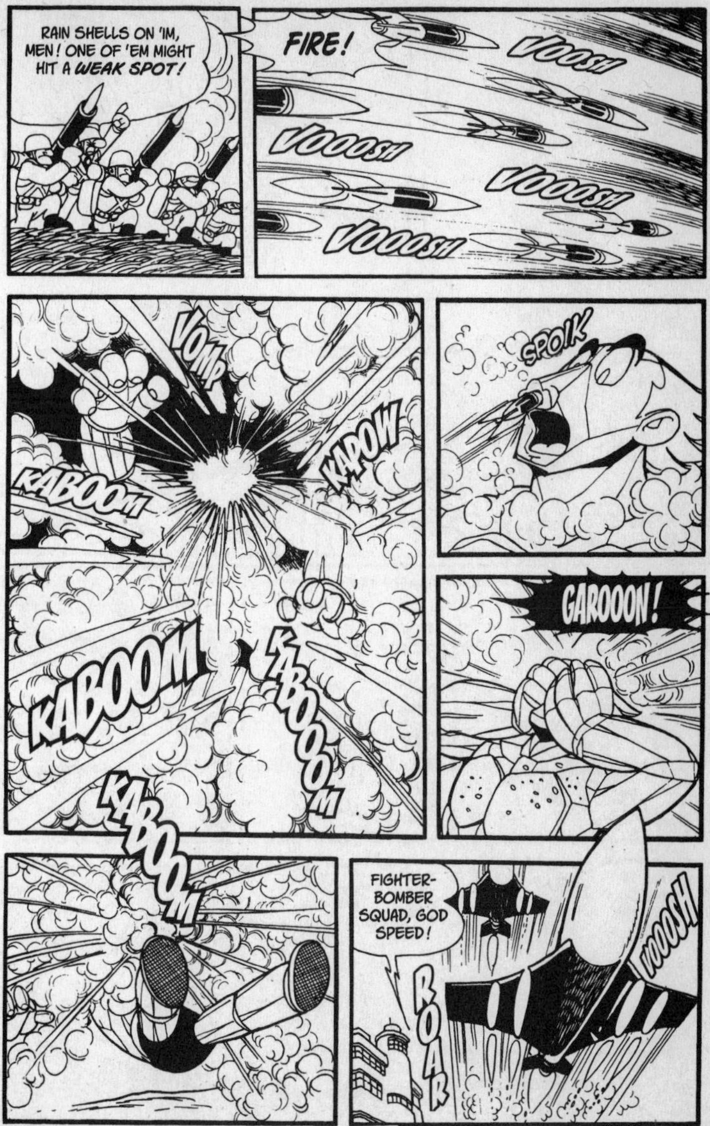
RAIN SHELLS ON 'IM, MEN! ONE OF 'EM MIGHT HIT A WEAK SPOT!
FIRE!
VOOOSH
VOOOSH
VOOOSH
VOOOSH
VOMP
KAPOW
KABOOM
KABOOM
KABOOOOOM
KABOOOM
SPOIK
GAROOON!
FIGHTER-BOMBER SQUAD, GOD SPEED!
ROAR
VOOOSH

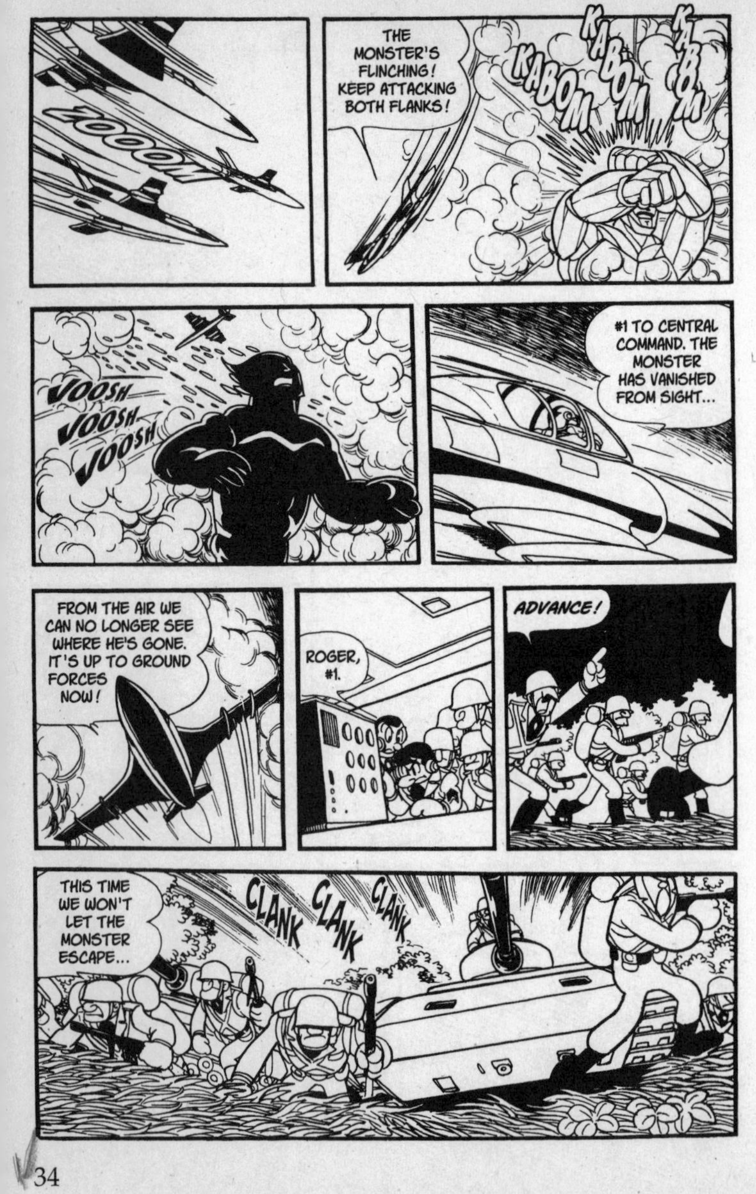
ZOOOOM
THE MONSTER'S FLINCHING! KEEP ATTACKING BOTH FLANKS!
KABOM KABOM KABOM
VOOSH VOOSH VOOSH
#1 TO CENTRAL COMMAND. THE MONSTER HAS VANISHED FROM SIGHT...
FROM THE AIR WE CAN NO LONGER SEE WHERE HE'S GONE. IT'S UP TO GROUND FORCES NOW!
ROGER, #1.
ADVANCE!
THIS TIME WE WON'T LET THE MONSTER ESCAPE...
CLANK CLANK CLANK

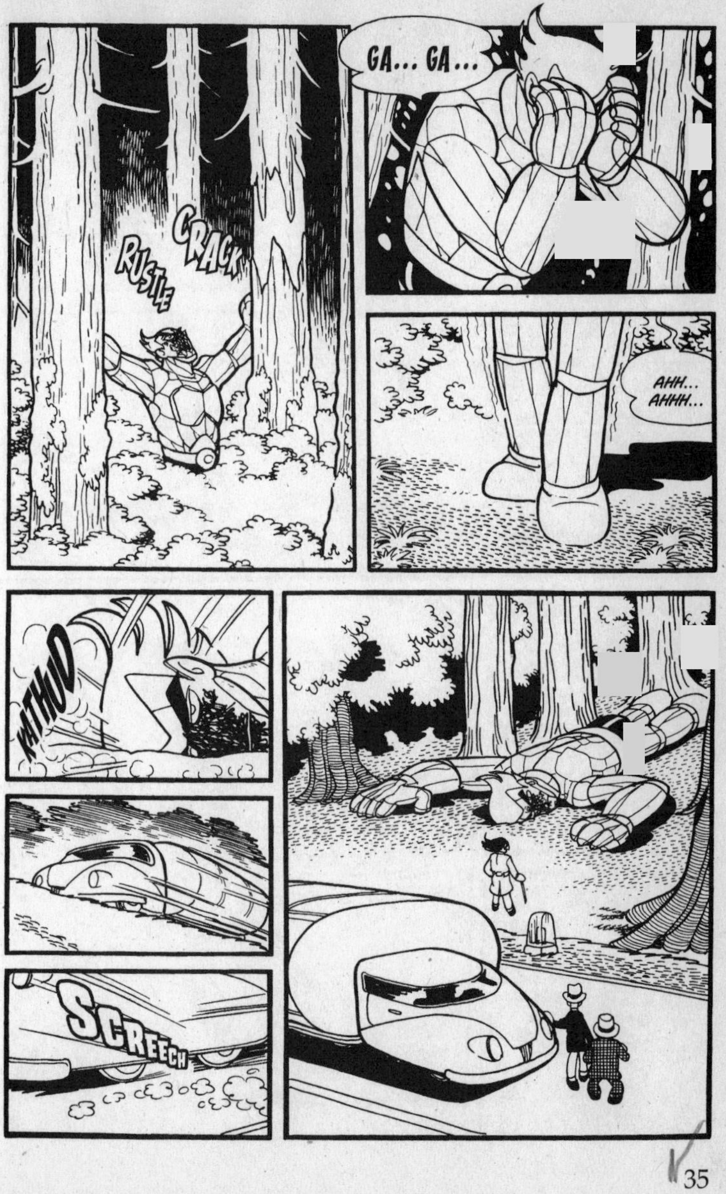
RUSTLE
CRACK
GA... GA...
AHH... AHHH...
KATHUD
SCREECH

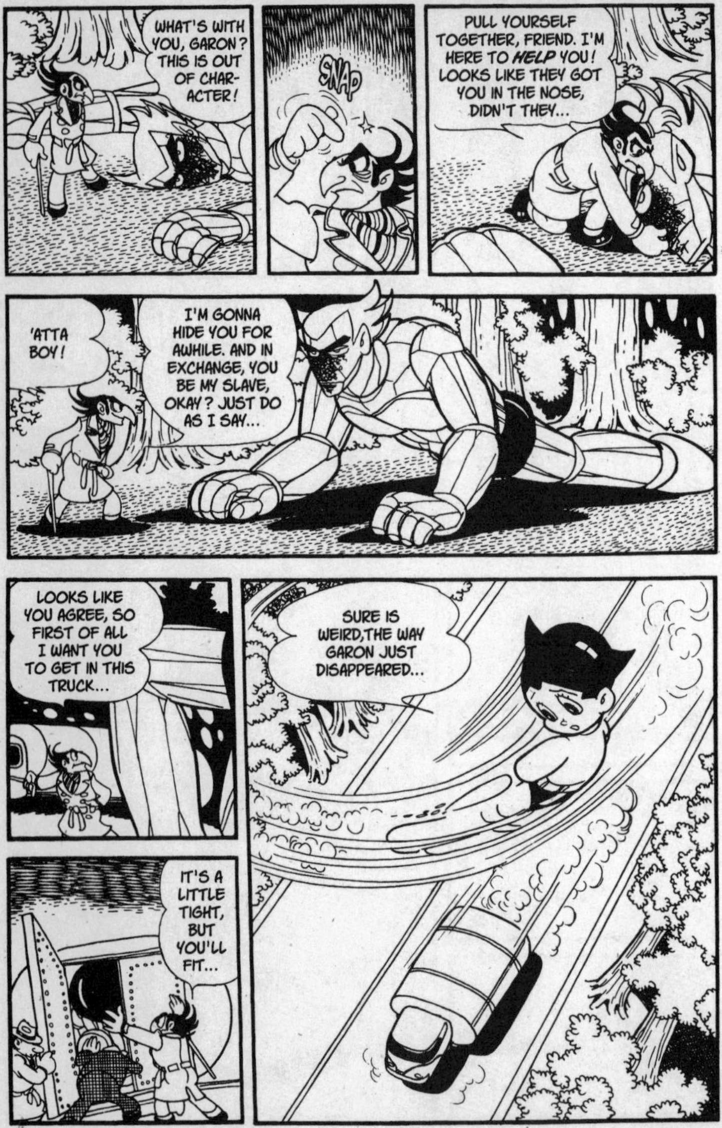
WHAT'S WITH YOU, GARON? THIS IS OUT OF CHAR-ACTER!
SNAP
PULL YOURSELF TOGETHER, FRIEND. I'M HERE TO **HELP** YOU! LOOKS LIKE THEY GOT YOU IN THE NOSE, DIDN'T THEY...
'ATTA BOY!
I'M GONNA HIDE YOU FOR AWHILE. AND IN EXCHANGE, YOU BE MY SLAVE, OKAY? JUST DO AS I SAY...
LOOKS LIKE YOU AGREE, SO FIRST OF ALL I WANT YOU TO GET IN THIS TRUCK...
IT'S A LITTLE TIGHT, BUT YOU'LL FIT...
SURE IS WEIRD, THE WAY GARON JUST DISAPPEARED...

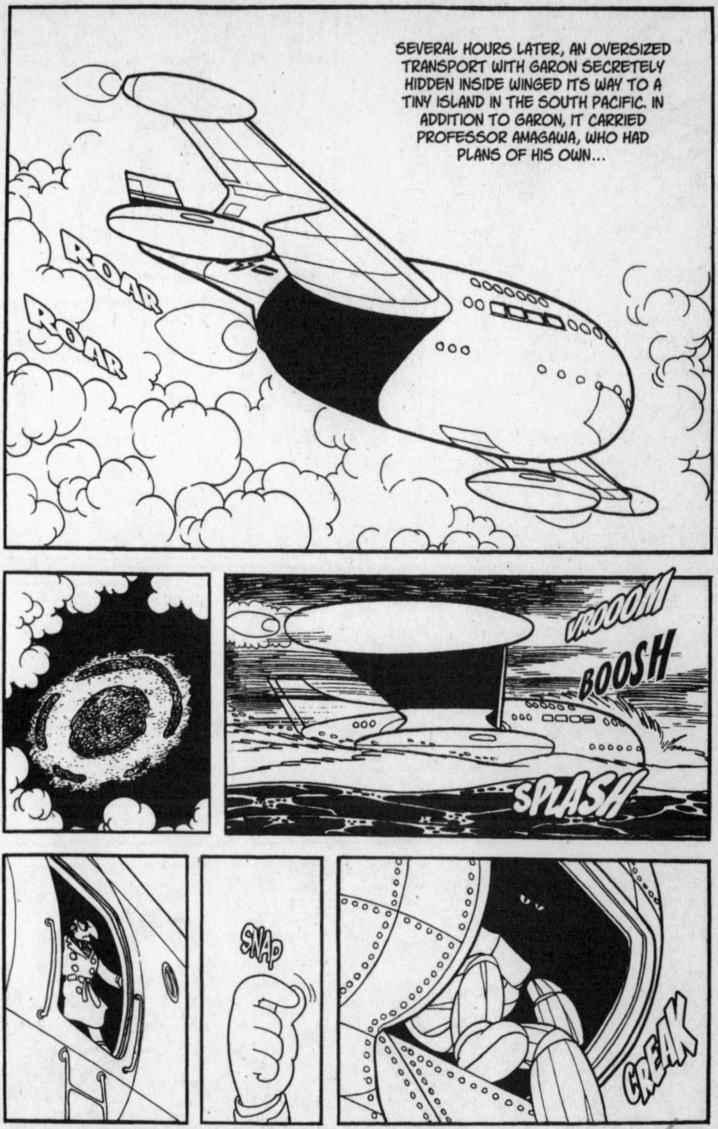
SEVERAL HOURS LATER, AN OVERSIZED TRANSPORT WITH GARON SECRETELY HIDDEN INSIDE WINGED ITS WAY TO A TINY ISLAND IN THE SOUTH PACIFIC. IN ADDITION TO GARON, IT CARRIED PROFESSOR AMAGAWA, WHO HAD PLANS OF HIS OWN...
ROAR
ROAR
VROOOM
BOOSH
SPLASH
SNAP
CREAK

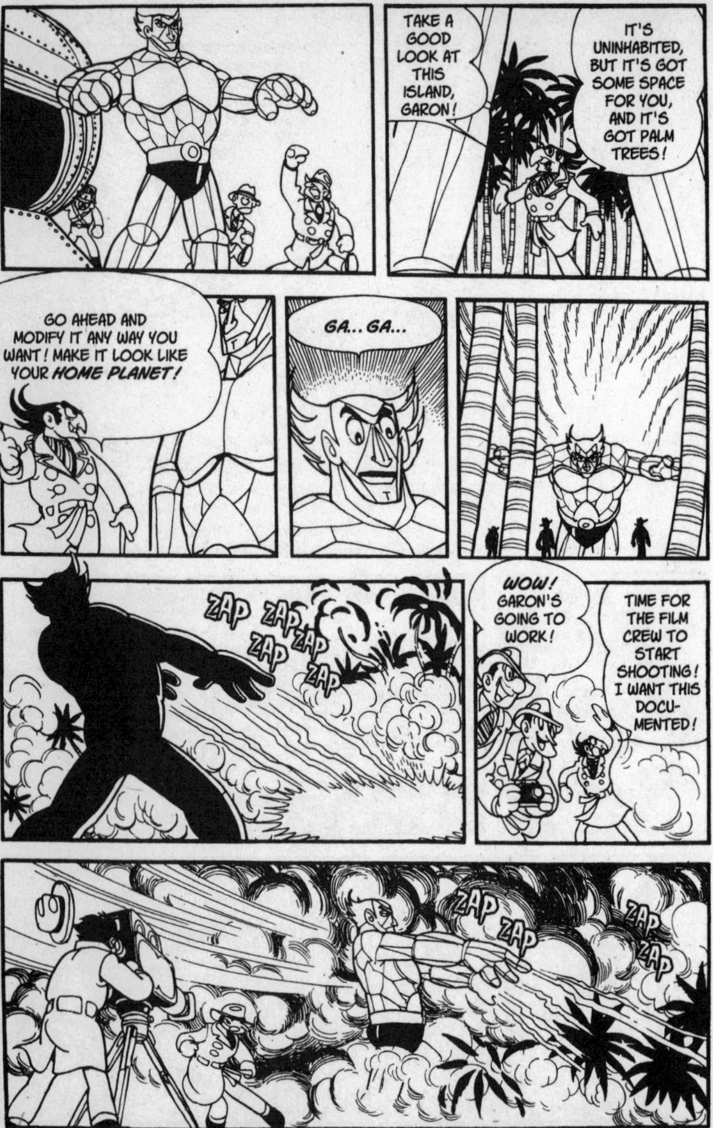
TAKE A GOOD LOOK AT THIS ISLAND, GARON!
IT'S UNINHABITED, BUT IT'S GOT SOME SPACE FOR YOU, AND IT'S GOT PALM TREES!
GO AHEAD AND MODIFY IT ANY WAY YOU WANT! MAKE IT LOOK LIKE YOUR HOME PLANET!
GA... GA...
ZAP ZAP ZAP ZAP ZAP
WOW! GARON'S GOING TO WORK!
TIME FOR THE FILM CREW TO START SHOOTING! I WANT THIS DOCU-MENTED!
ZAP ZAP
ZAP ZAP

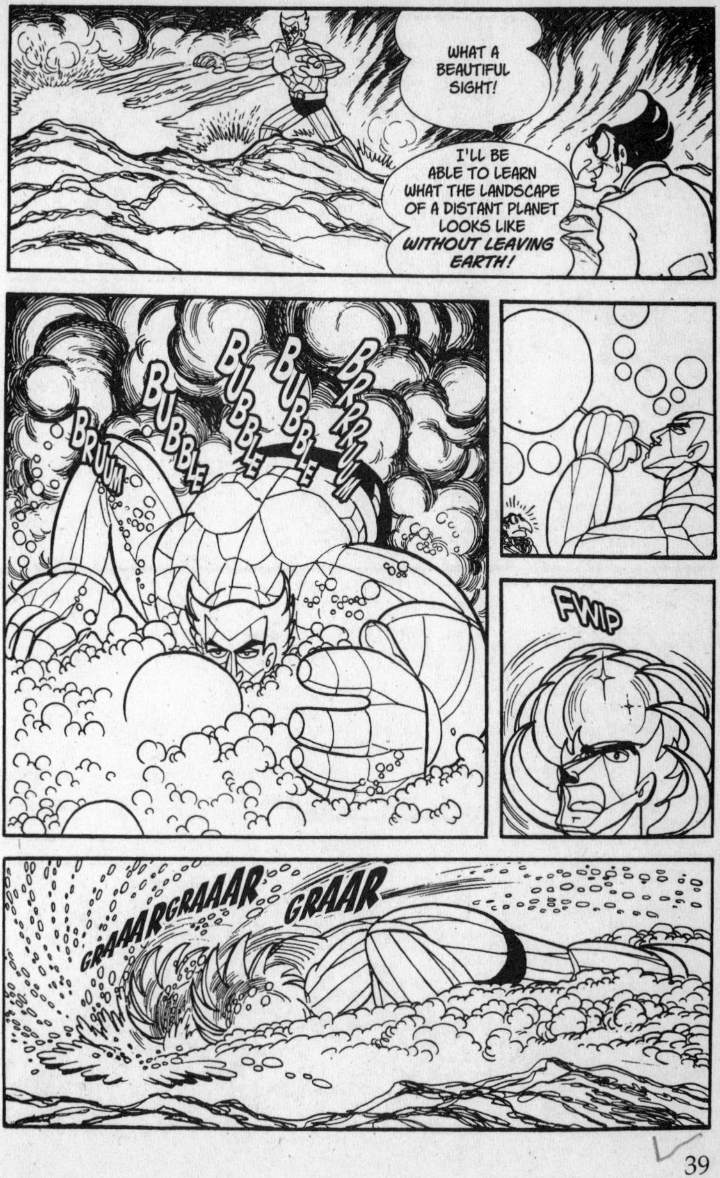
WHAT A BEAUTIFUL SIGHT!
I'LL BE ABLE TO LEARN WHAT THE LANDSCAPE OF A DISTANT PLANET LOOKS LIKE ***WITHOUT LEAVING EARTH!***
BRUUM
BUBBLE
BUBBLE
BUBBLE
BRRUM
FWIP
GRAAARGRAAAR
GRAAR

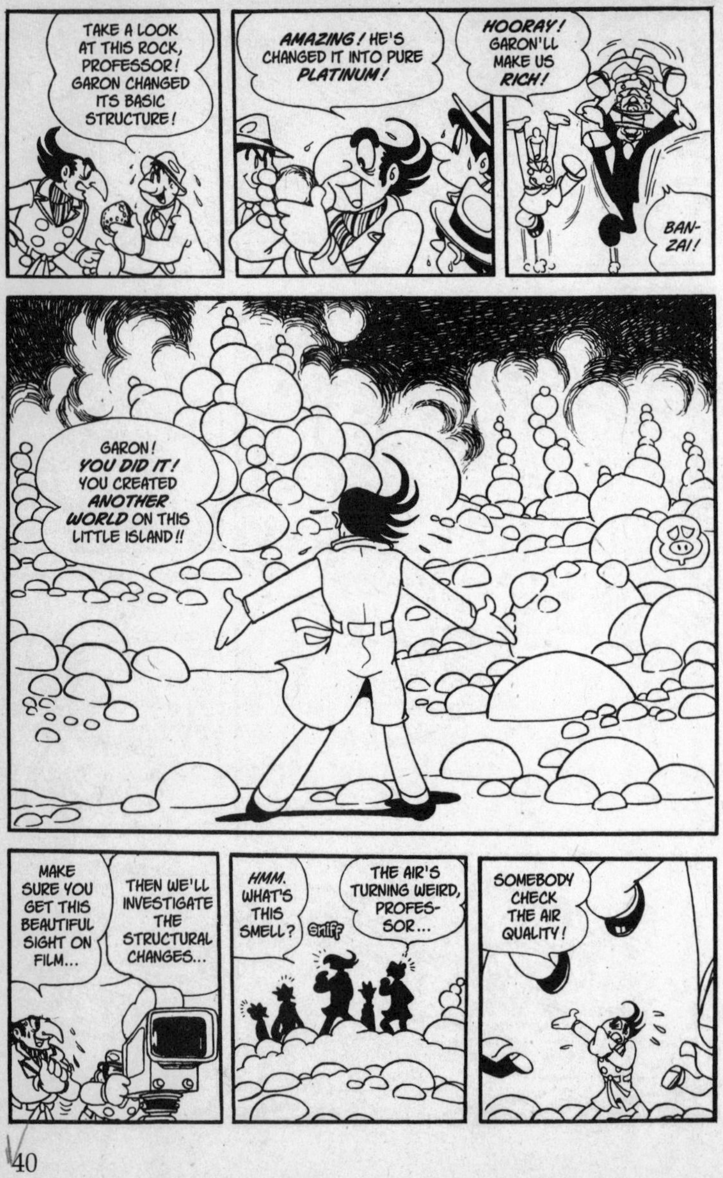
TAKE A LOOK AT THIS ROCK, PROFESSOR! GARON CHANGED ITS BASIC STRUCTURE!
AMAZING! HE'S CHANGED IT INTO PURE PLATINUM!
HOORAY! GARON'LL MAKE US RICH!
BAN-ZAI!
GARON! YOU DID IT! YOU CREATED ANOTHER WORLD ON THIS LITTLE ISLAND!!
MAKE SURE YOU GET THIS BEAUTIFUL SIGHT ON FILM...
THEN WE'LL INVESTIGATE THE STRUCTURAL CHANGES...
HMM. WHAT'S THIS SMELL?
SNIFF
THE AIR'S TURNING WEIRD, PROFES-SOR...
SOMEBODY CHECK THE AIR QUALITY!

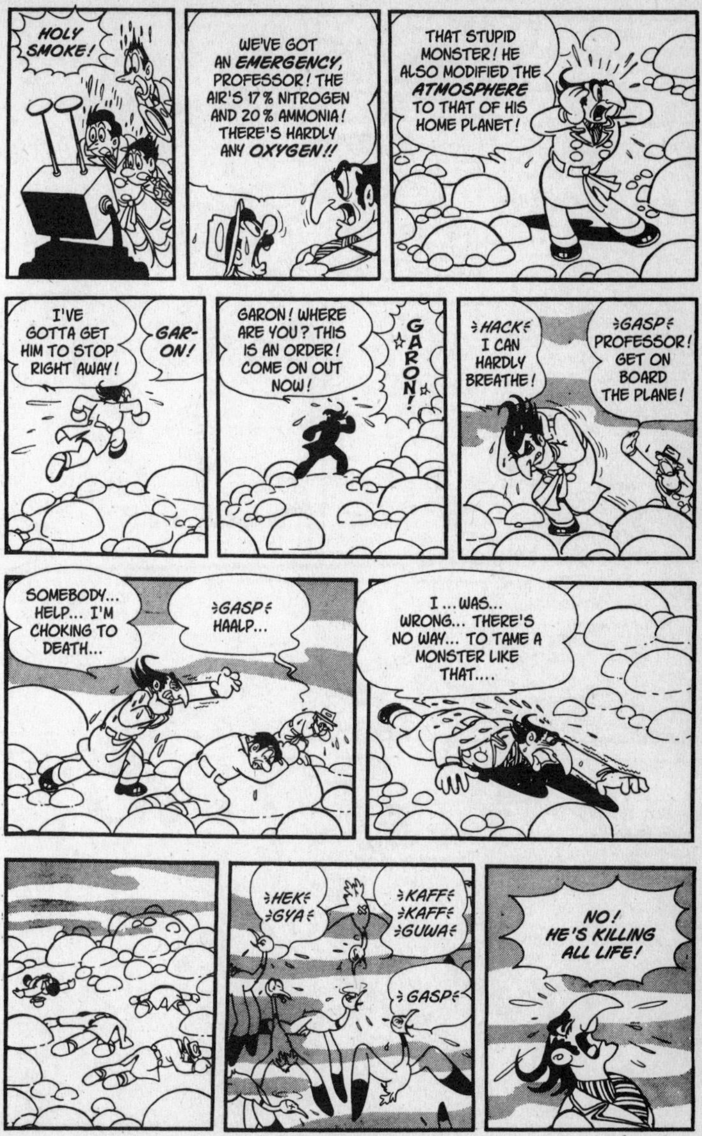
HOLY SMOKE!
WE'VE GOT AN EMERGENCY, PROFESSOR! THE AIR'S 17% NITROGEN AND 20% AMMONIA! THERE'S HARDLY ANY OXYGEN!!
THAT STUPID MONSTER! HE ALSO MODIFIED THE ATMOSPHERE TO THAT OF HIS HOME PLANET!
I'VE GOTTA GET HIM TO STOP RIGHT AWAY!
GAR-ON!
GARON! WHERE ARE YOU? THIS IS AN ORDER! COME ON OUT NOW!
GARON!
HACK I CAN HARDLY BREATHE!
GASP PROFESSOR! GET ON BOARD THE PLANE!
SOMEBODY... HELP... I'M CHOKING TO DEATH...
GASP HAALP...
I ... WAS... WRONG... THERE'S NO WAY... TO TAME A MONSTER LIKE THAT....
HEK GYA
KAFF KAFF GUWA
GASP
NO! HE'S KILLING ALL LIFE!

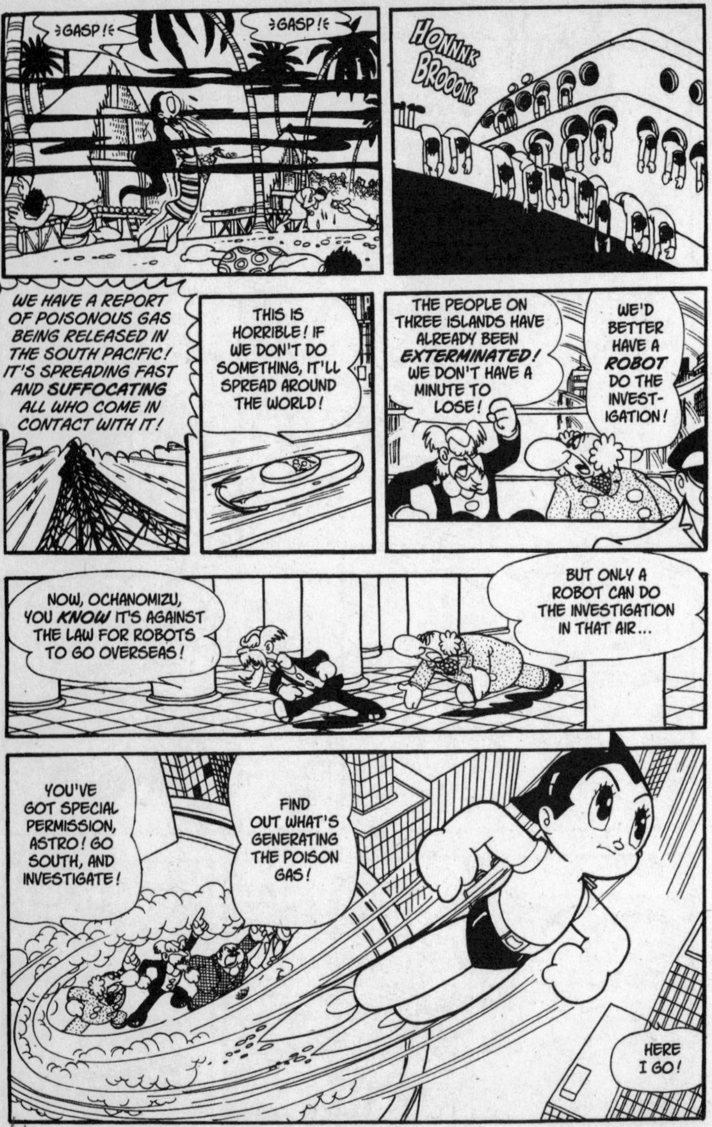

GASP!
GASP!
HONNNK BROOONK
WE HAVE A REPORT OF POISONOUS GAS BEING RELEASED IN THE SOUTH PACIFIC! IT'S SPREADING FAST AND SUFFOCATING ALL WHO COME IN CONTACT WITH IT!
THIS IS HORRIBLE! IF WE DON'T DO SOMETHING, IT'LL SPREAD AROUND THE WORLD!
THE PEOPLE ON THREE ISLANDS HAVE ALREADY BEEN EXTERMINATED! WE DON'T HAVE A MINUTE TO LOSE!
WE'D BETTER HAVE A ROBOT DO THE INVESTIGATION!
NOW, OCHANOMIZU, YOU KNOW IT'S AGAINST THE LAW FOR ROBOTS TO GO OVERSEAS!
BUT ONLY A ROBOT CAN DO THE INVESTIGATION IN THAT AIR...
YOU'VE GOT SPECIAL PERMISSION, ASTRO! GO SOUTH, AND INVESTIGATE!
FIND OUT WHAT'S GENERATING THE POISON GAS!
HERE I GO!

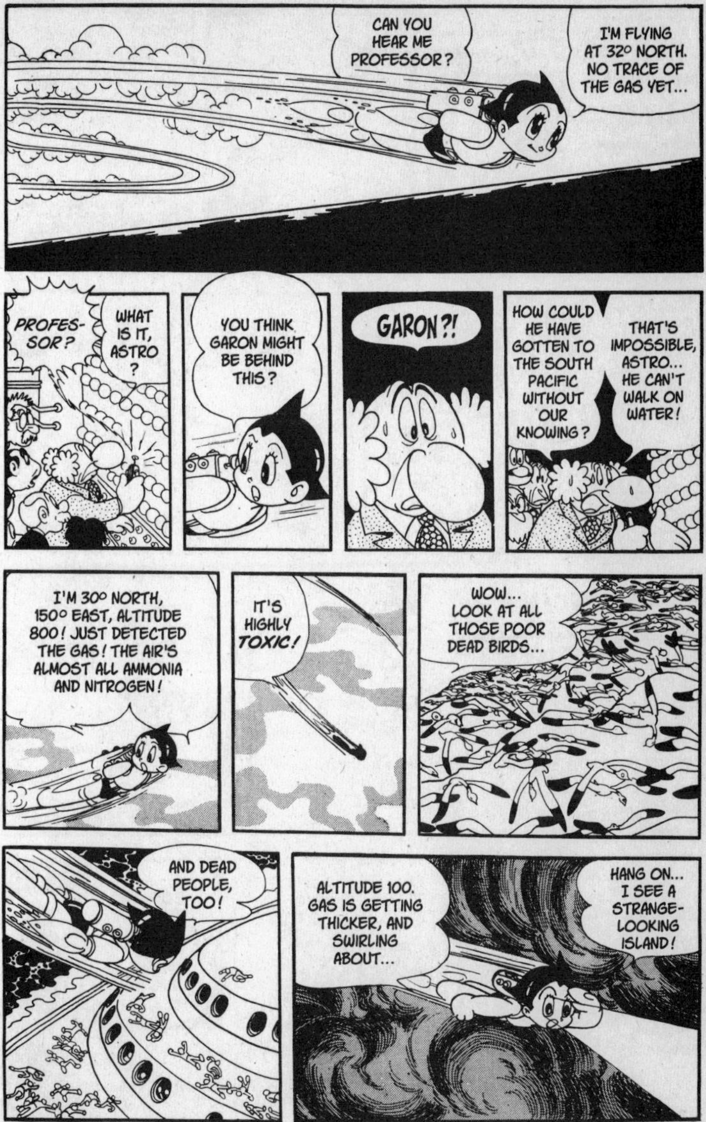
CAN YOU HEAR ME PROFESSOR?
I'M FLYING AT 32° NORTH. NO TRACE OF THE GAS YET...
PROFES-SOR?
WHAT IS IT, ASTRO?
YOU THINK GARON MIGHT BE BEHIND THIS?
GARON?!
HOW COULD HE HAVE GOTTEN TO THE SOUTH PACIFIC WITHOUT OUR KNOWING?
THAT'S IMPOSSIBLE, ASTRO... HE CAN'T WALK ON WATER!
I'M 30° NORTH, 150° EAST, ALTITUDE 800! JUST DETECTED THE GAS! THE AIR'S ALMOST ALL AMMONIA AND NITROGEN!
IT'S HIGHLY *TOXIC!*
WOW... LOOK AT ALL THOSE POOR DEAD BIRDS...
AND DEAD PEOPLE, TOO!
ALTITUDE 100. GAS IS GETTING THICKER, AND SWIRLING ABOUT...
HANG ON... I SEE A STRANGE-LOOKING ISLAND!

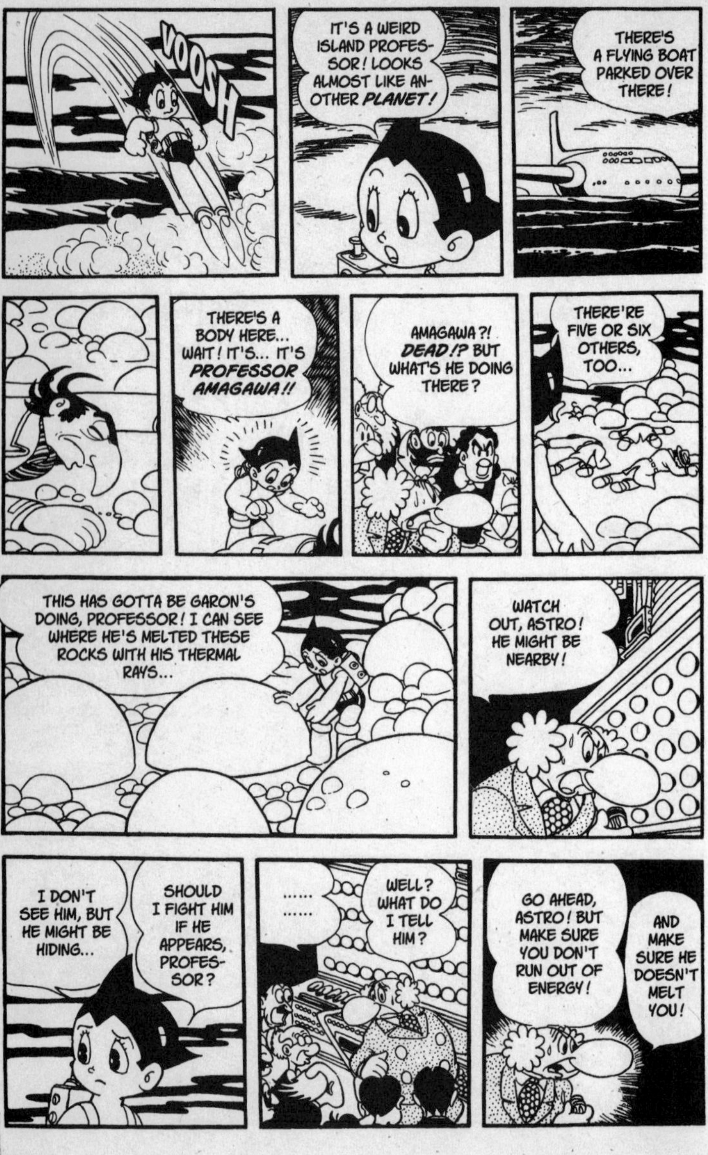
VOOSH
IT'S A WEIRD ISLAND PROFESSOR! LOOKS ALMOST LIKE ANOTHER PLANET!
THERE'S A FLYING BOAT PARKED OVER THERE!
THERE'S A BODY HERE... WAIT! IT'S... IT'S PROFESSOR AMAGAWA!!
AMAGAWA?! DEAD!? BUT WHAT'S HE DOING THERE?
THERE'RE FIVE OR SIX OTHERS, TOO...
THIS HAS GOTTA BE GARON'S DOING, PROFESSOR! I CAN SEE WHERE HE'S MELTED THESE ROCKS WITH HIS THERMAL RAYS...
WATCH OUT, ASTRO! HE MIGHT BE NEARBY!
I DON'T SEE HIM, BUT HE MIGHT BE HIDING...
SHOULD I FIGHT HIM IF HE APPEARS, PROFESSOR?
....
WELL? WHAT DO I TELL HIM?
GO AHEAD, ASTRO! BUT MAKE SURE YOU DON'T RUN OUT OF ENERGY!
AND MAKE SURE HE DOESN'T MELT YOU!

43

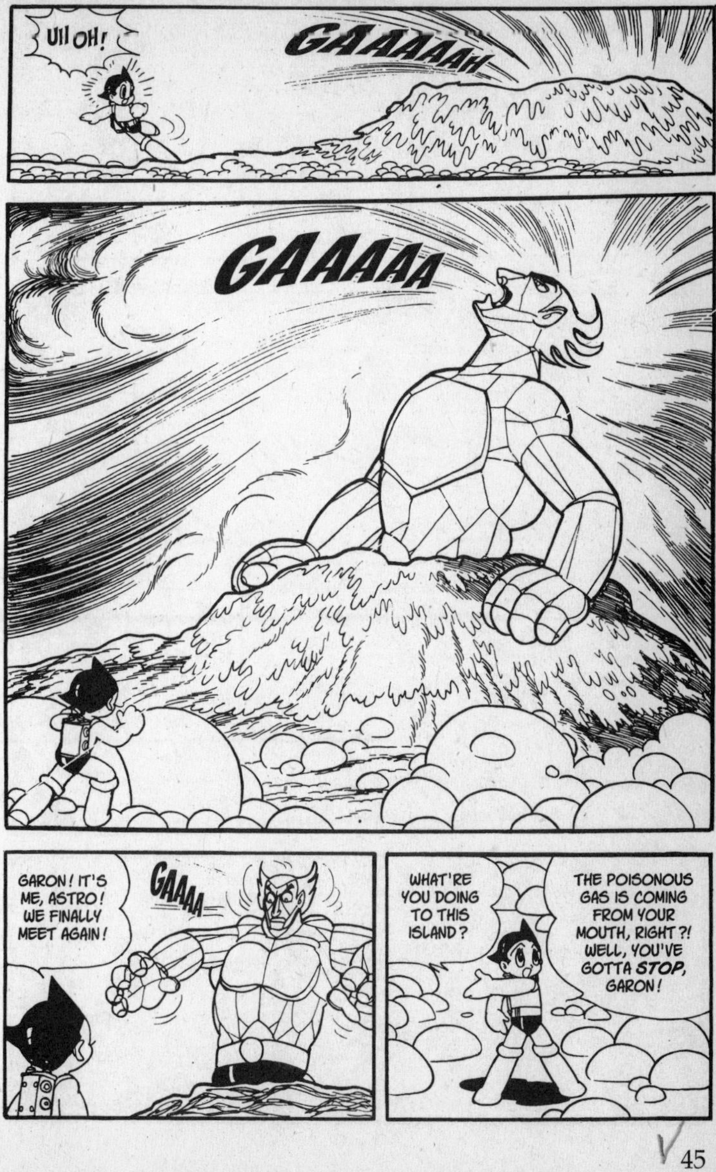
UII OH!
GAAAAAAH
GAAAAA
GARON! IT'S ME, ASTRO! WE FINALLY MEET AGAIN!
GAAAA
WHAT'RE YOU DOING TO THIS ISLAND?
THE POISONOUS GAS IS COMING FROM YOUR MOUTH, RIGHT?! WELL, YOU'VE GOTTA STOP, GARON!

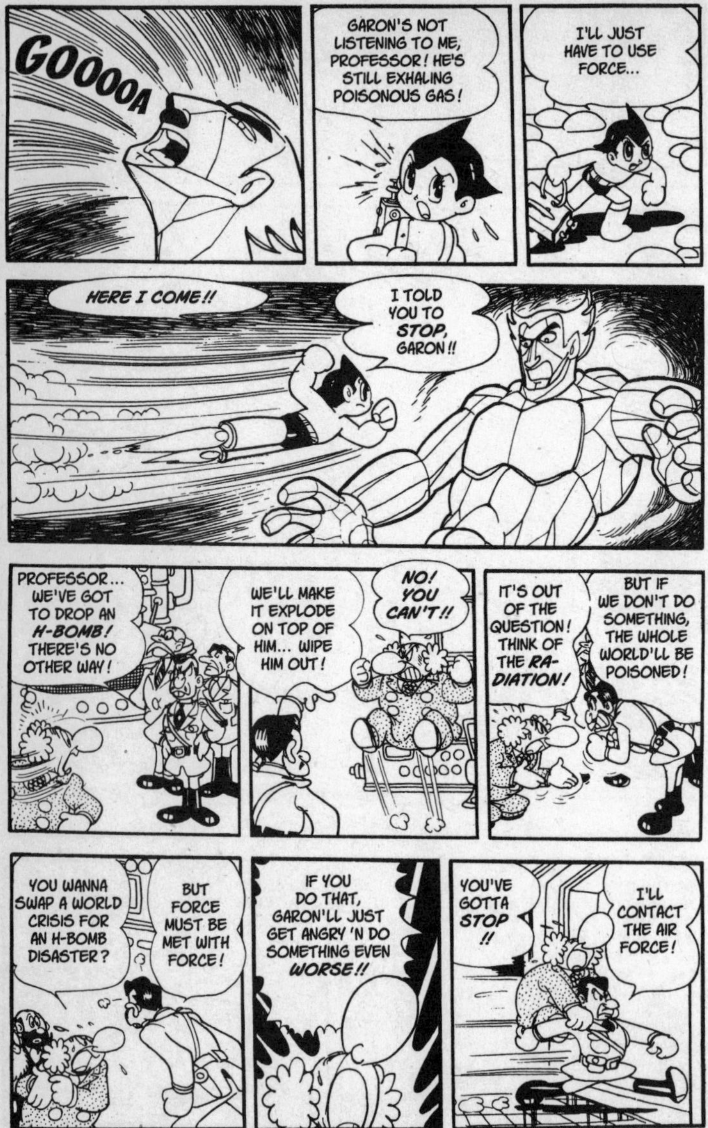
GOOOOA
GARON'S NOT LISTENING TO ME, PROFESSOR! HE'S STILL EXHALING POISONOUS GAS!
I'LL JUST HAVE TO USE FORCE...
HERE I COME!!
I TOLD YOU TO STOP, GARON!!
PROFESSOR... WE'VE GOT TO DROP AN H-BOMB! THERE'S NO OTHER WAY!
WE'LL MAKE IT EXPLODE ON TOP OF HIM... WIPE HIM OUT!
NO! YOU CAN'T!!
IT'S OUT OF THE QUESTION! THINK OF THE RA-DIATION!
BUT IF WE DON'T DO SOMETHING, THE WHOLE WORLD'LL BE POISONED!
YOU WANNA SWAP A WORLD CRISIS FOR AN H-BOMB DISASTER?
BUT FORCE MUST BE MET WITH FORCE!
IF YOU DO THAT, GARON'LL JUST GET ANGRY 'N DO SOMETHING EVEN WORSE!!
YOU'VE GOTTA STOP!!
I'LL CONTACT THE AIR FORCE!

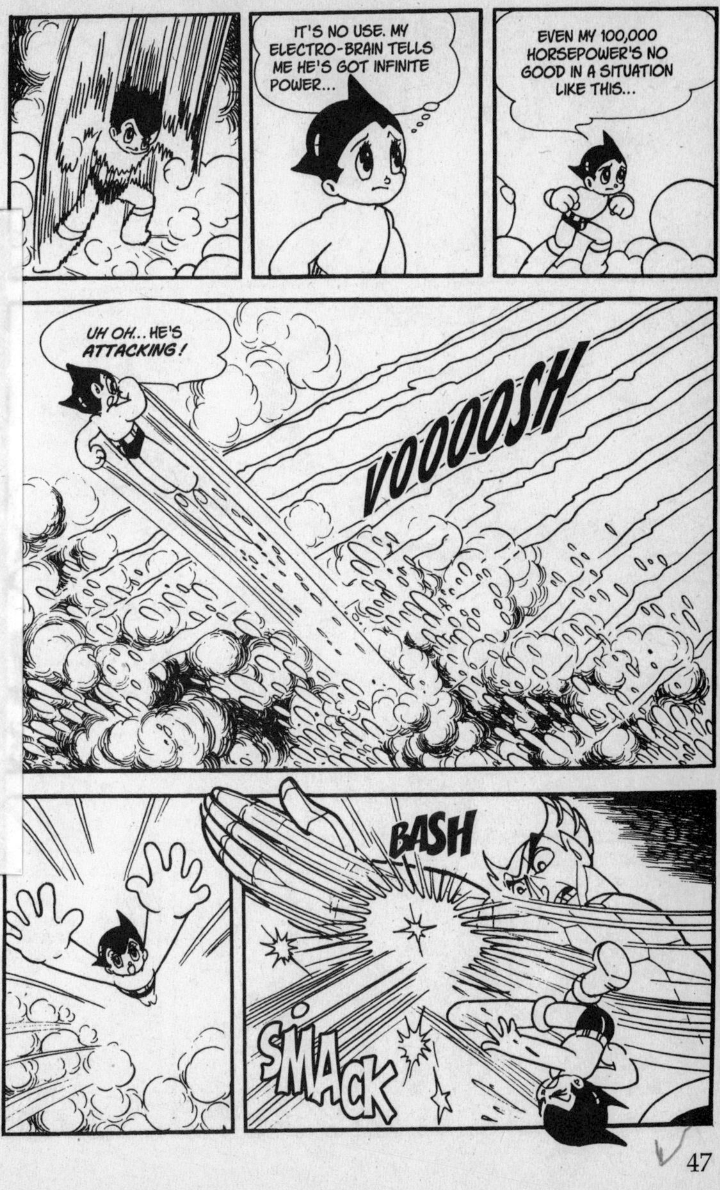
IT'S NO USE. MY ELECTRO-BRAIN TELLS ME HE'S GOT INFINITE POWER...
EVEN MY 100,000 HORSEPOWER'S NO GOOD IN A SITUATION LIKE THIS...
UH OH... HE'S ATTACKING!
VOOOOOSH
BASH
SMACK

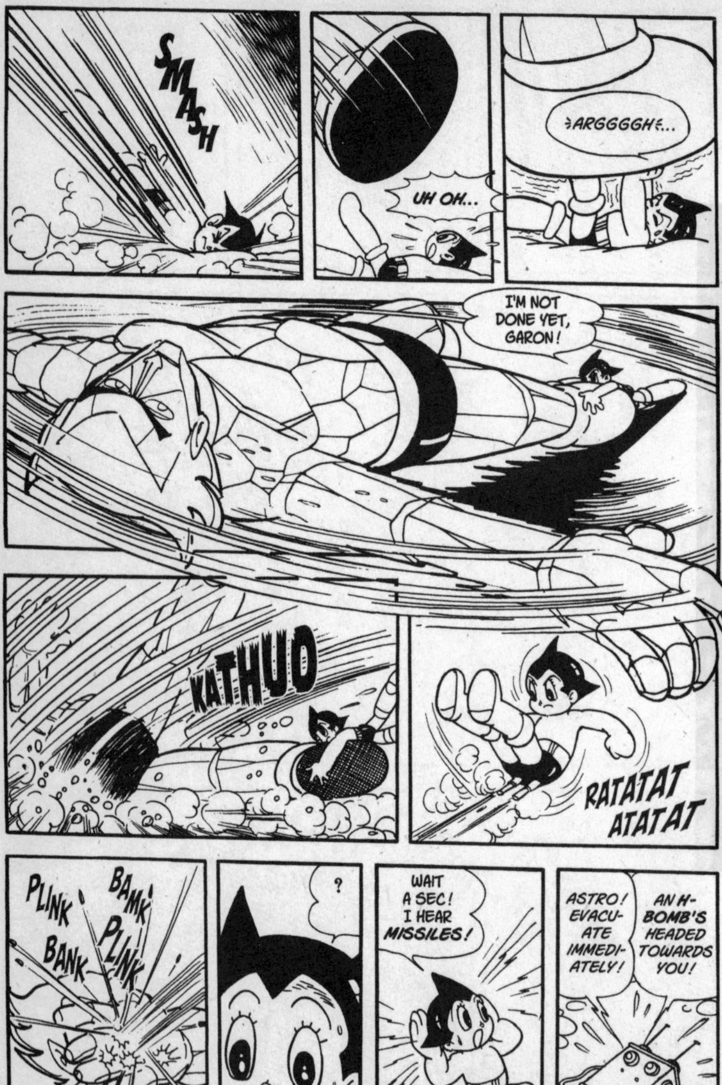
SMASH
UH OH...
ARGGGGH...
I'M NOT DONE YET, GARON!
KATHUD
RATATAT ATATAT
PLINK
BAMK
BANK
PLINK
?
WAIT A SEC! I HEAR MISSILES!
ASTRO! EVACUATE IMMEDIATELY!
AN H-BOMB'S HEADED TOWARDS YOU!

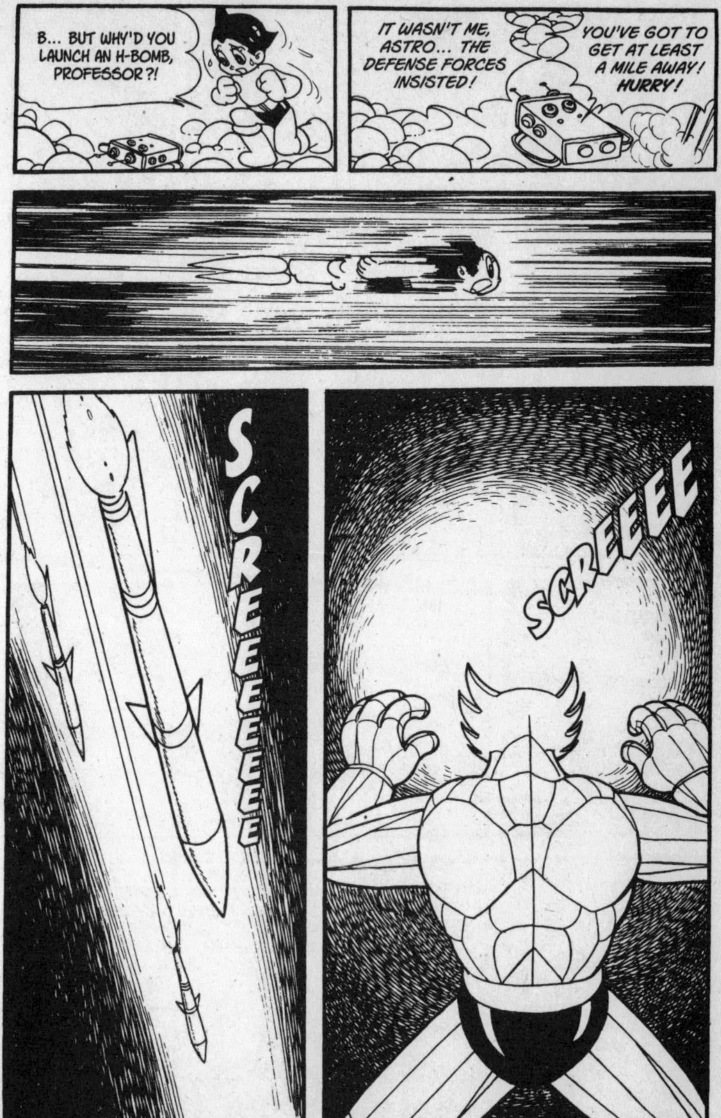

B... BUT WHY'D YOU LAUNCH AN H-BOMB, PROFESSOR?!
IT WASN'T ME, ASTRO... THE DEFENSE FORCES INSISTED!
YOU'VE GOT TO GET AT LEAST A MILE AWAY! HURRY!
SCREEEEEEEE
SCREEEE

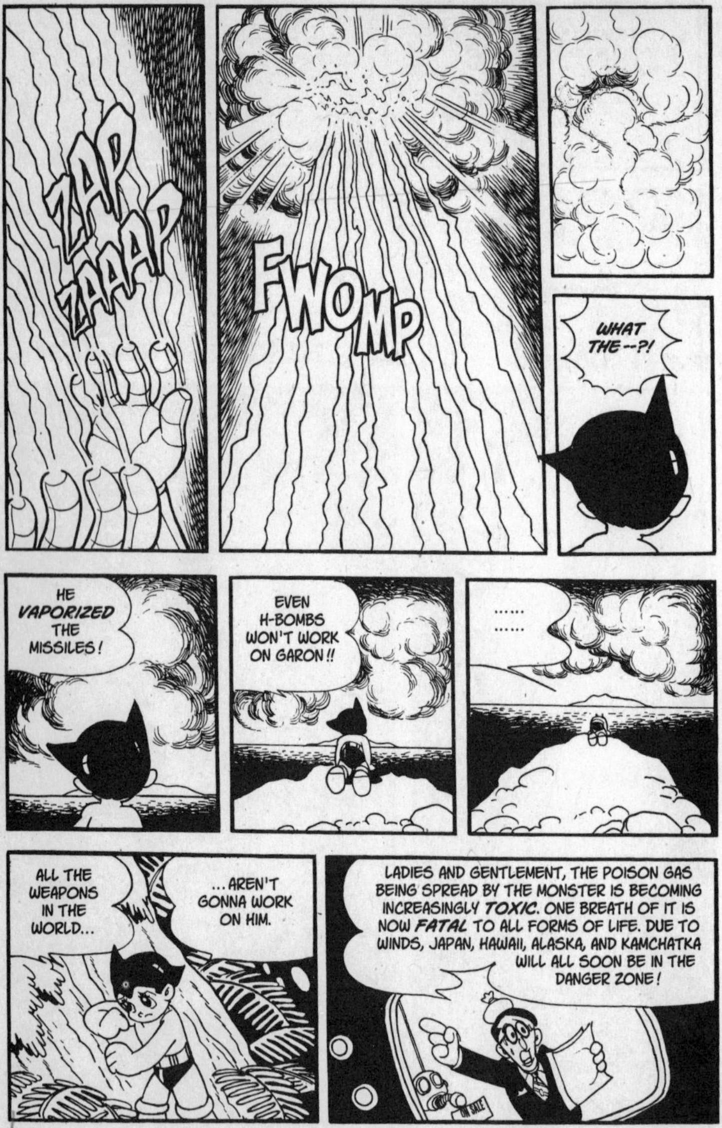
ZAP
ZAAAP
FWOMP
WHAT THE--?!
HE *VAPORIZED* THE MISSILES!
EVEN H-BOMBS WON'T WORK ON GARON!!
......
......
ALL THE WEAPONS IN THE WORLD...
...AREN'T GONNA WORK ON HIM.
LADIES AND GENTLEMENT, THE POISON GAS BEING SPREAD BY THE MONSTER IS BECOMING INCREASINGLY *TOXIC*. ONE BREATH OF IT IS NOW *FATAL* TO ALL FORMS OF LIFE. DUE TO WINDS, JAPAN, HAWAII, ALASKA, AND KAMCHATKA WILL ALL SOON BE IN THE DANGER ZONE!
ON SALE

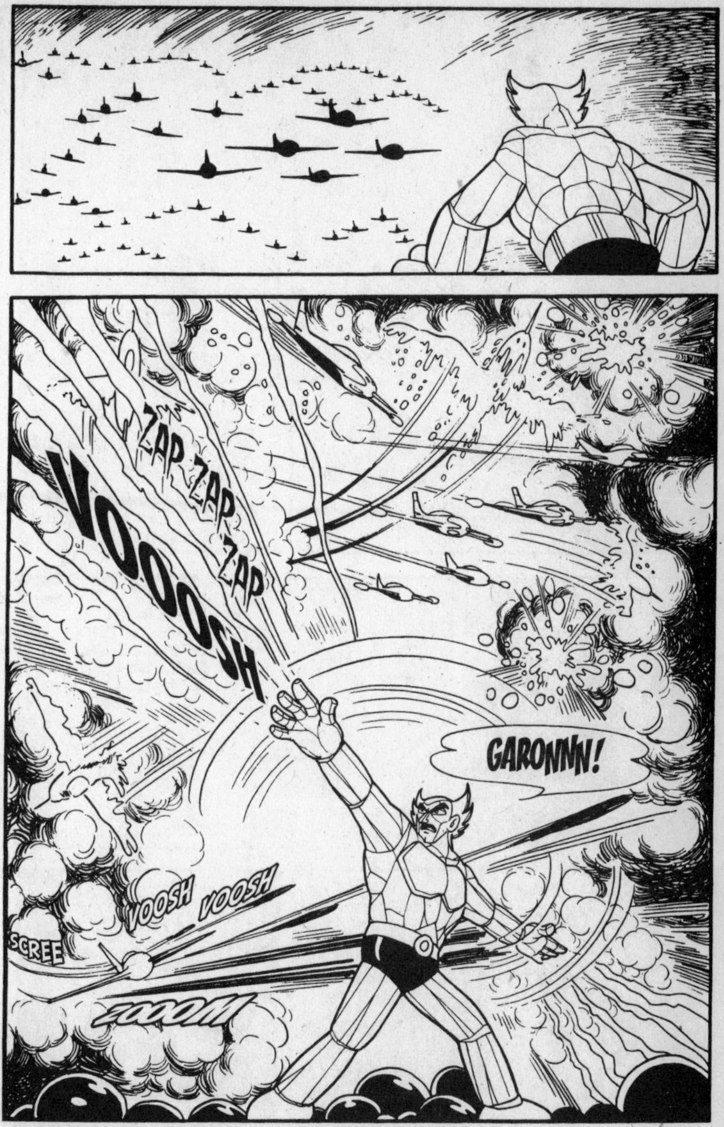
ZAP ZAP ZAP
VOOOOSH
GARONNN!
VOOSH VOOSH
SCREE
ZOOOM

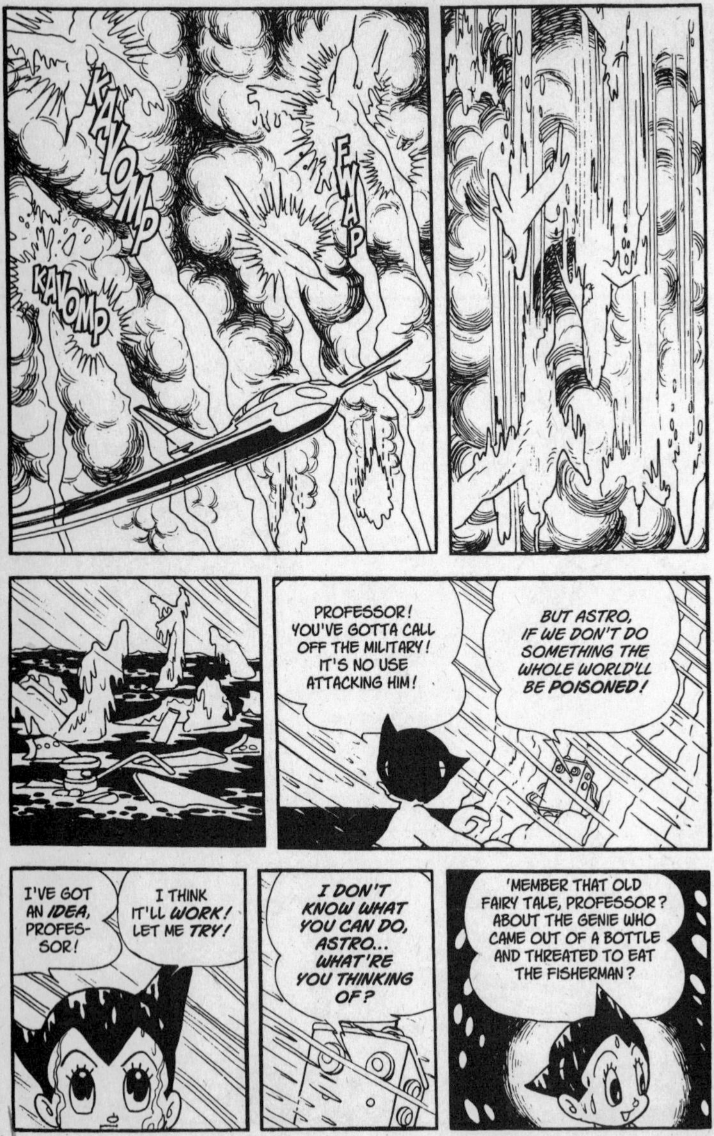
KAVOMP
KAVOMP
FWAP
PROFESSOR! YOU'VE GOTTA CALL OFF THE MILITARY! IT'S NO USE ATTACKING HIM!
BUT ASTRO, IF WE DON'T DO SOMETHING THE WHOLE WORLD'LL BE *POISONED*!
I'VE GOT AN *IDEA*, PROFES-SOR!
I THINK IT'LL *WORK*! LET ME *TRY*!
I DON'T KNOW WHAT YOU CAN DO, ASTRO... WHAT'RE YOU THINKING OF?
'MEMBER THAT OLD FAIRY TALE, PROFESSOR? ABOUT THE GENIE WHO CAME OUT OF A BOTTLE AND THREATED TO EAT THE FISHERMAN?

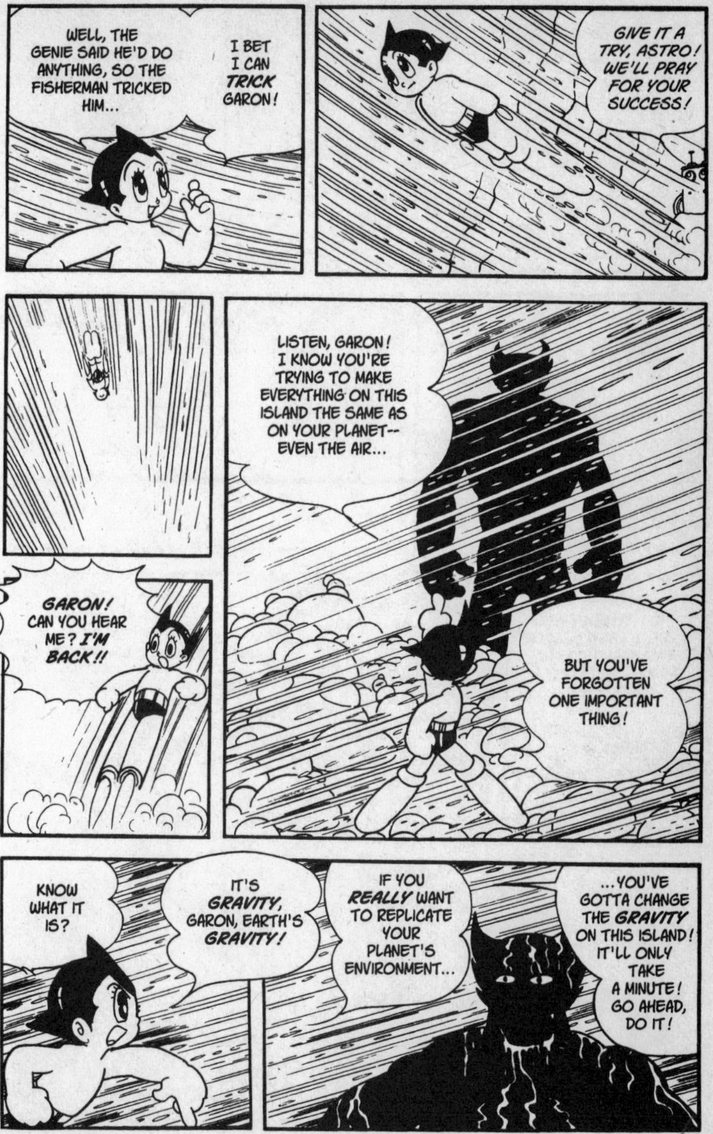
WELL, THE GENIE SAID HE'D DO ANYTHING, SO THE FISHERMAN TRICKED HIM...
I BET I CAN TRICK GARON!
GIVE IT A TRY, ASTRO! WE'LL PRAY FOR YOUR SUCCESS!
GARON! CAN YOU HEAR ME? I'M BACK!!
LISTEN, GARON! I KNOW YOU'RE TRYING TO MAKE EVERYTHING ON THIS ISLAND THE SAME AS ON YOUR PLANET-- EVEN THE AIR...
BUT YOU'VE FORGOTTEN ONE IMPORTANT THING!
KNOW WHAT IT IS?
IT'S GRAVITY, GARON, EARTH'S GRAVITY!
IF YOU REALLY WANT TO REPLICATE YOUR PLANET'S ENVIRONMENT...
...YOU'VE GOTTA CHANGE THE GRAVITY ON THIS ISLAND! IT'LL ONLY TAKE A MINUTE! GO AHEAD, DO IT!

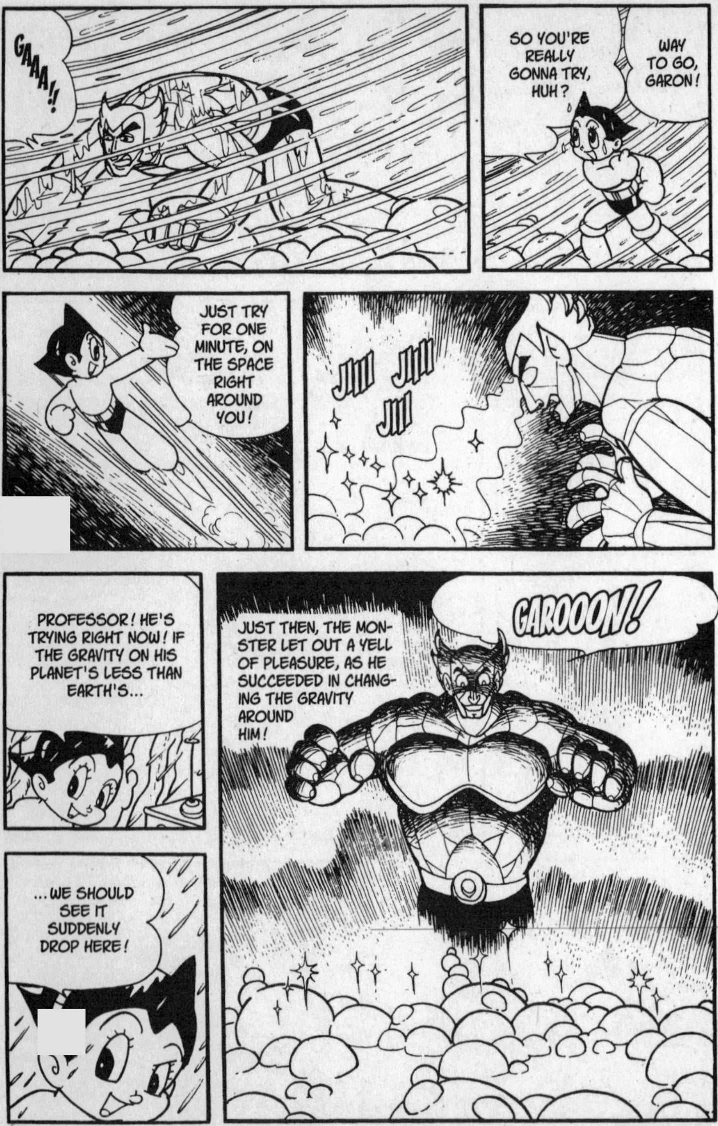
GAAA!!
SO YOU'RE REALLY GONNA TRY, HUH?
WAY TO GO, GARON!
JUST TRY FOR ONE MINUTE, ON THE SPACE RIGHT AROUND YOU!
JIIII JIIII JIII
PROFESSOR! HE'S TRYING RIGHT NOW! IF THE GRAVITY ON HIS PLANET'S LESS THAN EARTH'S...
...WE SHOULD SEE IT SUDDENLY DROP HERE!
JUST THEN, THE MONSTER LET OUT A YELL OF PLEASURE, AS HE SUCCEEDED IN CHANGING THE GRAVITY AROUND HIM!
GAROOON!

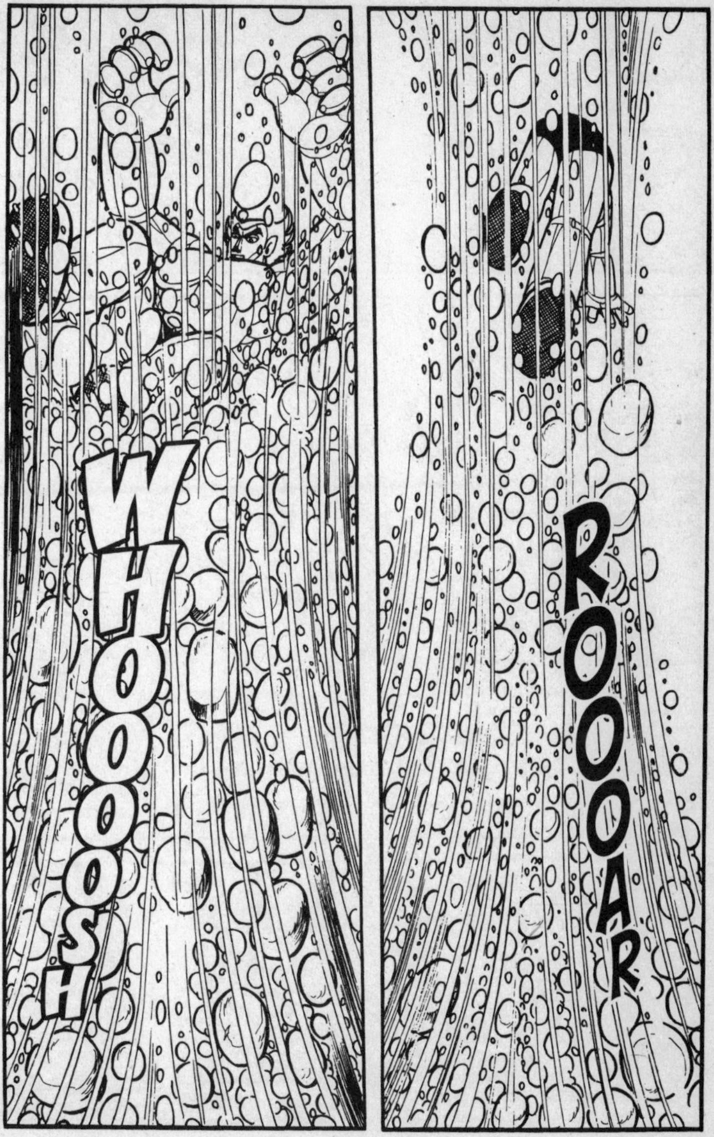
WHOOOOOSH
ROOOAR

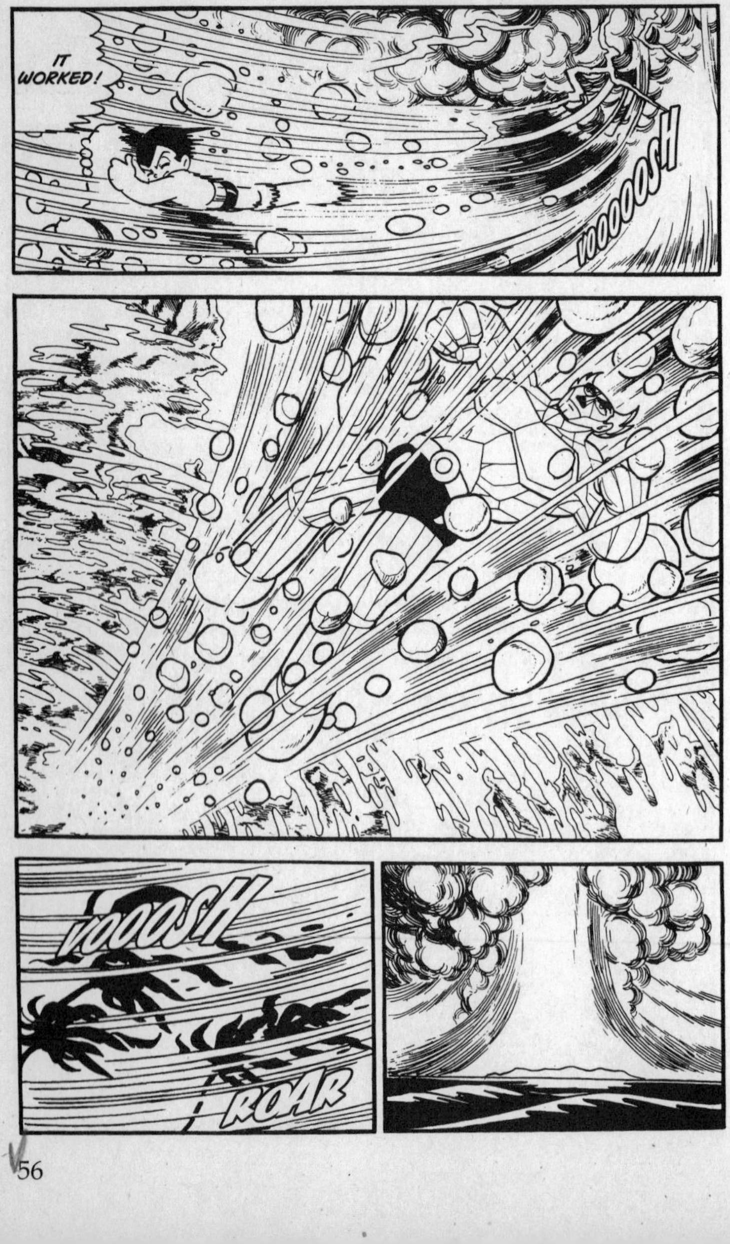
IT WORKED!
VOOOOOSH
VOOOSH
ROAR

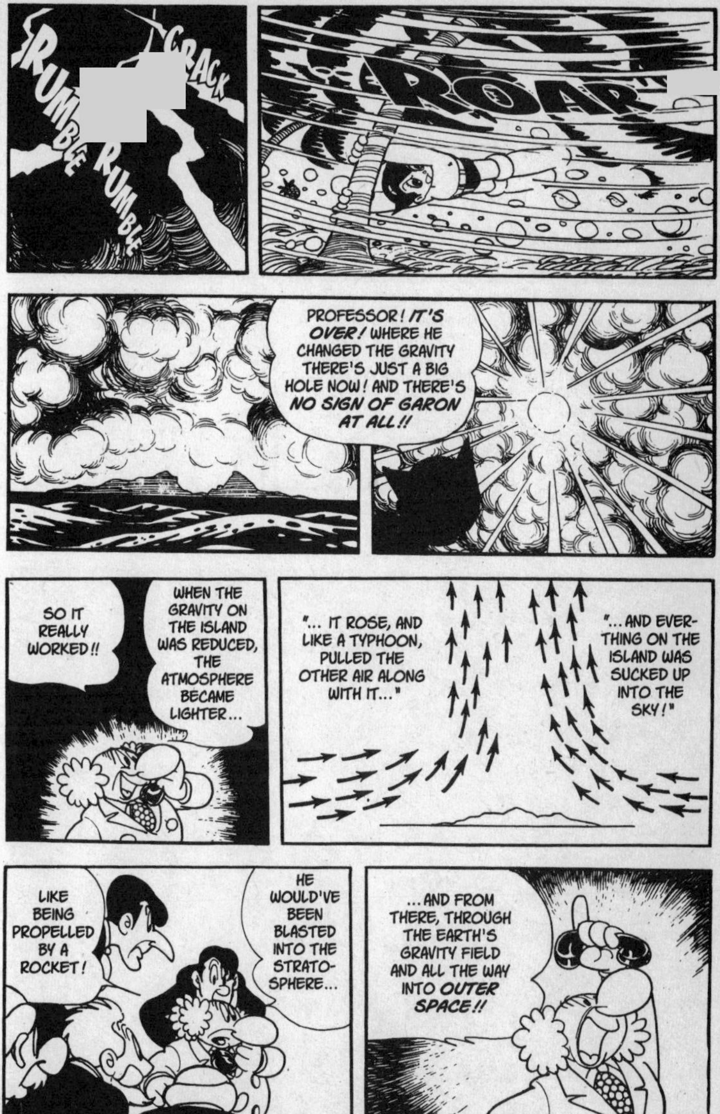

RUMBLE RUMBLE
CRACK
ROAR
PROFESSOR! *IT'S OVER!* WHERE HE CHANGED THE GRAVITY THERE'S JUST A BIG HOLE NOW! AND THERE'S *NO SIGN OF GARON AT ALL!!*
SO IT REALLY WORKED!!
WHEN THE GRAVITY ON THE ISLAND WAS REDUCED, THE ATMOSPHERE BECAME LIGHTER...
"... IT ROSE, AND LIKE A TYPHOON, PULLED THE OTHER AIR ALONG WITH IT..."
"... AND EVER-THING ON THE ISLAND WAS SUCKED UP INTO THE SKY!"
LIKE BEING PROPELLED BY A ROCKET!
HE WOULD'VE BEEN BLASTED INTO THE STRATO-SPHERE...
... AND FROM THERE, THROUGH THE EARTH'S GRAVITY FIELD AND ALL THE WAY INTO *OUTER SPACE!!*

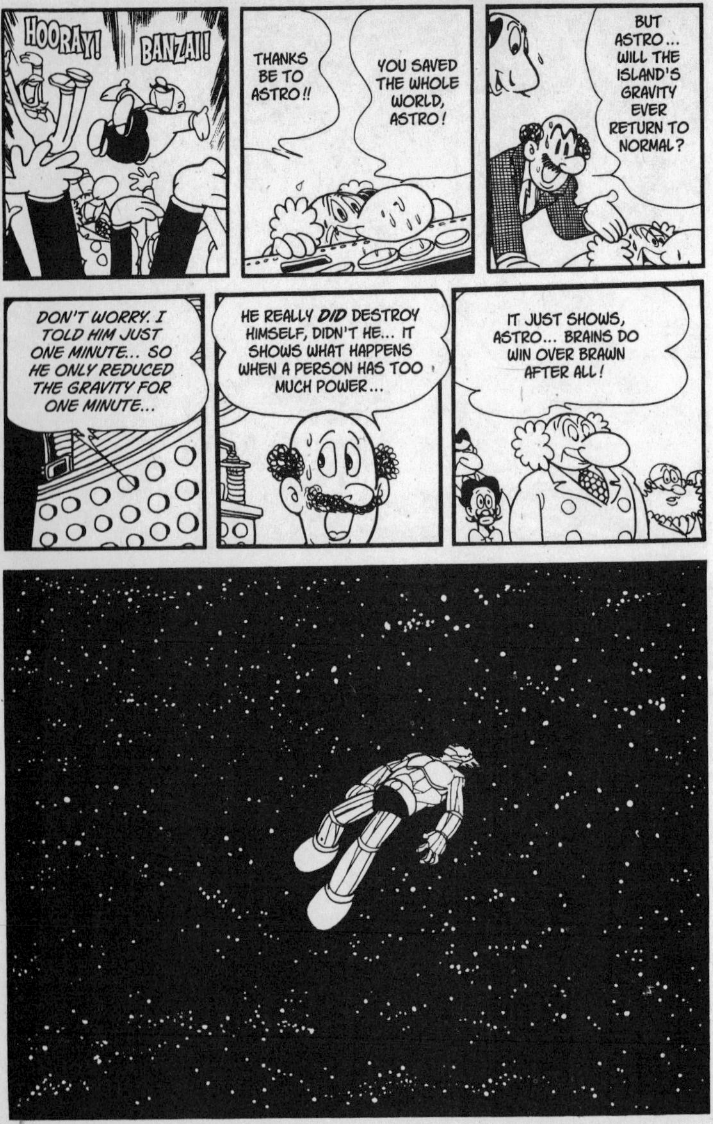
HOORAY!
BANZAI!
THANKS BE TO ASTRO!!
YOU SAVED THE WHOLE WORLD, ASTRO!
BUT ASTRO... WILL THE ISLAND'S GRAVITY EVER RETURN TO NORMAL?
DON'T WORRY. I TOLD HIM JUST ONE MINUTE... SO HE ONLY REDUCED THE GRAVITY FOR ONE MINUTE...
HE REALLY DID DESTROY HIMSELF, DIDN'T HE... IT SHOWS WHAT HAPPENS WHEN A PERSON HAS TOO MUCH POWER...
IT JUST SHOWS, ASTRO... BRAINS DO WIN OVER BRAWN AFTER ALL!

YELLOW HORSE

First serialized from October 1955 to February 1956 in *Shonen* magazine.

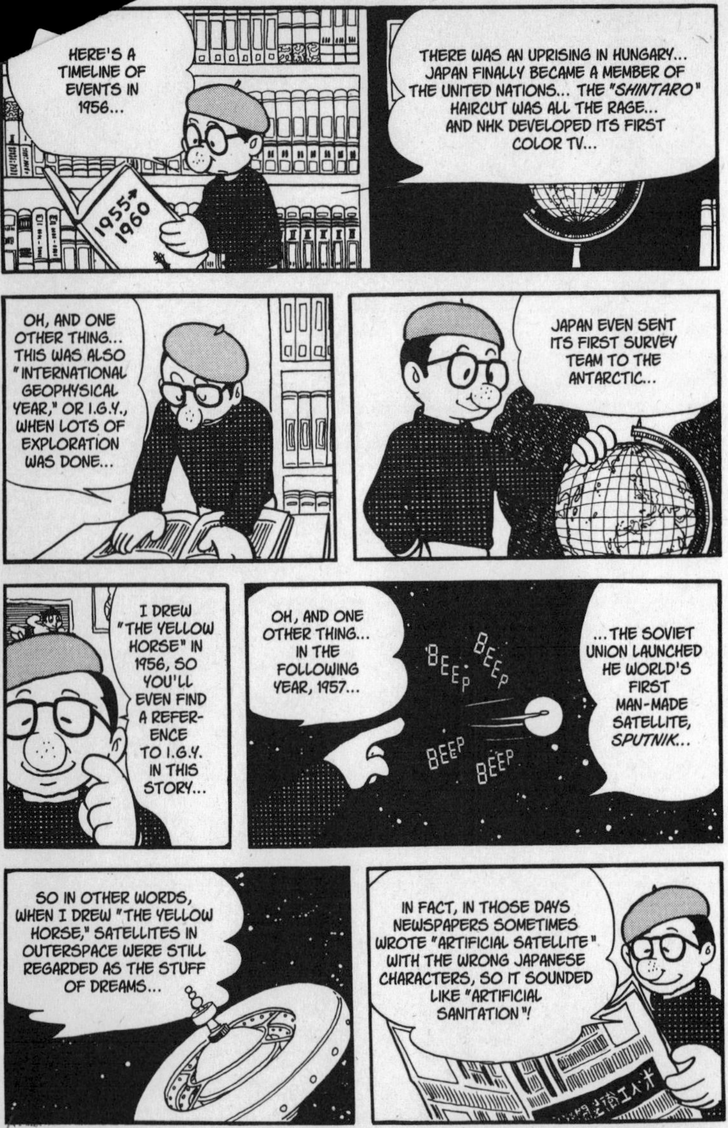
HERE'S A TIMELINE OF EVENTS IN 1956...
1955→1960
THERE WAS AN UPRISING IN HUNGARY... JAPAN FINALLY BECAME A MEMBER OF THE UNITED NATIONS... THE "SHINTARO" HAIRCUT WAS ALL THE RAGE... AND NHK DEVELOPED ITS FIRST COLOR TV...
OH, AND ONE OTHER THING... THIS WAS ALSO "INTERNATIONAL GEOPHYSICAL YEAR," OR I.G.Y., WHEN LOTS OF EXPLORATION WAS DONE...
JAPAN EVEN SENT ITS FIRST SURVEY TEAM TO THE ANTARCTIC...
I DREW "THE YELLOW HORSE" IN 1956, SO YOU'LL EVEN FIND A REFER-ENCE TO I.G.Y. IN THIS STORY...
OH, AND ONE OTHER THING... IN THE FOLLOWING YEAR, 1957...
BEEP BEEP
BEEP BEEP
...THE SOVIET UNION LAUNCHED HE WORLD'S FIRST MAN-MADE SATELLITE, SPUTNIK...
SO IN OTHER WORDS, WHEN I DREW "THE YELLOW HORSE," SATELLITES IN OUTERSPACE WERE STILL REGARDED AS THE STUFF OF DREAMS...
IN FACT, IN THOSE DAYS NEWSPAPERS SOMETIMES WROTE "ARTIFICIAL SATELLITE" WITH THE WRONG JAPANESE CHARACTERS, SO IT SOUNDED LIKE "ARTIFICIAL SANITATION"!

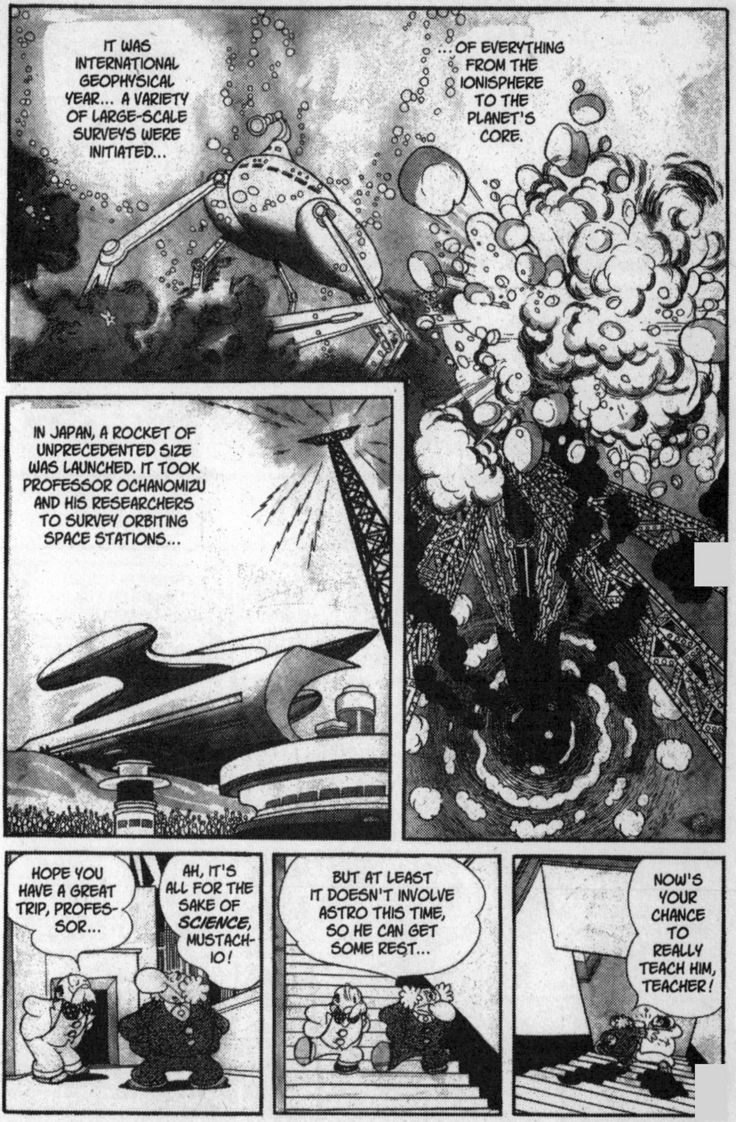
IT WAS INTERNATIONAL GEOPHYSICAL YEAR... A VARIETY OF LARGE-SCALE SURVEYS WERE INITIATED...
...OF EVERYTHING FROM THE IONISPHERE TO THE PLANET'S CORE.
IN JAPAN, A ROCKET OF UNPRECEDENTED SIZE WAS LAUNCHED. IT TOOK PROFESSOR OCHANOMIZU AND HIS RESEARCHERS TO SURVEY ORBITING SPACE STATIONS...
HOPE YOU HAVE A GREAT TRIP, PROFES-SOR...
AH, IT'S ALL FOR THE SAKE OF *SCIENCE*, MUSTACH-IO!
BUT AT LEAST IT DOESN'T INVOLVE ASTRO THIS TIME, SO HE CAN GET SOME REST...
NOW'S YOUR CHANCE TO REALLY TEACH HIM, TEACHER!

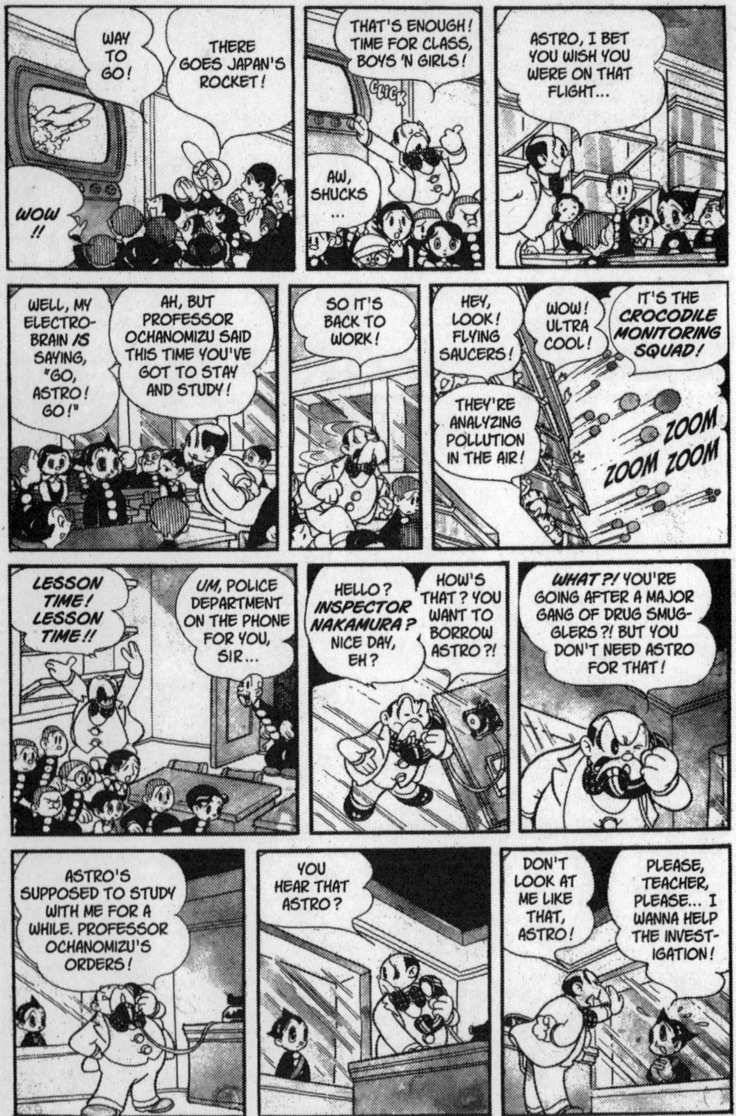
WAY TO GO!
THERE GOES JAPAN'S ROCKET!
WOW!!
THAT'S ENOUGH! TIME FOR CLASS, BOYS 'N GIRLS!
CLICK
AW, SHUCKS ...
ASTRO, I BET YOU WISH YOU WERE ON THAT FLIGHT...
WELL, MY ELECTRO-BRAIN *IS* SAYING, "GO, ASTRO! GO!"
AH, BUT PROFESSOR OCHANOMIZU SAID THIS TIME YOU'VE GOT TO STAY AND STUDY!
SO IT'S BACK TO WORK!
HEY, LOOK! FLYING SAUCERS!
WOW! ULTRA COOL!
IT'S THE *CROCODILE MONITORING SQUAD!*
THEY'RE ANALYZING POLLUTION IN THE AIR!
ZOOM ZOOM ZOOM
LESSON TIME! LESSON TIME!!
UM, POLICE DEPARTMENT ON THE PHONE FOR YOU, SIR...
HELLO? *INSPECTOR NAKAMURA?* NICE DAY, EH?
HOW'S THAT? YOU WANT TO BORROW ASTRO?!
WHAT?! YOU'RE GOING AFTER A MAJOR GANG OF DRUG SMUG-GLERS?! BUT YOU DON'T NEED ASTRO FOR THAT!
ASTRO'S SUPPOSED TO STUDY WITH ME FOR A WHILE. PROFESSOR OCHANOMIZU'S ORDERS!
YOU HEAR THAT ASTRO?
DON'T LOOK AT ME LIKE THAT, ASTRO!
PLEASE, TEACHER, PLEASE... I WANNA HELP THE INVEST-IGATION!

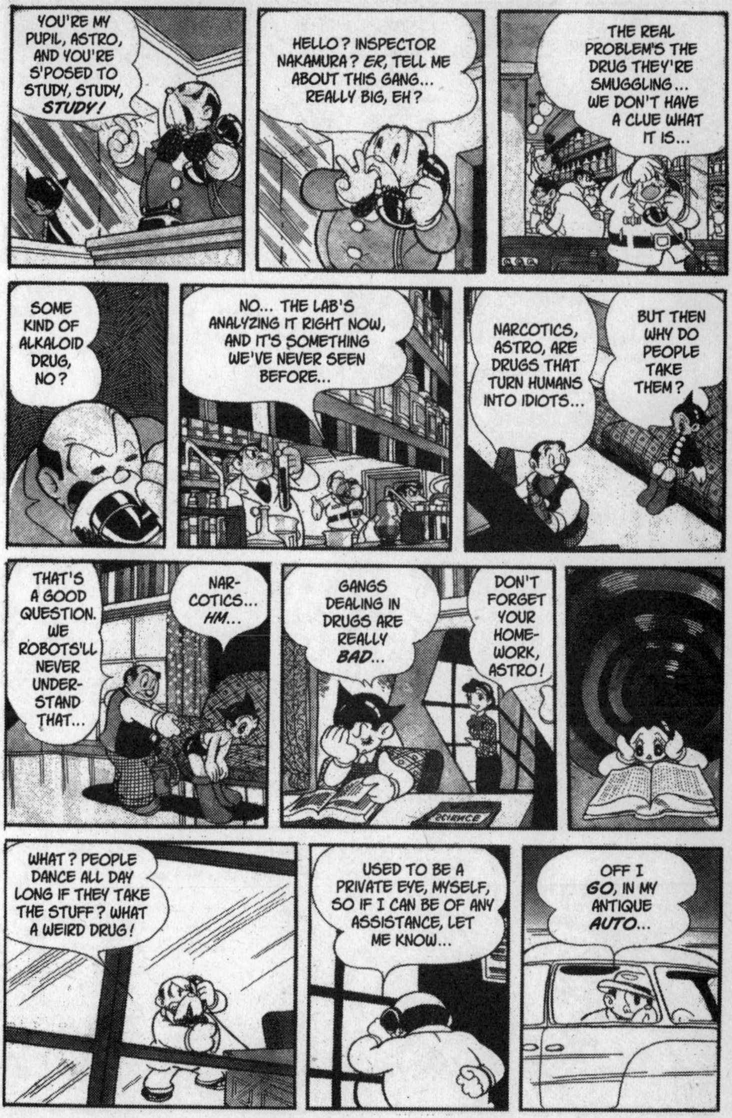
YOU'RE MY PUPIL, ASTRO, AND YOU'RE S'POSED TO STUDY, STUDY, STUDY!
HELLO? INSPECTOR NAKAMURA? ER, TELL ME ABOUT THIS GANG... REALLY BIG, EH?
THE REAL PROBLEM'S THE DRUG THEY'RE SMUGGLING... WE DON'T HAVE A CLUE WHAT IT IS...
SOME KIND OF ALKALOID DRUG, NO?
NO... THE LAB'S ANALYZING IT RIGHT NOW, AND IT'S SOMETHING WE'VE NEVER SEEN BEFORE...
NARCOTICS, ASTRO, ARE DRUGS THAT TURN HUMANS INTO IDIOTS...
BUT THEN WHY DO PEOPLE TAKE THEM?
THAT'S A GOOD QUESTION. WE ROBOTS'LL NEVER UNDER-STAND THAT...
NAR-COTICS... HM...
GANGS DEALING IN DRUGS ARE REALLY BAD...
DON'T FORGET YOUR HOME-WORK, ASTRO!
SCIENCE
WHAT? PEOPLE DANCE ALL DAY LONG IF THEY TAKE THE STUFF? WHAT A WEIRD DRUG!
USED TO BE A PRIVATE EYE, MYSELF, SO IF I CAN BE OF ANY ASSISTANCE, LET ME KNOW...
OFF I GO, IN MY ANTIQUE AUTO...

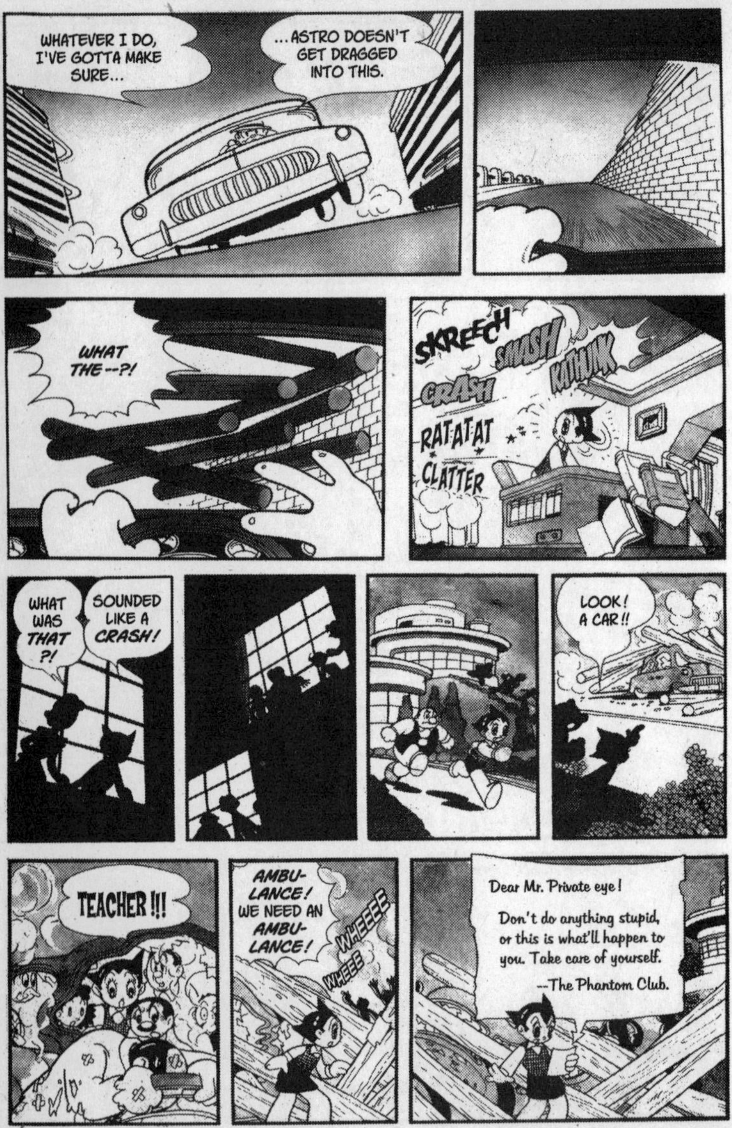
WHATEVER I DO, I'VE GOTTA MAKE SURE...
...ASTRO DOESN'T GET DRAGGED INTO THIS.
WHAT THE--?!
SKREECH
SMASH
KATHUNK
CRASH
RAT-AT-AT
CLATTER
WHAT WAS THAT ?!
SOUNDED LIKE A CRASH!
LOOK! A CAR!!
TEACHER !!!
AMBULANCE! WE NEED AN AMBULANCE!
WHEEEE
WHEEE
Dear Mr. Private eye!
Don't do anything stupid, or this is what'll happen to you. Take care of yourself.
--The Phantom Club.

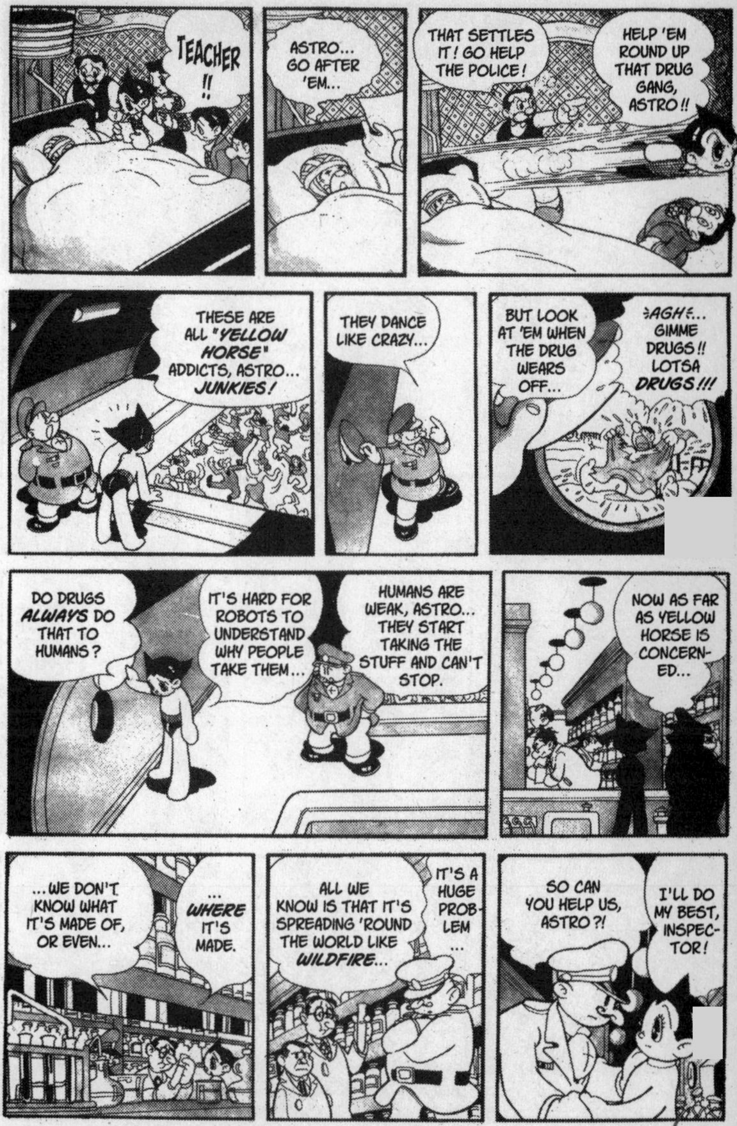
TEACHER !!
ASTRO... GO AFTER 'EM...
THAT SETTLES IT! GO HELP THE POLICE!
HELP 'EM ROUND UP THAT DRUG GANG, ASTRO!!
THESE ARE ALL "YELLOW HORSE" ADDICTS, ASTRO... JUNKIES!
THEY DANCE LIKE CRAZY...
BUT LOOK AT 'EM WHEN THE DRUG WEARS OFF...
AGH... GIMME DRUGS!! LOTSA DRUGS!!!
DO DRUGS ALWAYS DO THAT TO HUMANS?
IT'S HARD FOR ROBOTS TO UNDERSTAND WHY PEOPLE TAKE THEM...
HUMANS ARE WEAK, ASTRO... THEY START TAKING THE STUFF AND CAN'T STOP.
NOW AS FAR AS YELLOW HORSE IS CONCERN-ED...
...WE DON'T KNOW WHAT IT'S MADE OF, OR EVEN...
...WHERE IT'S MADE.
ALL WE KNOW IS THAT IT'S SPREADING 'ROUND THE WORLD LIKE WILDFIRE...
IT'S A HUGE PROB-LEM...
SO CAN YOU HELP US, ASTRO?!
I'LL DO MY BEST, INSPEC-TOR!

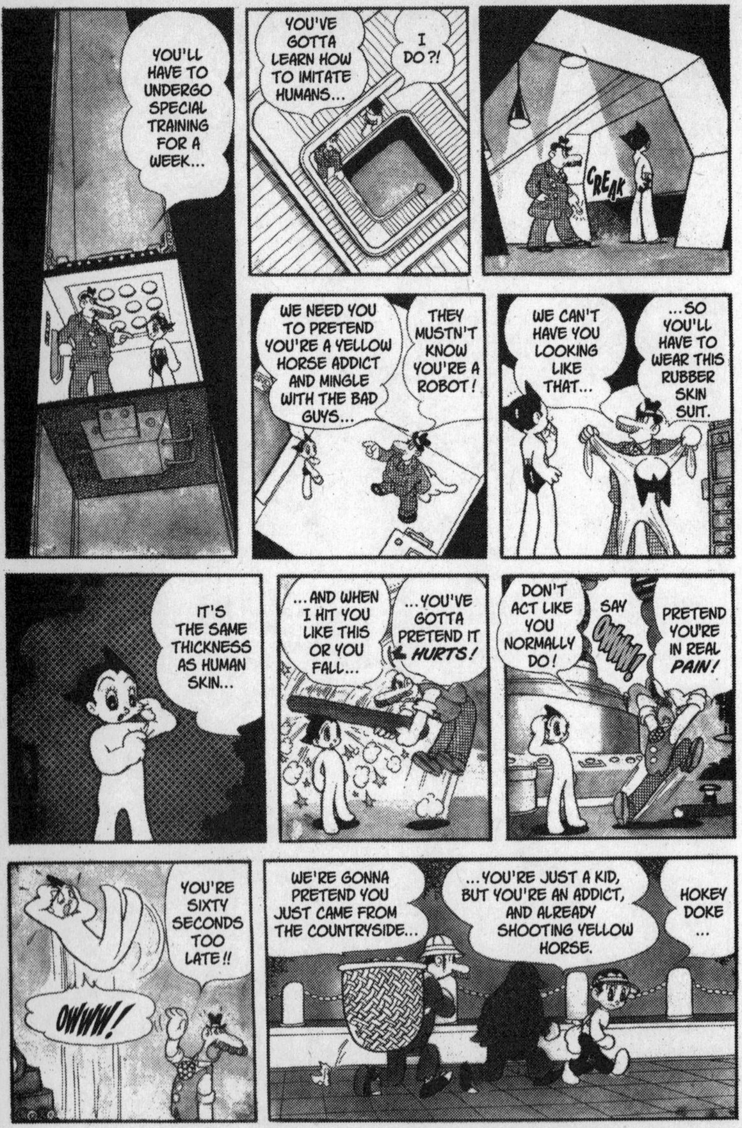
YOU'LL HAVE TO UNDERGO SPECIAL TRAINING FOR A WEEK...
YOU'VE GOTTA LEARN HOW TO IMITATE HUMANS...
I DO?!
CREAK
WE NEED YOU TO PRETEND YOU'RE A YELLOW HORSE ADDICT AND MINGLE WITH THE BAD GUYS...
THEY MUSTN'T KNOW YOU'RE A ROBOT!
WE CAN'T HAVE YOU LOOKING LIKE THAT...
...SO YOU'LL HAVE TO WEAR THIS RUBBER SKIN SUIT.
IT'S THE SAME THICKNESS AS HUMAN SKIN...
...AND WHEN I HIT YOU LIKE THIS OR YOU FALL...
...YOU'VE GOTTA PRETEND IT HURTS!
DON'T ACT LIKE YOU NORMALLY DO!
SAY OWWW!
PRETEND YOU'RE IN REAL PAIN!
YOU'RE SIXTY SECONDS TOO LATE!!
OWWW!
WE'RE GONNA PRETEND YOU JUST CAME FROM THE COUNTRYSIDE...
...YOU'RE JUST A KID, BUT YOU'RE AN ADDICT, AND ALREADY SHOOTING YELLOW HORSE.
HOKEY DOKE ...

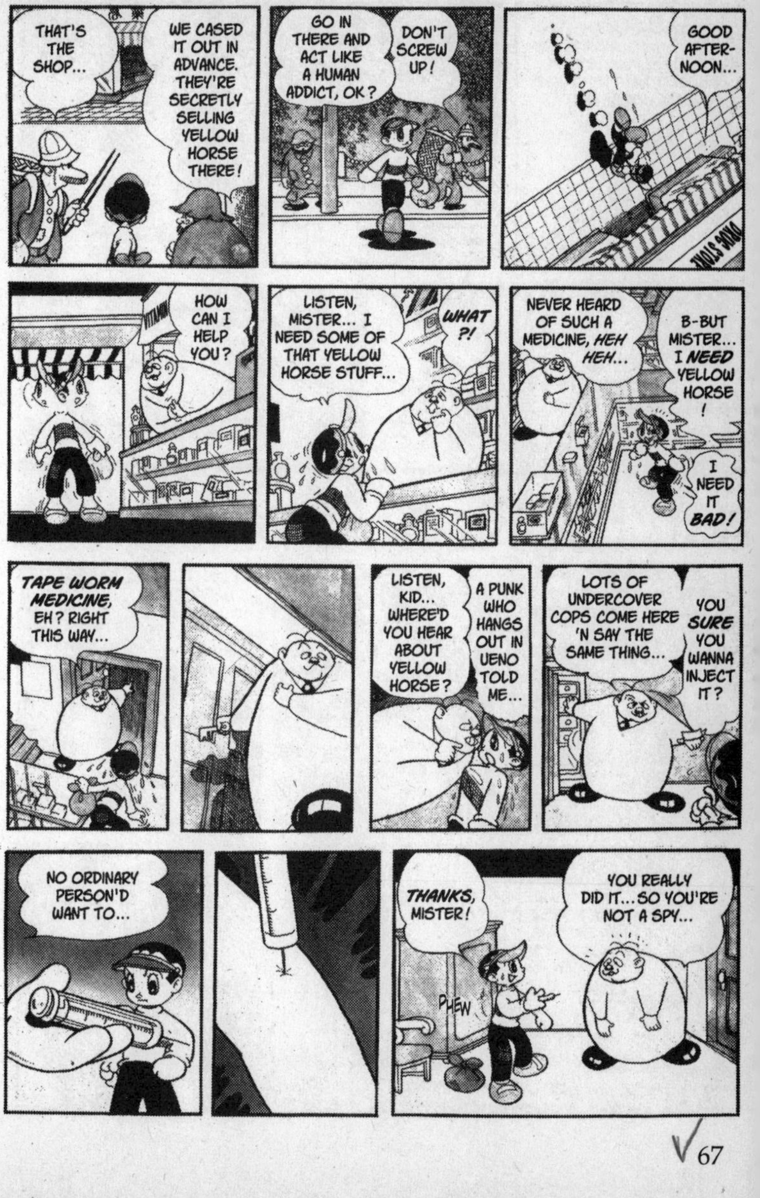
THAT'S THE SHOP...
WE CASED IT OUT IN ADVANCE. THEY'RE SECRETLY SELLING YELLOW HORSE THERE!
GO IN THERE AND ACT LIKE A HUMAN ADDICT, OK?
DON'T SCREW UP!
GOOD AFTER-NOON...
HOW CAN I HELP YOU?
LISTEN, MISTER... I NEED SOME OF THAT YELLOW HORSE STUFF...
WHAT?!
NEVER HEARD OF SUCH A MEDICINE, HEH HEH...
B-BUT MISTER... I NEED YELLOW HORSE!
I NEED IT BAD!
TAPE WORM MEDICINE, EH? RIGHT THIS WAY...
LISTEN, KID... WHERE'D YOU HEAR ABOUT YELLOW HORSE?
A PUNK WHO HANGS OUT IN UENO TOLD ME...
LOTS OF UNDERCOVER COPS COME HERE 'N SAY THE SAME THING...
YOU SURE YOU WANNA INJECT IT?
NO ORDINARY PERSON'D WANT TO...
THANKS, MISTER!
PHEW
YOU REALLY DID IT... SO YOU'RE NOT A SPY...

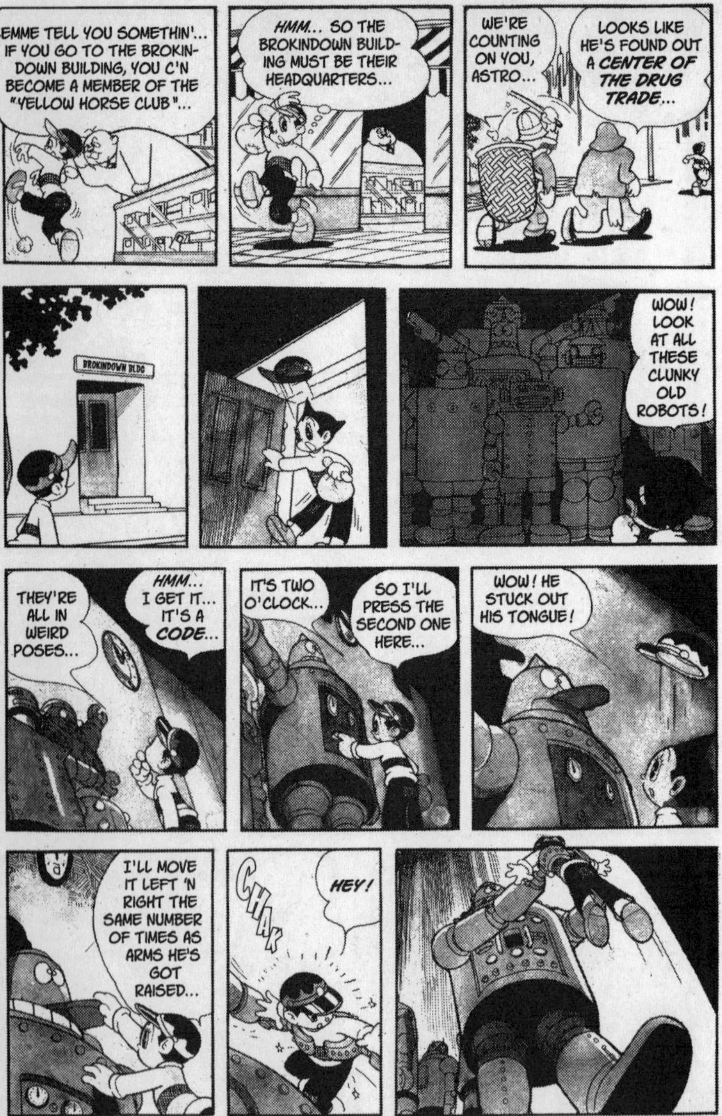
LEMME TELL YOU SOMETHIN'... IF YOU GO TO THE BROKINDOWN BUILDING, YOU C'N BECOME A MEMBER OF THE "YELLOW HORSE CLUB"...
HMM... SO THE BROKINDOWN BUILDING MUST BE THEIR HEADQUARTERS...
WE'RE COUNTING ON YOU, ASTRO...
LOOKS LIKE HE'S FOUND OUT A CENTER OF THE DRUG TRADE...
BROKINDOWN BLDG
WOW! LOOK AT ALL THESE CLUNKY OLD ROBOTS!
THEY'RE ALL IN WEIRD POSES...
HMM... I GET IT... IT'S A CODE...
IT'S TWO O'CLOCK...
SO I'LL PRESS THE SECOND ONE HERE...
WOW! HE STUCK OUT HIS TONGUE!
I'LL MOVE IT LEFT 'N RIGHT THE SAME NUMBER OF TIMES AS ARMS HE'S GOT RAISED...
CHAK
HEY!

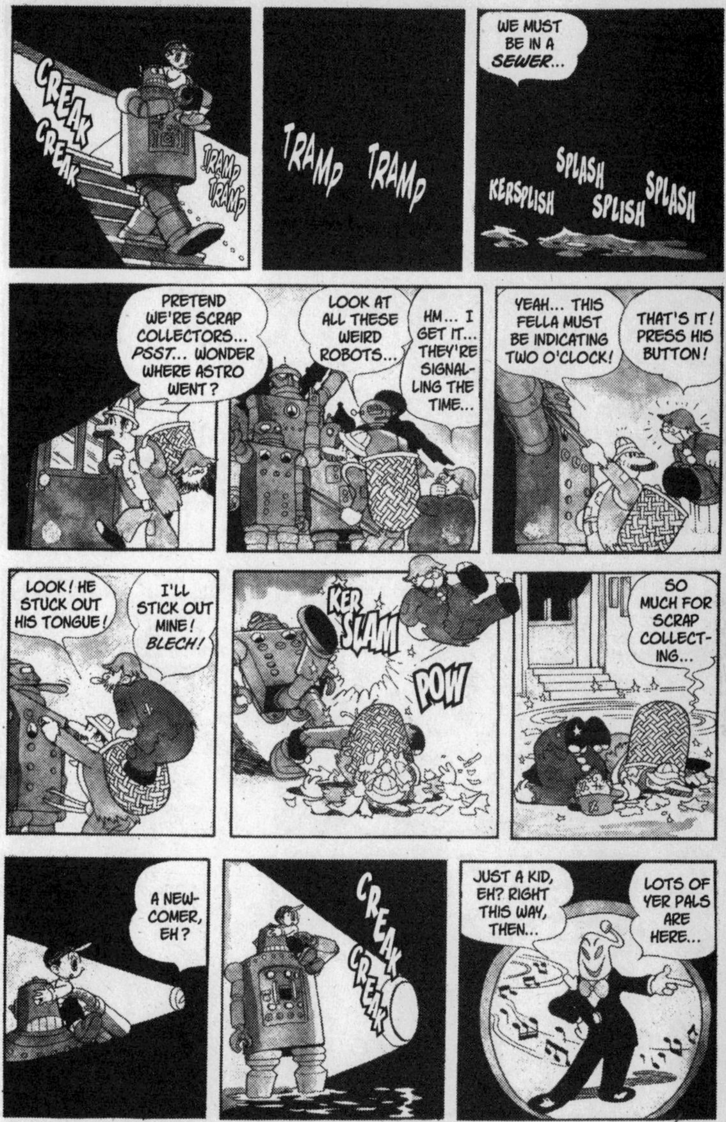
CREAK CREAK
TRAMP TRAMP
TRAMP TRAMP
WE MUST BE IN A SEWER...
KERSPLISH SPLASH SPLISH SPLASH
PRETEND WE'RE SCRAP COLLECTORS... PSST... WONDER WHERE ASTRO WENT?
LOOK AT ALL THESE WEIRD ROBOTS...
HM... I GET IT... THEY'RE SIGNAL-LING THE TIME...
YEAH... THIS FELLA MUST BE INDICATING TWO O'CLOCK!
THAT'S IT! PRESS HIS BUTTON!
LOOK! HE STUCK OUT HIS TONGUE!
I'LL STICK OUT MINE! BLECH!
KER SLAM
POW
SO MUCH FOR SCRAP COLLECT-ING...
A NEW-COMER, EH?
CREAK CREAK
JUST A KID, EH? RIGHT THIS WAY, THEN...
LOTS OF YER PALS ARE HERE...

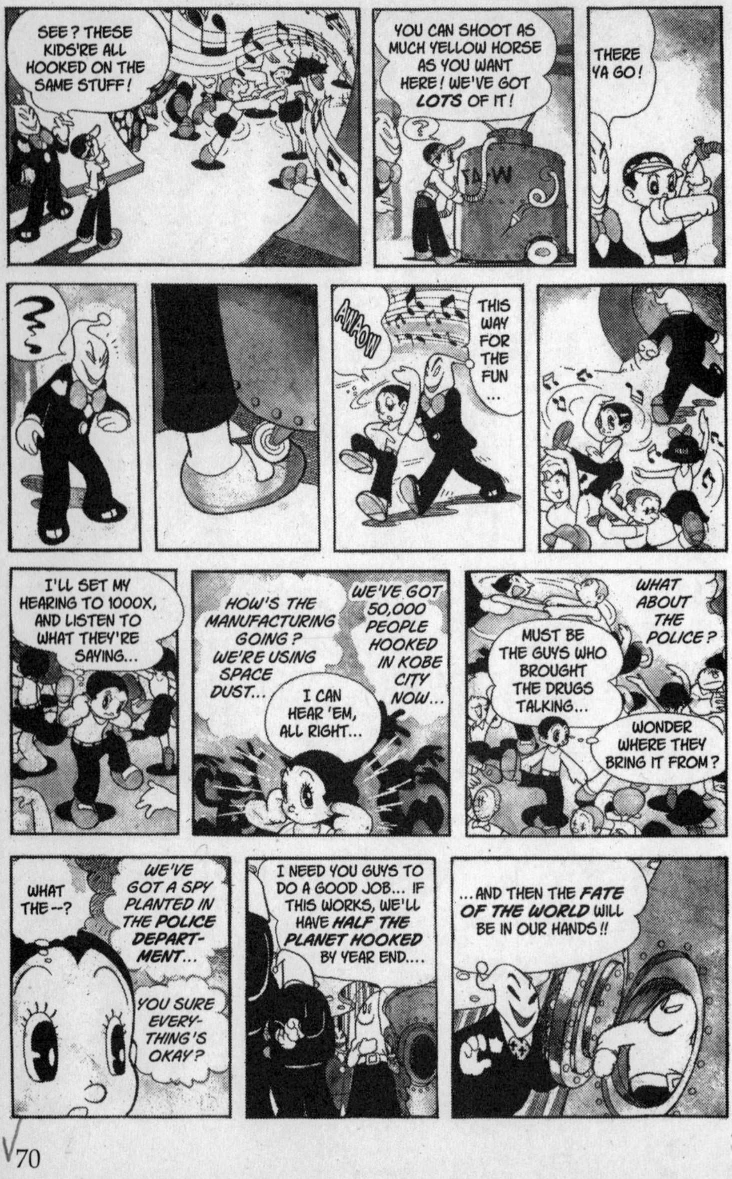
SEE? THESE KIDS'RE ALL HOOKED ON THE SAME STUFF!
YOU CAN SHOOT AS MUCH YELLOW HORSE AS YOU WANT HERE! WE'VE GOT LOTS OF IT!
?
THERE YA GO!
AWOW
THIS WAY FOR THE FUN ...
I'LL SET MY HEARING TO 1000X, AND LISTEN TO WHAT THEY'RE SAYING...
HOW'S THE MANUFACTURING GOING? WE'RE USING SPACE DUST...
WE'VE GOT 50,000 PEOPLE HOOKED IN KOBE CITY NOW...
I CAN HEAR 'EM, ALL RIGHT...
WHAT ABOUT THE POLICE?
MUST BE THE GUYS WHO BROUGHT THE DRUGS TALKING...
WONDER WHERE THEY BRING IT FROM?
WHAT THE--?
WE'VE GOT A SPY PLANTED IN THE POLICE DEPART-MENT...
YOU SURE EVERY-THING'S OKAY?
I NEED YOU GUYS TO DO A GOOD JOB... IF THIS WORKS, WE'LL HAVE HALF THE PLANET HOOKED BY YEAR END....
...AND THEN THE FATE OF THE WORLD WILL BE IN OUR HANDS!!

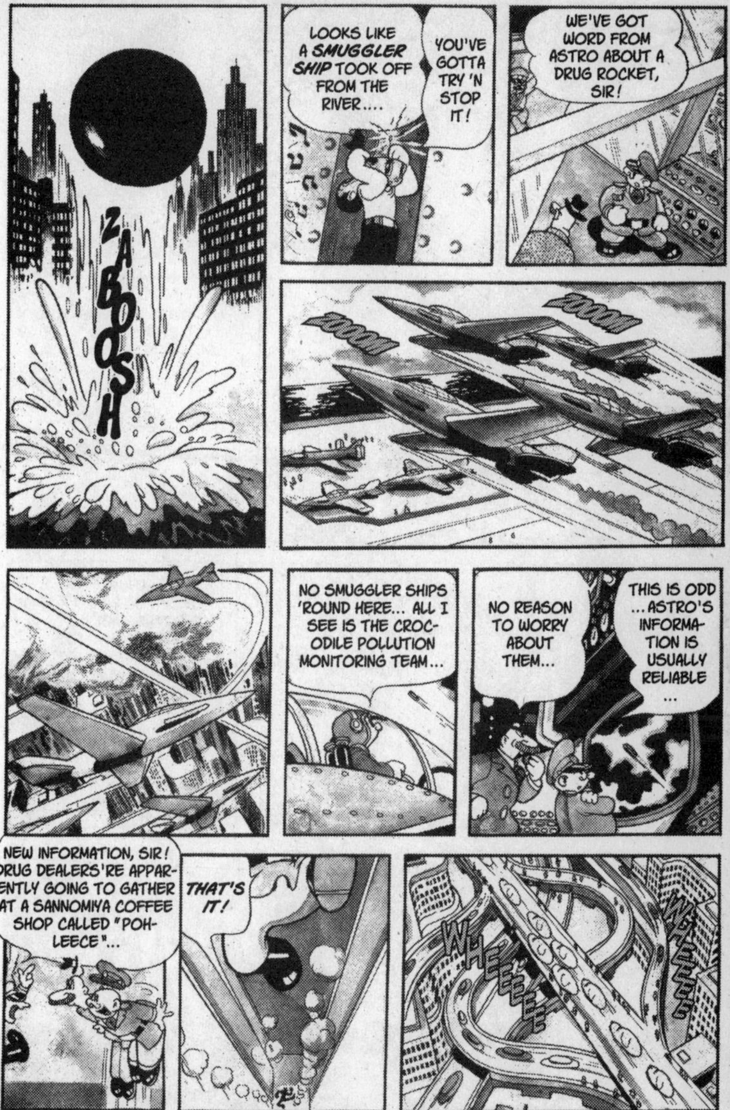
ZABOOSH
LOOKS LIKE A SMUGGLER SHIP TOOK OFF FROM THE RIVER....
YOU'VE GOTTA TRY 'N STOP IT!
WE'VE GOT WORD FROM ASTRO ABOUT A DRUG ROCKET, SIR!
NO SMUGGLER SHIPS 'ROUND HERE... ALL I SEE IS THE CROC-ODILE POLLUTION MONITORING TEAM...
NO REASON TO WORRY ABOUT THEM...
THIS IS ODD ...ASTRO'S INFORMA-TION IS USUALLY RELIABLE ...
NEW INFORMATION, SIR! DRUG DEALERS'RE APPAR-ENTLY GOING TO GATHER AT A SANNOMIYA COFFEE SHOP CALLED "POH-LEECE"...
THAT'S IT!
WHEEEEE

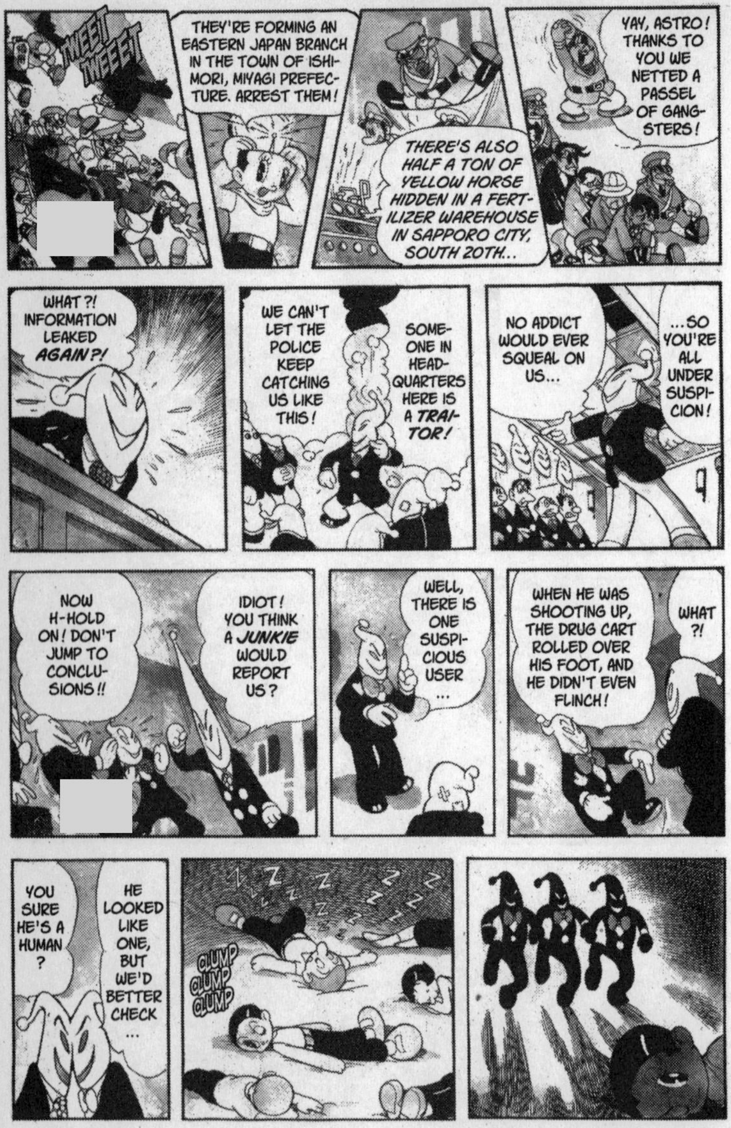
TWEEET TWEEEET
THEY'RE FORMING AN EASTERN JAPAN BRANCH IN THE TOWN OF ISHI-MORI, MIYAGI PREFEC-TURE. ARREST THEM!
THERE'S ALSO HALF A TON OF YELLOW HORSE HIDDEN IN A FERT-ILIZER WAREHOUSE IN SAPPORO CITY, SOUTH 20TH...
YAY, ASTRO! THANKS TO YOU WE NETTED A PASSEL OF GANG-STERS!
WHAT?! INFORMATION LEAKED AGAIN?!
WE CAN'T LET THE POLICE KEEP CATCHING US LIKE THIS!
SOME-ONE IN HEAD-QUARTERS HERE IS A TRAI-TOR!
NO ADDICT WOULD EVER SQUEAL ON US...
...SO YOU'RE ALL UNDER SUSPI-CION!
NOW H-HOLD ON! DON'T JUMP TO CONCLU-SIONS!!
IDIOT! YOU THINK A JUNKIE WOULD REPORT US?
WELL, THERE IS ONE SUSPI-CIOUS USER ...
WHEN HE WAS SHOOTING UP, THE DRUG CART ROLLED OVER HIS FOOT, AND HE DIDN'T EVEN FLINCH!
WHAT ?!
YOU SURE HE'S A HUMAN ?
HE LOOKED LIKE ONE, BUT WE'D BETTER CHECK ...
CLUMP CLUMP CLUMP

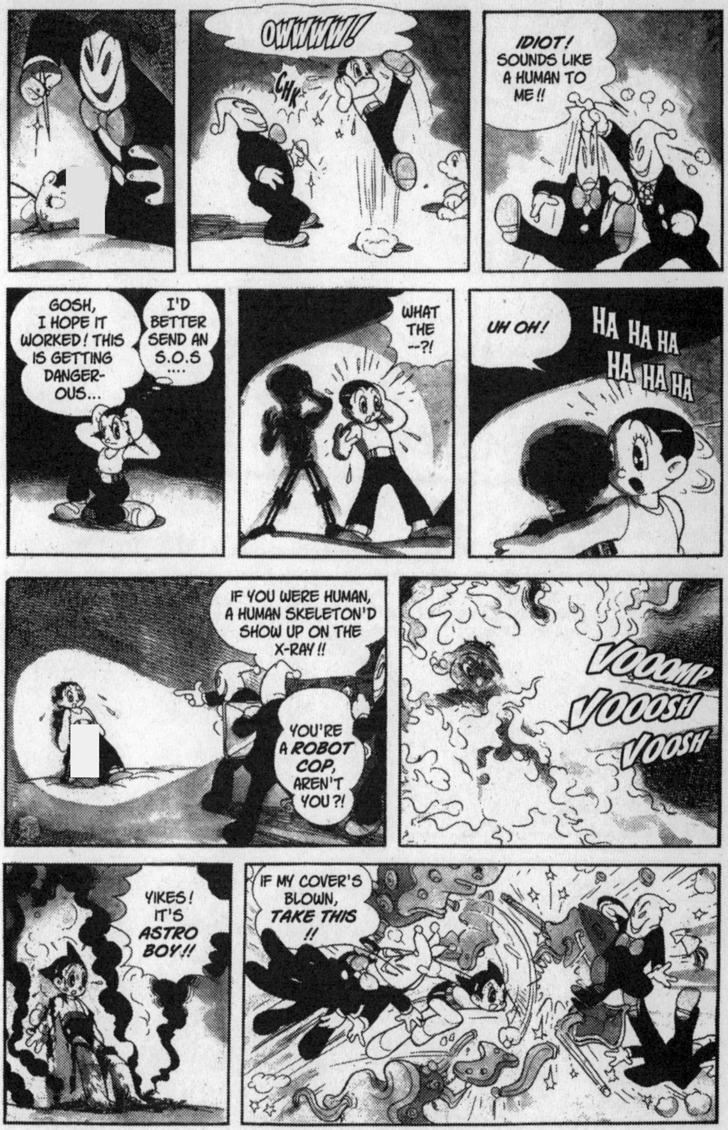
OWWWW!
CHK
IDIOT! SOUNDS LIKE A HUMAN TO ME!!
GOSH, I HOPE IT WORKED! THIS IS GETTING DANGER-OUS...
I'D BETTER SEND AN S.O.S ....
WHAT THE --?!
UH OH!
HA HA HA HA HA HA
IF YOU WERE HUMAN, A HUMAN SKELETON'D SHOW UP ON THE X-RAY!!
YOU'RE A ROBOT COP, AREN'T YOU?!
VOOOMP
VOOOSH
VOOSH
YIKES! IT'S ASTRO BOY!!
IF MY COVER'S BLOWN, TAKE THIS!!

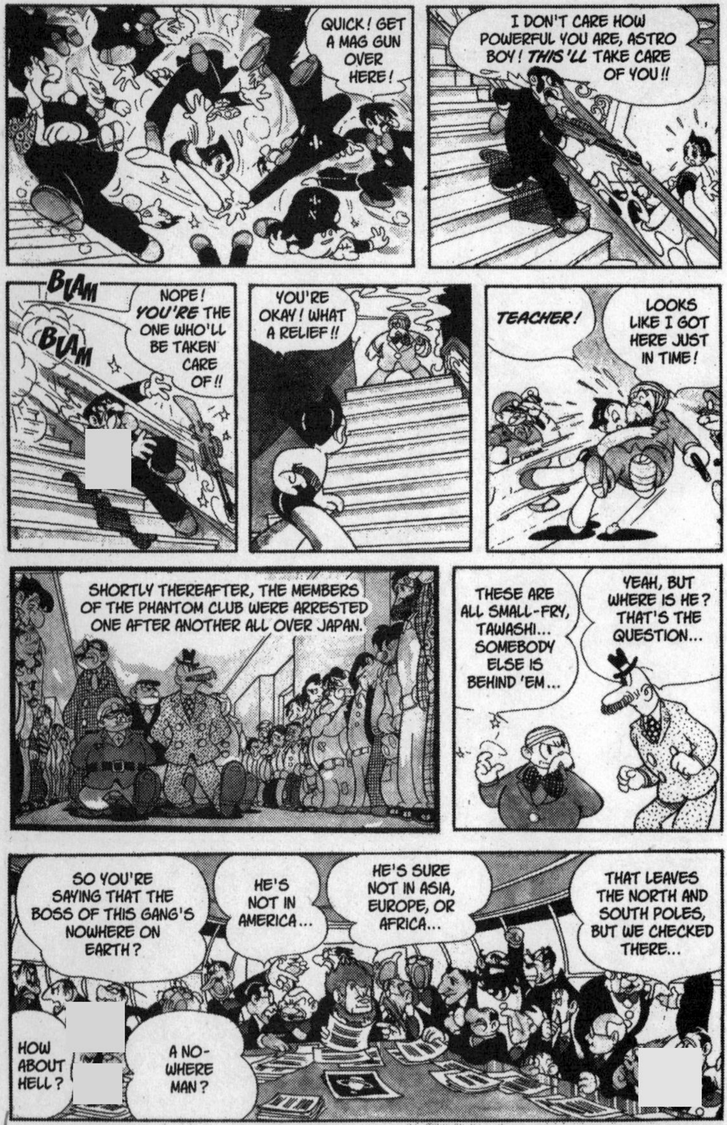
QUICK! GET A MAG GUN OVER HERE!
I DON'T CARE HOW POWERFUL YOU ARE, ASTRO BOY! THIS'LL TAKE CARE OF YOU!!
BLAM
BLAM
NOPE! YOU'RE THE ONE WHO'LL BE TAKEN CARE OF!!
YOU'RE OKAY! WHAT A RELIEF!!
TEACHER!
LOOKS LIKE I GOT HERE JUST IN TIME!
SHORTLY THEREAFTER, THE MEMBERS OF THE PHANTOM CLUB WERE ARRESTED ONE AFTER ANOTHER ALL OVER JAPAN.
THESE ARE ALL SMALL-FRY, TAWASHI... SOMEBODY ELSE IS BEHIND 'EM...
YEAH, BUT WHERE IS HE? THAT'S THE QUESTION...
SO YOU'RE SAYING THAT THE BOSS OF THIS GANG'S NOWHERE ON EARTH?
HE'S NOT IN AMERICA...
HE'S SURE NOT IN ASIA, EUROPE, OR AFRICA...
THAT LEAVES THE NORTH AND SOUTH POLES, BUT WE CHECKED THERE...
HOW ABOUT HELL?
A NO-WHERE MAN?

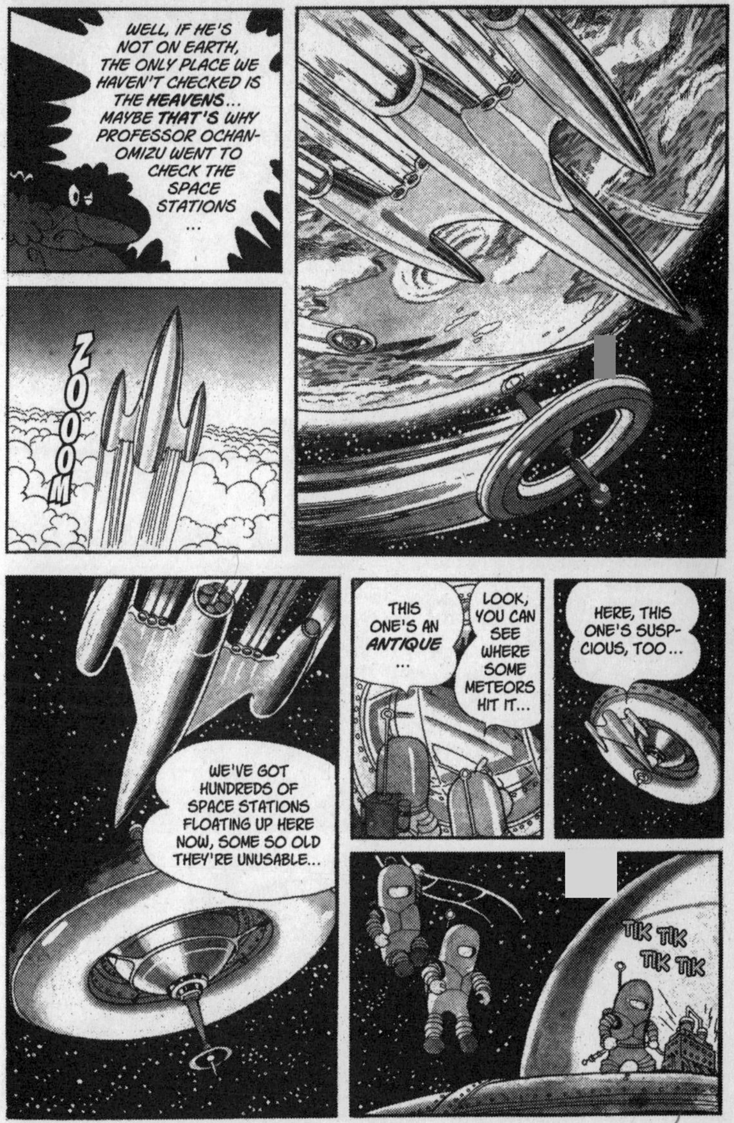
WELL, IF HE'S NOT ON EARTH, THE ONLY PLACE WE HAVEN'T CHECKED IS THE **HEAVENS**... MAYBE **THAT'S** WHY PROFESSOR OCHAN-OMIZU WENT TO CHECK THE SPACE STATIONS ...
ZOOOOM
WE'VE GOT HUNDREDS OF SPACE STATIONS FLOATING UP HERE NOW, SOME SO OLD THEY'RE UNUSABLE...
THIS ONE'S AN ***ANTIQUE*** ...
LOOK, YOU CAN SEE WHERE SOME METEORS HIT IT...
HERE, THIS ONE'S SUSP-CIOUS, TOO...
TIK TIK
TIK TIK

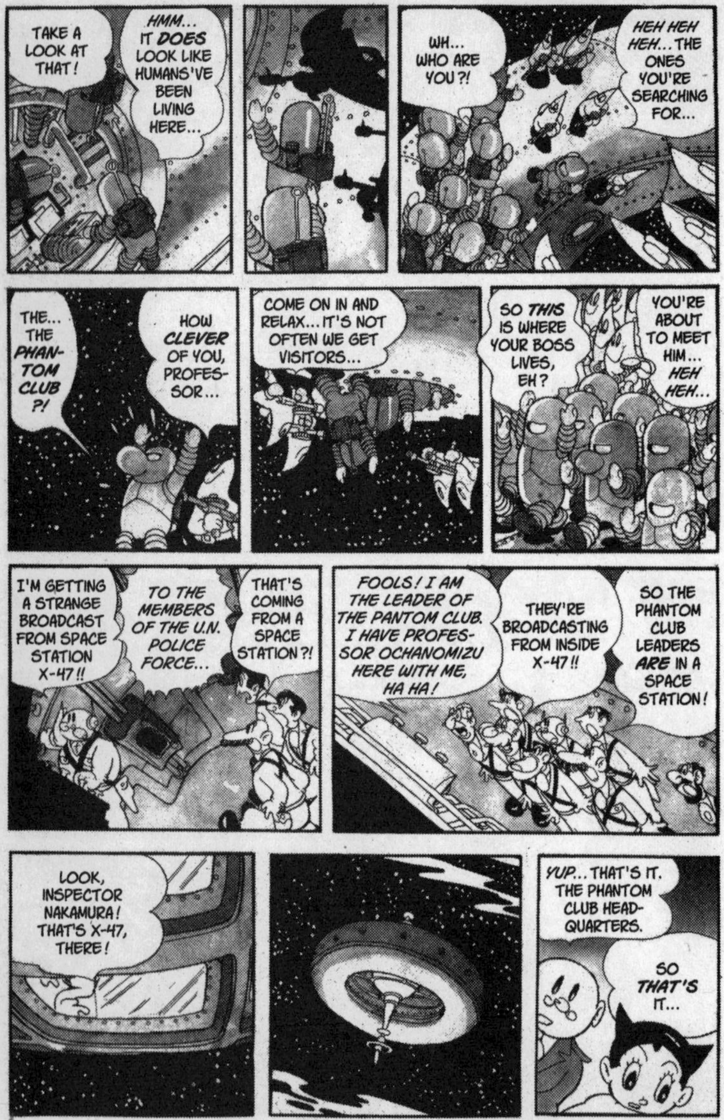

TAKE A LOOK AT THAT!
HMM... IT DOES LOOK LIKE HUMANS'VE BEEN LIVING HERE...
WH... WHO ARE YOU?!
HEH HEH HEH... THE ONES YOU'RE SEARCHING FOR...
THE... THE PHANTOM CLUB?!
HOW CLEVER OF YOU, PROFESSOR...
COME ON IN AND RELAX... IT'S NOT OFTEN WE GET VISITORS...
SO THIS IS WHERE YOUR BOSS LIVES, EH?
YOU'RE ABOUT TO MEET HIM... HEH HEH...
I'M GETTING A STRANGE BROADCAST FROM SPACE STATION X-47!!
TO THE MEMBERS OF THE U.N. POLICE FORCE...
THAT'S COMING FROM A SPACE STATION?!
FOOLS! I AM THE LEADER OF THE PANTOM CLUB. I HAVE PROFESSOR OCHANOMIZU HERE WITH ME, HA HA!
THEY'RE BROADCASTING FROM INSIDE X-47!!
SO THE PHANTOM CLUB LEADERS ARE IN A SPACE STATION!
LOOK, INSPECTOR NAKAMURA! THAT'S X-47, THERE!
YUP... THAT'S IT. THE PHANTOM CLUB HEADQUARTERS.
SO THAT'S IT...

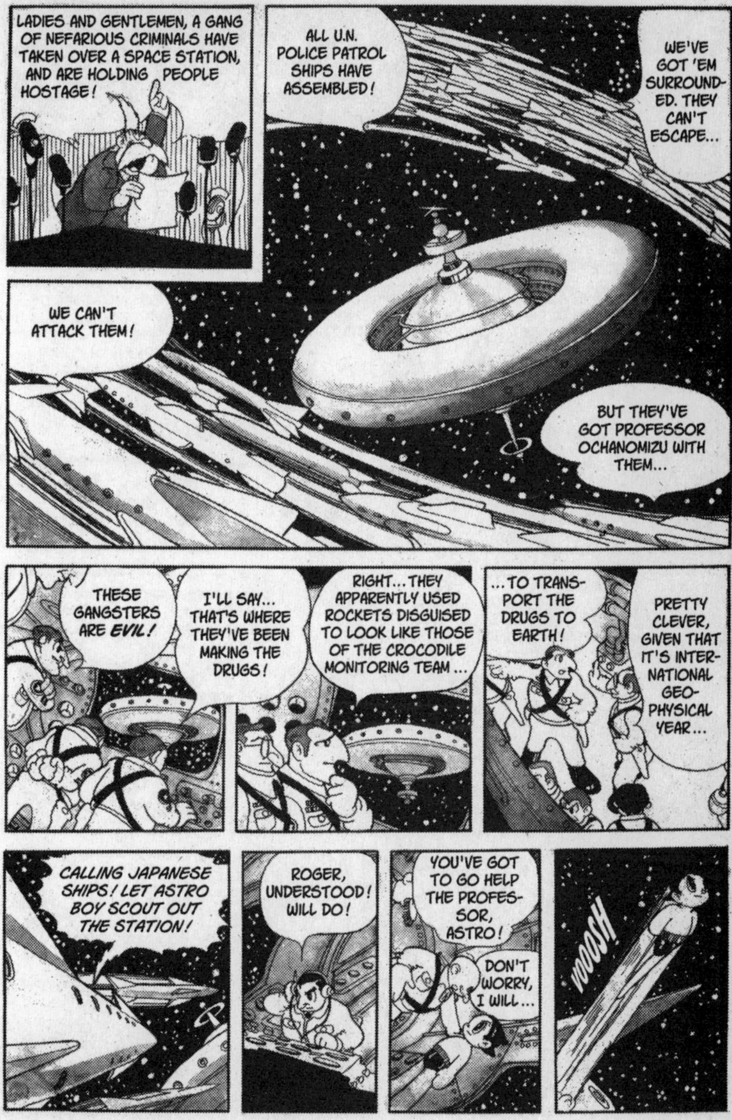
LADIES AND GENTLEMEN, A GANG OF NEFARIOUS CRIMINALS HAVE TAKEN OVER A SPACE STATION, AND ARE HOLDING PEOPLE HOSTAGE!
ALL U.N. POLICE PATROL SHIPS HAVE ASSEMBLED!
WE'VE GOT 'EM SURROUNDED. THEY CAN'T ESCAPE...
WE CAN'T ATTACK THEM!
BUT THEY'VE GOT PROFESSOR OCHANOMIZU WITH THEM...
THESE GANGSTERS ARE *EVIL*!
I'LL SAY... THAT'S WHERE THEY'VE BEEN MAKING THE DRUGS!
RIGHT... THEY APPARENTLY USED ROCKETS DISGUISED TO LOOK LIKE THOSE OF THE CROCODILE MONITORING TEAM ...
...TO TRANSPORT THE DRUGS TO EARTH!
PRETTY CLEVER, GIVEN THAT IT'S INTERNATIONAL GEOPHYSICAL YEAR...
CALLING JAPANESE SHIPS! LET ASTRO BOY SCOUT OUT THE STATION!
ROGER, UNDERSTOOD! WILL DO!
YOU'VE GOT TO GO HELP THE PROFESSOR, ASTRO!
DON'T WORRY, I WILL...
VOOOSH

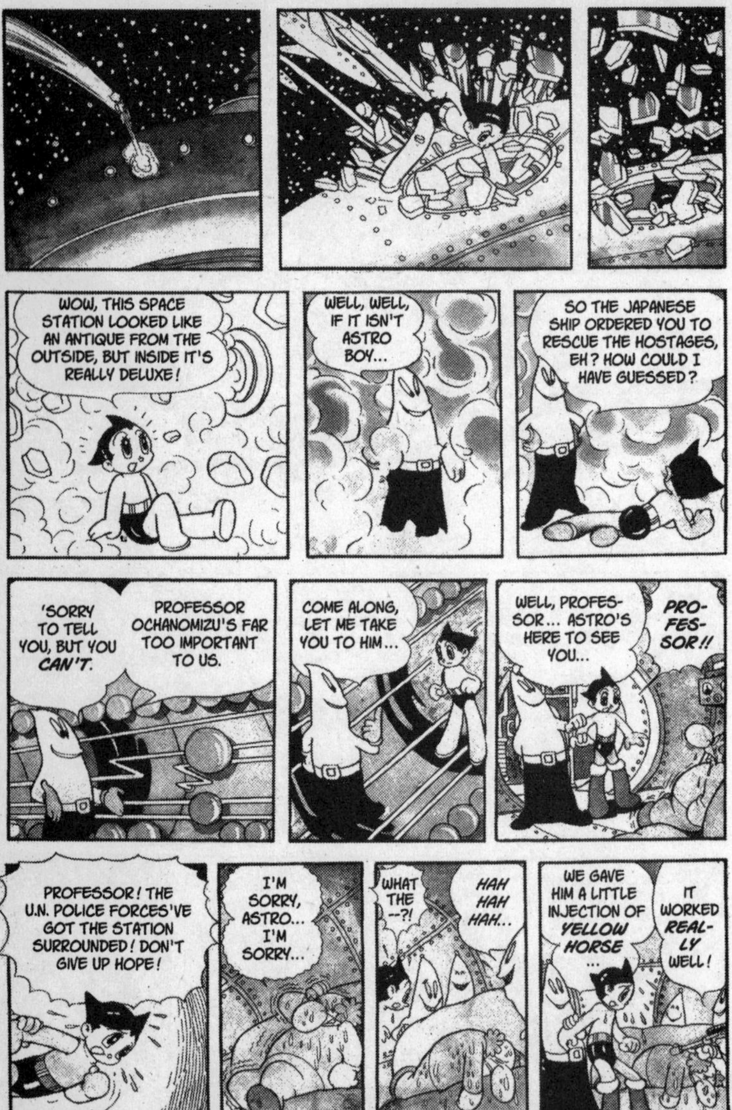
WOW, THIS SPACE STATION LOOKED LIKE AN ANTIQUE FROM THE OUTSIDE, BUT INSIDE IT'S REALLY DELUXE!
WELL, WELL, IF IT ISN'T ASTRO BOY...
SO THE JAPANESE SHIP ORDERED YOU TO RESCUE THE HOSTAGES, EH? HOW COULD I HAVE GUESSED?
'SORRY TO TELL YOU, BUT YOU CAN'T.
PROFESSOR OCHANOMIZU'S FAR TOO IMPORTANT TO US.
COME ALONG, LET ME TAKE YOU TO HIM...
WELL, PROFESSOR... ASTRO'S HERE TO SEE YOU...
PROFESSOR!!
PROFESSOR! THE U.N. POLICE FORCES'VE GOT THE STATION SURROUNDED! DON'T GIVE UP HOPE!
I'M SORRY, ASTRO... I'M SORRY...
WHAT THE --?!
HAH HAH HAH...
WE GAVE HIM A LITTLE INJECTION OF YELLOW HORSE...
IT WORKED REALLY WELL!

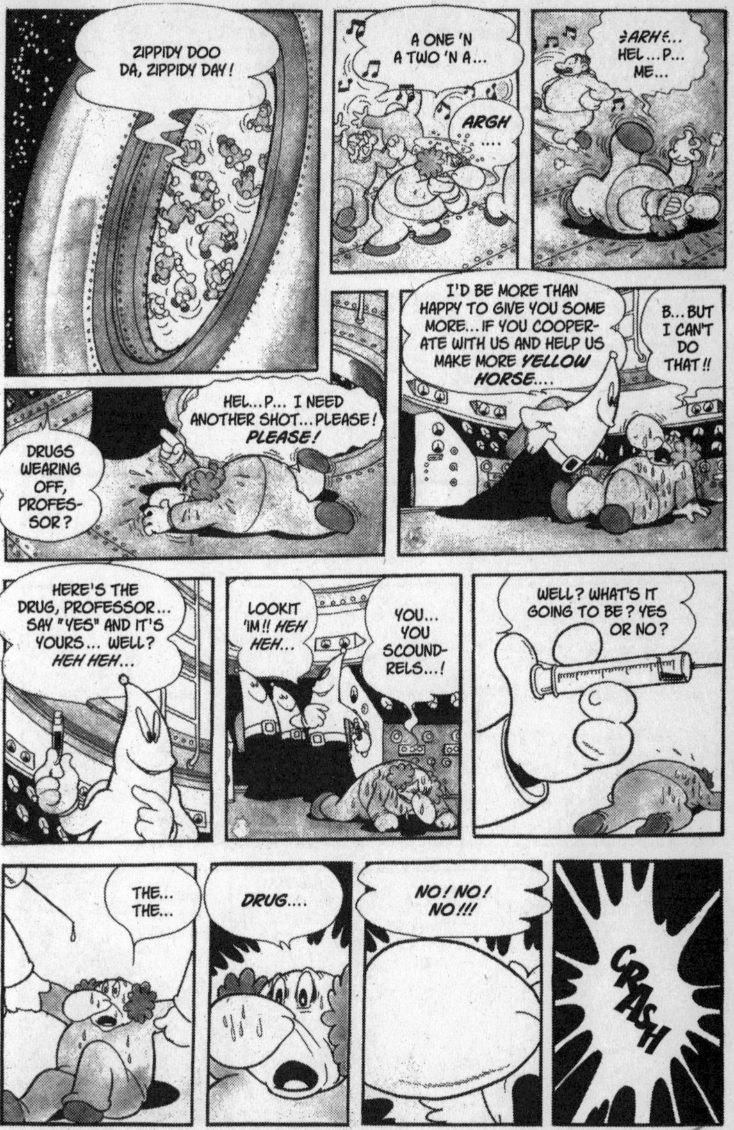

ZIPPIDY DOO DA, ZIPPIDY DAY!
A ONE 'N A TWO 'N A...
ARGH ....
ARH... HEL...P... ME...
DRUGS WEARING OFF, PROFESSOR?
HEL...P... I NEED ANOTHER SHOT...PLEASE! PLEASE!
I'D BE MORE THAN HAPPY TO GIVE YOU SOME MORE... IF YOU COOPERATE WITH US AND HELP US MAKE MORE YELLOW HORSE....
B...BUT I CAN'T DO THAT!!
HERE'S THE DRUG, PROFESSOR... SAY "YES" AND IT'S YOURS... WELL? HEH HEH...
LOOKIT 'IM!! HEH HEH...
YOU... YOU SCOUNDRELS...!
WELL? WHAT'S IT GOING TO BE? YES OR NO?
THE... THE...
DRUG....
NO! NO! NO!!!
CRASH

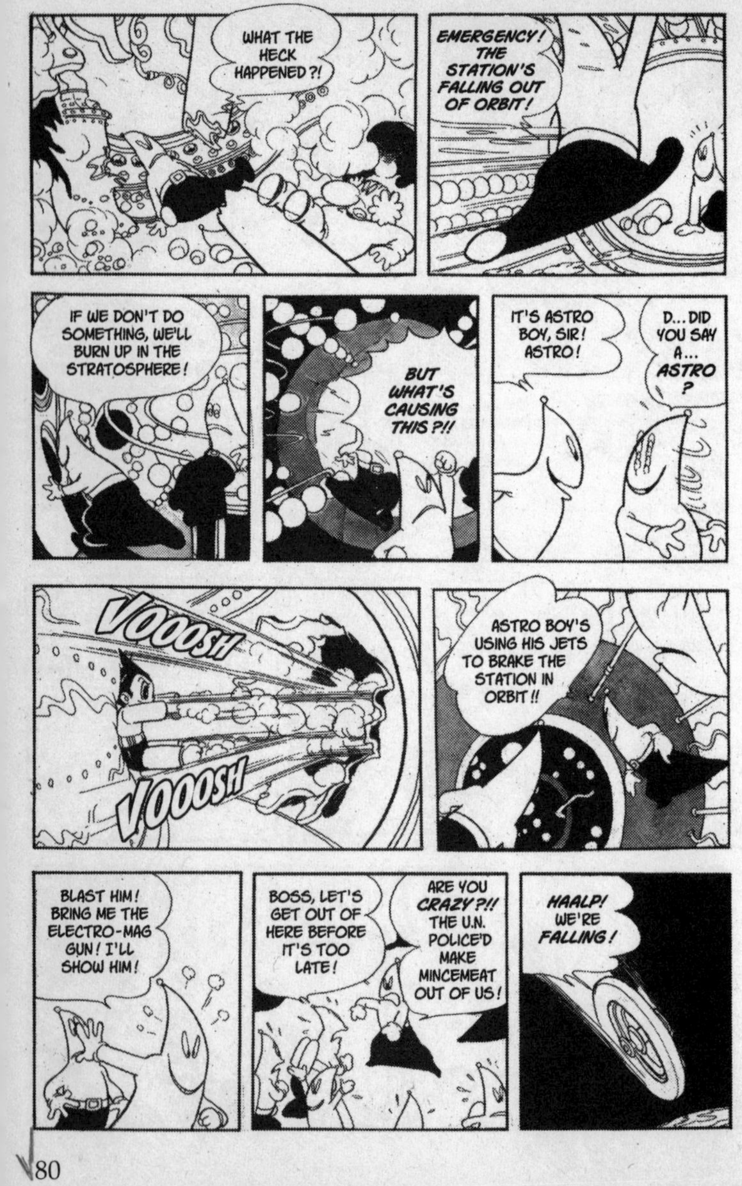
WHAT THE HECK HAPPENED?!
EMERGENCY! THE STATION'S FALLING OUT OF ORBIT!
IF WE DON'T DO SOMETHING, WE'LL BURN UP IN THE STRATOSPHERE!
BUT WHAT'S CAUSING THIS?!!
IT'S ASTRO BOY, SIR! ASTRO!
D... DID YOU SAY A... ASTRO?
VOOOSH
VOOOSH
ASTRO BOY'S USING HIS JETS TO BRAKE THE STATION IN ORBIT!!
BLAST HIM! BRING ME THE ELECTRO-MAG GUN! I'LL SHOW HIM!
BOSS, LET'S GET OUT OF HERE BEFORE IT'S TOO LATE!
ARE YOU CRAZY?!! THE U.N. POLICE'D MAKE MINCEMEAT OUT OF US!
HAALP! WE'RE FALLING!

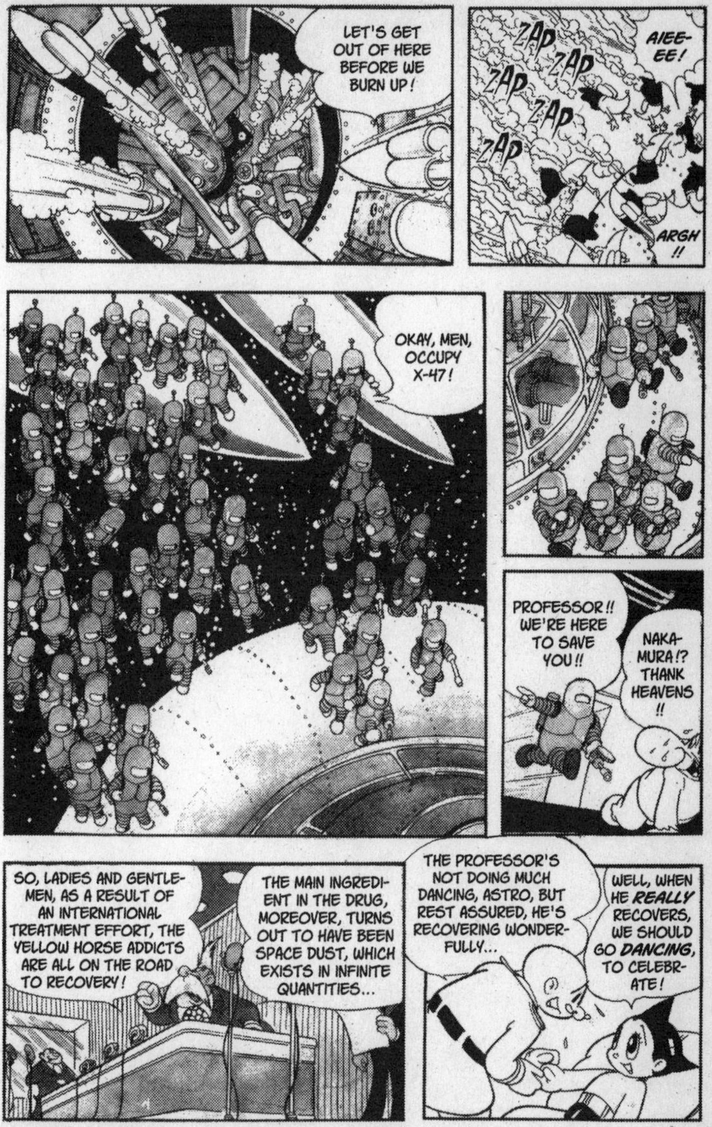
LET'S GET OUT OF HERE BEFORE WE BURN UP!
ZAP ZAP ZAP ZAP ZAP
AIEEE-EE!
ARGH!!
OKAY, MEN, OCCUPY X-47!
PROFESSOR!! WE'RE HERE TO SAVE YOU!!
NAKA-MURA!? THANK HEAVENS!!
SO, LADIES AND GENTLE-MEN, AS A RESULT OF AN INTERNATIONAL TREATMENT EFFORT, THE YELLOW HORSE ADDICTS ARE ALL ON THE ROAD TO RECOVERY!
THE MAIN INGREDI-ENT IN THE DRUG, MOREOVER, TURNS OUT TO HAVE BEEN SPACE DUST, WHICH EXISTS IN INFINITE QUANTITIES...
THE PROFESSOR'S NOT DOING MUCH DANCING, ASTRO, BUT REST ASSURED, HE'S RECOVERING WONDER-FULLY...
WELL, WHEN HE *REALLY* RECOVERS, WE SHOULD GO *DANCING*, TO CELEBR-ATE!

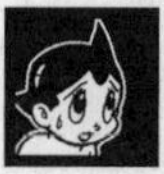

THE 100 MILLION YEAR OLD CRIME

First serialized from March to April 1967 in *Shonen* magazine.

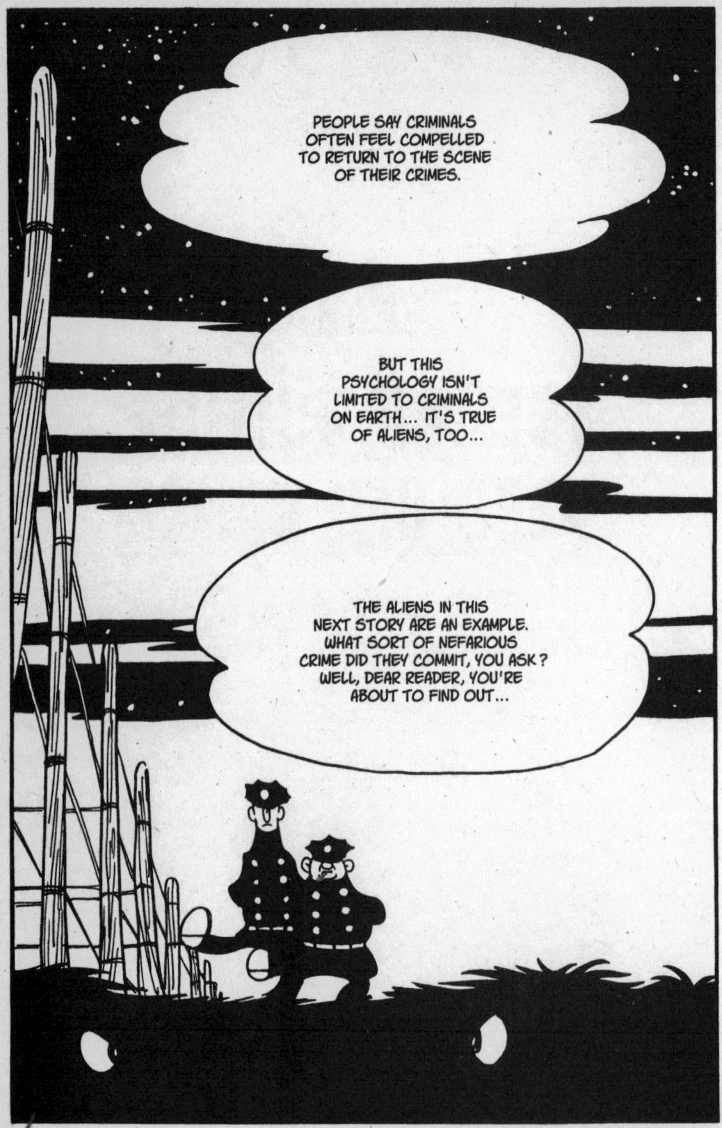
PEOPLE SAY CRIMINALS OFTEN FEEL COMPELLED TO RETURN TO THE SCENE OF THEIR CRIMES.
BUT THIS PSYCHOLOGY ISN'T LIMITED TO CRIMINALS ON EARTH... IT'S TRUE OF ALIENS, TOO...
THE ALIENS IN THIS NEXT STORY ARE AN EXAMPLE. WHAT SORT OF NEFARIOUS CRIME DID THEY COMMIT, YOU ASK? WELL, DEAR READER, YOU'RE ABOUT TO FIND OUT...

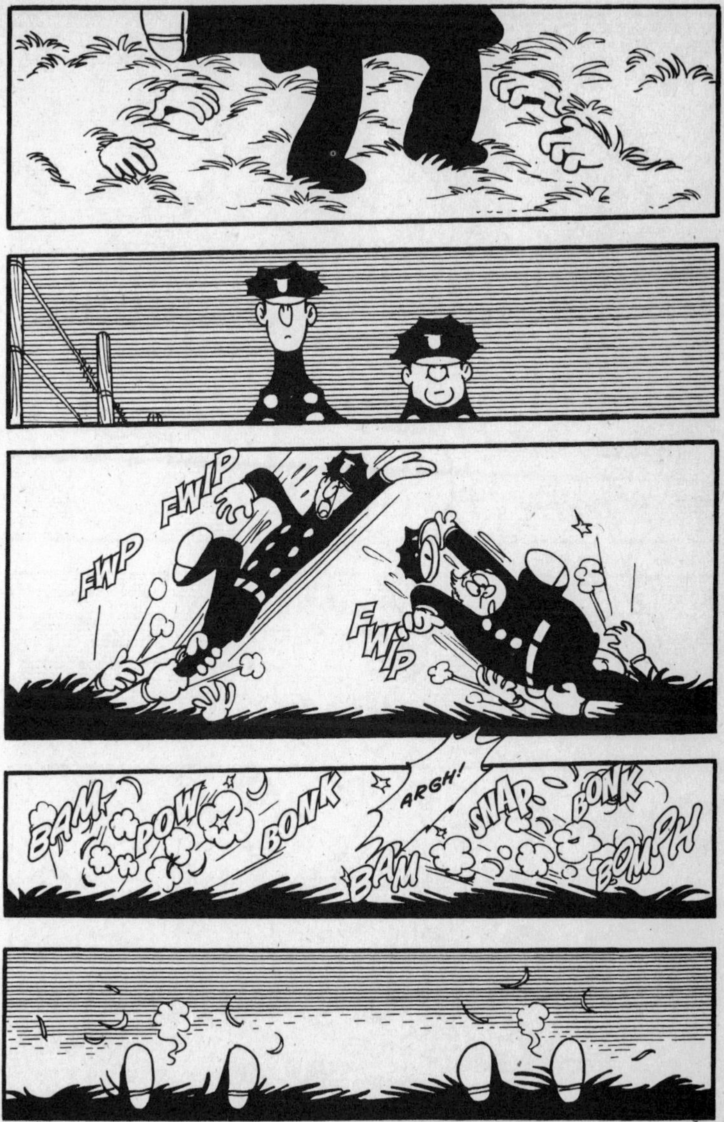
FWP
FWIP
FWIP
BAM
POW
BONK
ARGH!
BAM
SNAP
BONK
BOMPH

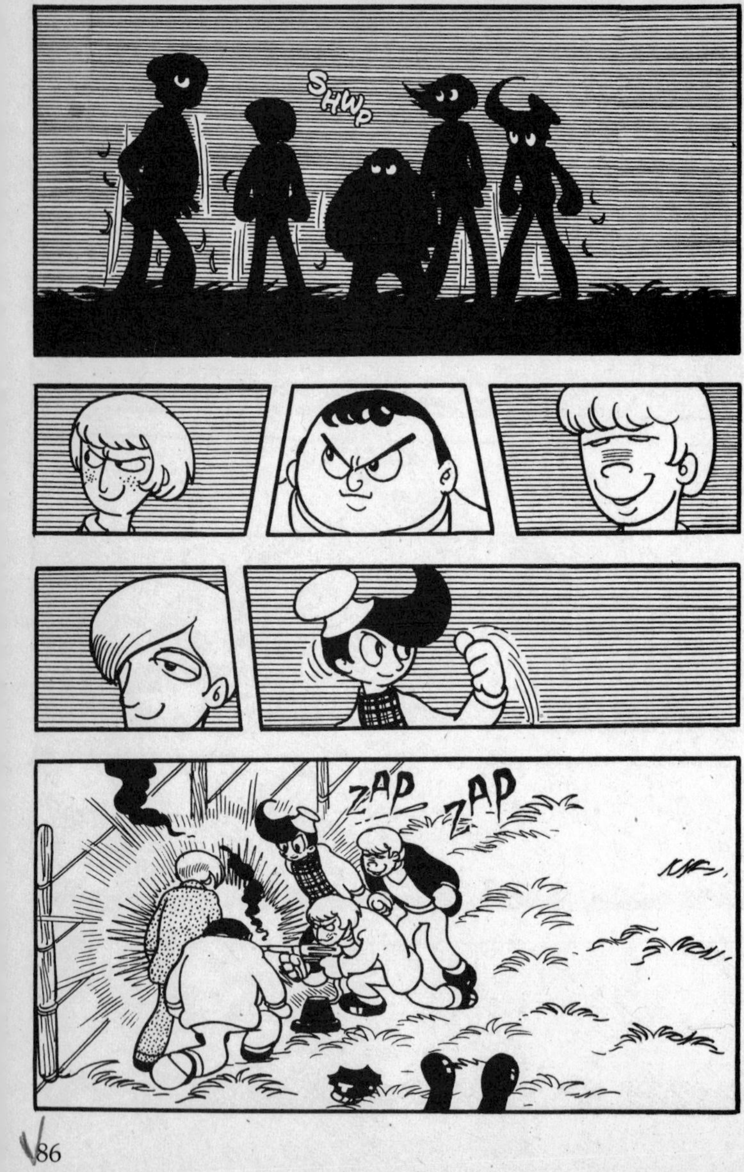
SHWP
ZAP
ZAP

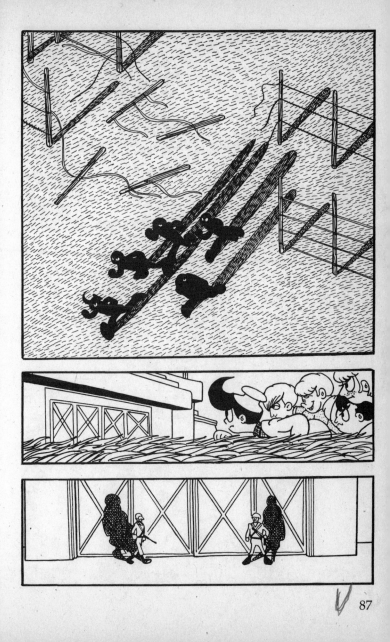

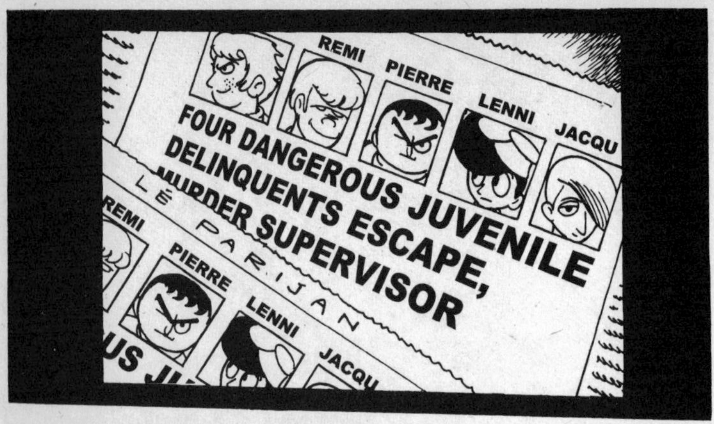
REMI
PIERRE
LENNI
JACQU
FOUR DANGEROUS JUVENILE
DELINQUENTS ESCAPE,
MURDER SUPERVISOR
LÉ PARIJAN

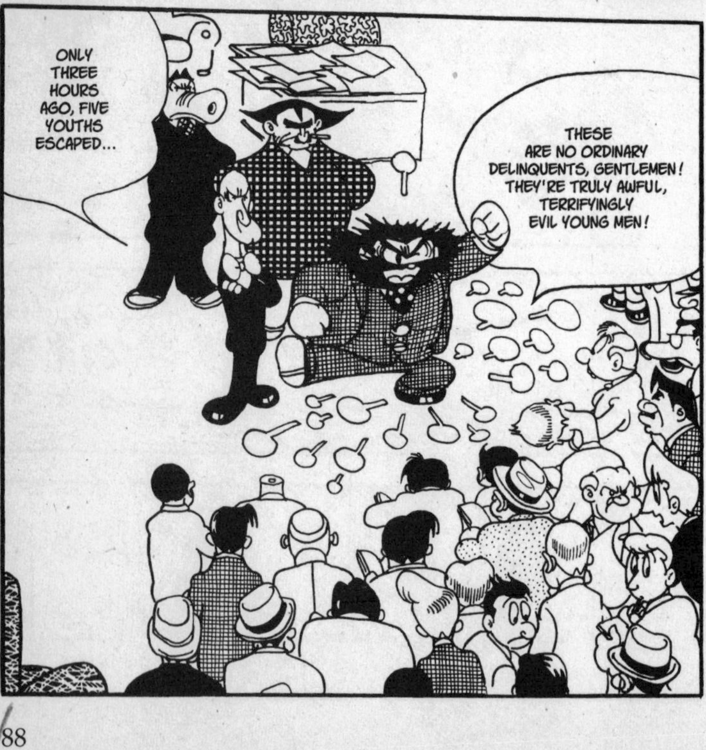
ONLY THREE HOURS AGO, FIVE YOUTHS ESCAPED...
THESE ARE NO ORDINARY DELINQUENTS, GENTLEMEN! THEY'RE TRULY AWFUL, TERRIFYINGLY EVIL YOUNG MEN!

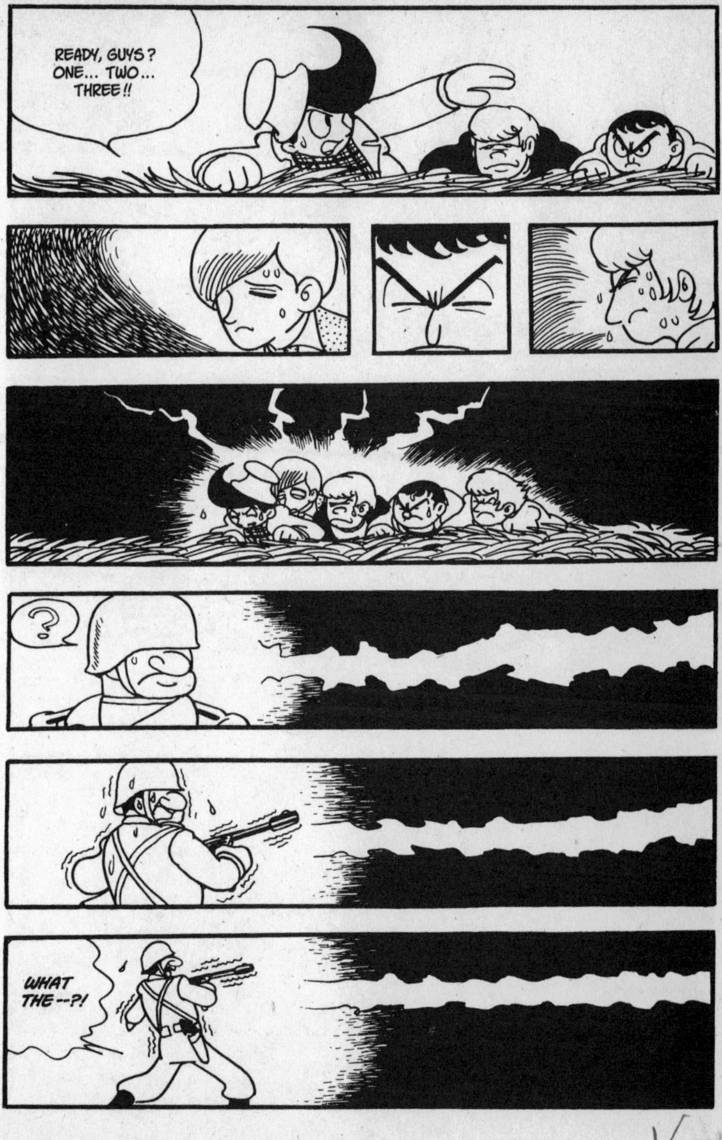
READY, GUYS? ONE... TWO... THREE!!
?
WHAT THE--?!

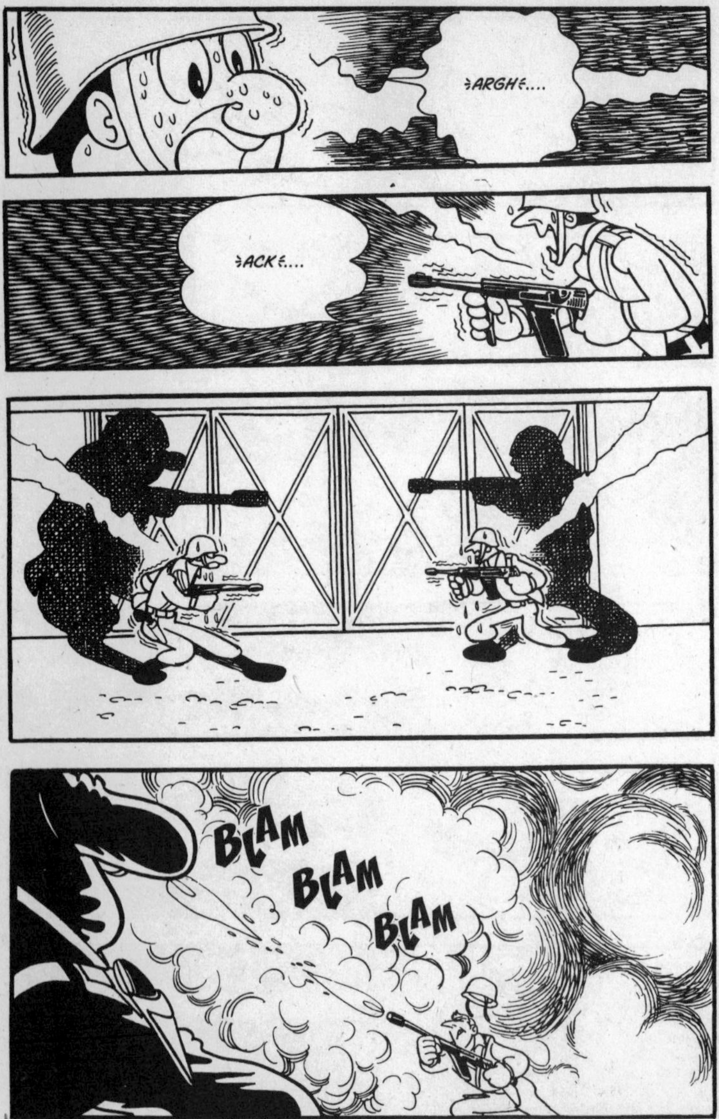
ARGH....
ACK....
BLAM
BLAM
BLAM

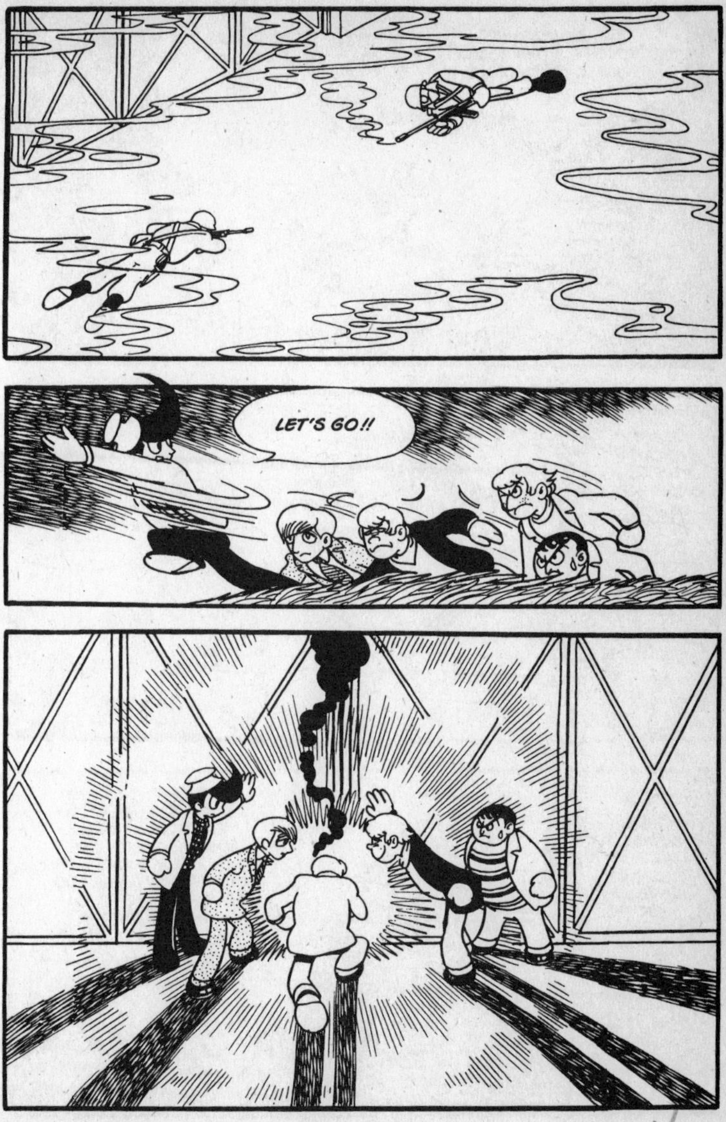
LET'S GO!!

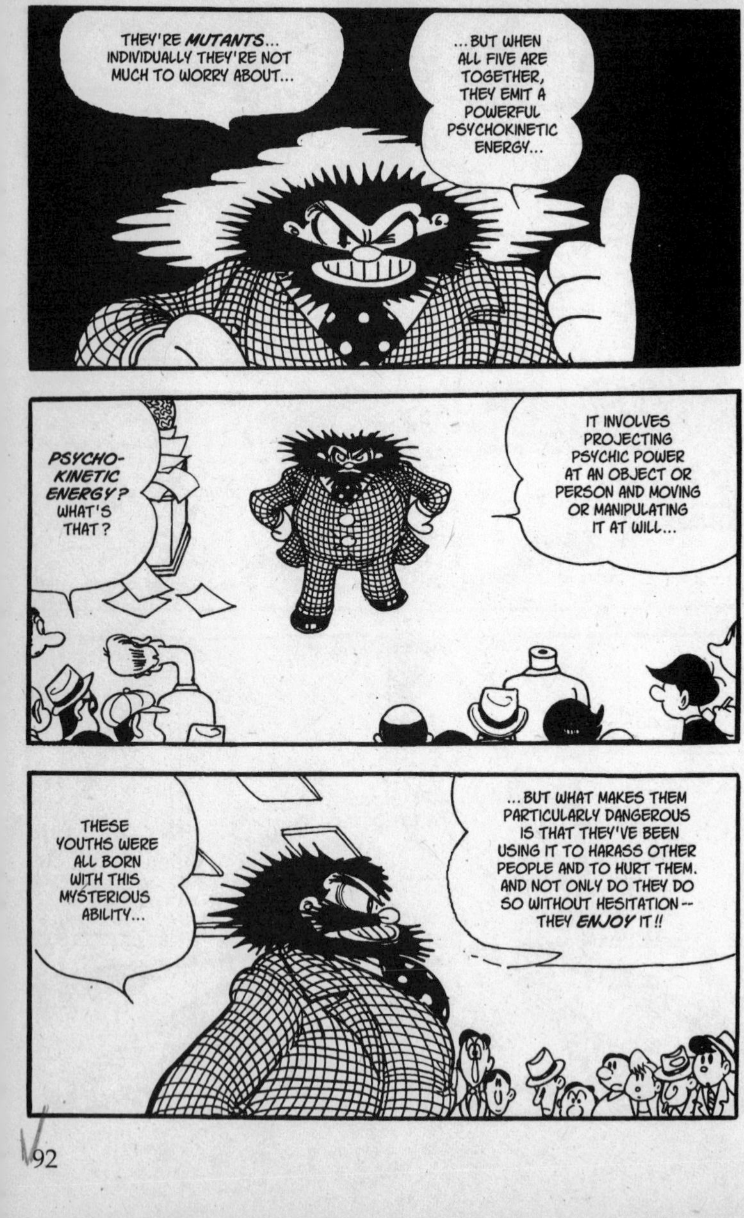
THEY'RE MUTANTS... INDIVIDUALLY THEY'RE NOT MUCH TO WORRY ABOUT...
...BUT WHEN ALL FIVE ARE TOGETHER, THEY EMIT A POWERFUL PSYCHOKINETIC ENERGY...
PSYCHO-KINETIC ENERGY? WHAT'S THAT?
IT INVOLVES PROJECTING PSYCHIC POWER AT AN OBJECT OR PERSON AND MOVING OR MANIPULATING IT AT WILL...
THESE YOUTHS WERE ALL BORN WITH THIS MYSTERIOUS ABILITY...
...BUT WHAT MAKES THEM PARTICULARLY DANGEROUS IS THAT THEY'VE BEEN USING IT TO HARASS OTHER PEOPLE AND TO HURT THEM. AND NOT ONLY DO THEY DO SO WITHOUT HESITATION -- THEY ENJOY IT!!

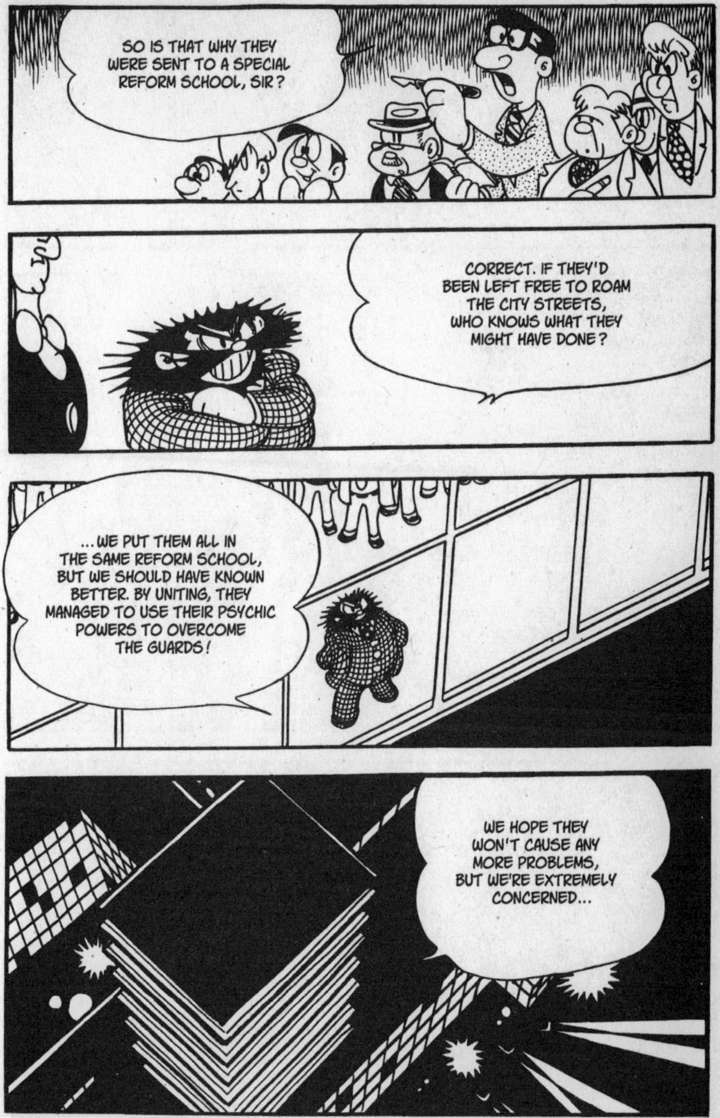
SO IS THAT WHY THEY WERE SENT TO A SPECIAL REFORM SCHOOL, SIR?
CORRECT. IF THEY'D BEEN LEFT FREE TO ROAM THE CITY STREETS, WHO KNOWS WHAT THEY MIGHT HAVE DONE?
...WE PUT THEM ALL IN THE SAME REFORM SCHOOL, BUT WE SHOULD HAVE KNOWN BETTER. BY UNITING, THEY MANAGED TO USE THEIR PSYCHIC POWERS TO OVERCOME THE GUARDS!
WE HOPE THEY WON'T CAUSE ANY MORE PROBLEMS, BUT WE'RE EXTREMELY CONCERNED...

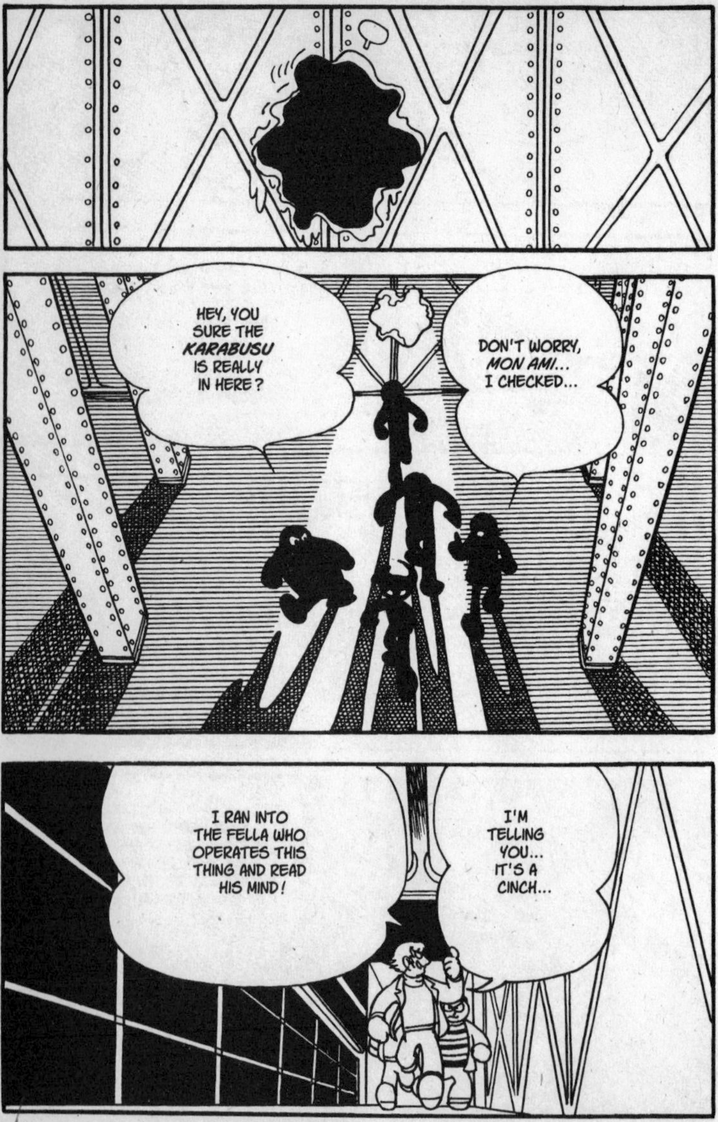
HEY, YOU SURE THE KARABUSU IS REALLY IN HERE?
DON'T WORRY, MON AMI... I CHECKED...
I RAN INTO THE FELLA WHO OPERATES THIS THING AND READ HIS MIND!
I'M TELLING YOU... IT'S A CINCH...

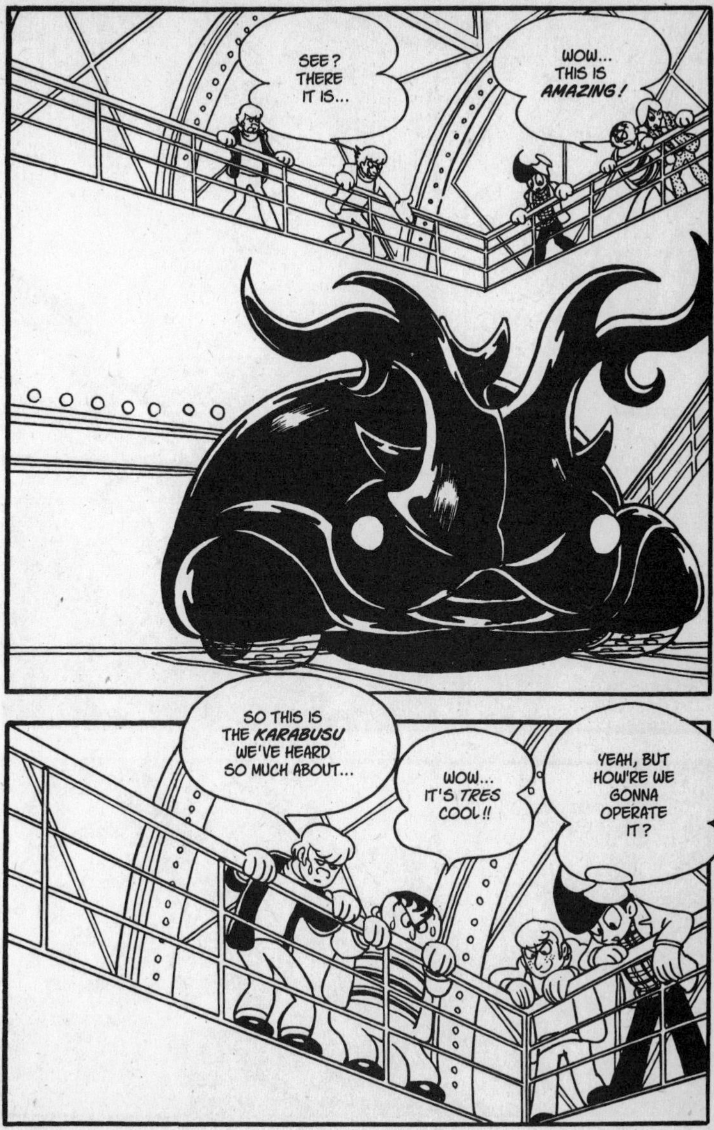
SEE? THERE IT IS...
WOW... THIS IS AMAZING!
SO THIS IS THE KARABUSU WE'VE HEARD SO MUCH ABOUT...
WOW... IT'S TRES COOL!!
YEAH, BUT HOW'RE WE GONNA OPERATE IT?

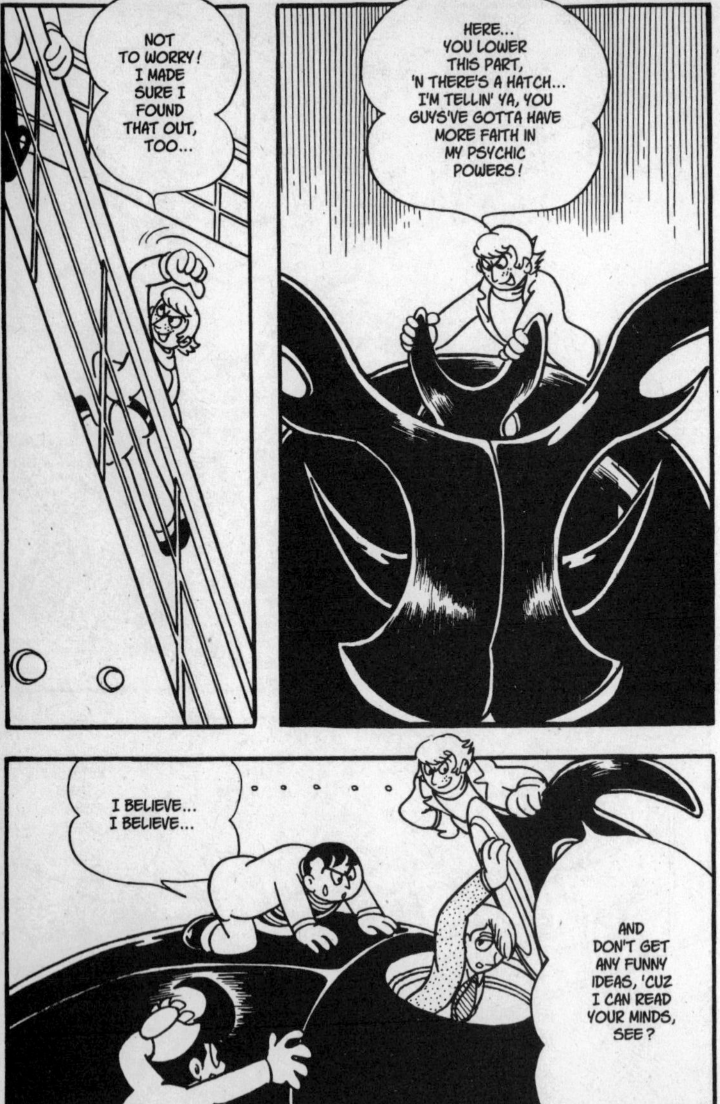
NOT TO WORRY! I MADE SURE I FOUND THAT OUT, TOO...
HERE... YOU LOWER THIS PART, 'N THERE'S A HATCH... I'M TELLIN' YA, YOU GUYS'VE GOTTA HAVE MORE FAITH IN MY PSYCHIC POWERS!
I BELIEVE... I BELIEVE...
. . . . .
AND DON'T GET ANY FUNNY IDEAS, 'CUZ I CAN READ YOUR MINDS, SEE?

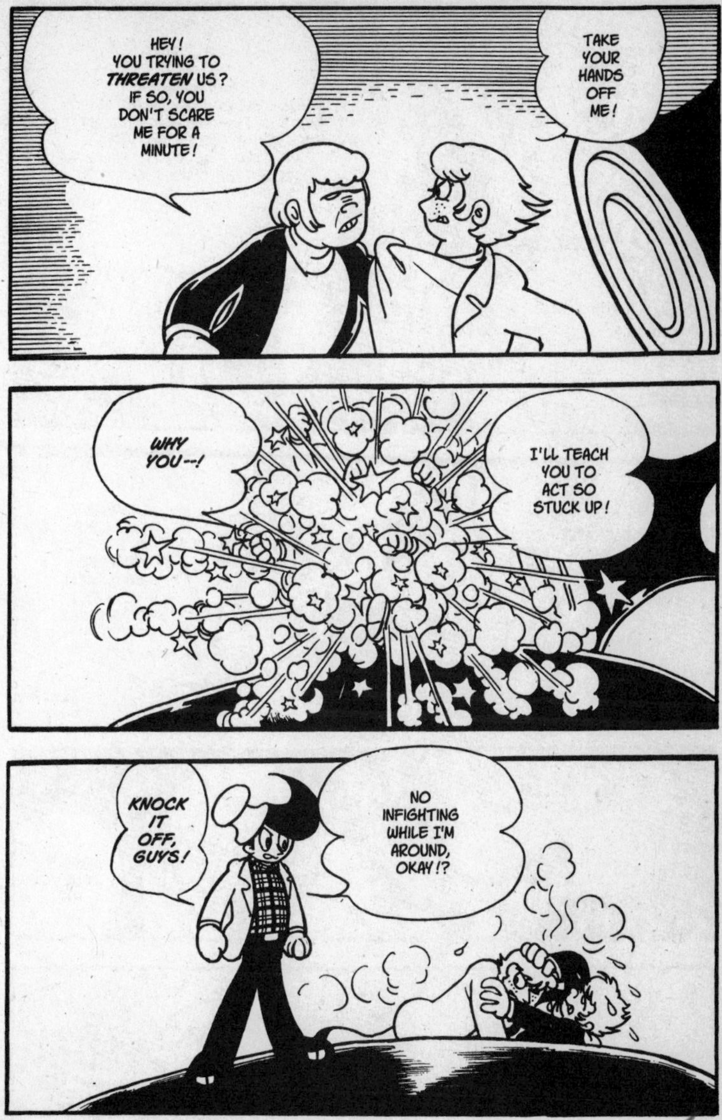
HEY! YOU TRYING TO THREATEN US? IF SO, YOU DON'T SCARE ME FOR A MINUTE!
TAKE YOUR HANDS OFF ME!
WHY YOU--!
I'LL TEACH YOU TO ACT SO STUCK UP!
KNOCK IT OFF, GUYS!
NO INFIGHTING WHILE I'M AROUND, OKAY!?

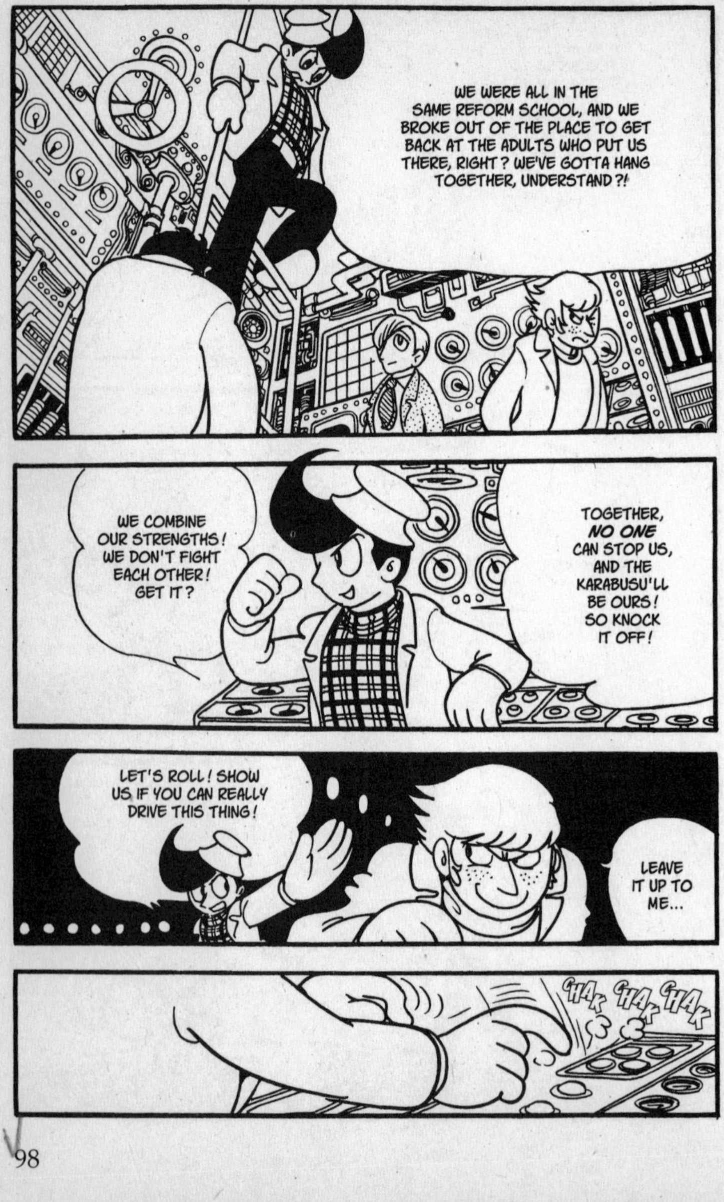
WE WERE ALL IN THE SAME REFORM SCHOOL, AND WE BROKE OUT OF THE PLACE TO GET BACK AT THE ADULTS WHO PUT US THERE, RIGHT? WE'VE GOTTA HANG TOGETHER, UNDERSTAND?!
WE COMBINE OUR STRENGTHS! WE DON'T FIGHT EACH OTHER! GET IT?
TOGETHER, *NO ONE* CAN STOP US, AND THE KARABUSU'LL BE OURS! SO KNOCK IT OFF!
LET'S ROLL! SHOW US IF YOU CAN REALLY DRIVE THIS THING!
LEAVE IT UP TO ME...
CHAK CHAK CHAK

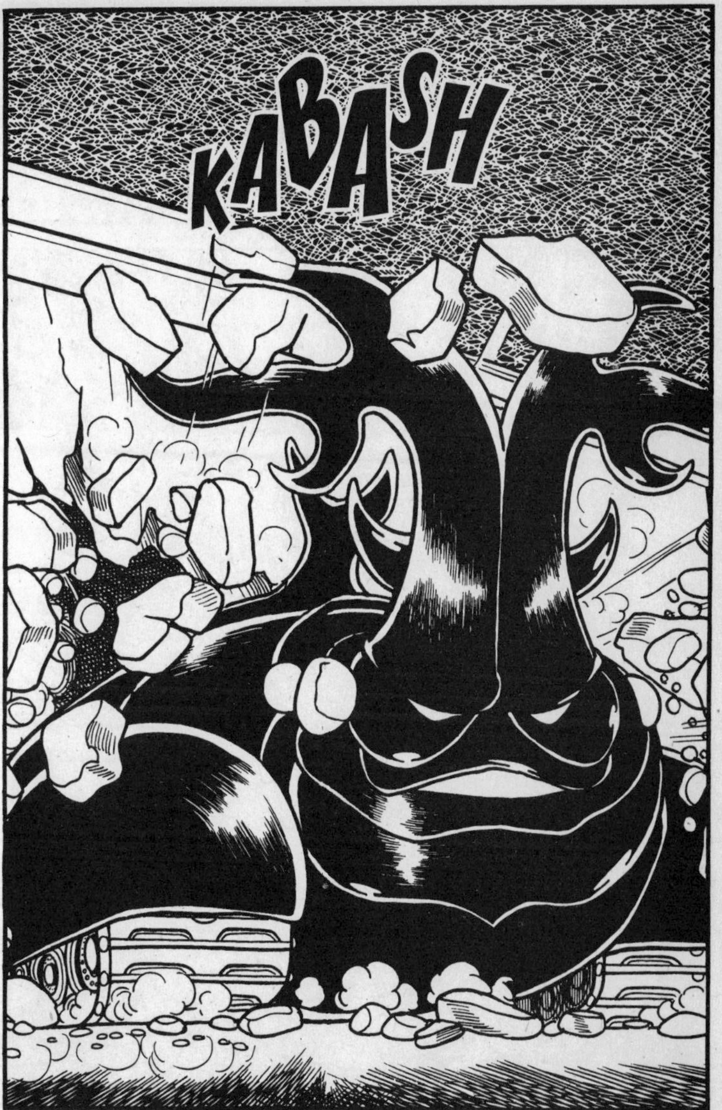
KABASH

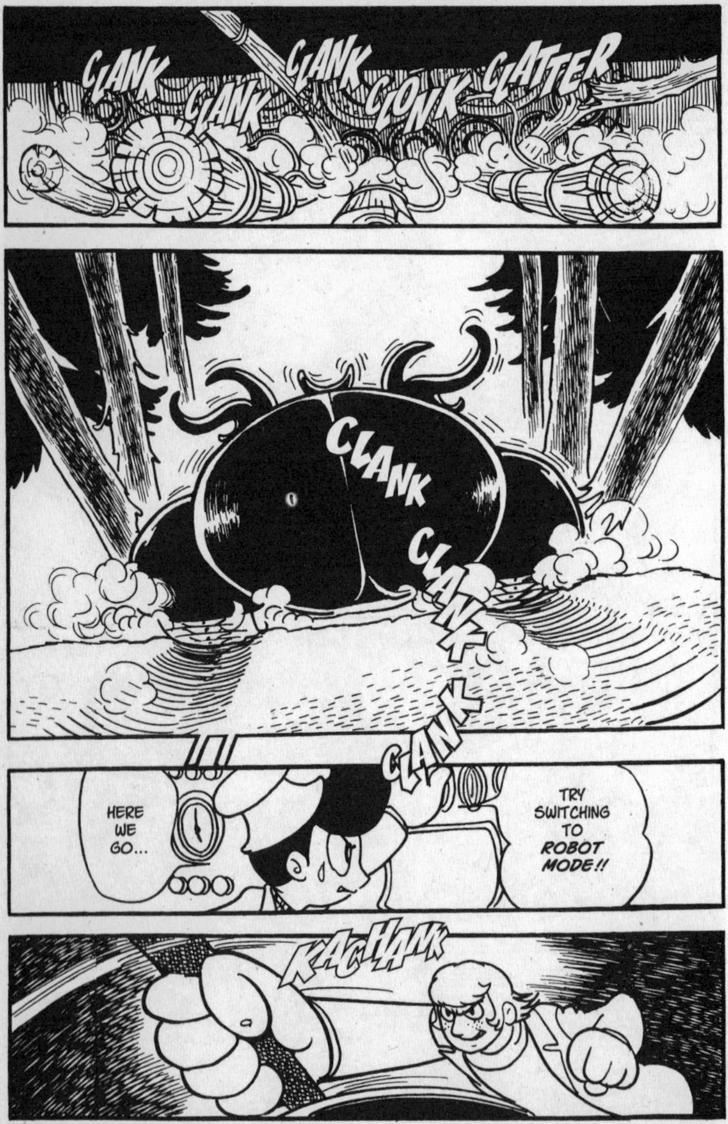
CLANK
CLANK
CLANK
CLONK
CLATTER
CLANK
CLANK
CLANK
CLANK
CLANK
HERE WE GO...
TRY SWITCHING TO *ROBOT MODE!!*
KACHANK

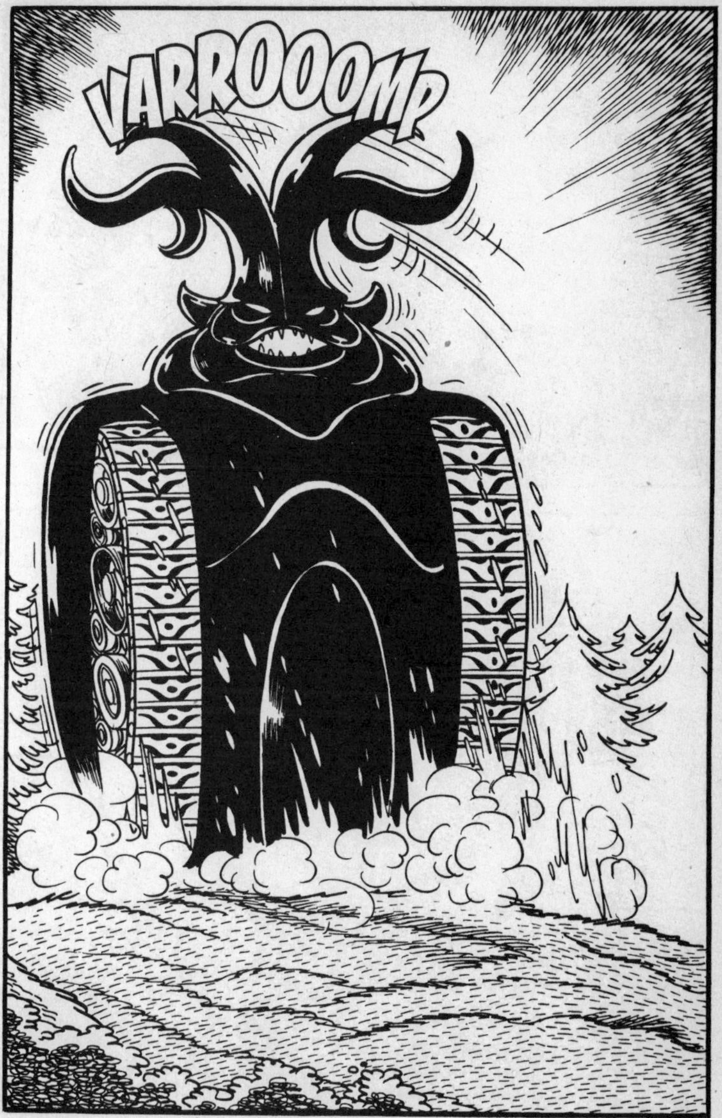
VARROOOMP

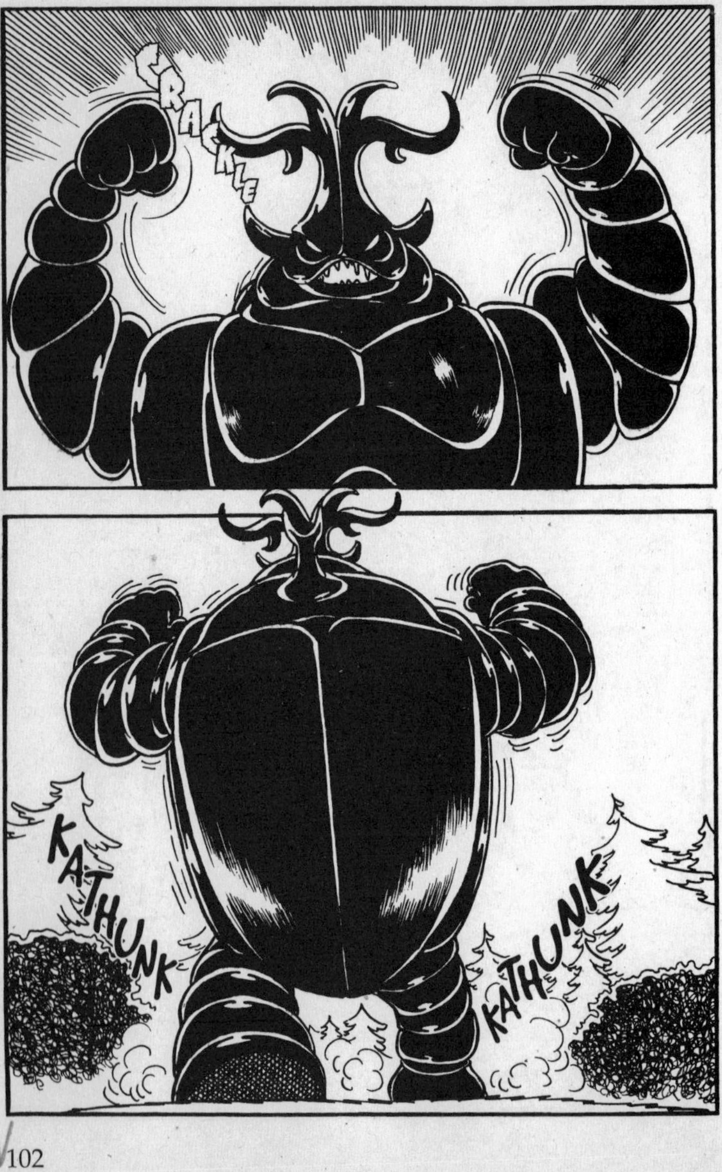
CRACKLE
KATHUNK
KATHUNK

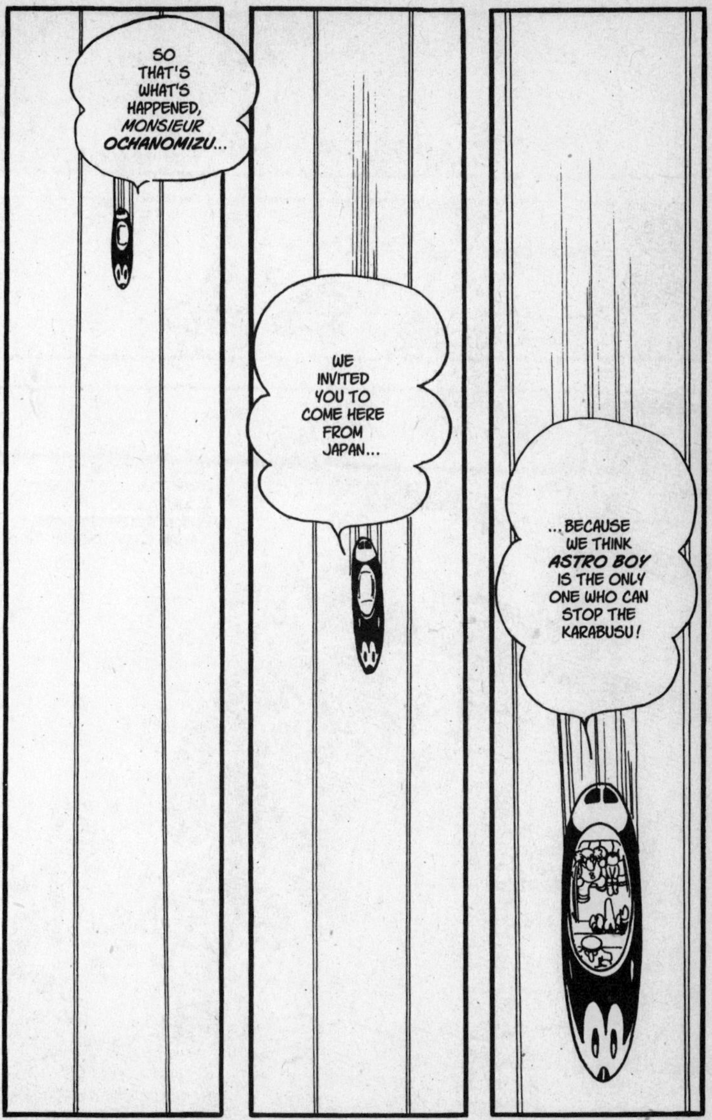
SO THAT'S WHAT'S HAPPENED, MONSIEUR OCHANOMIZU...
WE INVITED YOU TO COME HERE FROM JAPAN...
...BECAUSE WE THINK ASTRO BOY IS THE ONLY ONE WHO CAN STOP THE KARABUSU!

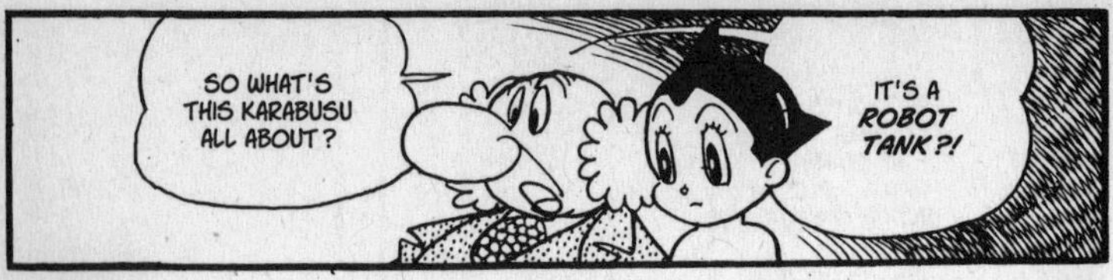
SO WHAT'S THIS KARABUSU ALL ABOUT?
IT'S A *ROBOT TANK*?!

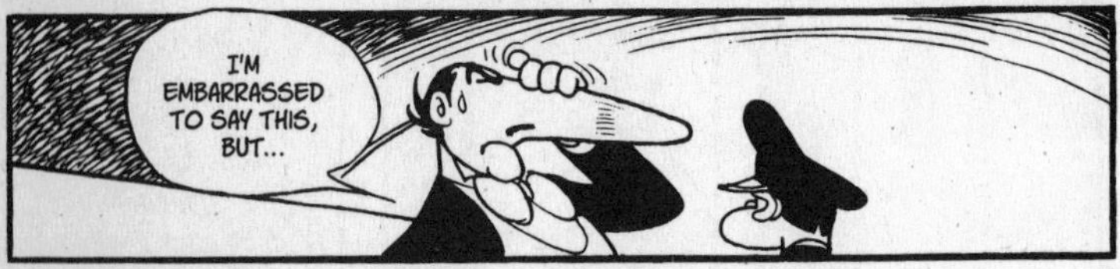
I'M EMBARRASSED TO SAY THIS, BUT...

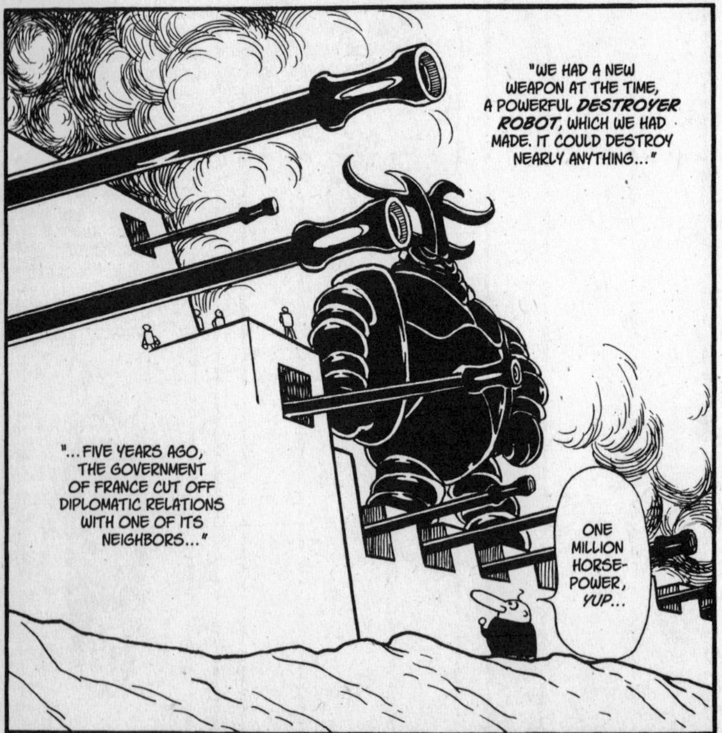
"...FIVE YEARS AGO, THE GOVERNMENT OF FRANCE CUT OFF DIPLOMATIC RELATIONS WITH ONE OF ITS NEIGHBORS..."
"WE HAD A NEW WEAPON AT THE TIME, A POWERFUL ***DESTROYER ROBOT***, WHICH WE HAD MADE. IT COULD DESTROY NEARLY ANYTHING..."
ONE MILLION HORSE-POWER, *YUP*...

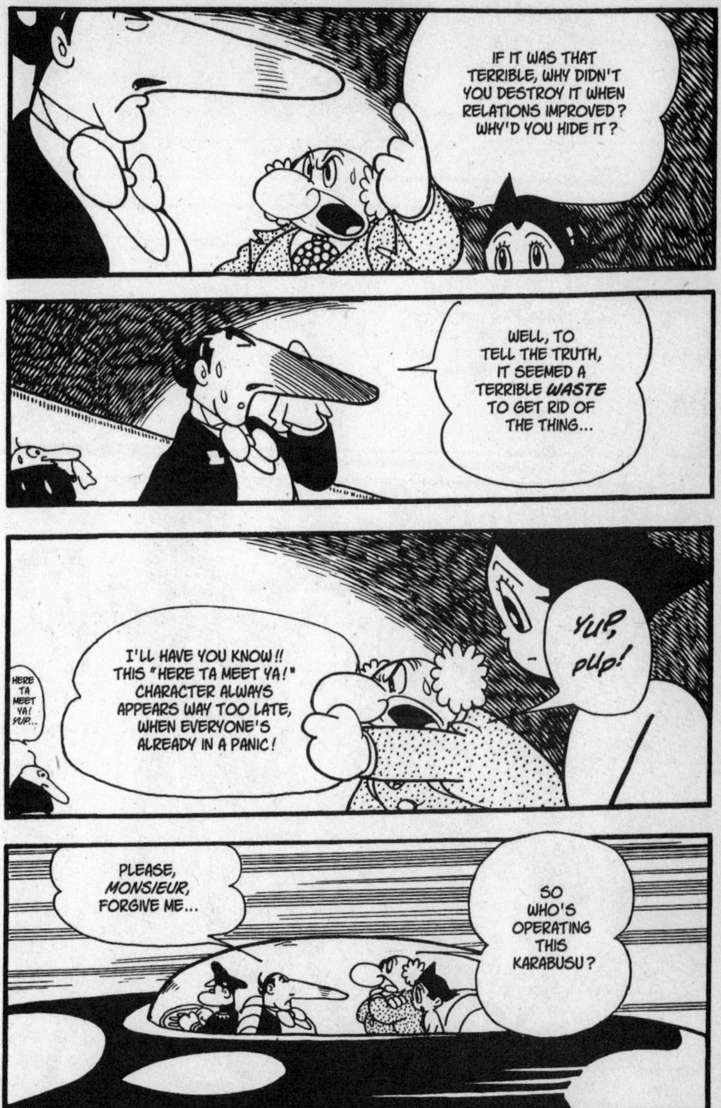
IF IT WAS THAT TERRIBLE, WHY DIDN'T YOU DESTROY IT WHEN RELATIONS IMPROVED? WHY'D YOU HIDE IT?
WELL, TO TELL THE TRUTH, IT SEEMED A TERRIBLE *WASTE* TO GET RID OF THE THING...
HERE TA MEET YA! YUP...
I'LL HAVE YOU KNOW!! THIS "HERE TA MEET YA!" CHARACTER ALWAYS APPEARS WAY TOO LATE, WHEN EVERYONE'S ALREADY IN A PANIC!
YUP, PUP!
PLEASE, *MONSIEUR*, FORGIVE ME...
SO WHO'S OPERATING THIS KARABUSU?

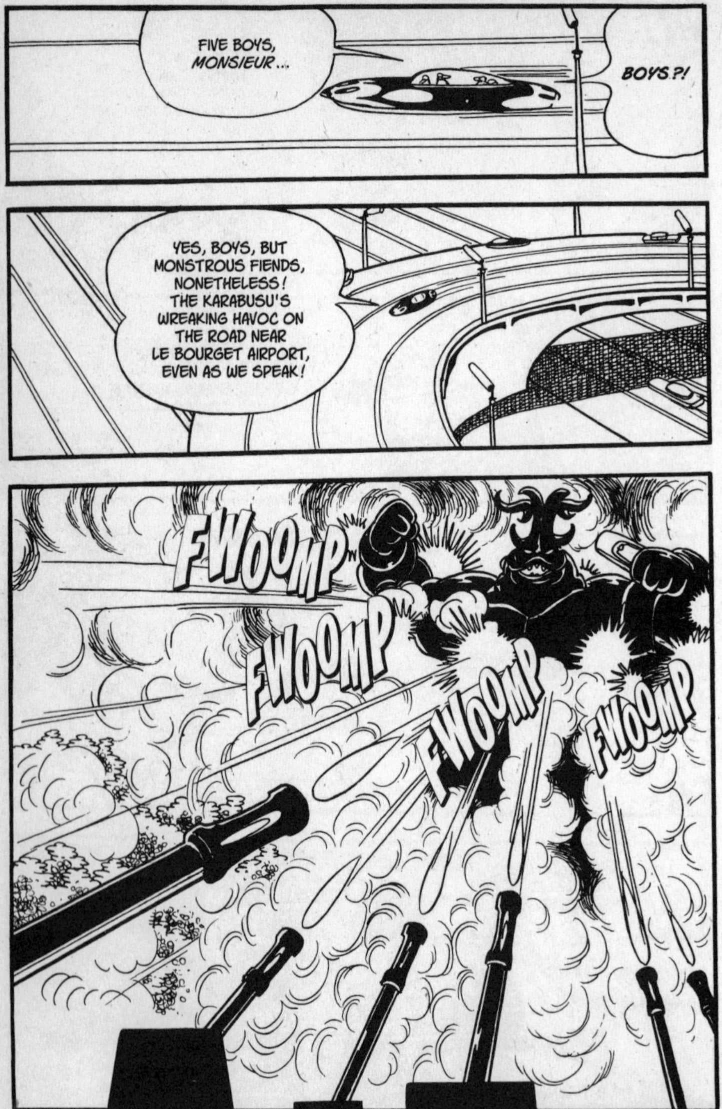
FIVE BOYS, MONSIEUR...
BOYS?!
YES, BOYS, BUT MONSTROUS FIENDS, NONETHELESS! THE KARABUSU'S WREAKING HAVOC ON THE ROAD NEAR LE BOURGET AIRPORT, EVEN AS WE SPEAK!
FWOOMP
FWOOMP
FWOOMP
FWOOMP

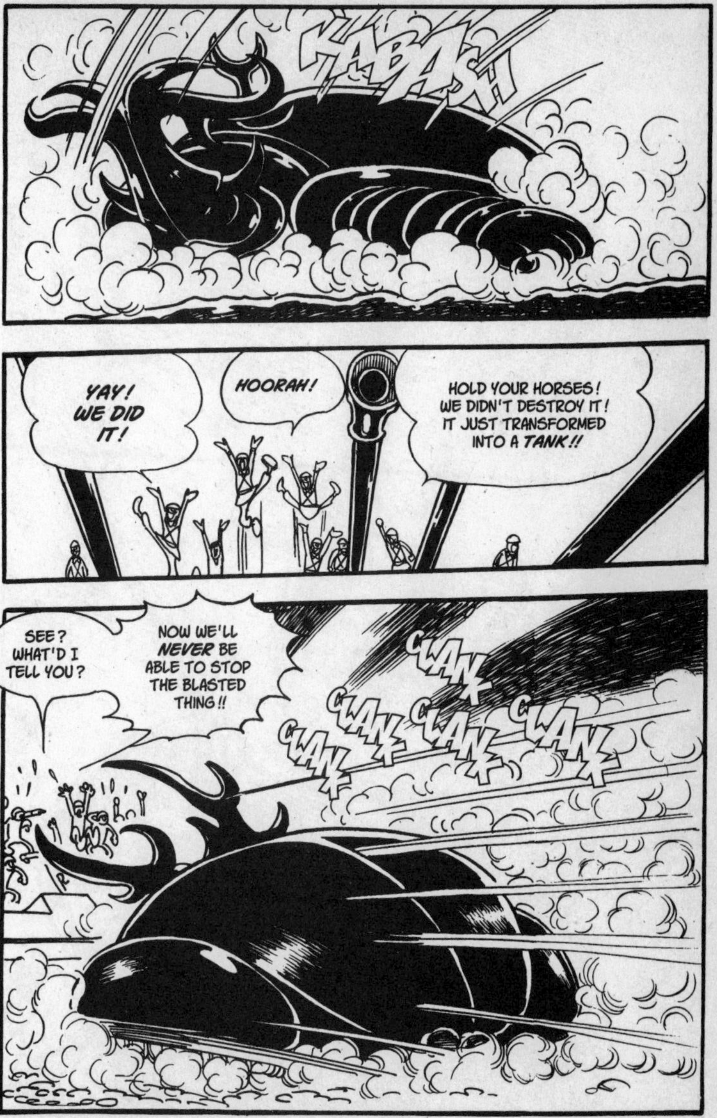
KABASH
YAY! WE DID IT!
HOORAH!
HOLD YOUR HORSES! WE DIDN'T DESTROY IT! IT JUST TRANSFORMED INTO A *TANK*!!
SEE? WHAT'D I TELL YOU?
NOW WE'LL *NEVER* BE ABLE TO STOP THE BLASTED THING!!
CLANK
CLANK
CLANK
CLANK
CLANK

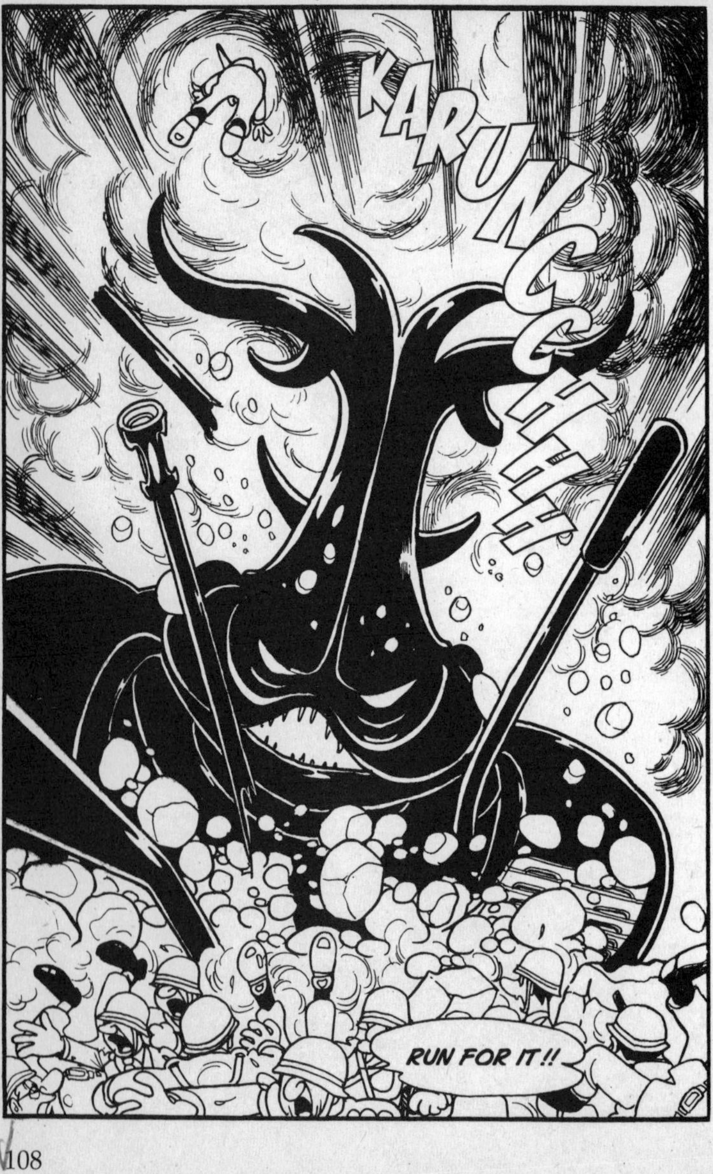
KARUNCCHHH!!
RUN FOR IT!!

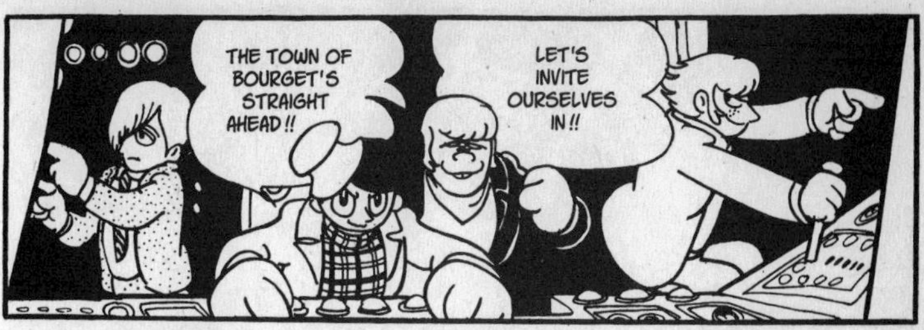
THE TOWN OF BOURGET'S STRAIGHT AHEAD!!
LET'S INVITE OURSELVES IN!!
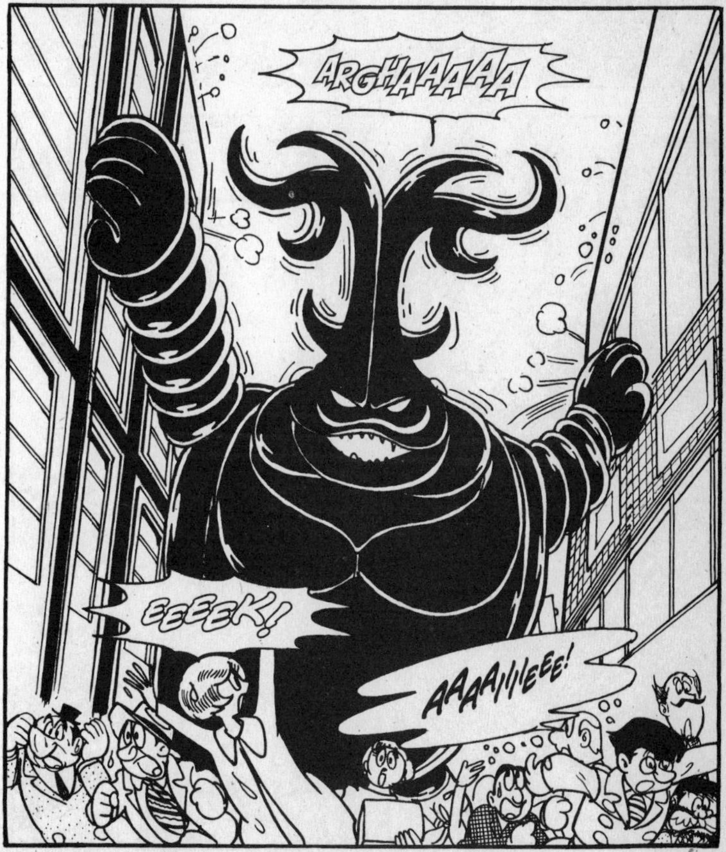
ARGHAAAAA
EEEEK!
AAAAIIIEEE!

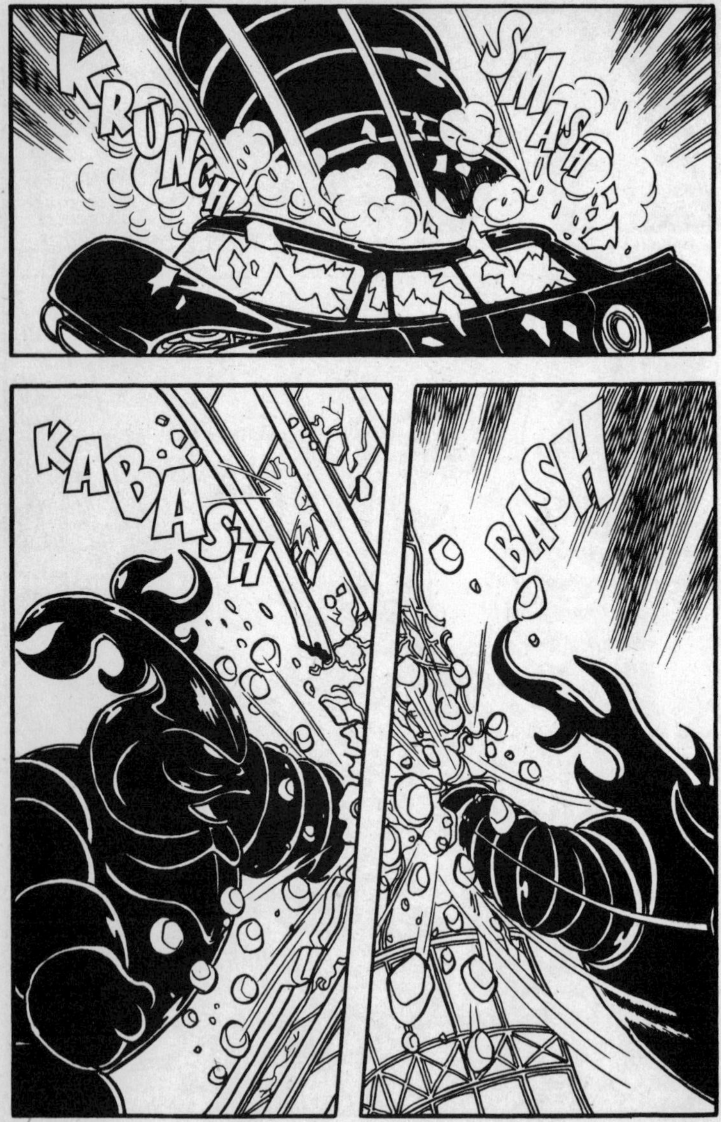
KRUNCH
SMASH
KABASH
BASH

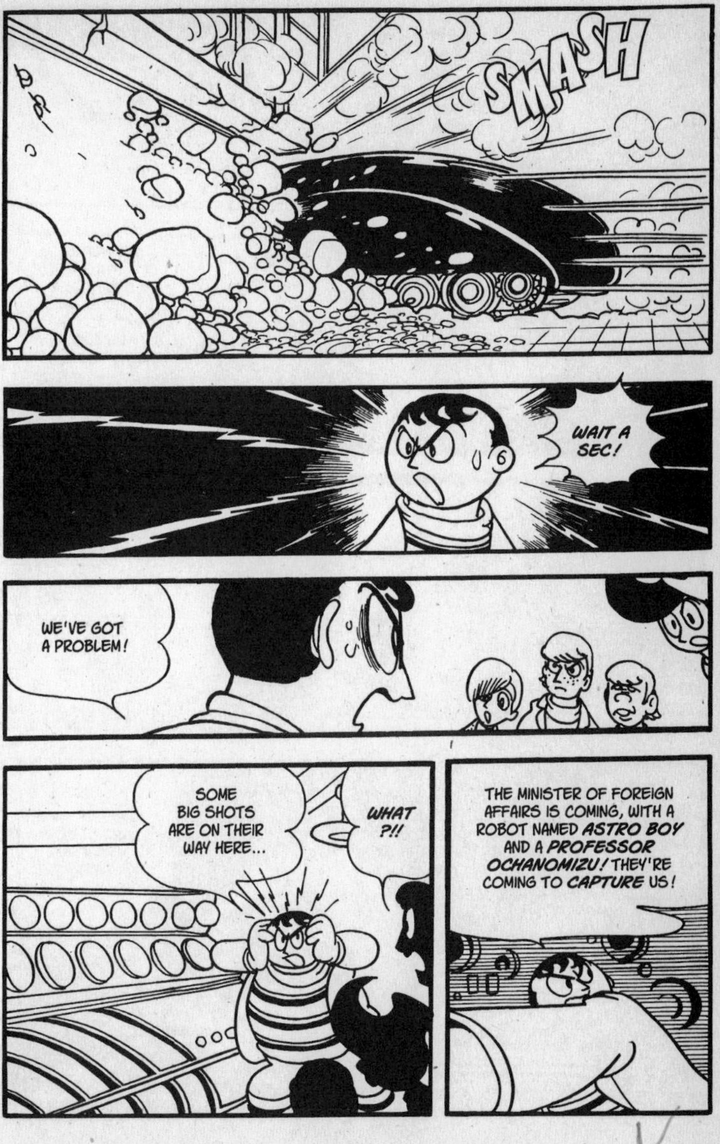
SMASH
WAIT A SEC!
WE'VE GOT A PROBLEM!
SOME BIG SHOTS ARE ON THEIR WAY HERE...
WHAT ?!!
THE MINISTER OF FOREIGN AFFAIRS IS COMING, WITH A ROBOT NAMED ASTRO BOY AND A PROFESSOR OCHANOMIZU! THEY'RE COMING TO CAPTURE US!

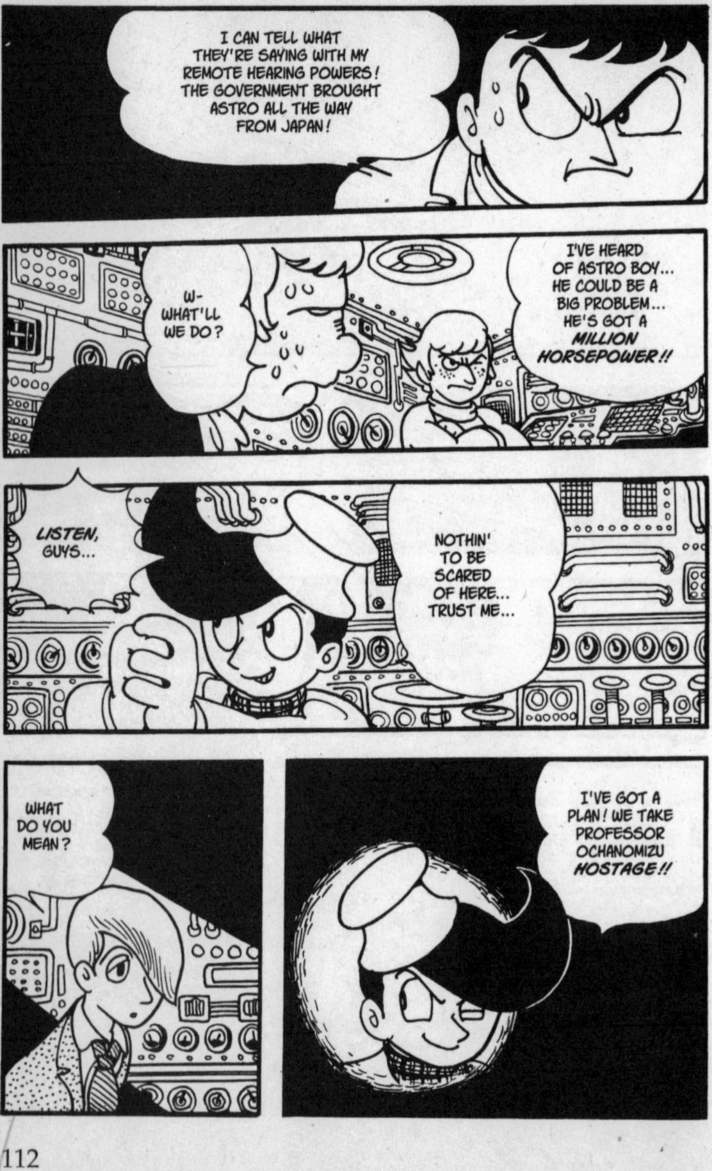
I CAN TELL WHAT THEY'RE SAYING WITH MY REMOTE HEARING POWERS! THE GOVERNMENT BROUGHT ASTRO ALL THE WAY FROM JAPAN!
W- WHAT'LL WE DO?
I'VE HEARD OF ASTRO BOY... HE COULD BE A BIG PROBLEM... HE'S GOT A MILLION HORSEPOWER!!
LISTEN, GUYS...
NOTHIN' TO BE SCARED OF HERE... TRUST ME...
WHAT DO YOU MEAN?
I'VE GOT A PLAN! WE TAKE PROFESSOR OCHANOMIZU HOSTAGE!!

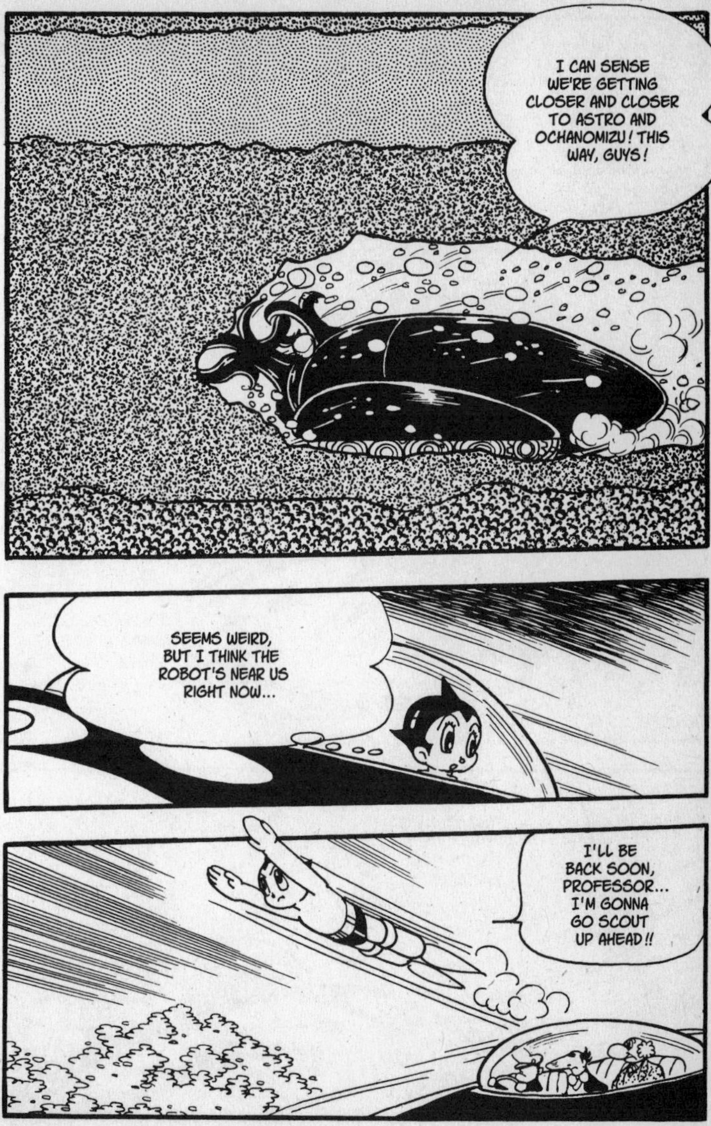
I CAN SENSE WE'RE GETTING CLOSER AND CLOSER TO ASTRO AND OCHANOMIZU! THIS WAY, GUYS!
SEEMS WEIRD, BUT I THINK THE ROBOT'S NEAR US RIGHT NOW...
I'LL BE BACK SOON, PROFESSOR... I'M GONNA GO SCOUT UP AHEAD!!

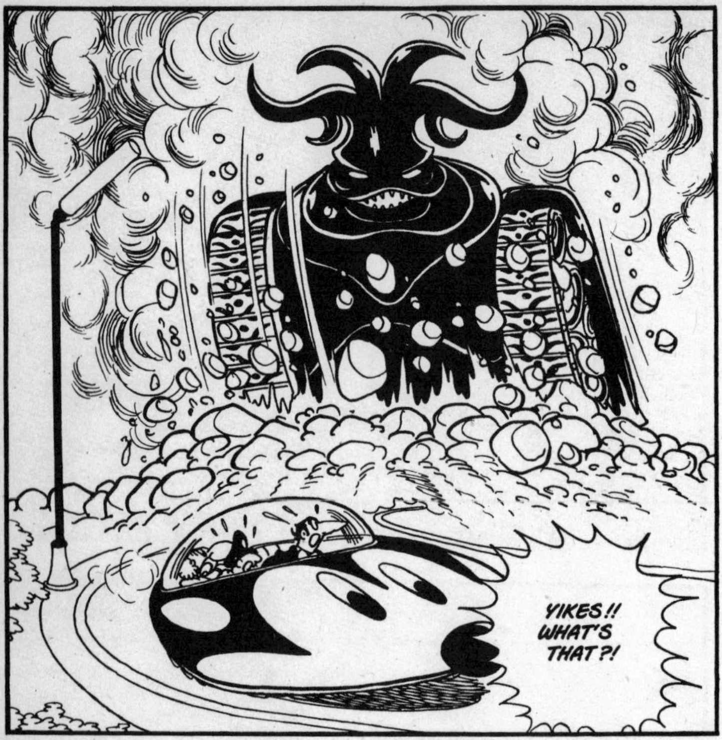
YIKES!! WHAT'S THAT?!
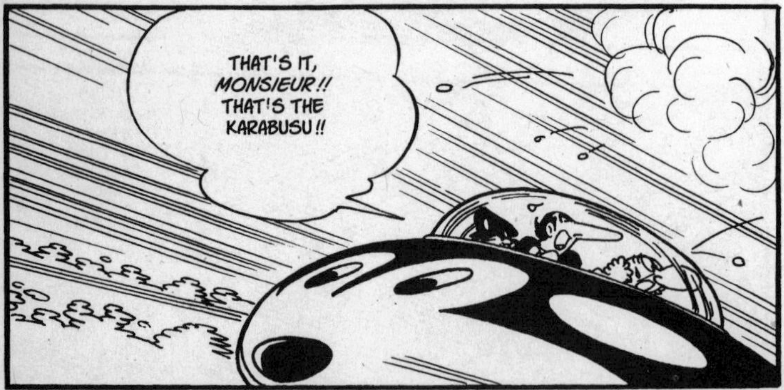
THAT'S IT, MONSIEUR!! THAT'S THE KARABUSU!!

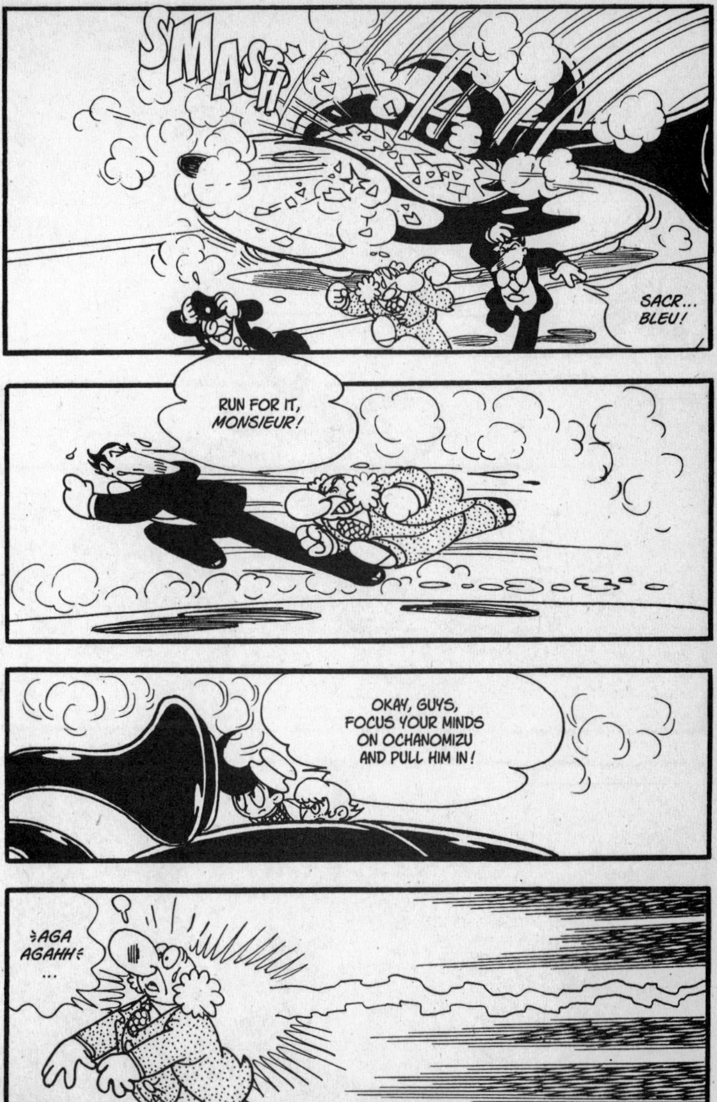
SMASH
SACR... BLEU!
RUN FOR IT, MONSIEUR!
OKAY, GUYS, FOCUS YOUR MINDS ON OCHANOMIZU AND PULL HIM IN!
AGA AGAHH ...

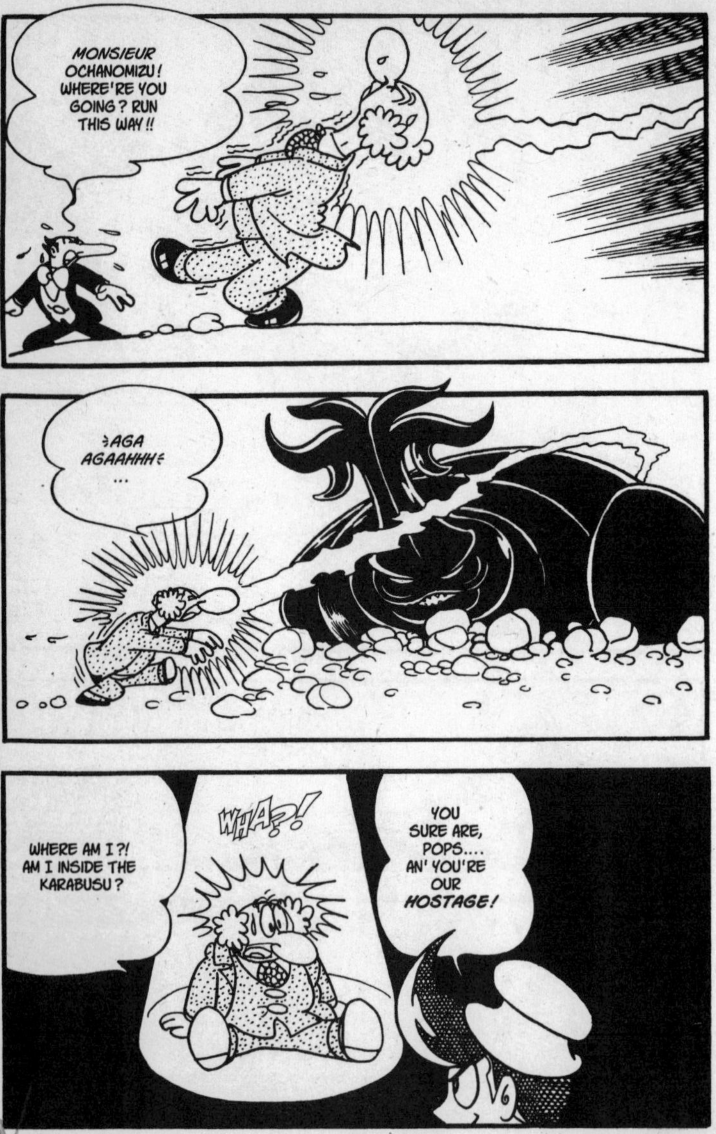
MONSIEUR OCHANOMIZU! WHERE'RE YOU GOING? RUN THIS WAY!!
≷AGA AGAAHHH≶ ...
WHERE AM I?! AM I INSIDE THE KARABUSU?
WHA?!
YOU SURE ARE, POPS.... AN' YOU'RE OUR HOSTAGE!

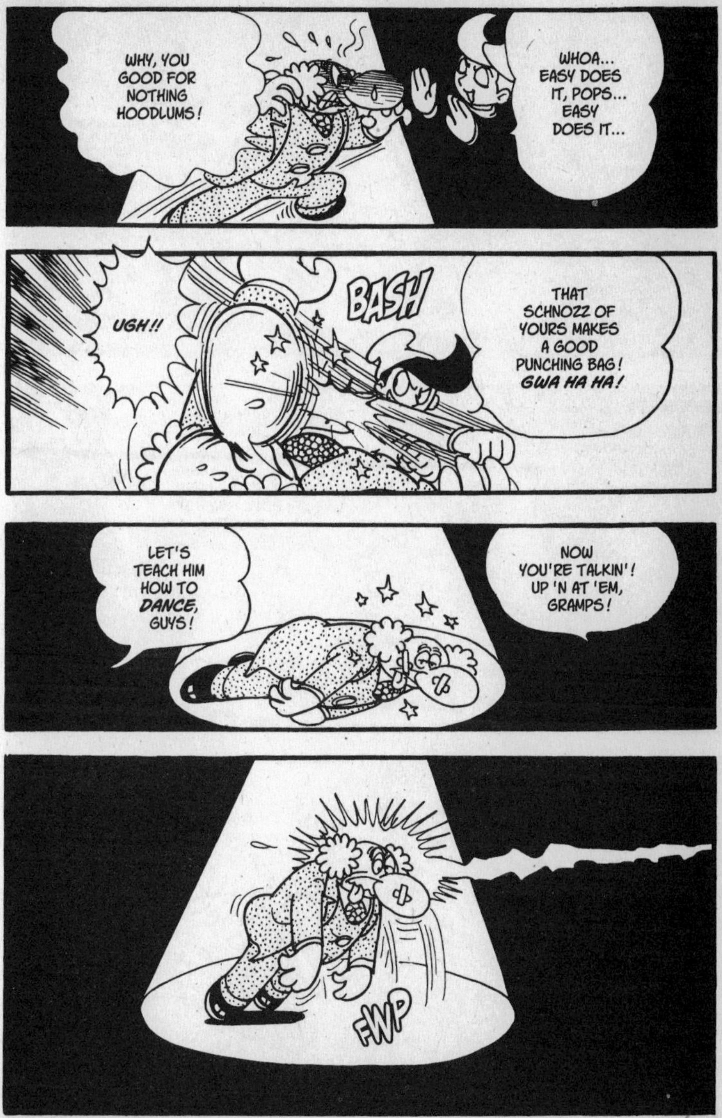
WHY, YOU GOOD FOR NOTHING HOODLUMS!
WHOA... EASY DOES IT, POPS... EASY DOES IT...
UGH!!
BASH
THAT SCHNOZZ OF YOURS MAKES A GOOD PUNCHING BAG! GWA HA HA!
LET'S TEACH HIM HOW TO DANCE, GUYS!
NOW YOU'RE TALKIN'! UP 'N AT 'EM, GRAMPS!
FWP

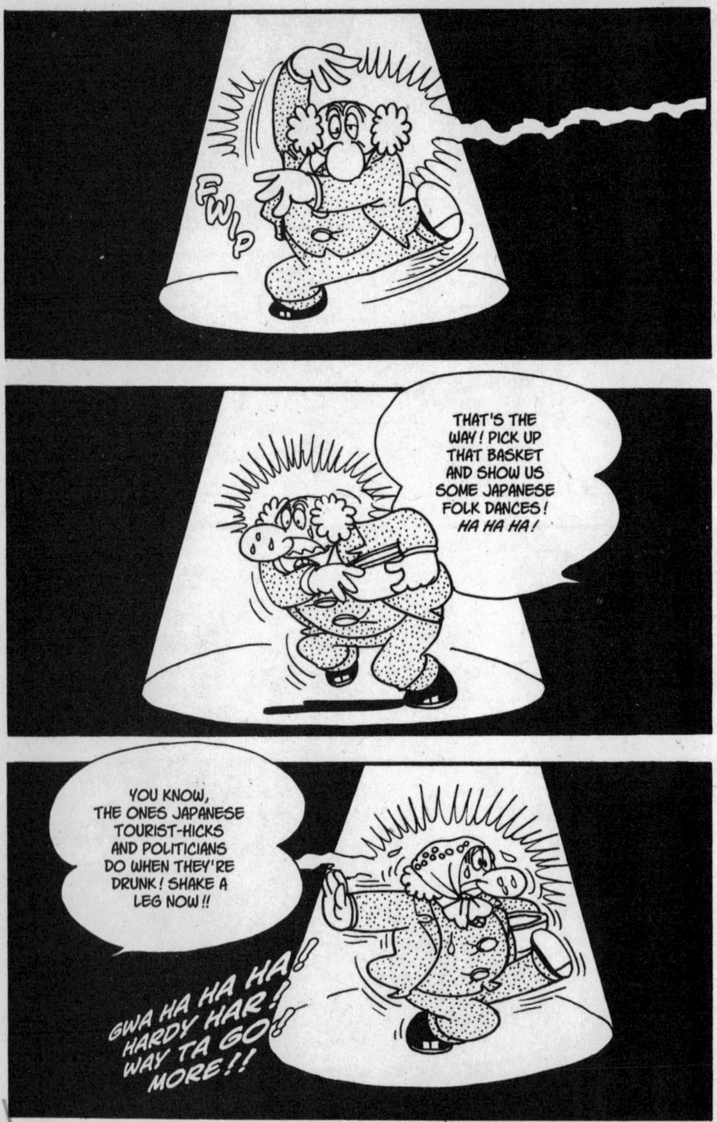
FWIP
THAT'S THE WAY! PICK UP THAT BASKET AND SHOW US SOME JAPANESE FOLK DANCES! HA HA HA!
YOU KNOW, THE ONES JAPANESE TOURIST-HICKS AND POLITICIANS DO WHEN THEY'RE DRUNK! SHAKE A LEG NOW!!
GWA HA HA HA! HARDY HAR! WAY TA GO! MORE!!

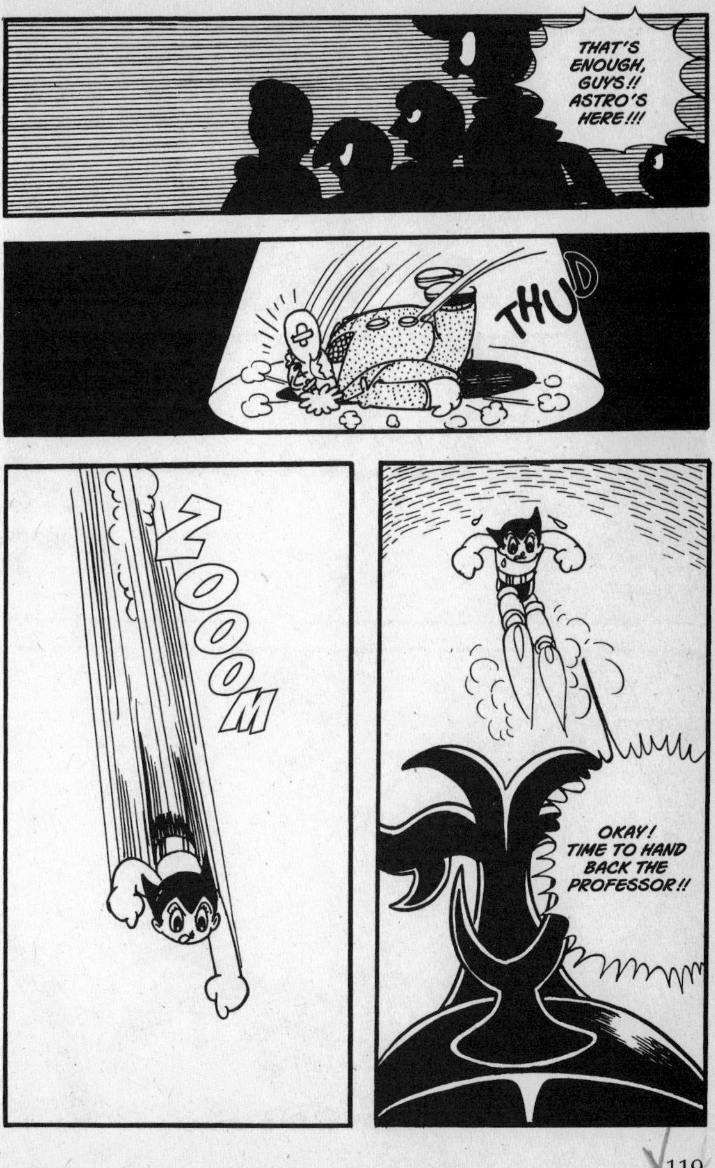
THAT'S ENOUGH, GUYS!! ASTRO'S HERE!!!
THUD
ZOOOOM
OKAY! TIME TO HAND BACK THE PROFESSOR!!

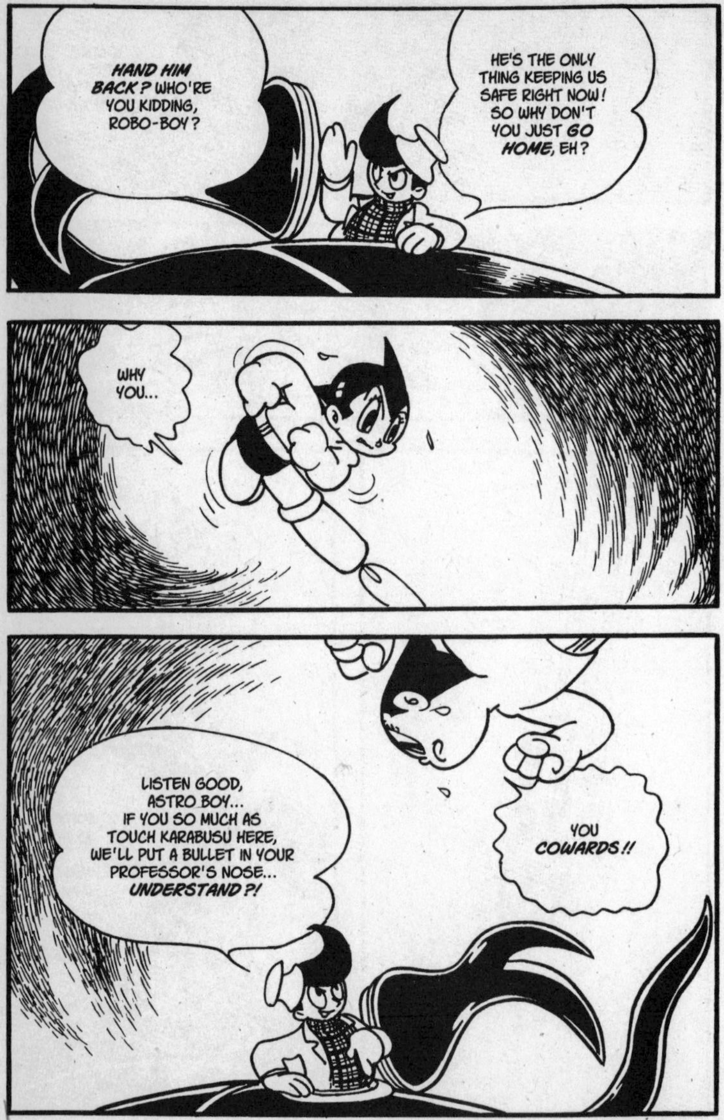
HAND HIM BACK? WHO'RE YOU KIDDING, ROBO-BOY?
HE'S THE ONLY THING KEEPING US SAFE RIGHT NOW! SO WHY DON'T YOU JUST GO HOME, EH?
WHY YOU...
LISTEN GOOD, ASTRO BOY... IF YOU SO MUCH AS TOUCH KARABUSU HERE, WE'LL PUT A BULLET IN YOUR PROFESSOR'S NOSE... UNDERSTAND?!
YOU COWARDS!!

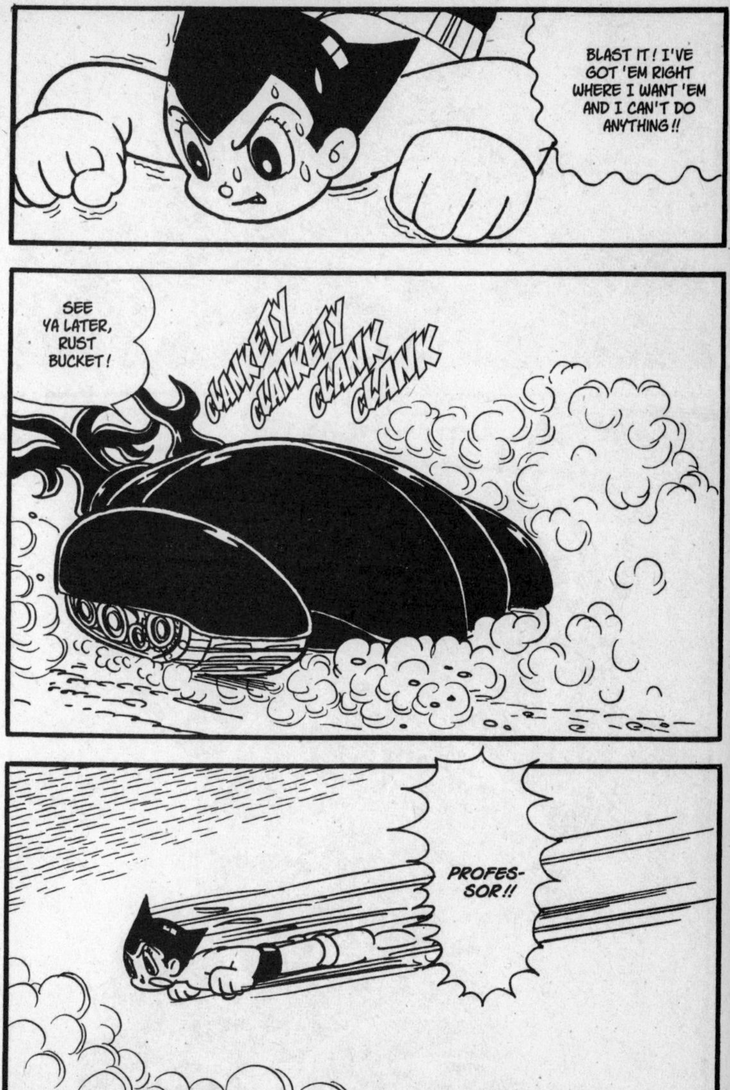

BLAST IT! I'VE GOT 'EM RIGHT WHERE I WANT 'EM AND I CAN'T DO ANYTHING!!
SEE YA LATER, RUST BUCKET!
CLANKETY CLANKETY CLANK CLANK
PROFES-SOR!!

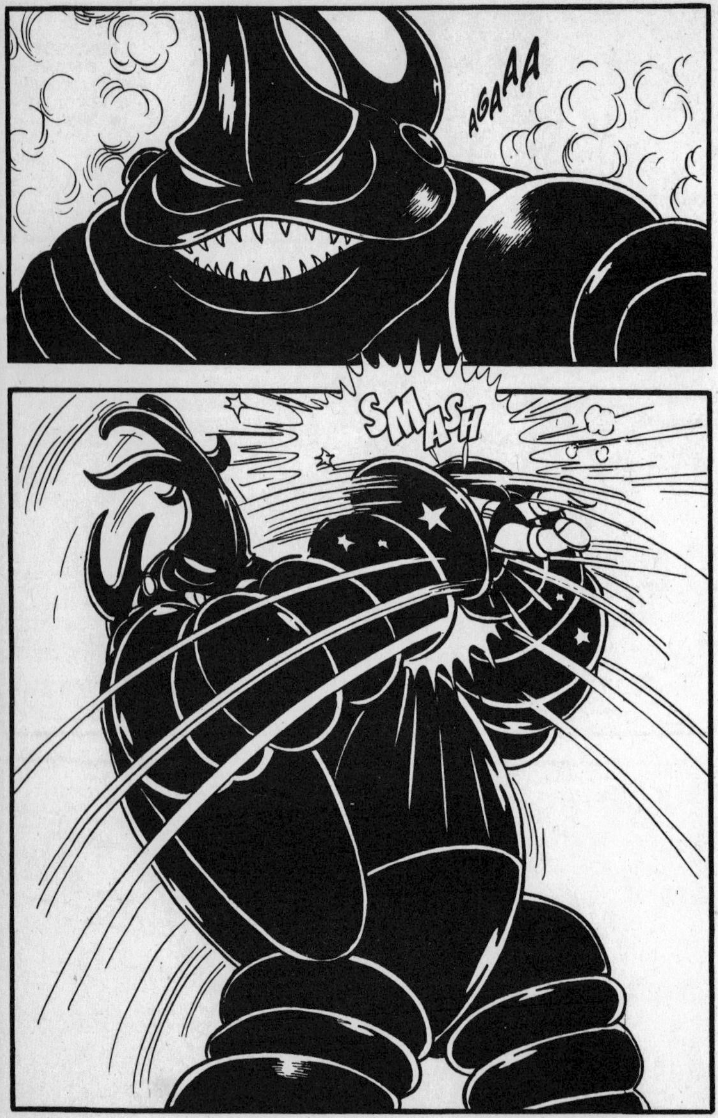
AGAAAA
SMASH

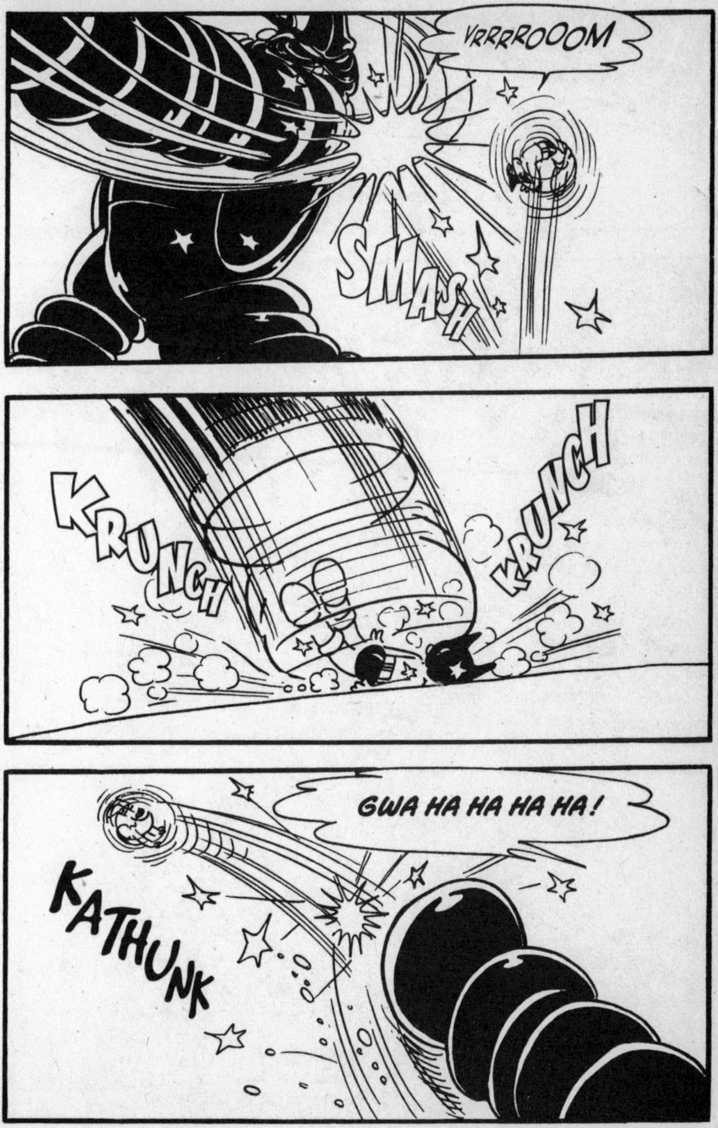
VRRRROOOM
SMASH
KRUNCH
KRUNCH
GWA HA HA HA HA!
KATHUNK

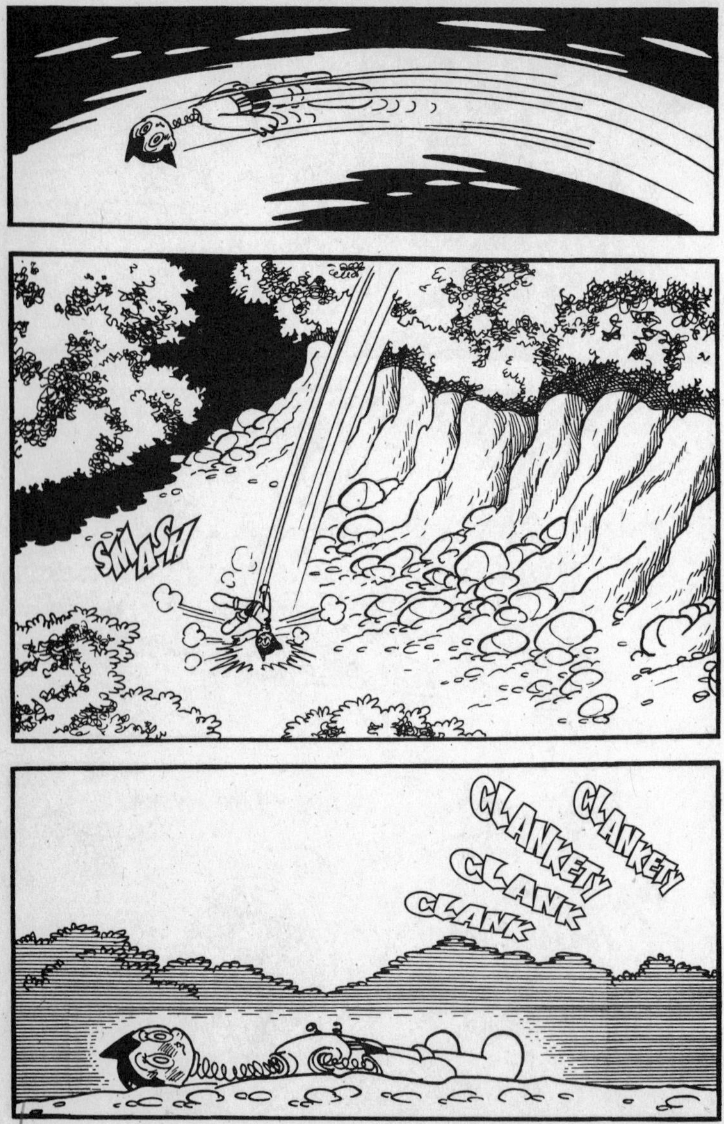
SMASH
CLANKETY
CLANKETY
CLANK
CLANK

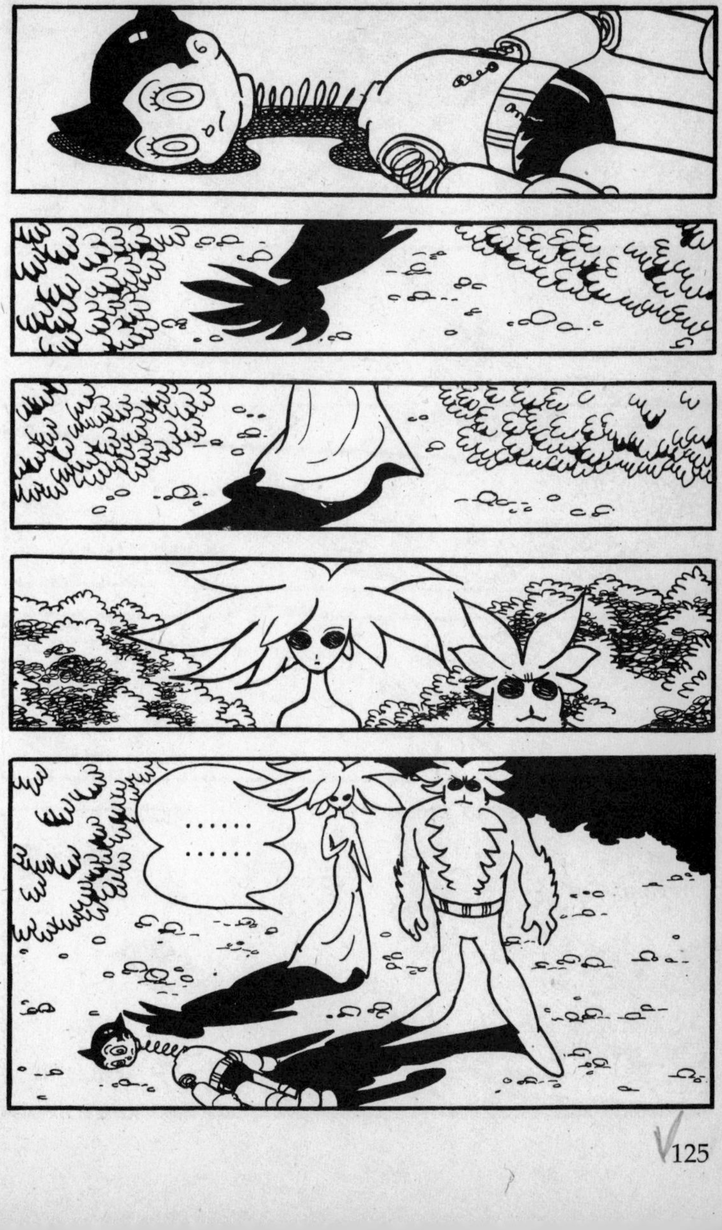
…… ……

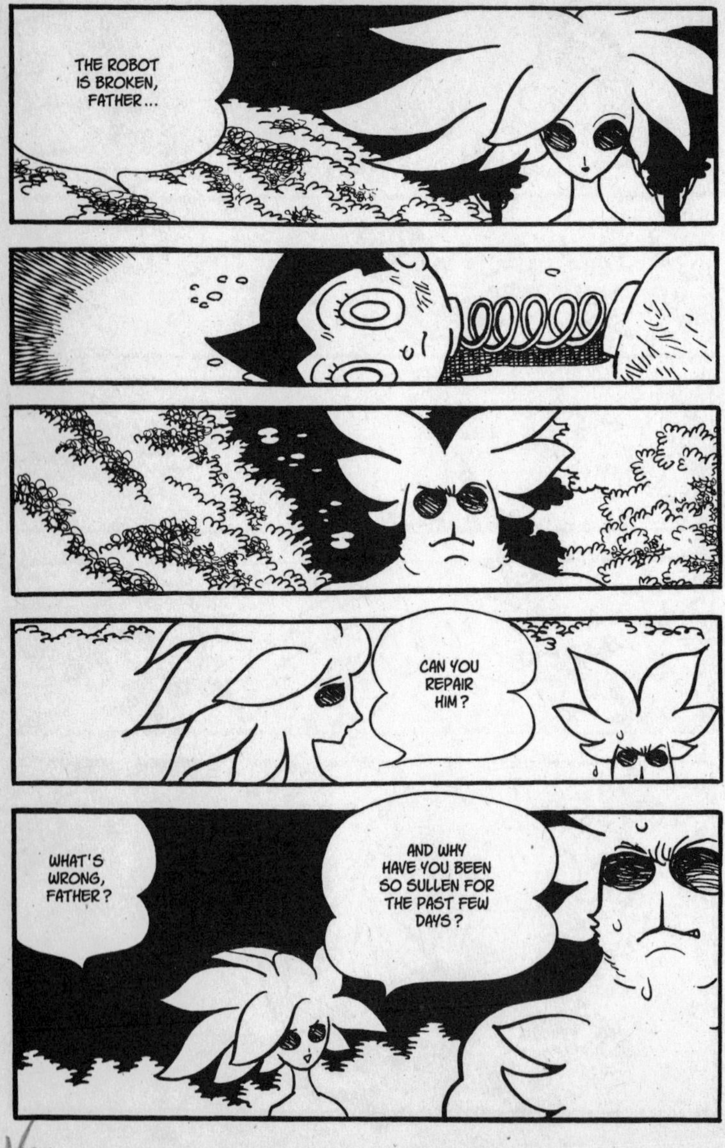
THE ROBOT IS BROKEN, FATHER...
CAN YOU REPAIR HIM?
WHAT'S WRONG, FATHER?
AND WHY HAVE YOU BEEN SO SULLEN FOR THE PAST FEW DAYS?

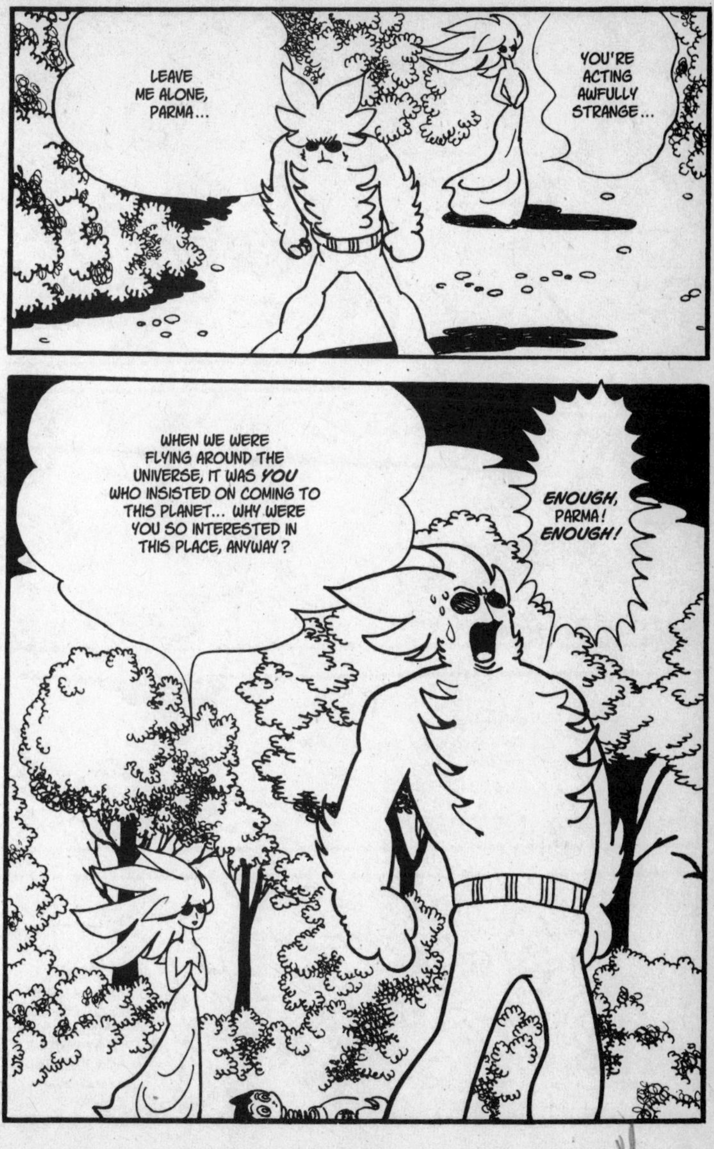
LEAVE ME ALONE, PARMA...
YOU'RE ACTING AWFULLY STRANGE...
WHEN WE WERE FLYING AROUND THE UNIVERSE, IT WAS *YOU* WHO INSISTED ON COMING TO THIS PLANET... WHY WERE YOU SO INTERESTED IN THIS PLACE, ANYWAY?
ENOUGH, PARMA! *ENOUGH!*

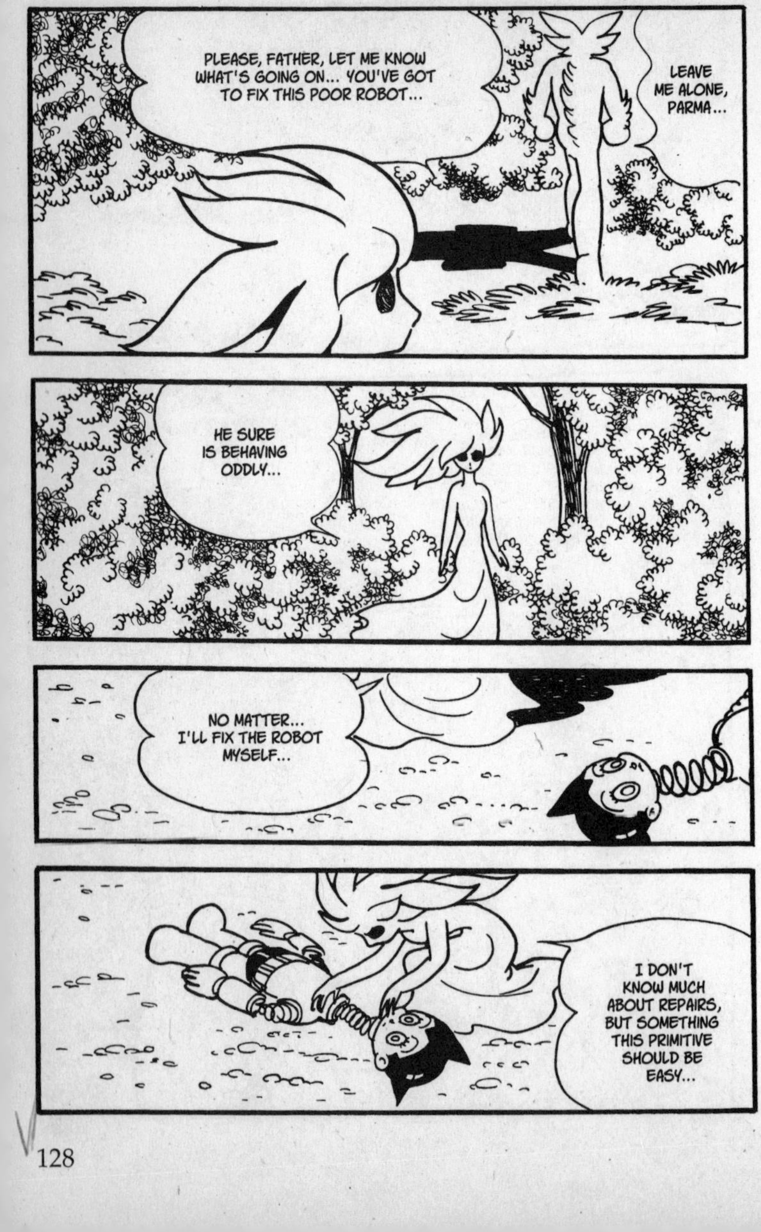
PLEASE, FATHER, LET ME KNOW WHAT'S GOING ON... YOU'VE GOT TO FIX THIS POOR ROBOT...
LEAVE ME ALONE, PARMA...
HE SURE IS BEHAVING ODDLY...
NO MATTER... I'LL FIX THE ROBOT MYSELF...
I DON'T KNOW MUCH ABOUT REPAIRS, BUT SOMETHING THIS PRIMITIVE SHOULD BE EASY...

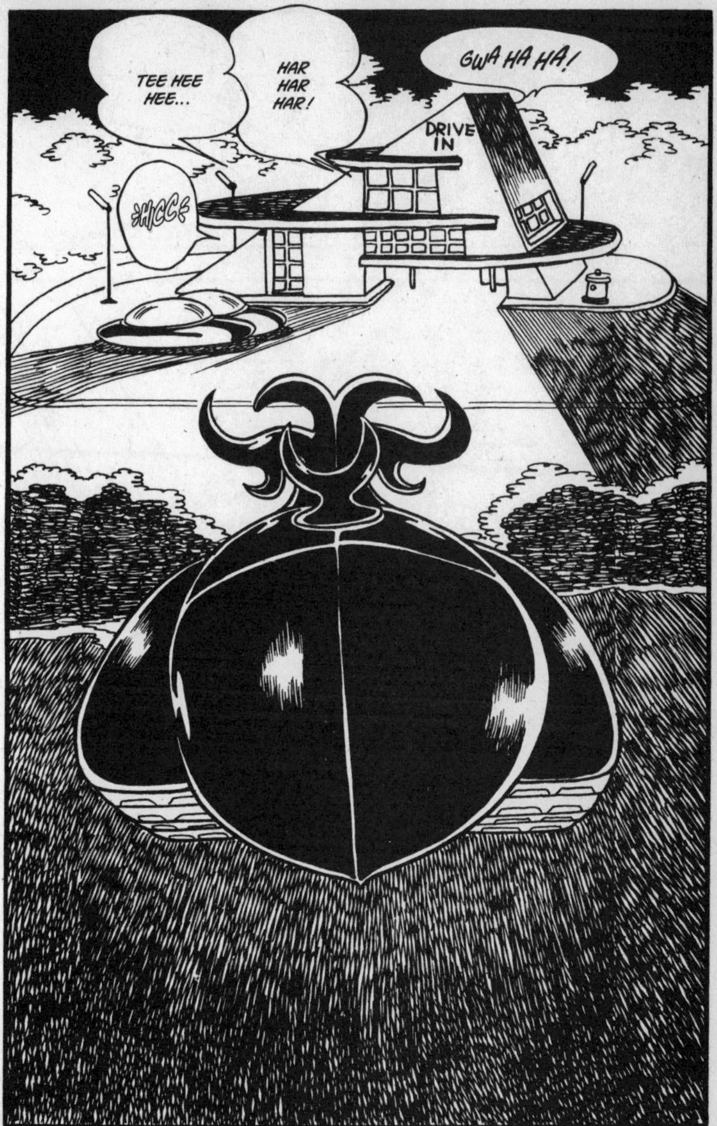
TEE HEE HEE...
HAR HAR HAR!
GWA HA HA!
HICC
DRIVE IN

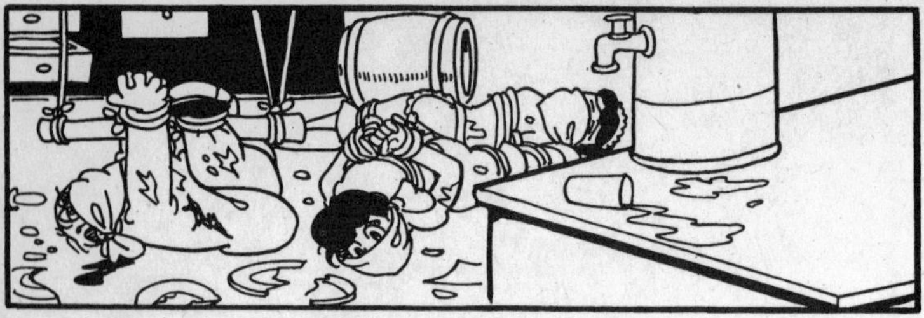

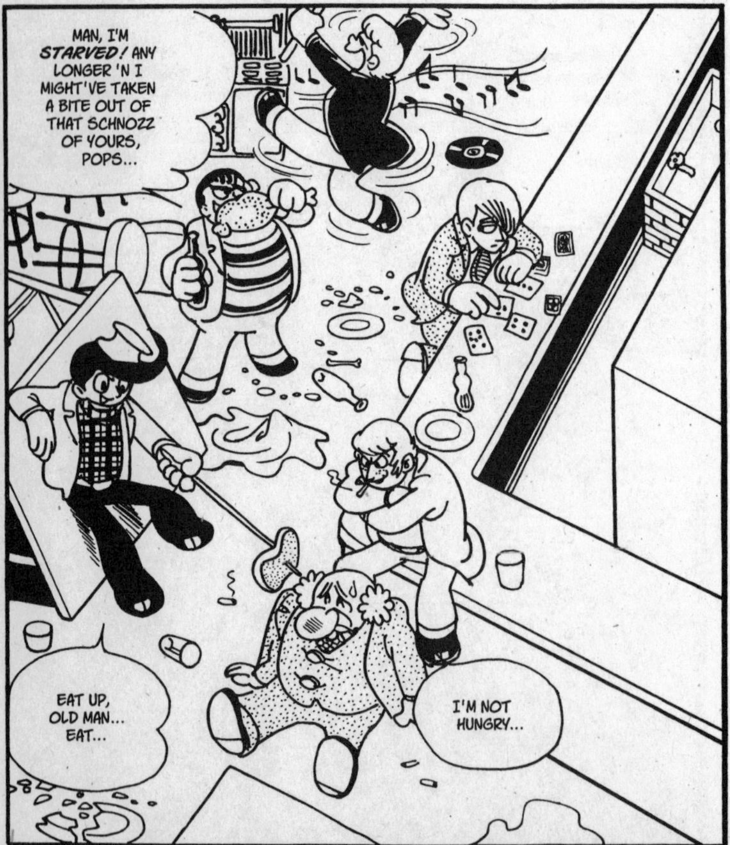
MAN, I'M **STARVED!** ANY LONGER 'N I MIGHT'VE TAKEN A BITE OUT OF THAT SCHNOZZ OF YOURS, POPS...
EAT UP, OLD MAN... EAT...
I'M NOT HUNGRY...

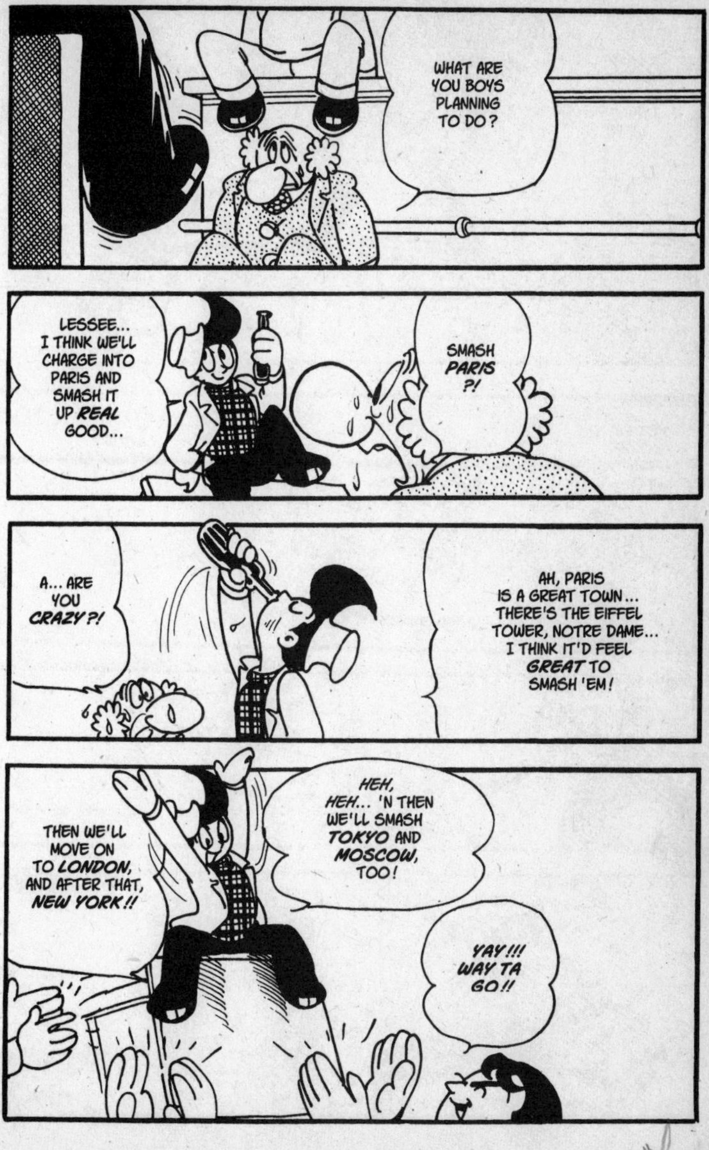
WHAT ARE YOU BOYS PLANNING TO DO?
LESSEE... I THINK WE'LL CHARGE INTO PARIS AND SMASH IT UP REAL GOOD...
SMASH PARIS ?!
A... ARE YOU CRAZY?!
AH, PARIS IS A GREAT TOWN... THERE'S THE EIFFEL TOWER, NOTRE DAME... I THINK IT'D FEEL GREAT TO SMASH 'EM!
THEN WE'LL MOVE ON TO LONDON, AND AFTER THAT, NEW YORK!!
HEH, HEH... 'N THEN WE'LL SMASH TOKYO AND MOSCOW, TOO!
YAY!!! WAY TA GO!!

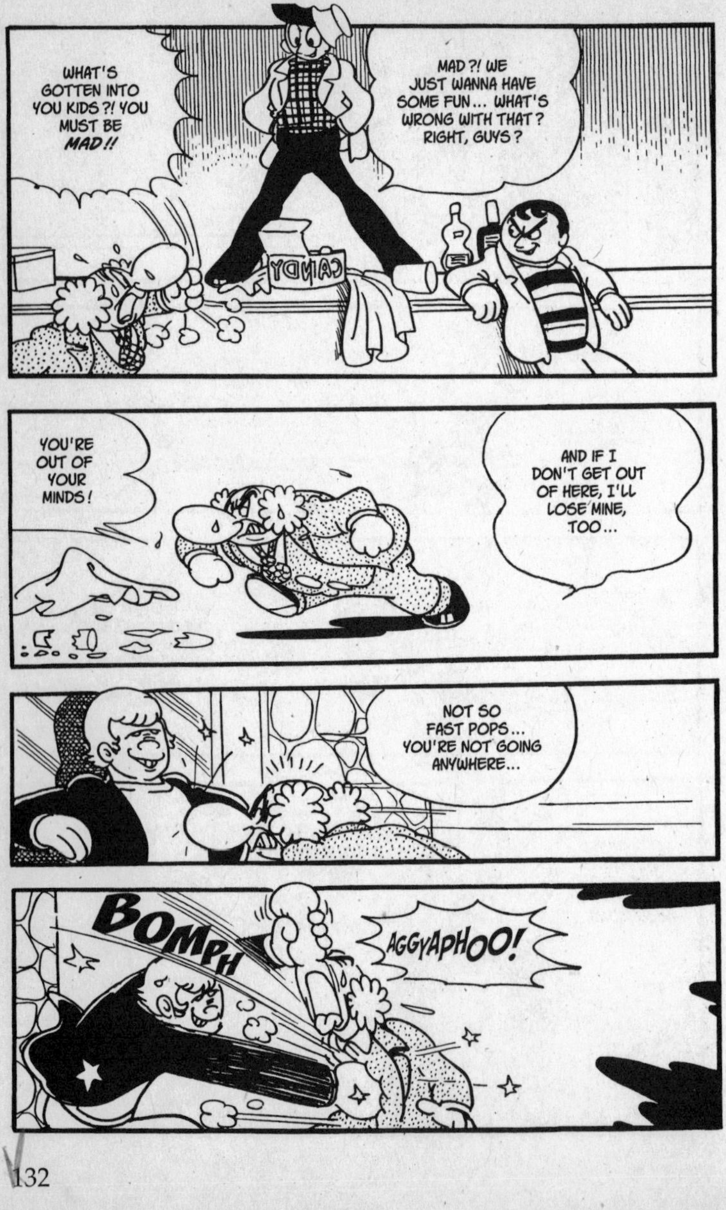
WHAT'S GOTTEN INTO YOU KIDS?! YOU MUST BE *MAD!!*
MAD?! WE JUST WANNA HAVE SOME FUN... WHAT'S WRONG WITH THAT? RIGHT, GUYS?
YOU'RE OUT OF YOUR MINDS!
AND IF I DON'T GET OUT OF HERE, I'LL LOSE MINE, TOO...
NOT SO FAST POPS... YOU'RE NOT GOING ANYWHERE...
BOMPH
AGGYAPHOO!

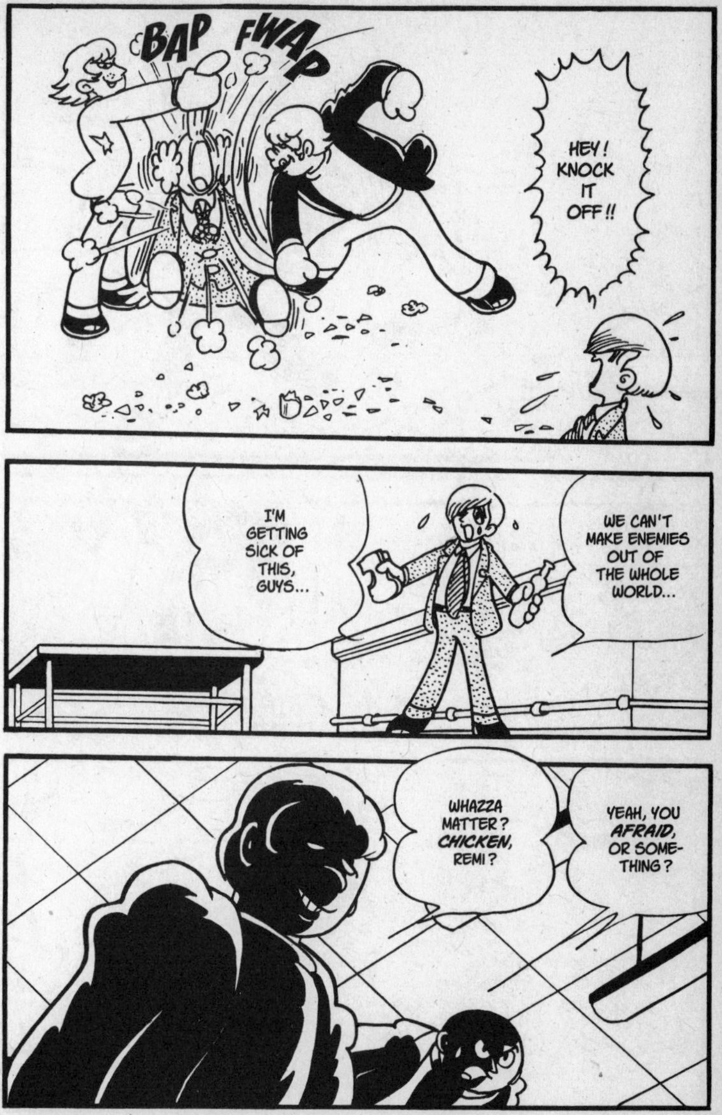
BAP FWAP
HEY! KNOCK IT OFF!!
I'M GETTING SICK OF THIS, GUYS...
WE CAN'T MAKE ENEMIES OUT OF THE WHOLE WORLD...
WHAZZA MATTER? CHICKEN, REMI?
YEAH, YOU AFRAID, OR SOME-THING?

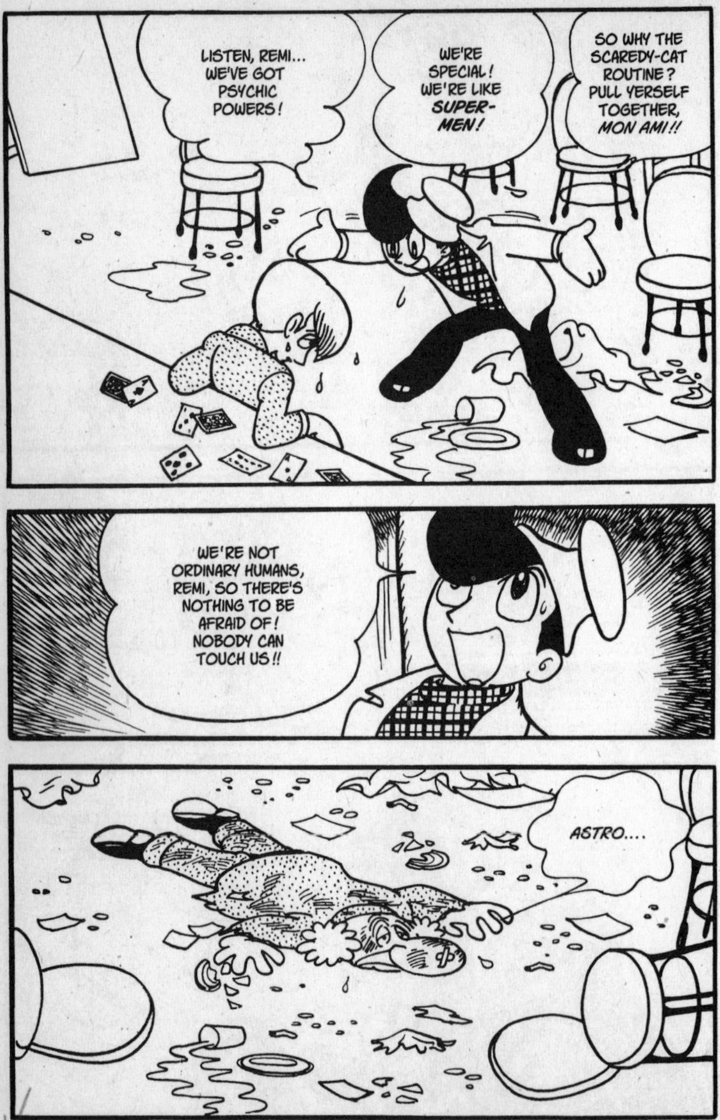
LISTEN, REMI... WE'VE GOT PSYCHIC POWERS!
WE'RE SPECIAL! WE'RE LIKE SUPER-MEN!
SO WHY THE SCAREDY-CAT ROUTINE? PULL YERSELF TOGETHER, MON AMI!!
WE'RE NOT ORDINARY HUMANS, REMI, SO THERE'S NOTHING TO BE AFRAID OF! NOBODY CAN TOUCH US!!
ASTRO....

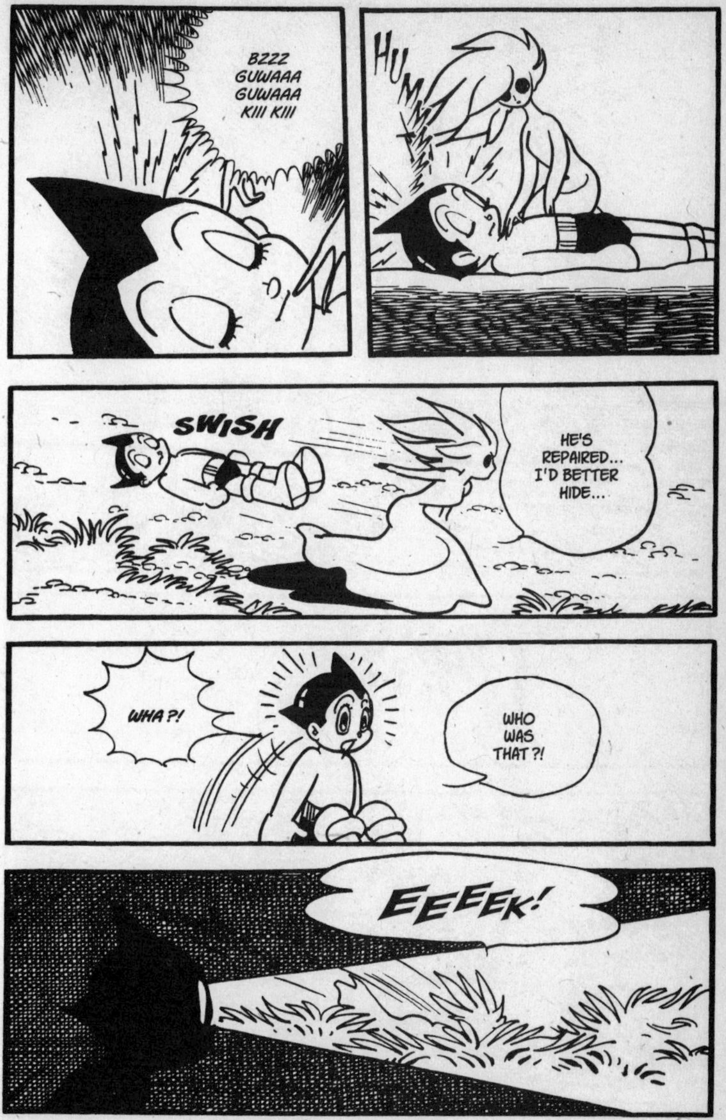
BZZZ
GUWAAA
GUWAAA
KIII KIII
HUMMMM
SWISH
HE'S REPAIRED... I'D BETTER HIDE...
WHA?!
WHO WAS THAT?!
EEEEK!

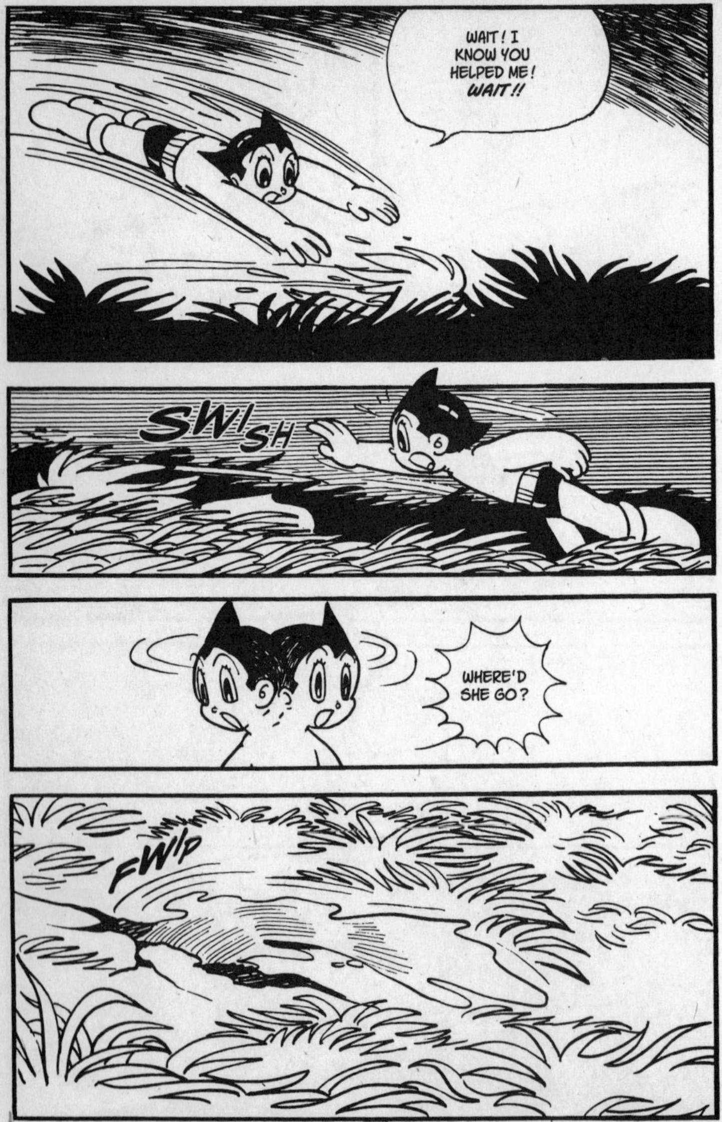
WAIT! I KNOW YOU HELPED ME! WAIT!!
SWISH
WHERE'D SHE GO?
FWIP

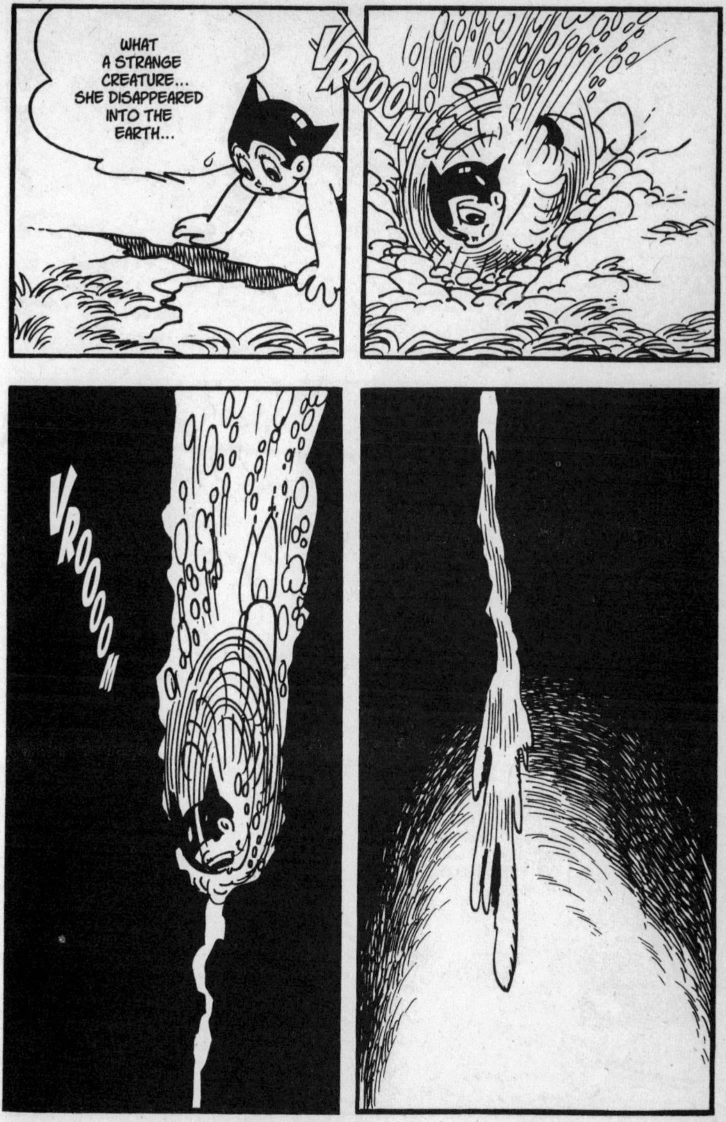
WHAT A STRANGE CREATURE... SHE DISAPPEARED INTO THE EARTH...
VROOOM
VROOOOM

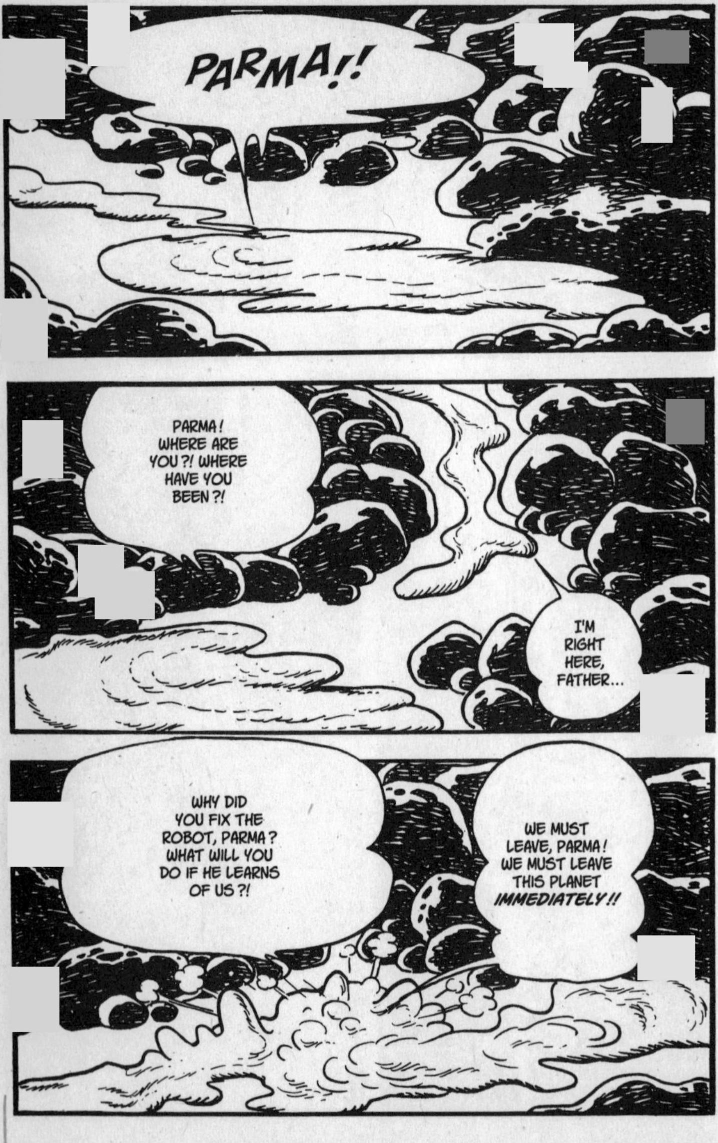
PARMA!!
PARMA! WHERE ARE YOU?! WHERE HAVE YOU BEEN?!
I'M RIGHT HERE, FATHER...
WHY DID YOU FIX THE ROBOT, PARMA? WHAT WILL YOU DO IF HE LEARNS OF US?!
WE MUST LEAVE, PARMA! WE MUST LEAVE THIS PLANET *IMMEDIATELY!!*

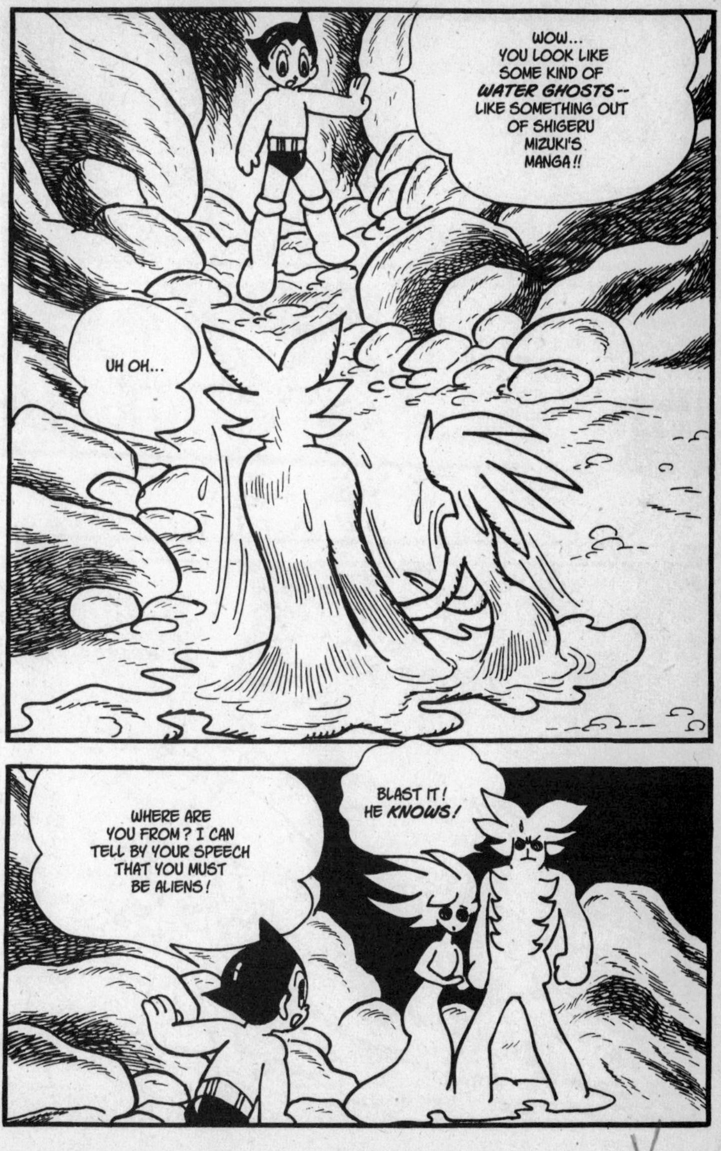
WOW... YOU LOOK LIKE SOME KIND OF WATER GHOSTS -- LIKE SOMETHING OUT OF SHIGERU MIZUKI'S MANGA!!
UH OH...
WHERE ARE YOU FROM? I CAN TELL BY YOUR SPEECH THAT YOU MUST BE ALIENS!
BLAST IT! HE KNOWS!

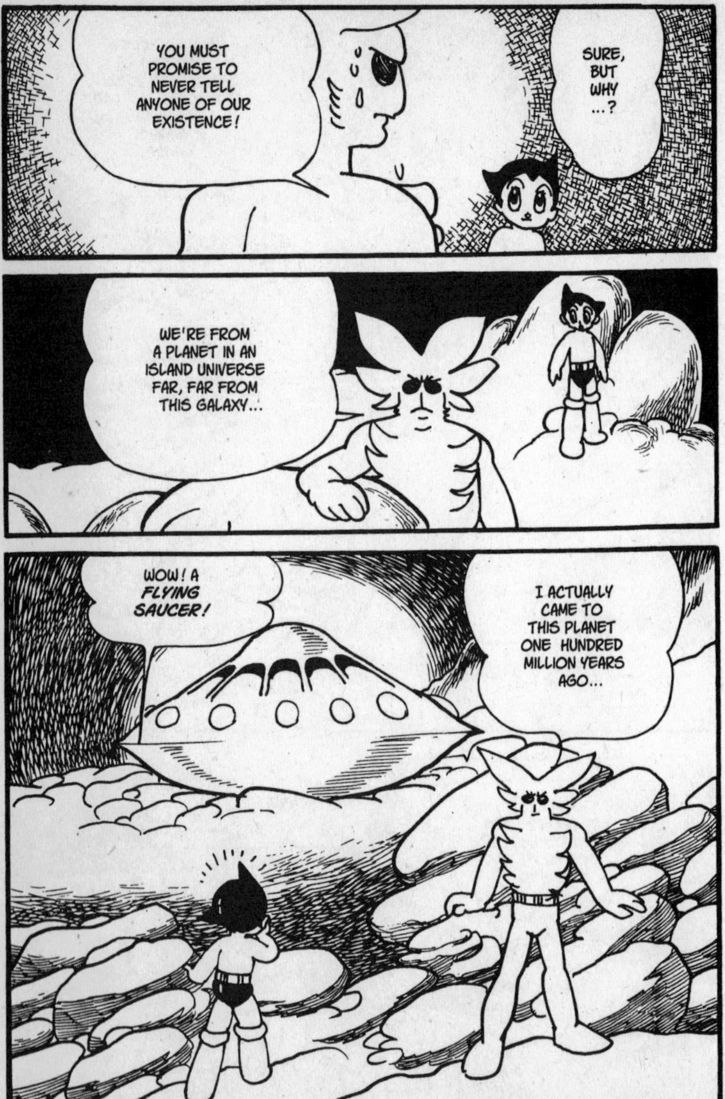
YOU MUST PROMISE TO NEVER TELL ANYONE OF OUR EXISTENCE!
SURE, BUT WHY ...?
WE'RE FROM A PLANET IN AN ISLAND UNIVERSE FAR, FAR FROM THIS GALAXY...
WOW! A *FLYING SAUCER!*
I ACTUALLY CAME TO THIS PLANET ONE HUNDRED MILLION YEARS AGO...

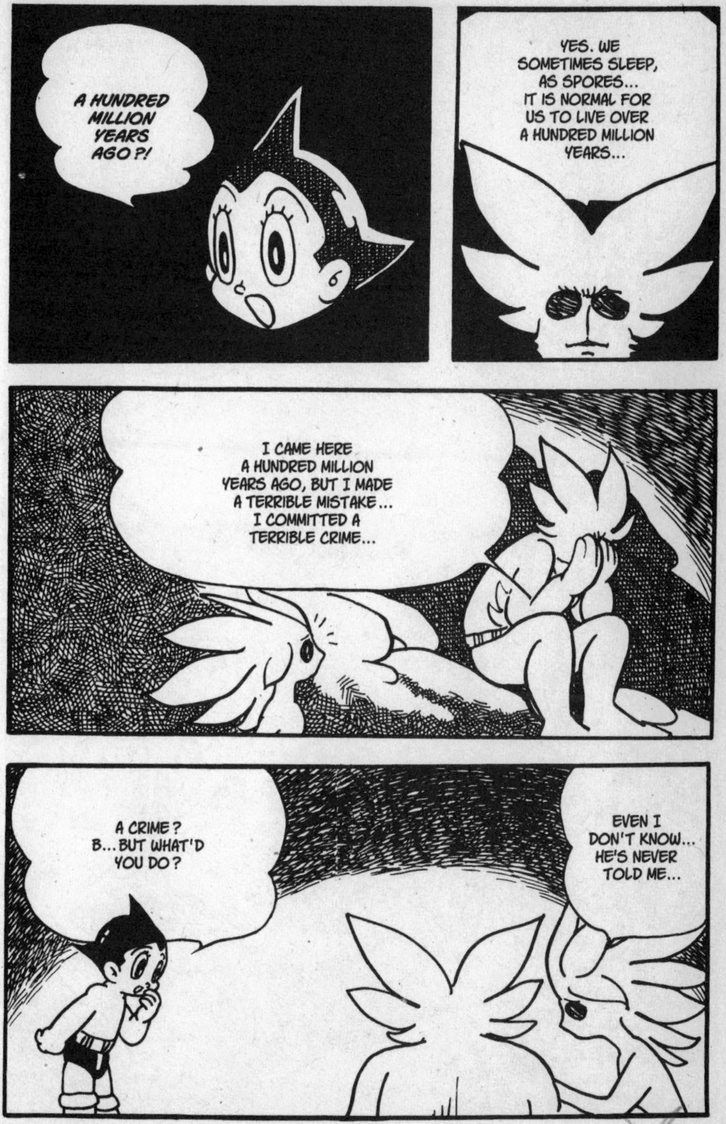
A HUNDRED MILLION YEARS AGO?!
YES. WE SOMETIMES SLEEP, AS SPORES... IT IS NORMAL FOR US TO LIVE OVER A HUNDRED MILLION YEARS...
I CAME HERE A HUNDRED MILLION YEARS AGO, BUT I MADE A TERRIBLE MISTAKE... I COMMITTED A TERRIBLE CRIME...
A CRIME? B...BUT WHAT'D YOU DO?
EVEN I DON'T KNOW... HE'S NEVER TOLD ME...

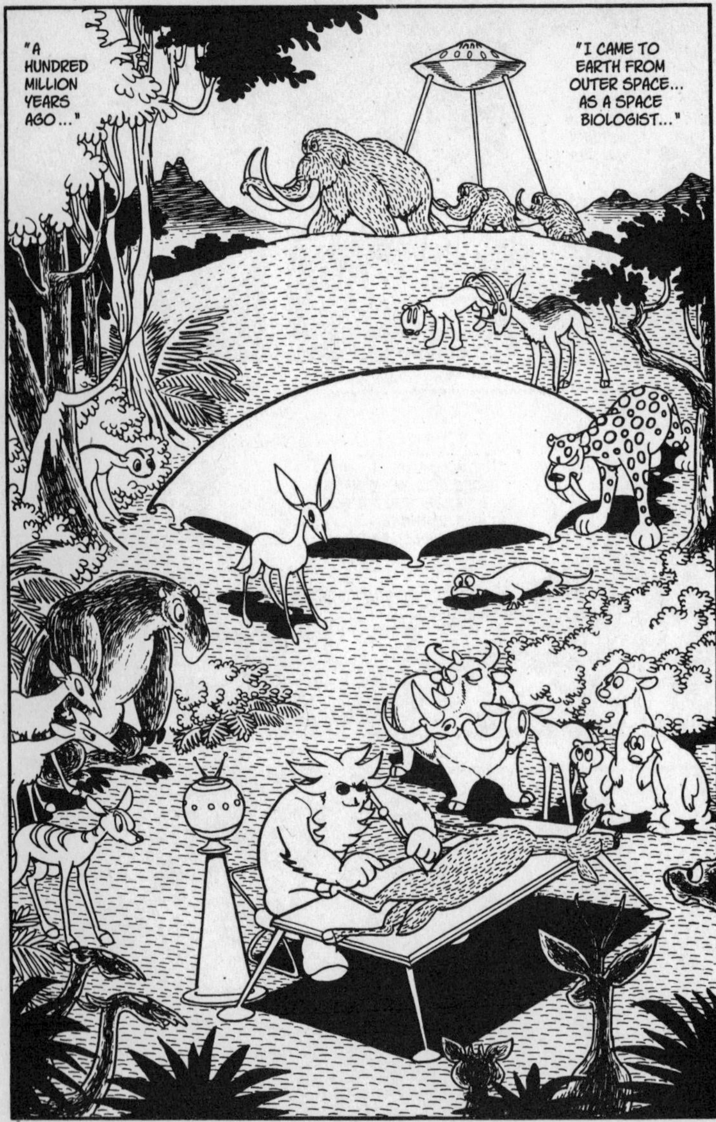
"A HUNDRED MILLION YEARS AGO..."
"I CAME TO EARTH FROM OUTER SPACE... AS A SPACE BIOLOGIST..."

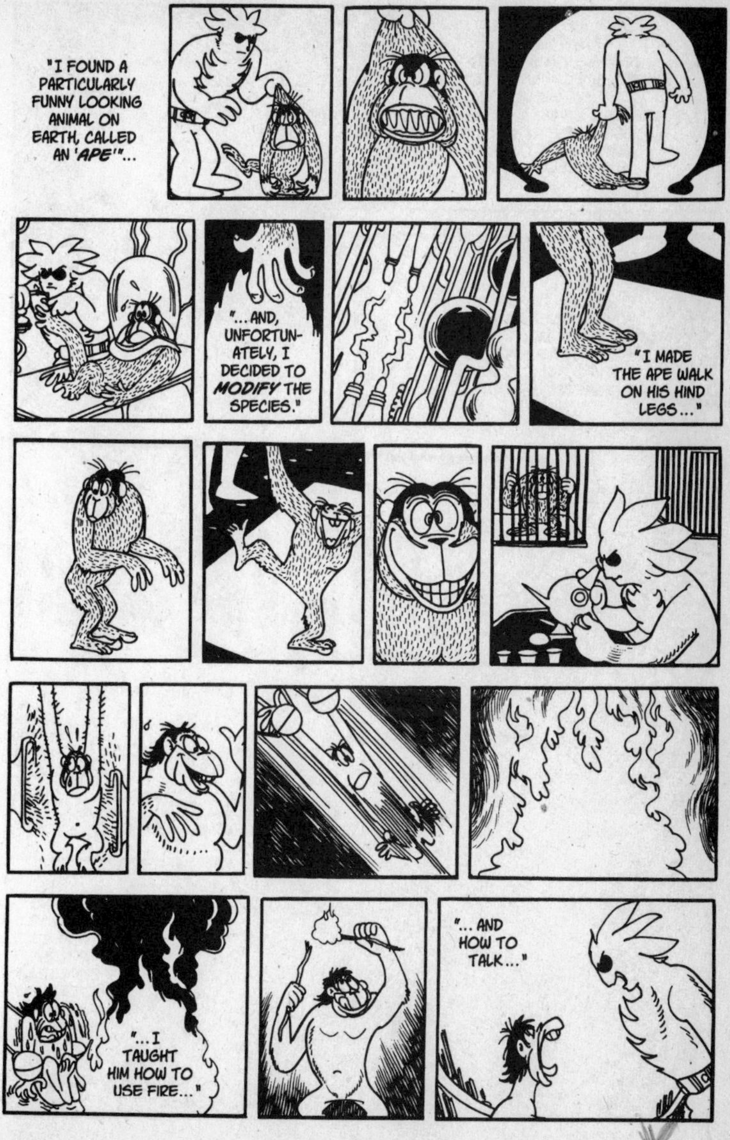
"I FOUND A PARTICULARLY FUNNY LOOKING ANIMAL ON EARTH, CALLED AN '*APE*'"...
"...AND, UNFORTUN-ATELY, I DECIDED TO *MODIFY* THE SPECIES."
"I MADE THE APE WALK ON HIS HIND LEGS..."
"...I TAUGHT HIM HOW TO USE FIRE..."
"...AND HOW TO TALK..."

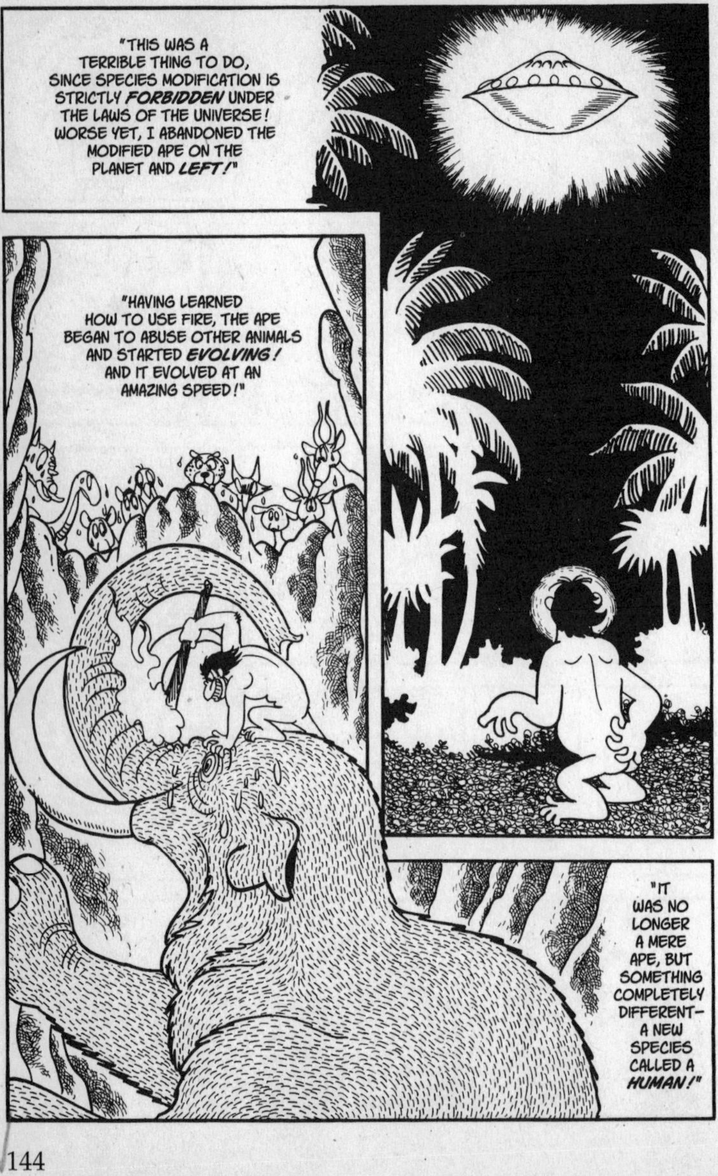
"THIS WAS A TERRIBLE THING TO DO, SINCE SPECIES MODIFICATION IS STRICTLY *FORBIDDEN* UNDER THE LAWS OF THE UNIVERSE! WORSE YET, I ABANDONED THE MODIFIED APE ON THE PLANET AND *LEFT!*"
"HAVING LEARNED HOW TO USE FIRE, THE APE BEGAN TO ABUSE OTHER ANIMALS AND STARTED *EVOLVING!* AND IT EVOLVED AT AN AMAZING SPEED!"
"IT WAS NO LONGER A MERE APE, BUT SOMETHING COMPLETELY DIFFERENT— A NEW SPECIES CALLED A *HUMAN!*"

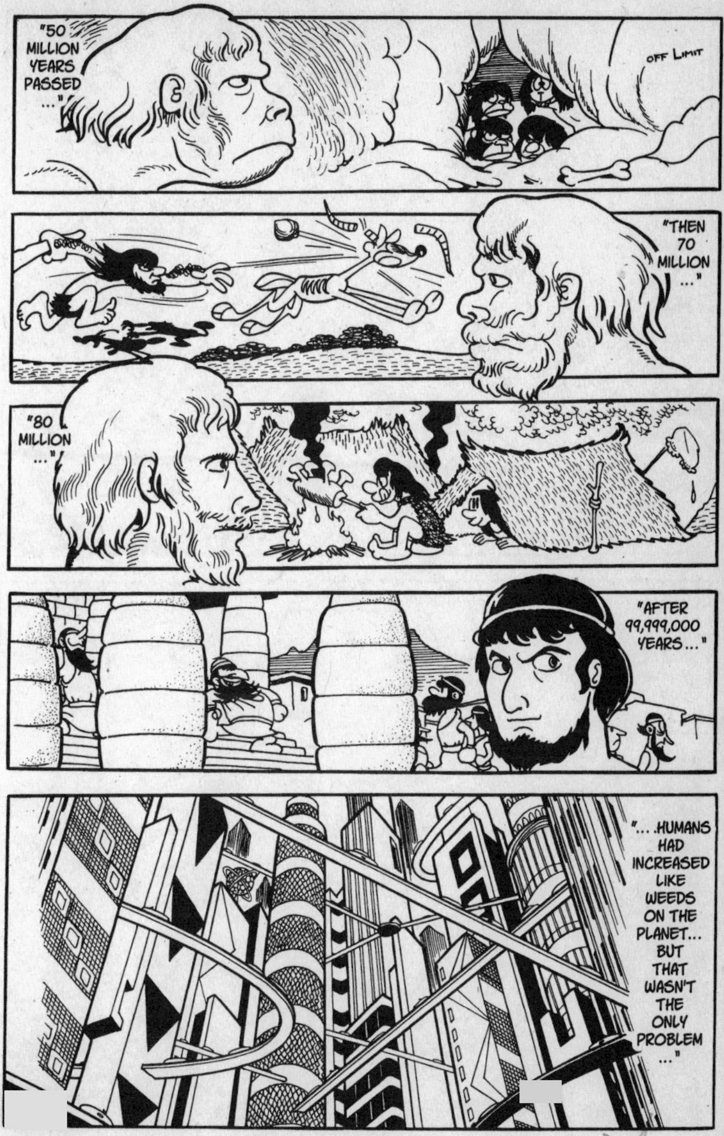
"50 MILLION YEARS PASSED ..."
OFF LIMIT
"THEN 70 MILLION ..."
"80 MILLION ..."
"AFTER 99,999,000 YEARS ..."
"... .HUMANS HAD INCREASED LIKE WEEDS ON THE PLANET... BUT THAT WASN'T THE ONLY PROBLEM ..."

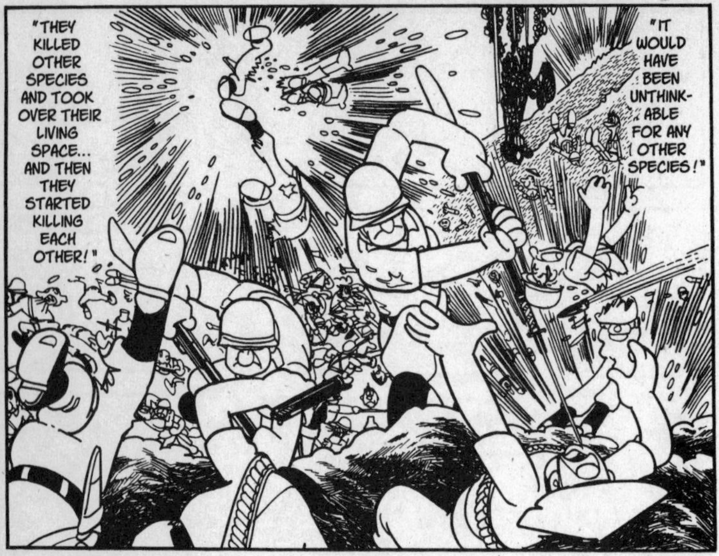
"THEY KILLED OTHER SPECIES AND TOOK OVER THEIR LIVING SPACE... AND THEN THEY STARTED KILLING EACH OTHER!"
"IT WOULD HAVE BEEN UNTHINK-ABLE FOR ANY OTHER SPECIES!"
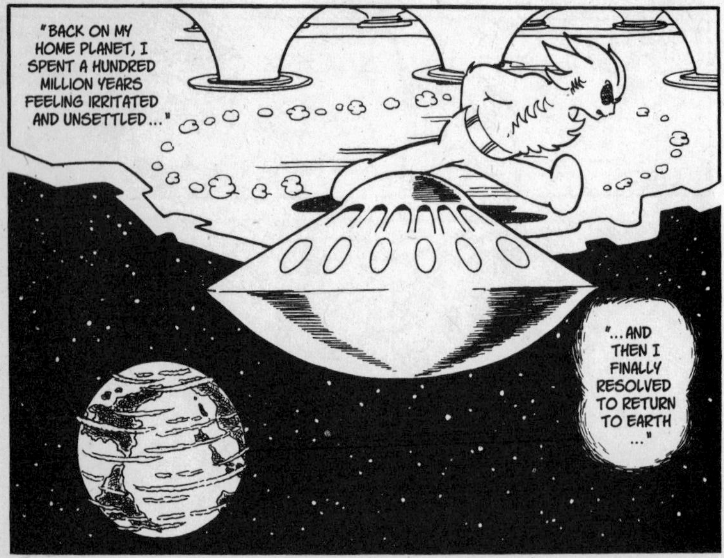
"BACK ON MY HOME PLANET, I SPENT A HUNDRED MILLION YEARS FEELING IRRITATED AND UNSETTLED..."
"...AND THEN I FINALLY RESOLVED TO RETURN TO EARTH..."

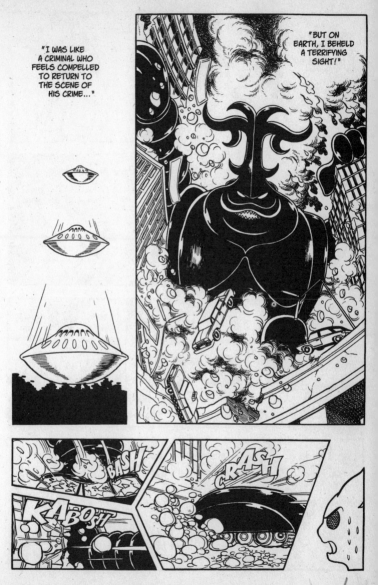

"I WAS LIKE A CRIMINAL WHO FEELS COMPELLED TO RETURN TO THE SCENE OF HIS CRIME..."

"BUT ON EARTH, I BEHELD A TERRIFYING SIGHT!"

147

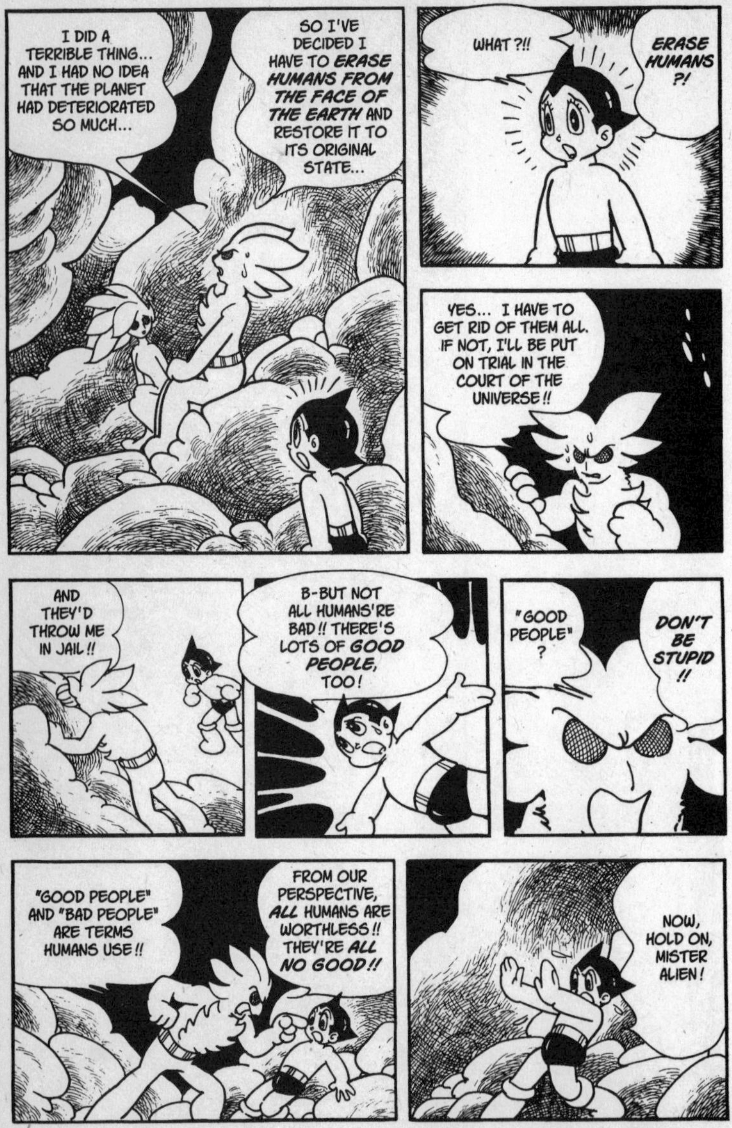
I DID A TERRIBLE THING... AND I HAD NO IDEA THAT THE PLANET HAD DETERIORATED SO MUCH...
SO I'VE DECIDED I HAVE TO *ERASE HUMANS FROM THE FACE OF THE EARTH* AND RESTORE IT TO ITS ORIGINAL STATE...
WHAT ?!!
ERASE HUMANS ?!
YES... I HAVE TO GET RID OF THEM ALL. IF NOT, I'LL BE PUT ON TRIAL IN THE COURT OF THE UNIVERSE !!
AND THEY'D THROW ME IN JAIL !!
B-BUT NOT ALL HUMANS'RE BAD !! THERE'S LOTS OF *GOOD PEOPLE*, TOO !
"GOOD PEOPLE" ?
DON'T BE STUPID !!
"GOOD PEOPLE" AND "BAD PEOPLE" ARE TERMS HUMANS USE !!
FROM OUR PERSPECTIVE, *ALL* HUMANS ARE WORTHLESS !! THEY'RE *ALL NO GOOD !!*
NOW, HOLD ON, MISTER ALIEN !

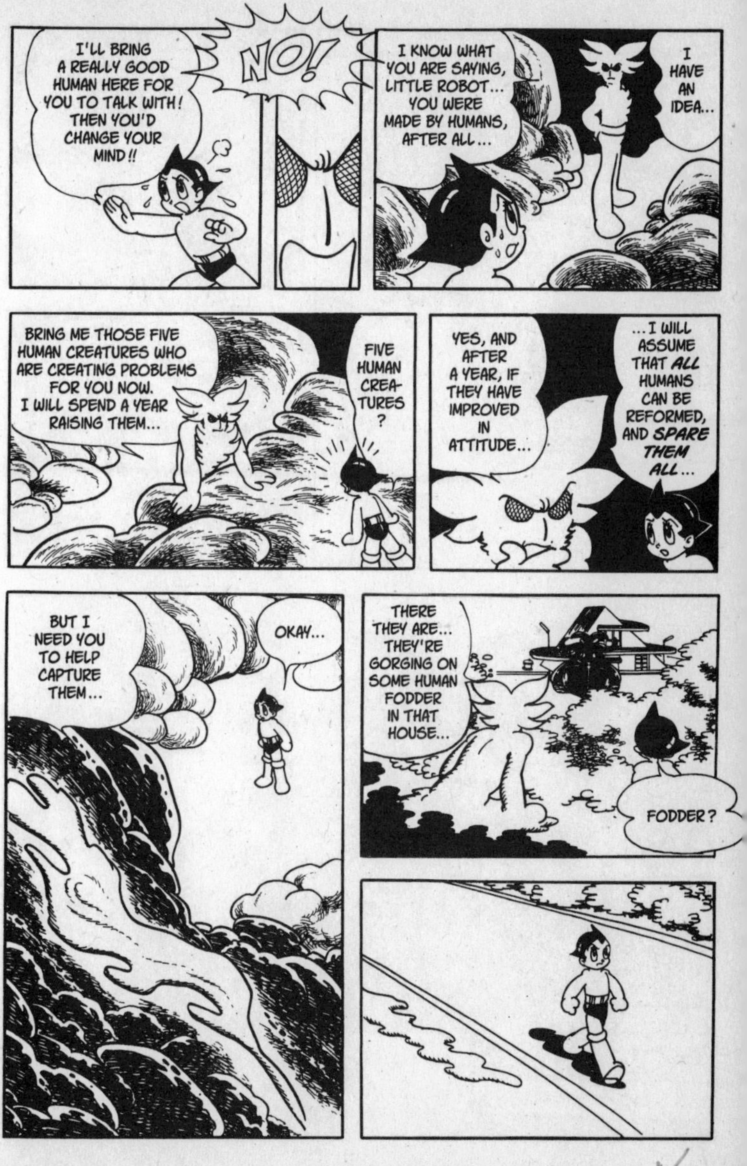

I'LL BRING A REALLY GOOD HUMAN HERE FOR YOU TO TALK WITH! THEN YOU'D CHANGE YOUR MIND!!
NO!
I KNOW WHAT YOU ARE SAYING, LITTLE ROBOT... YOU WERE MADE BY HUMANS, AFTER ALL...
I HAVE AN IDEA...
BRING ME THOSE FIVE HUMAN CREATURES WHO ARE CREATING PROBLEMS FOR YOU NOW. I WILL SPEND A YEAR RAISING THEM...
FIVE HUMAN CREA-TURES?
YES, AND AFTER A YEAR, IF THEY HAVE IMPROVED IN ATTITUDE...
...I WILL ASSUME THAT ALL HUMANS CAN BE REFORMED, AND SPARE THEM ALL...
BUT I NEED YOU TO HELP CAPTURE THEM...
OKAY...
THERE THEY ARE... THEY'RE GORGING ON SOME HUMAN FODDER IN THAT HOUSE...
FODDER?

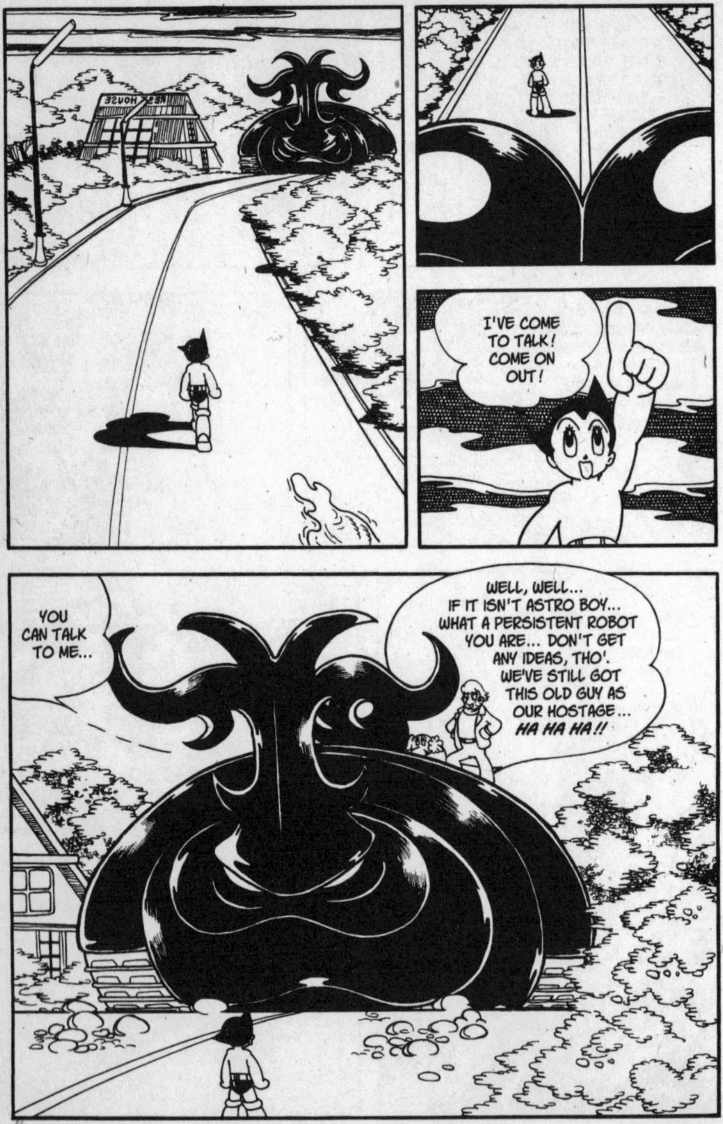
I'VE COME TO TALK! COME ON OUT!
YOU CAN TALK TO ME...
WELL, WELL... IF IT ISN'T ASTRO BOY... WHAT A PERSISTENT ROBOT YOU ARE... DON'T GET ANY IDEAS, THO'. WE'VE STILL GOT THIS OLD GUY AS OUR HOSTAGE... HA HA HA!!

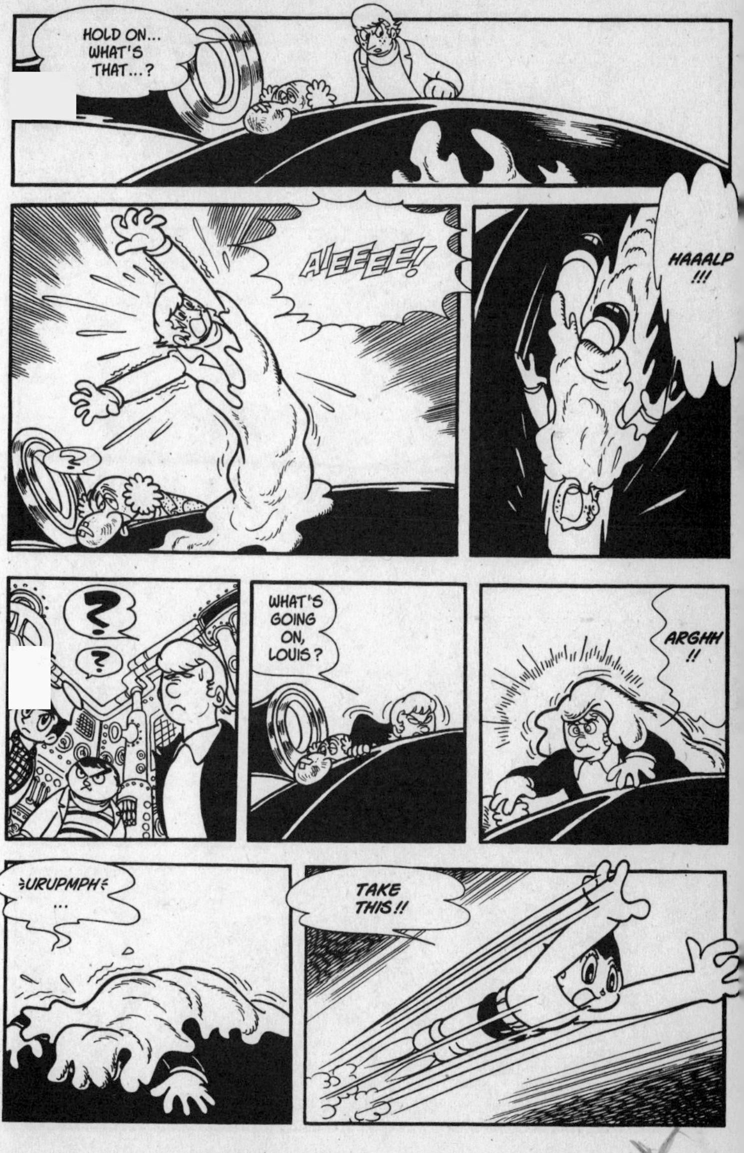
HOLD ON... WHAT'S THAT...?
AIEEEE!
?
HAAALP !!!
?
?
WHAT'S GOING ON, LOUIS?
ARGHH !!
URUPMPH ...
TAKE THIS!!

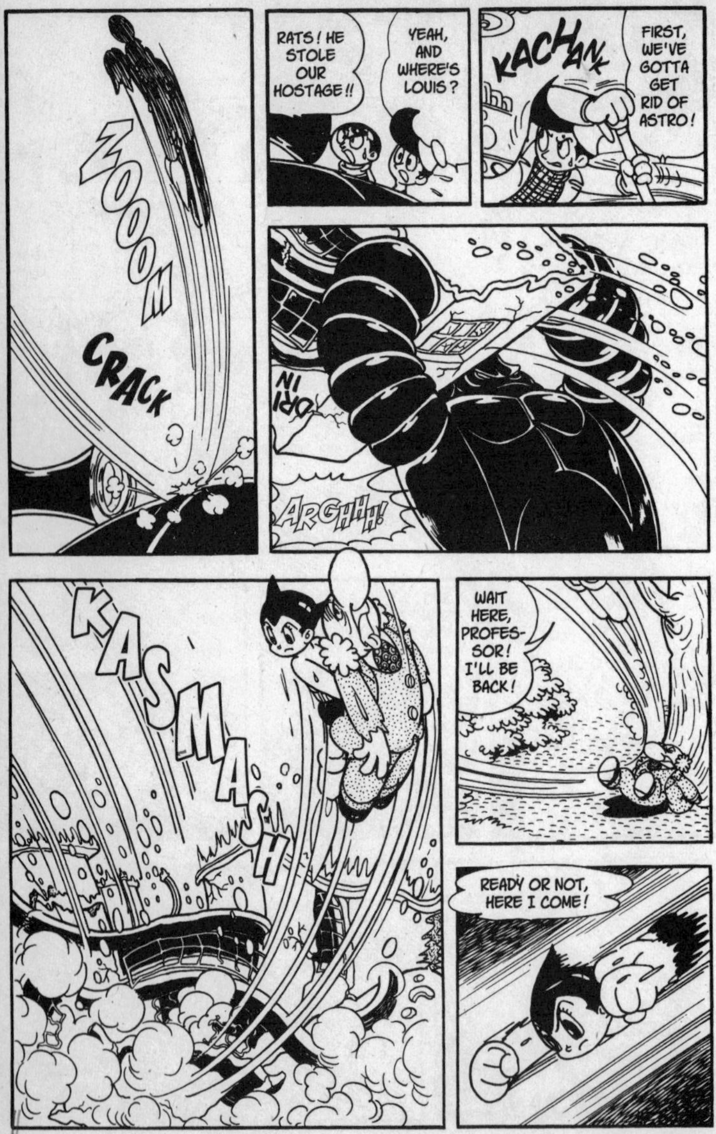
ZOOOOM
CRACK
RATS! HE STOLE OUR HOSTAGE!!
YEAH, AND WHERE'S LOUIS?
KACHANK
FIRST, WE'VE GOTTA GET RID OF ASTRO!
ARGHHH!
KASMASH
WAIT HERE, PROFES-SOR! I'LL BE BACK!
READY OR NOT, HERE I COME!

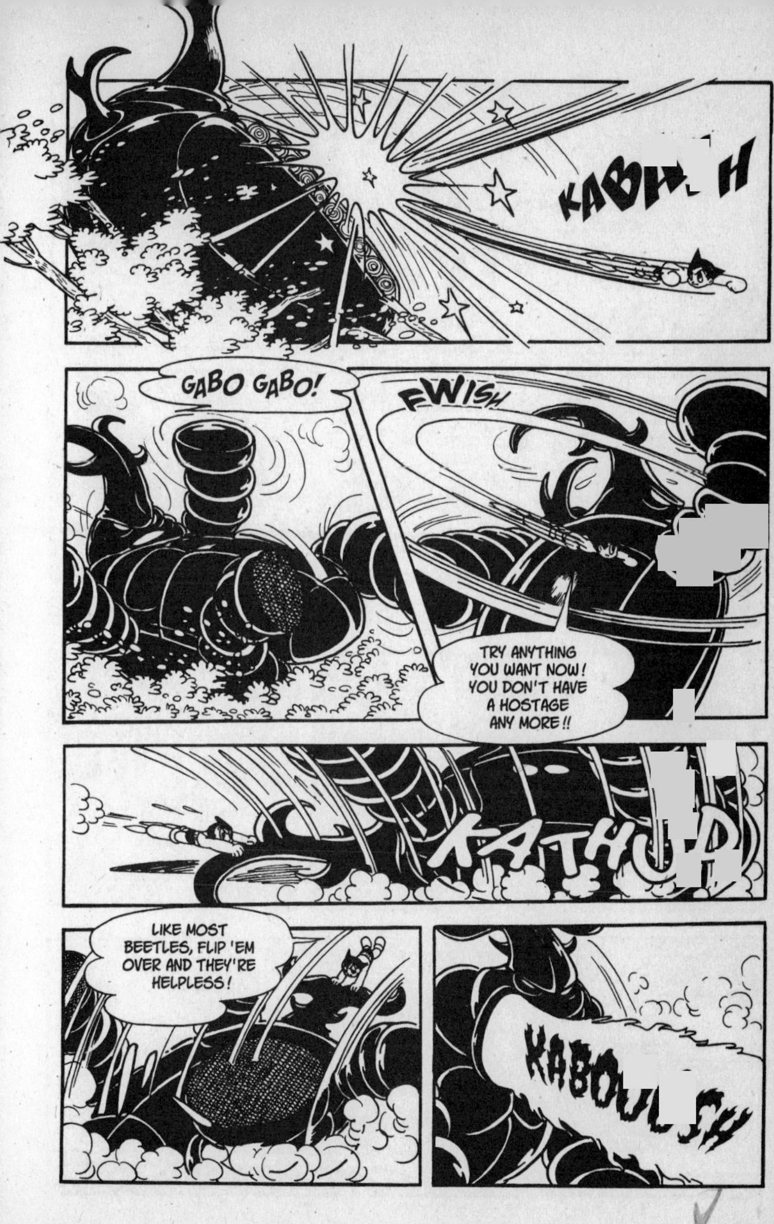
GABO GABO!
FWISH
TRY ANYTHING YOU WANT NOW! YOU DON'T HAVE A HOSTAGE ANY MORE!!
LIKE MOST BEETLES, FLIP 'EM OVER AND THEY'RE HELPLESS!

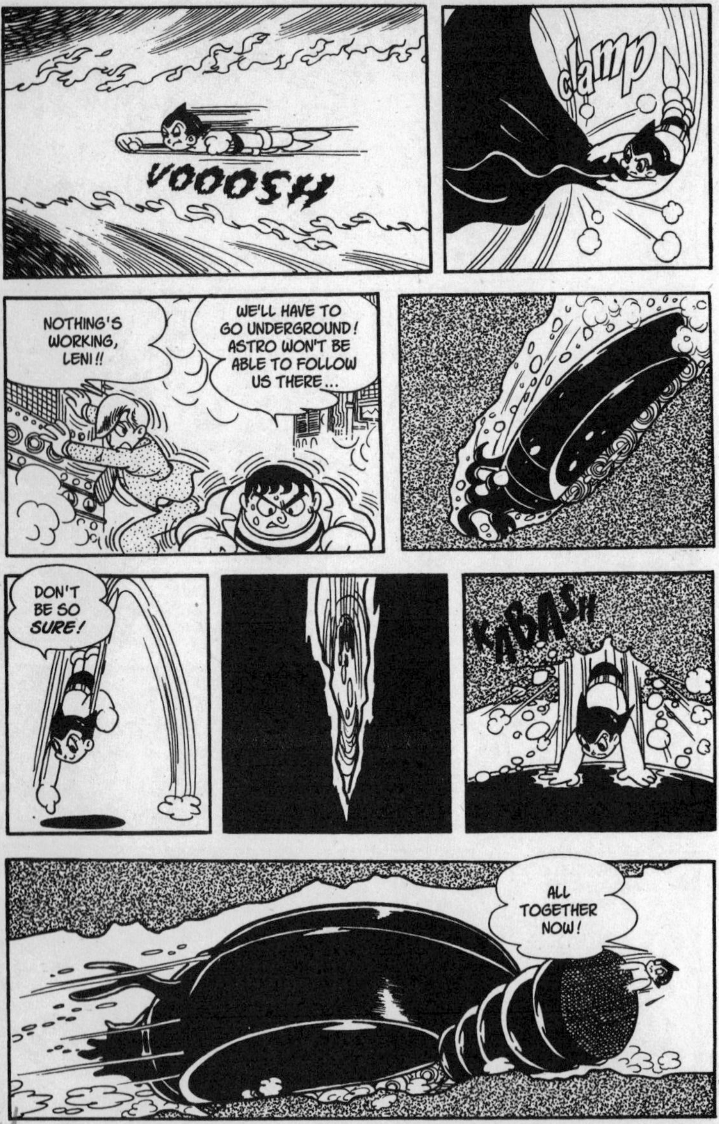
VOOOSH
clamp
NOTHING'S WORKING, LENI!!
WE'LL HAVE TO GO UNDERGROUND! ASTRO WON'T BE ABLE TO FOLLOW US THERE...
DON'T BE SO SURE!
KABASH
ALL TOGETHER NOW!

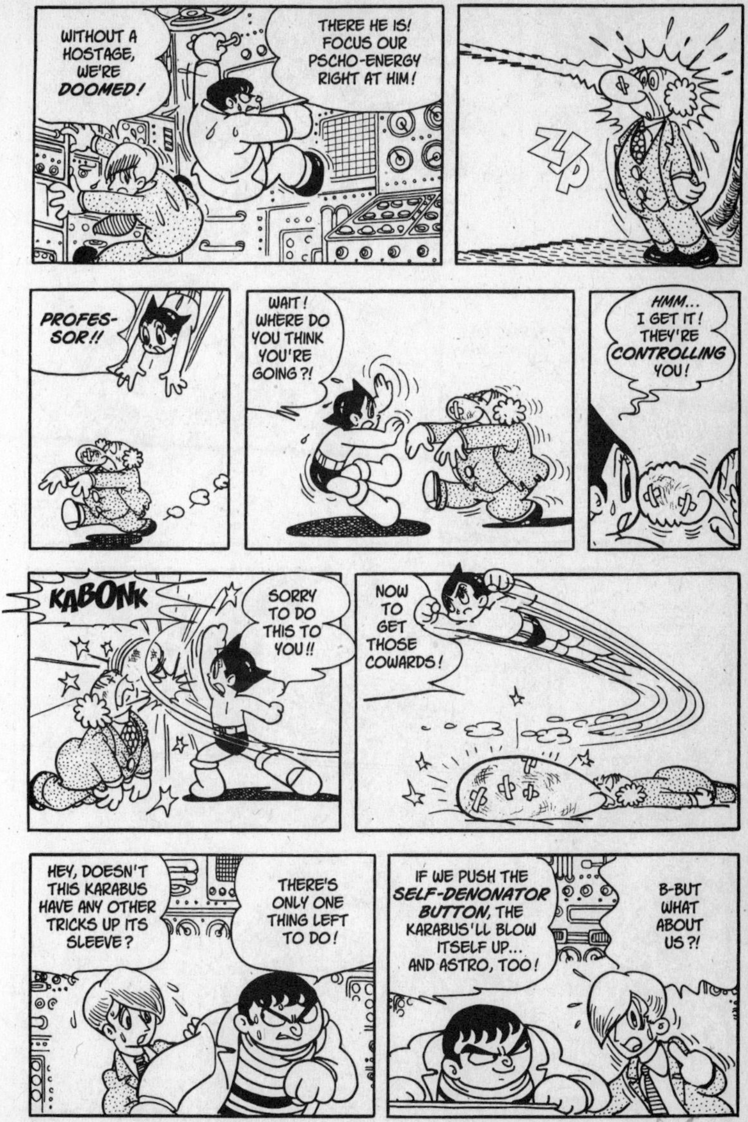
WITHOUT A HOSTAGE, WE'RE DOOMED!
THERE HE IS! FOCUS OUR PSCHO-ENERGY RIGHT AT HIM!
ZIP
PROFES-SOR!!
WAIT! WHERE DO YOU THINK YOU'RE GOING?!
HMM... I GET IT! THEY'RE CONTROLLING YOU!
KABONK
SORRY TO DO THIS TO YOU!!
NOW TO GET THOSE COWARDS!
HEY, DOESN'T THIS KARABUS HAVE ANY OTHER TRICKS UP ITS SLEEVE?
THERE'S ONLY ONE THING LEFT TO DO!
IF WE PUSH THE SELF-DENONATOR BUTTON, THE KARABUS'LL BLOW ITSELF UP... AND ASTRO, TOO!
B-BUT WHAT ABOUT US?!

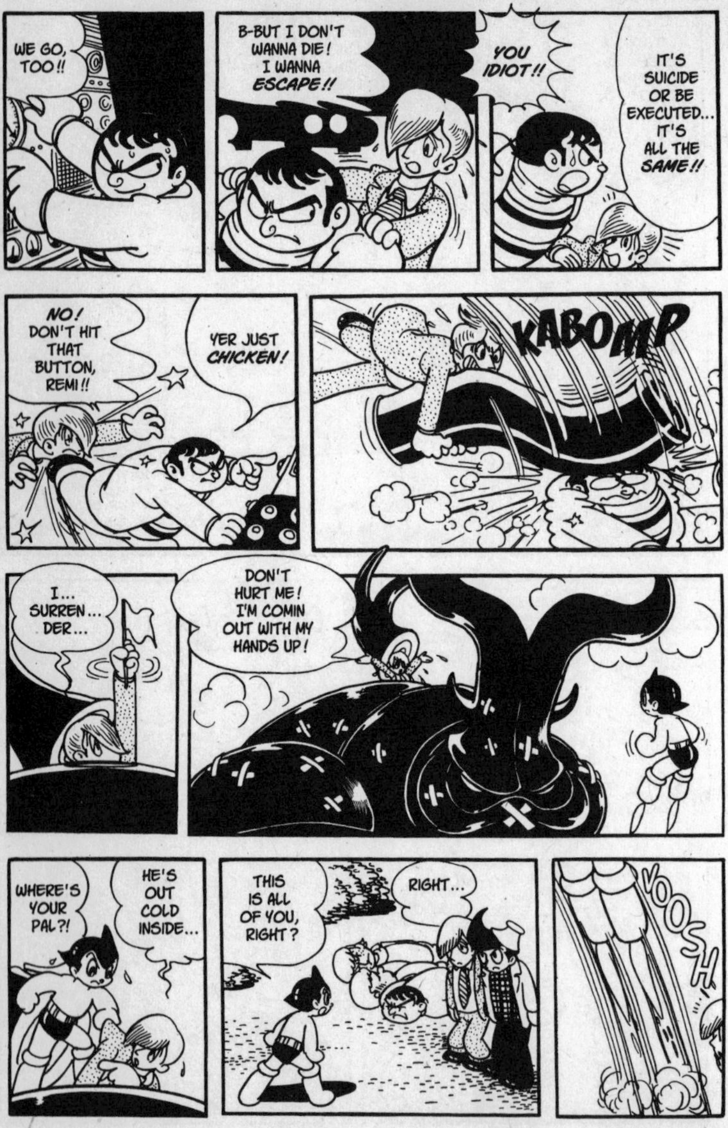
WE GO, TOO!!
B-BUT I DON'T WANNA DIE! I WANNA ESCAPE!!
YOU IDIOT!!
IT'S SUICIDE OR BE EXECUTED... IT'S ALL THE SAME!!
NO! DON'T HIT THAT BUTTON, REMI!!
YER JUST CHICKEN!
KABOMP
I... SURREN... DER...
DON'T HURT ME! I'M COMIN OUT WITH MY HANDS UP!
WHERE'S YOUR PAL?!
HE'S OUT COLD INSIDE...
THIS IS ALL OF YOU, RIGHT?
RIGHT...
VOOSH

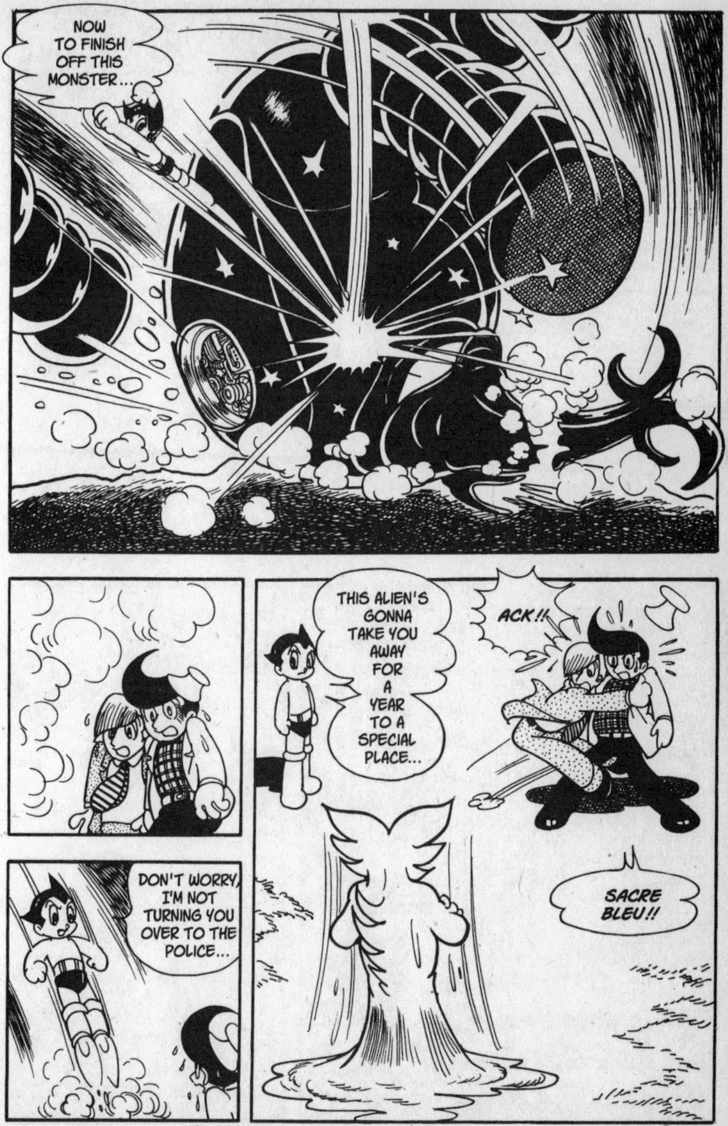
NOW TO FINISH OFF THIS MONSTER...
DON'T WORRY, I'M NOT TURNING YOU OVER TO THE POLICE...
THIS ALIEN'S GONNA TAKE YOU AWAY FOR A YEAR TO A SPECIAL PLACE...
ACK!!
SACRE BLEU!!

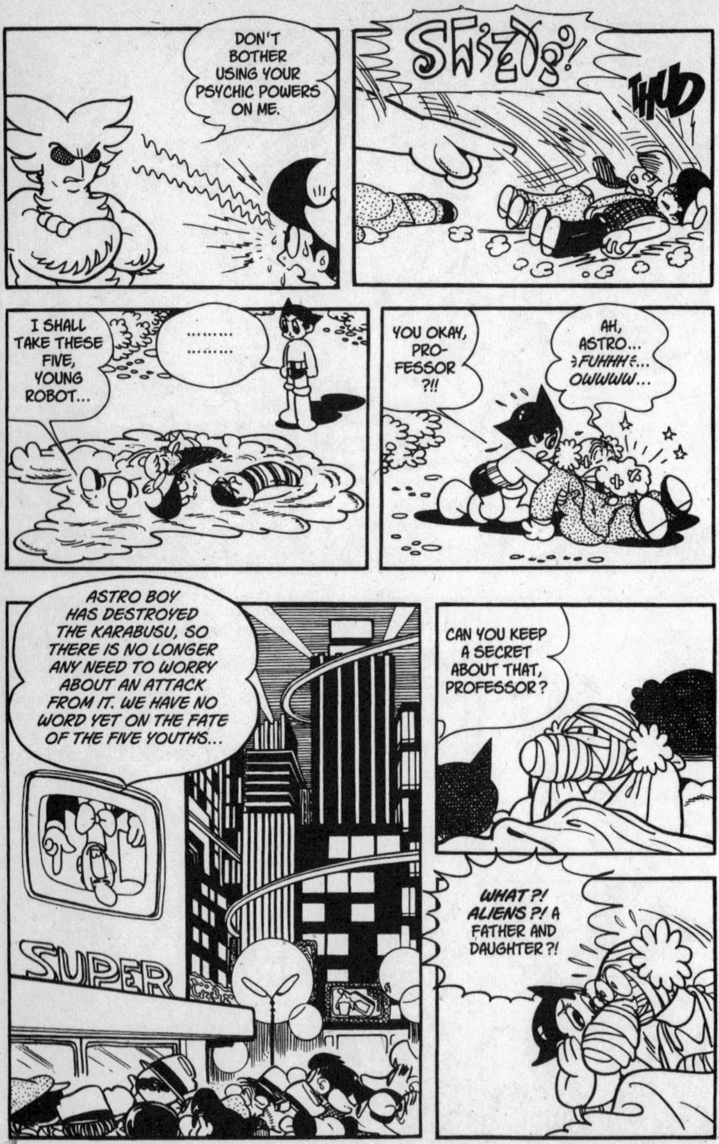
DON'T BOTHER USING YOUR PSYCHIC POWERS ON ME.
THUD
I SHALL TAKE THESE FIVE, YOUNG ROBOT...
....
....
YOU OKAY, PRO-FESSOR ?!!
AH, ASTRO... FUHHH... OWWWW...
ASTRO BOY HAS DESTROYED THE KARABUSU, SO THERE IS NO LONGER ANY NEED TO WORRY ABOUT AN ATTACK FROM IT. WE HAVE NO WORD YET ON THE FATE OF THE FIVE YOUTHS...
SUPER
CAN YOU KEEP A SECRET ABOUT THAT, PROFESSOR?
WHAT?! ALIENS?! A FATHER AND DAUGHTER?!

157

158

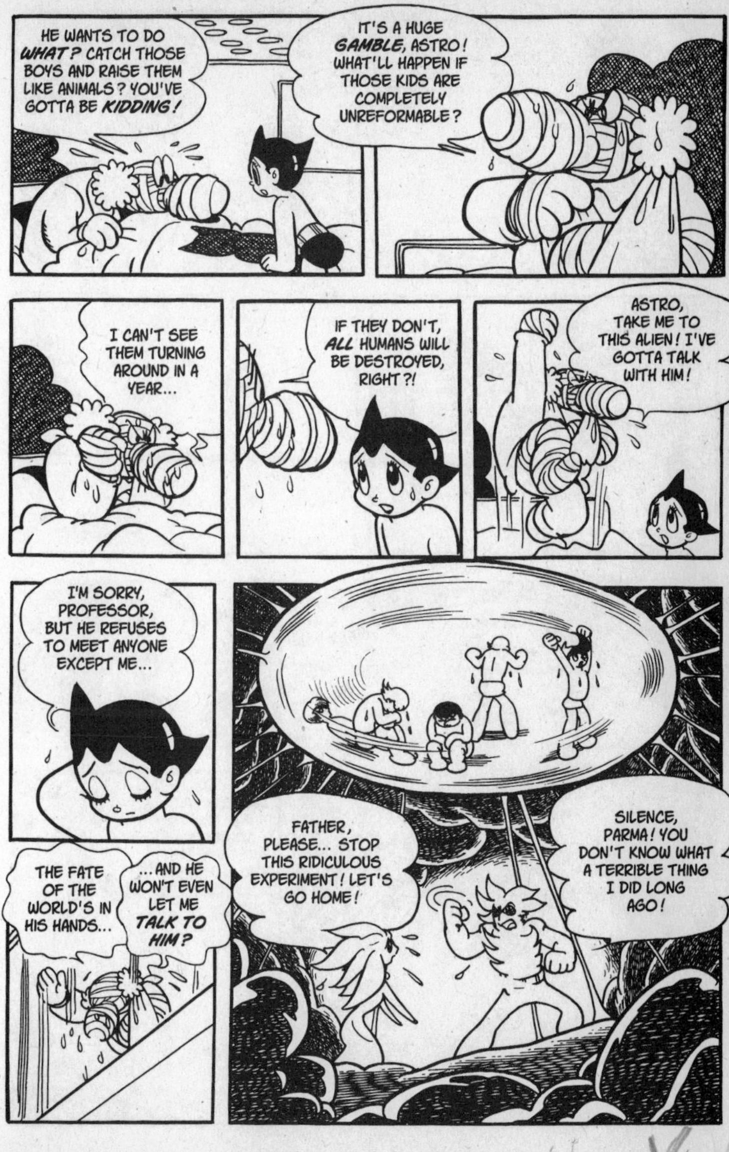
HE WANTS TO DO WHAT? CATCH THOSE BOYS AND RAISE THEM LIKE ANIMALS? YOU'VE GOTTA BE KIDDING!
IT'S A HUGE GAMBLE, ASTRO! WHAT'LL HAPPEN IF THOSE KIDS ARE COMPLETELY UNREFORMABLE?
I CAN'T SEE THEM TURNING AROUND IN A YEAR...
IF THEY DON'T, ALL HUMANS WILL BE DESTROYED, RIGHT?!
ASTRO, TAKE ME TO THIS ALIEN! I'VE GOTTA TALK WITH HIM!
I'M SORRY, PROFESSOR, BUT HE REFUSES TO MEET ANYONE EXCEPT ME...
THE FATE OF THE WORLD'S IN HIS HANDS...
...AND HE WON'T EVEN LET ME TALK TO HIM?
FATHER, PLEASE... STOP THIS RIDICULOUS EXPERIMENT! LET'S GO HOME!
SILENCE, PARMA! YOU DON'T KNOW WHAT A TERRIBLE THING I DID LONG AGO!

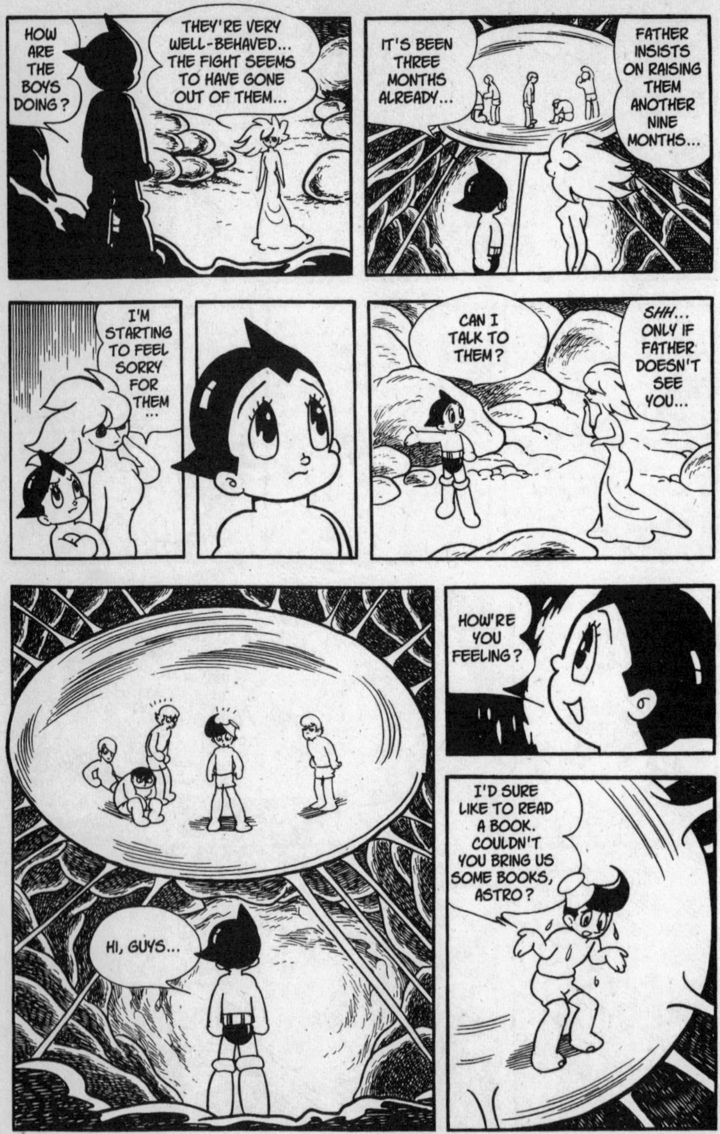
HOW ARE THE BOYS DOING?
THEY'RE VERY WELL-BEHAVED... THE FIGHT SEEMS TO HAVE GONE OUT OF THEM...
IT'S BEEN THREE MONTHS ALREADY...
FATHER INSISTS ON RAISING THEM ANOTHER NINE MONTHS...
I'M STARTING TO FEEL SORRY FOR THEM ...
CAN I TALK TO THEM?
SHH... ONLY IF FATHER DOESN'T SEE YOU...
HI, GUYS...
HOW'RE YOU FEELING?
I'D SURE LIKE TO READ A BOOK. COULDN'T YOU BRING US SOME BOOKS, ASTRO?

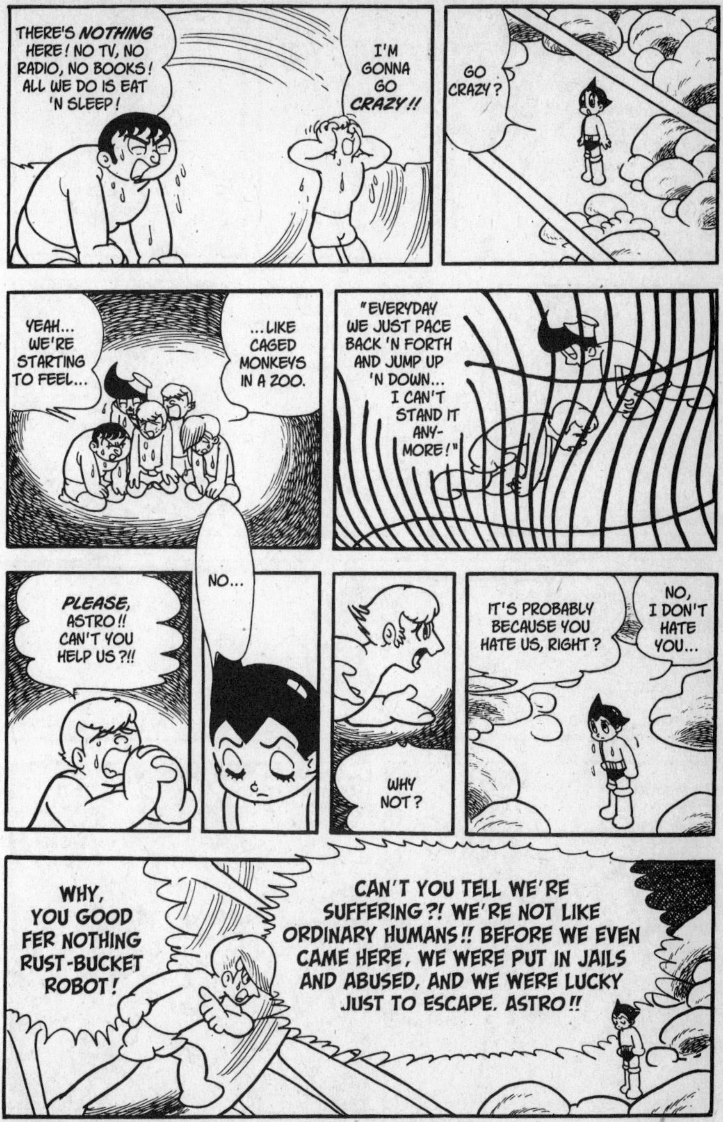
THERE'S NOTHING HERE! NO TV, NO RADIO, NO BOOKS! ALL WE DO IS EAT 'N SLEEP!
I'M GONNA GO CRAZY!!
GO CRAZY?
YEAH... WE'RE STARTING TO FEEL...
...LIKE CAGED MONKEYS IN A ZOO.
"EVERYDAY WE JUST PACE BACK 'N FORTH AND JUMP UP 'N DOWN... I CAN'T STAND IT ANY-MORE!"
PLEASE, ASTRO!! CAN'T YOU HELP US?!!
NO...
WHY NOT?
IT'S PROBABLY BECAUSE YOU HATE US, RIGHT?
NO, I DON'T HATE YOU...
WHY, YOU GOOD FER NOTHING RUST-BUCKET ROBOT!
CAN'T YOU TELL WE'RE SUFFERING?! WE'RE NOT LIKE ORDINARY HUMANS!! BEFORE WE EVEN CAME HERE, WE WERE PUT IN JAILS AND ABUSED, AND WE WERE LUCKY JUST TO ESCAPE, ASTRO!!

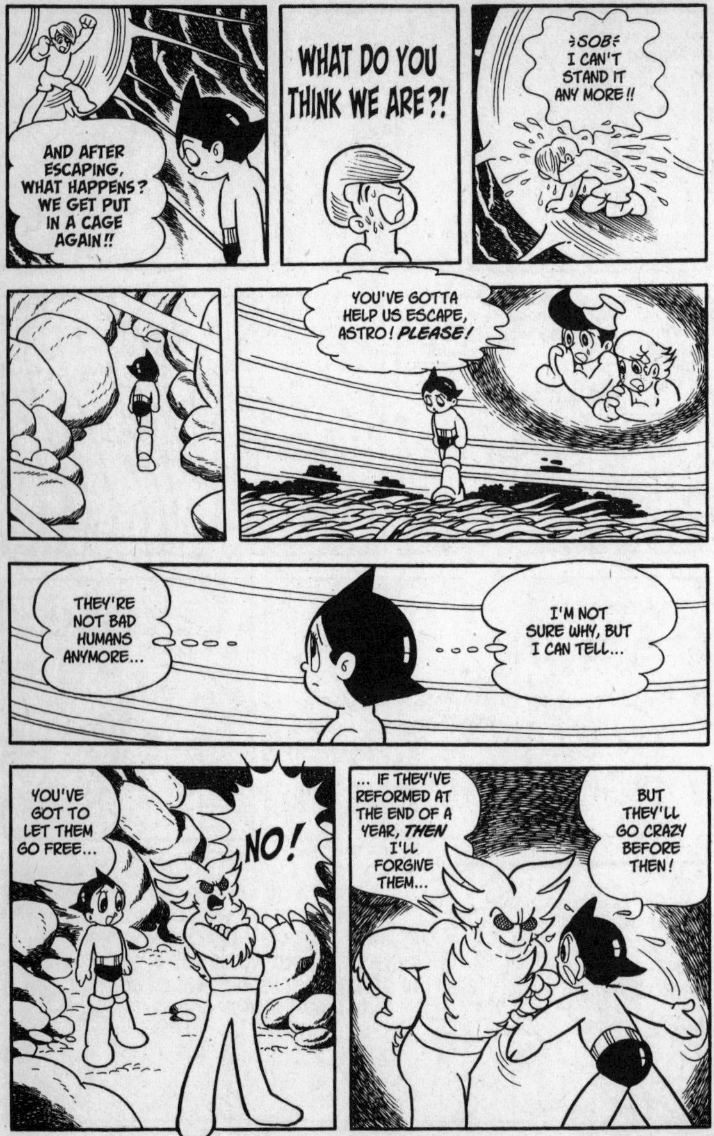
AND AFTER ESCAPING, WHAT HAPPENS? WE GET PUT IN A CAGE AGAIN!!
WHAT DO YOU THINK WE ARE?!
SOB
I CAN'T STAND IT ANY MORE!!
YOU'VE GOTTA HELP US ESCAPE, ASTRO! PLEASE!
THEY'RE NOT BAD HUMANS ANYMORE...
I'M NOT SURE WHY, BUT I CAN TELL...
YOU'VE GOT TO LET THEM GO FREE...
NO!
... IF THEY'VE REFORMED AT THE END OF A YEAR, THEN I'LL FORGIVE THEM...
BUT THEY'LL GO CRAZY BEFORE THEN!

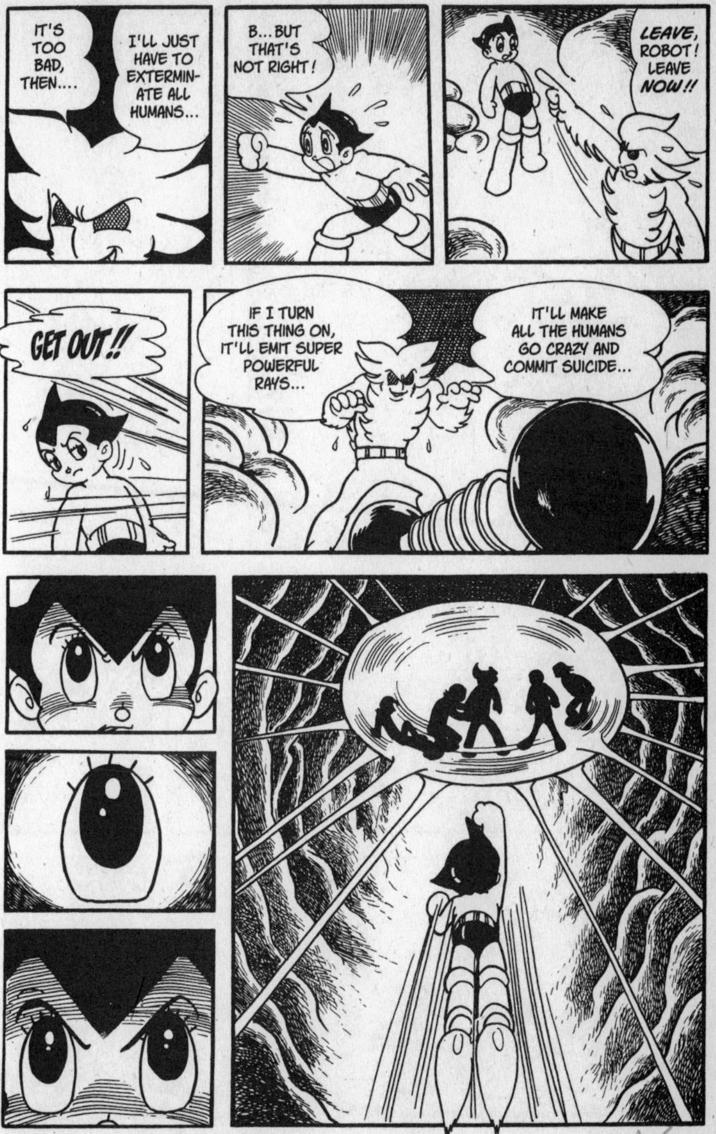
IT'S TOO BAD, THEN....
I'LL JUST HAVE TO EXTERMINATE ALL HUMANS...
B...BUT THAT'S NOT RIGHT!
LEAVE, ROBOT! LEAVE NOW!!
GET OUT!!
IF I TURN THIS THING ON, IT'LL EMIT SUPER POWERFUL RAYS...
IT'LL MAKE ALL THE HUMANS GO CRAZY AND COMMIT SUICIDE...

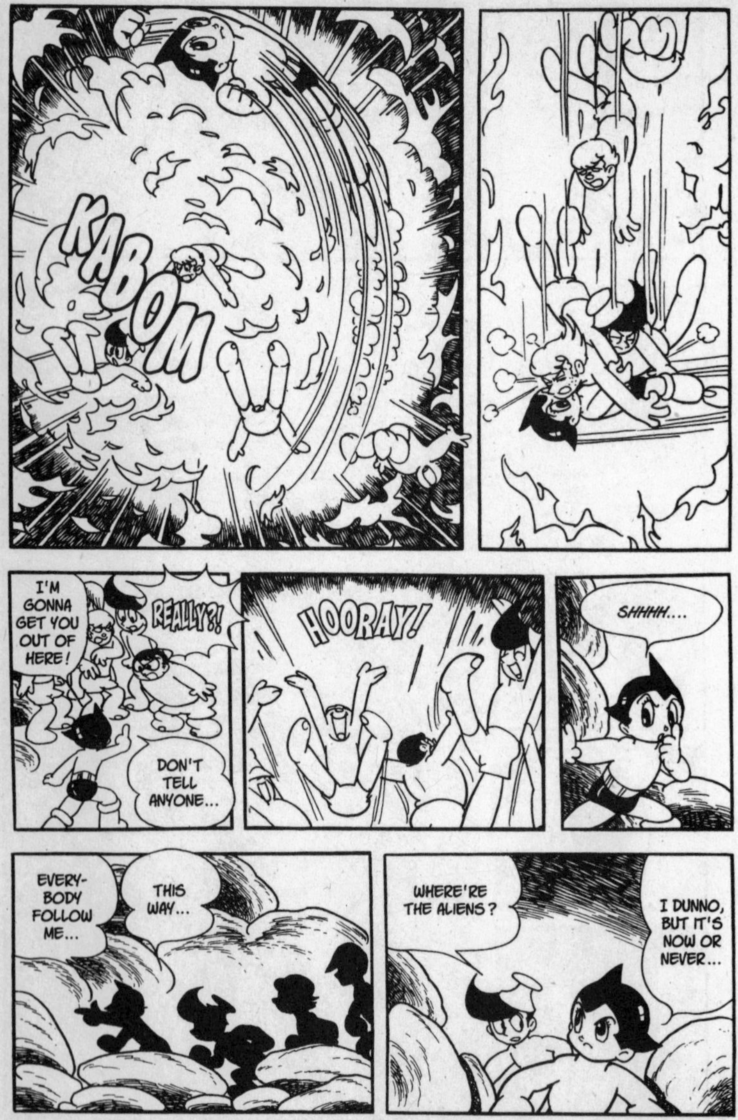
KABOOM
I'M GONNA GET YOU OUT OF HERE!
REALLY?!
DON'T TELL ANYONE...
HOORAY!
SHHHH....
EVERY-BODY FOLLOW ME...
THIS WAY...
WHERE'RE THE ALIENS?
I DUNNO, BUT IT'S NOW OR NEVER...

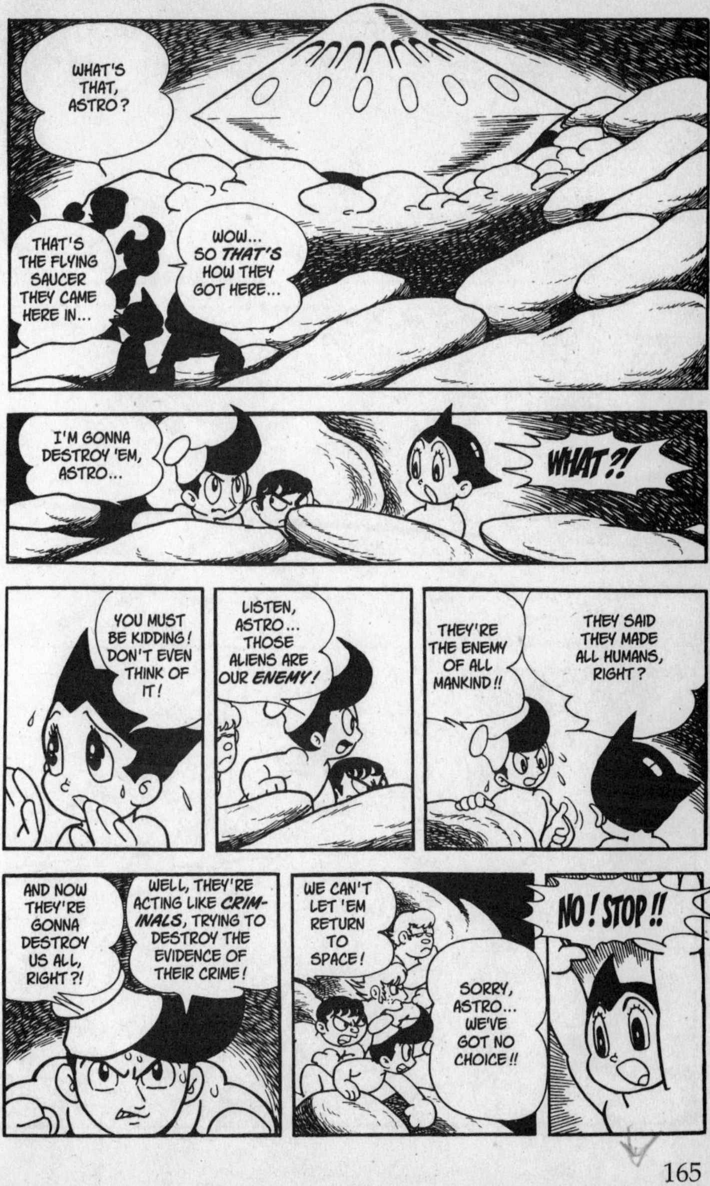
WHAT'S THAT, ASTRO?
THAT'S THE FLYING SAUCER THEY CAME HERE IN...
WOW... SO *THAT'S* HOW THEY GOT HERE...
I'M GONNA DESTROY 'EM, ASTRO...
WHAT?!
YOU MUST BE KIDDING! DON'T EVEN THINK OF IT!
LISTEN, ASTRO... THOSE ALIENS ARE OUR *ENEMY*!
THEY'RE THE ENEMY OF ALL MANKIND!!
THEY SAID THEY MADE ALL HUMANS, RIGHT?
AND NOW THEY'RE GONNA DESTROY US ALL, RIGHT?!
WELL, THEY'RE ACTING LIKE *CRIMINALS*, TRYING TO DESTROY THE EVIDENCE OF THEIR CRIME!
WE CAN'T LET 'EM RETURN TO SPACE!
SORRY, ASTRO... WE'VE GOT NO CHOICE!!
NO! STOP!!

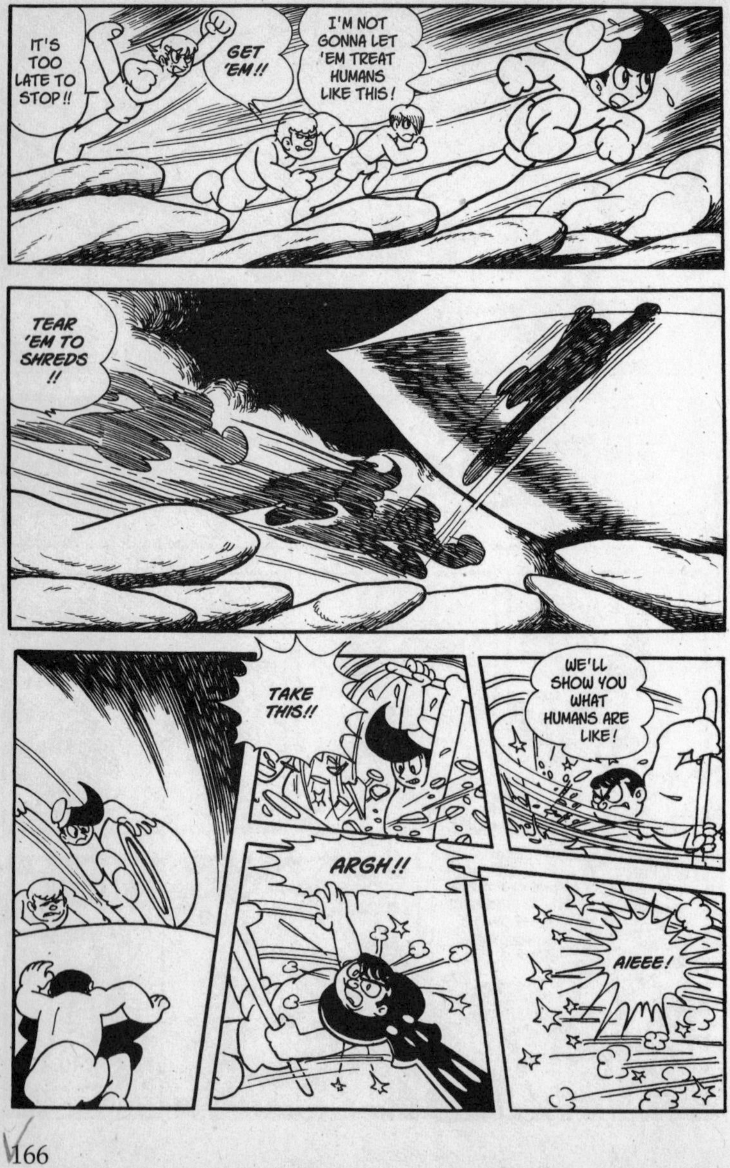
IT'S TOO LATE TO STOP!!
GET 'EM!!
I'M NOT GONNA LET 'EM TREAT HUMANS LIKE THIS!
TEAR 'EM TO SHREDS!!
TAKE THIS!!
WE'LL SHOW YOU WHAT HUMANS ARE LIKE!
ARGH!!
AIEEE!

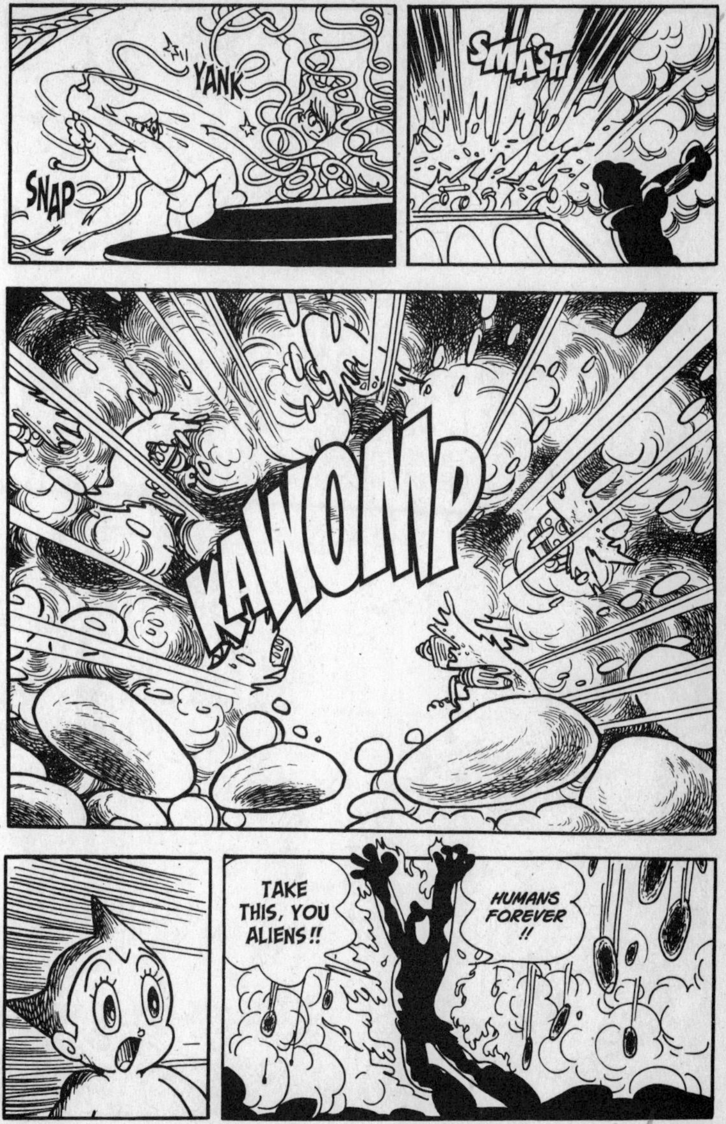
YANK
SNAP
SMASH
KAWOMP
TAKE THIS, YOU ALIENS!!
HUMANS FOREVER !!

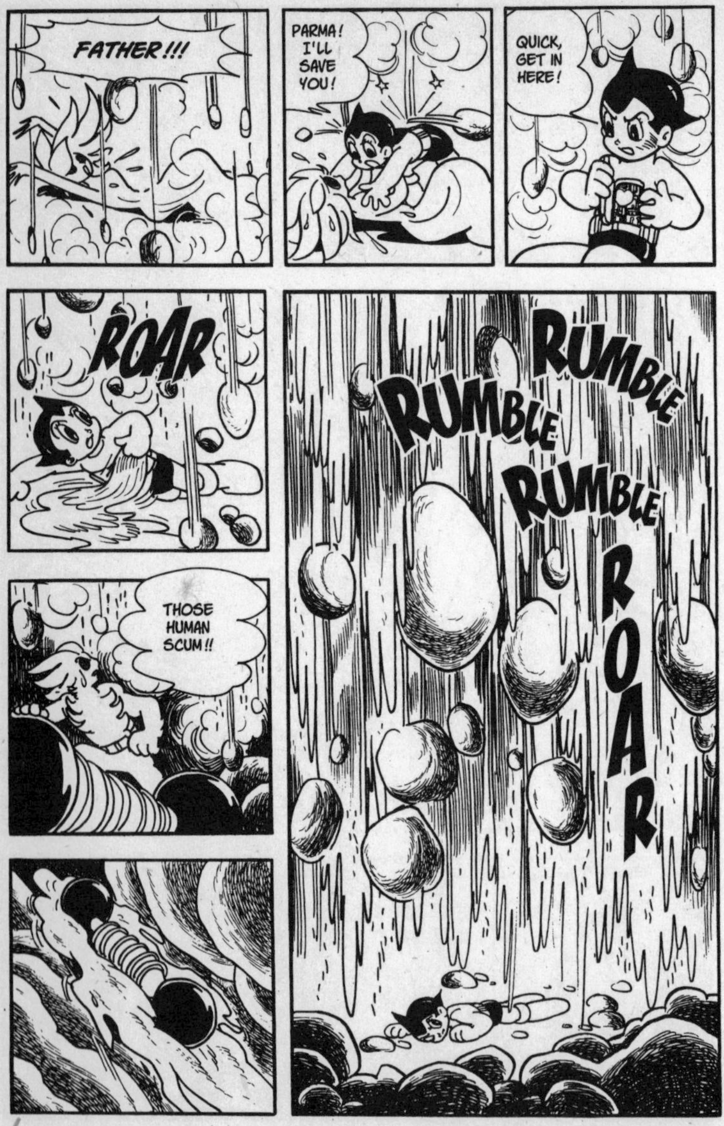
FATHER!!!
PARMA! I'LL SAVE YOU!
QUICK, GET IN HERE!
ROAR
THOSE HUMAN SCUM!!
RUMBLE
RUMBLE
RUMBLE
ROAR

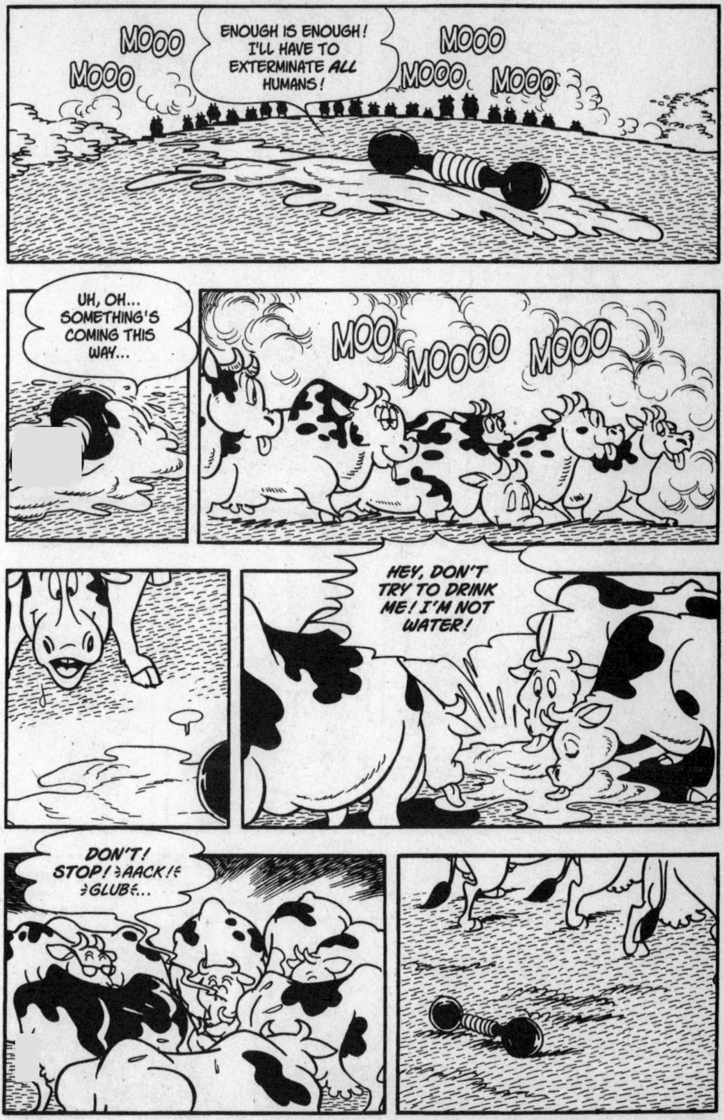
MOOO
MOOO
ENOUGH IS ENOUGH! I'LL HAVE TO EXTERMINATE ALL HUMANS!
MOOO
MOOO
MOOO
UH, OH... SOMETHING'S COMING THIS WAY...
MOO
MOOOO
MOOO
HEY, DON'T TRY TO DRINK ME! I'M NOT WATER!
DON'T! STOP! ≷AACK!≶ ≷GLUB≶...

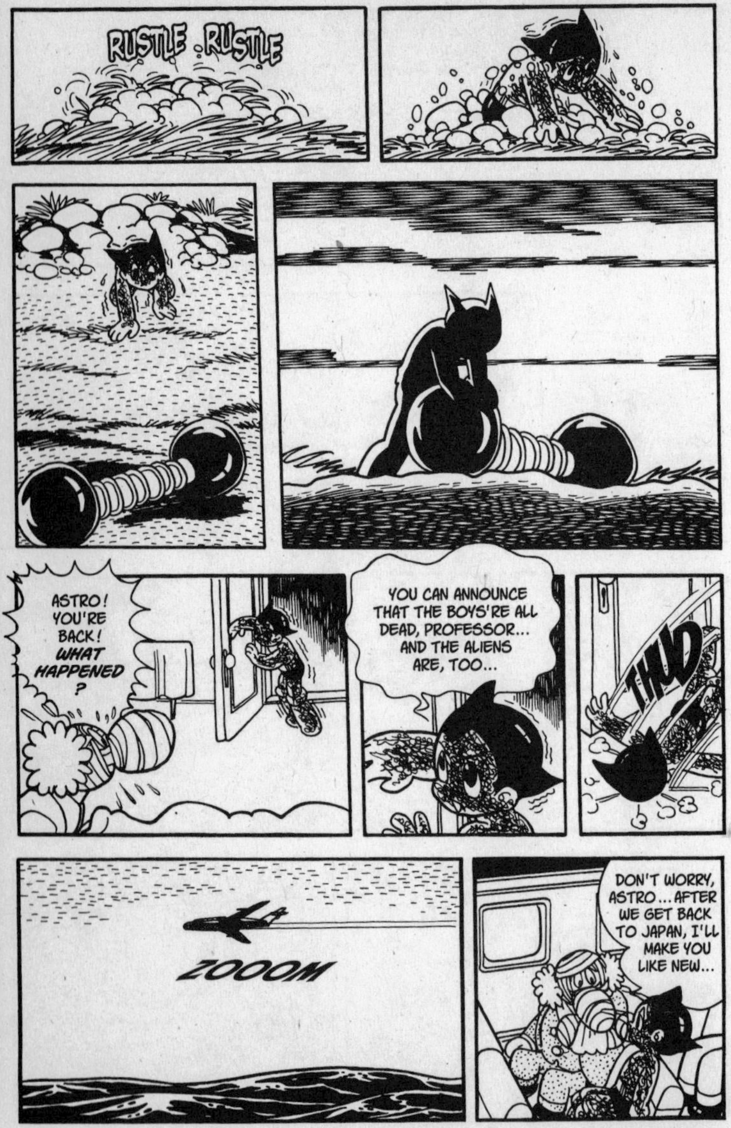
RUSTLE RUSTLE
ASTRO! YOU'RE BACK! WHAT HAPPENED?
YOU CAN ANNOUNCE THAT THE BOYS'RE ALL DEAD, PROFESSOR... AND THE ALIENS ARE, TOO...
THUD
ZOOOM
DON'T WORRY, ASTRO... AFTER WE GET BACK TO JAPAN, I'LL MAKE YOU LIKE NEW...

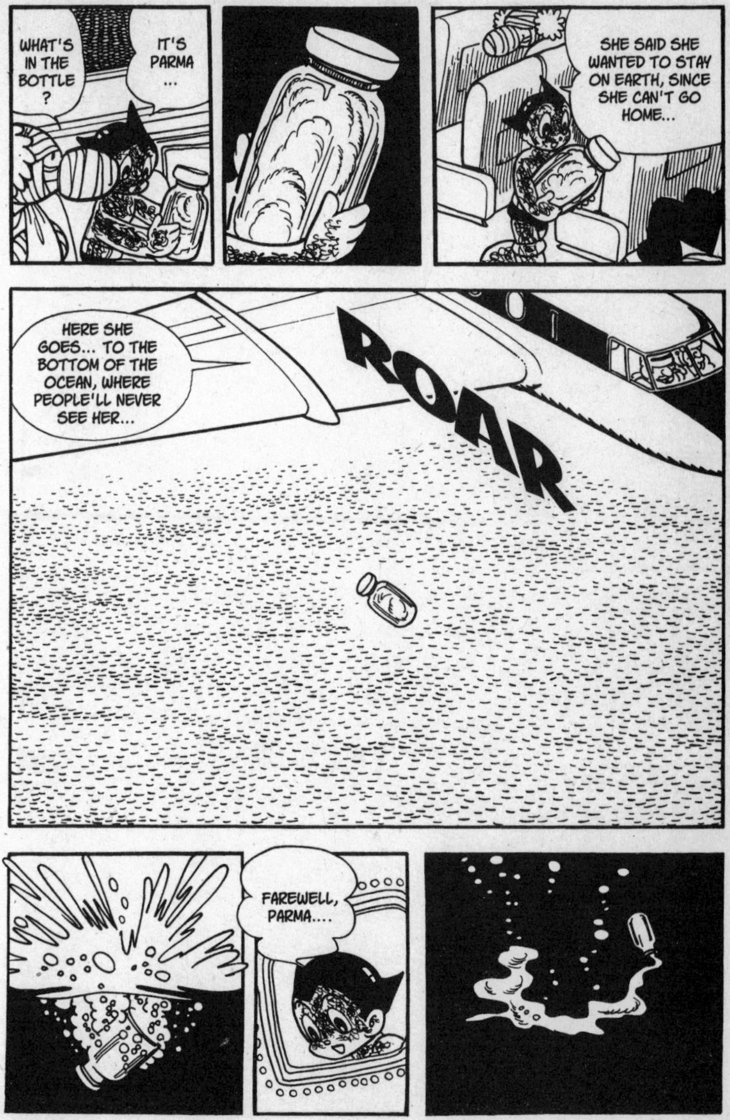
WHAT'S IN THE BOTTLE ?
IT'S PARMA ...
SHE SAID SHE WANTED TO STAY ON EARTH, SINCE SHE CAN'T GO HOME...
HERE SHE GOES... TO THE BOTTOM OF THE OCEAN, WHERE PEOPLE'LL NEVER SEE HER...
ROAR
FAREWELL, PARMA....

ASTRO'S BEEN STOLEN!

First serialized from June to September 1965
in *Tetsuwan Atom Kurabu* (Mighty Atom Club).

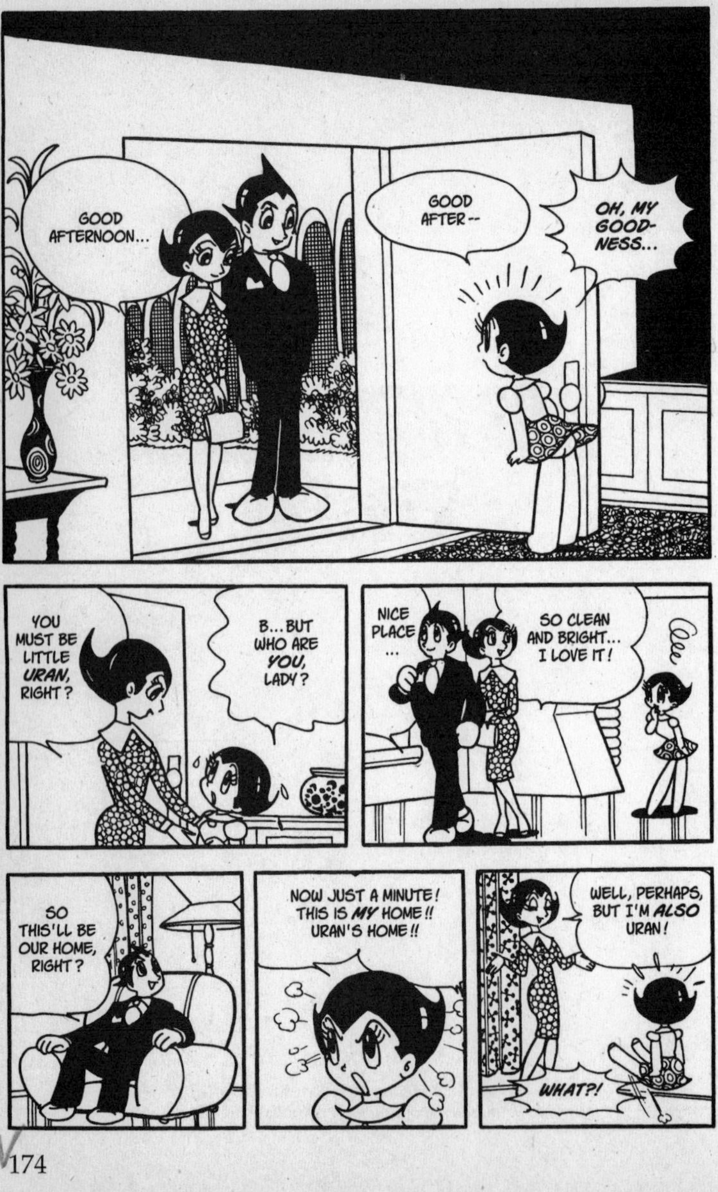
GOOD AFTERNOON...
GOOD AFTER--
OH, MY GOODNESS...
YOU MUST BE LITTLE URAN, RIGHT?
B... BUT WHO ARE YOU, LADY?
NICE PLACE ...
SO CLEAN AND BRIGHT... I LOVE IT!
SO THIS'LL BE OUR HOME, RIGHT?
NOW JUST A MINUTE! THIS IS MY HOME!! URAN'S HOME!!
WELL, PERHAPS, BUT I'M ALSO URAN!
WHAT?!

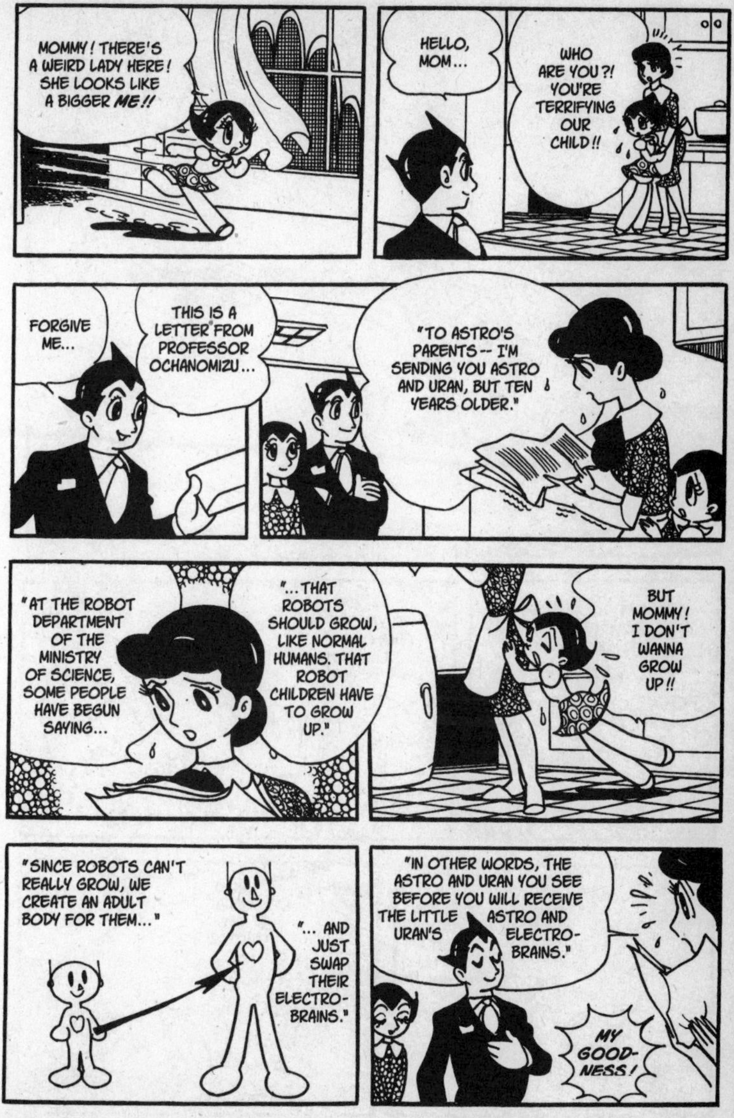
MOMMY! THERE'S A WEIRD LADY HERE! SHE LOOKS LIKE A BIGGER ME!!
HELLO, MOM...
WHO ARE YOU?! YOU'RE TERRIFYING OUR CHILD!!
FORGIVE ME...
THIS IS A LETTER FROM PROFESSOR OCHANOMIZU...
"TO ASTRO'S PARENTS -- I'M SENDING YOU ASTRO AND URAN, BUT TEN YEARS OLDER."
"AT THE ROBOT DEPARTMENT OF THE MINISTRY OF SCIENCE, SOME PEOPLE HAVE BEGUN SAYING...
"... THAT ROBOTS SHOULD GROW, LIKE NORMAL HUMANS. THAT ROBOT CHILDREN HAVE TO GROW UP."
BUT MOMMY! I DON'T WANNA GROW UP!!
"SINCE ROBOTS CAN'T REALLY GROW, WE CREATE AN ADULT BODY FOR THEM..."
"... AND JUST SWAP THEIR ELECTRO-BRAINS."
"IN OTHER WORDS, THE ASTRO AND URAN YOU SEE BEFORE YOU WILL RECEIVE THE LITTLE ASTRO AND URAN'S ELECTRO-BRAINS."
MY GOODNESS!

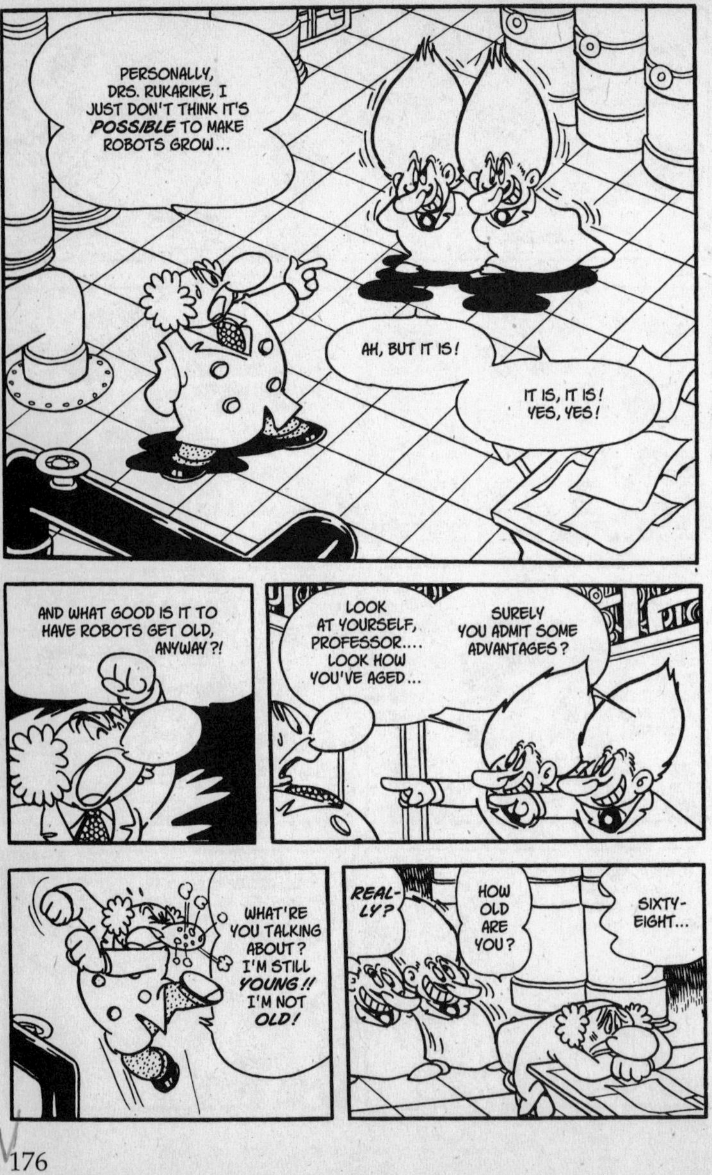
PERSONALLY, DRS. RUKARIKE, I JUST DON'T THINK IT'S *POSSIBLE* TO MAKE ROBOTS GROW...
AH, BUT IT IS!
IT IS, IT IS! YES, YES!
AND WHAT GOOD IS IT TO HAVE ROBOTS GET OLD, ANYWAY?!
LOOK AT YOURSELF, PROFESSOR.... LOOK HOW YOU'VE AGED...
SURELY YOU ADMIT SOME ADVANTAGES?
WHAT'RE YOU TALKING ABOUT? I'M STILL *YOUNG!!* I'M NOT *OLD!*
REAL-LY?
HOW OLD ARE YOU?
SIXTY-EIGHT...

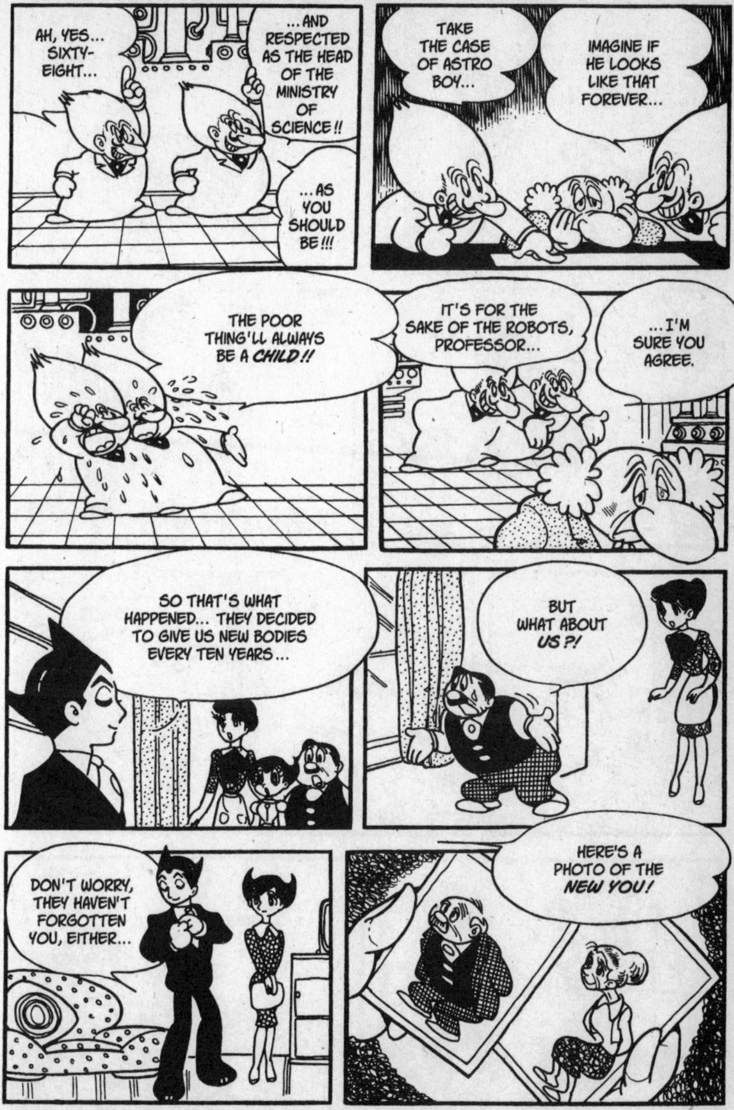
AH, YES... SIXTY-EIGHT...
...AND RESPECTED AS THE HEAD OF THE MINISTRY OF SCIENCE!!
...AS YOU SHOULD BE!!!
TAKE THE CASE OF ASTRO BOY...
IMAGINE IF HE LOOKS LIKE THAT FOREVER...
THE POOR THING'LL ALWAYS BE A CHILD!!
IT'S FOR THE SAKE OF THE ROBOTS, PROFESSOR...
...I'M SURE YOU AGREE.
SO THAT'S WHAT HAPPENED... THEY DECIDED TO GIVE US NEW BODIES EVERY TEN YEARS...
BUT WHAT ABOUT US?!
DON'T WORRY, THEY HAVEN'T FORGOTTEN YOU, EITHER...
HERE'S A PHOTO OF THE NEW YOU!

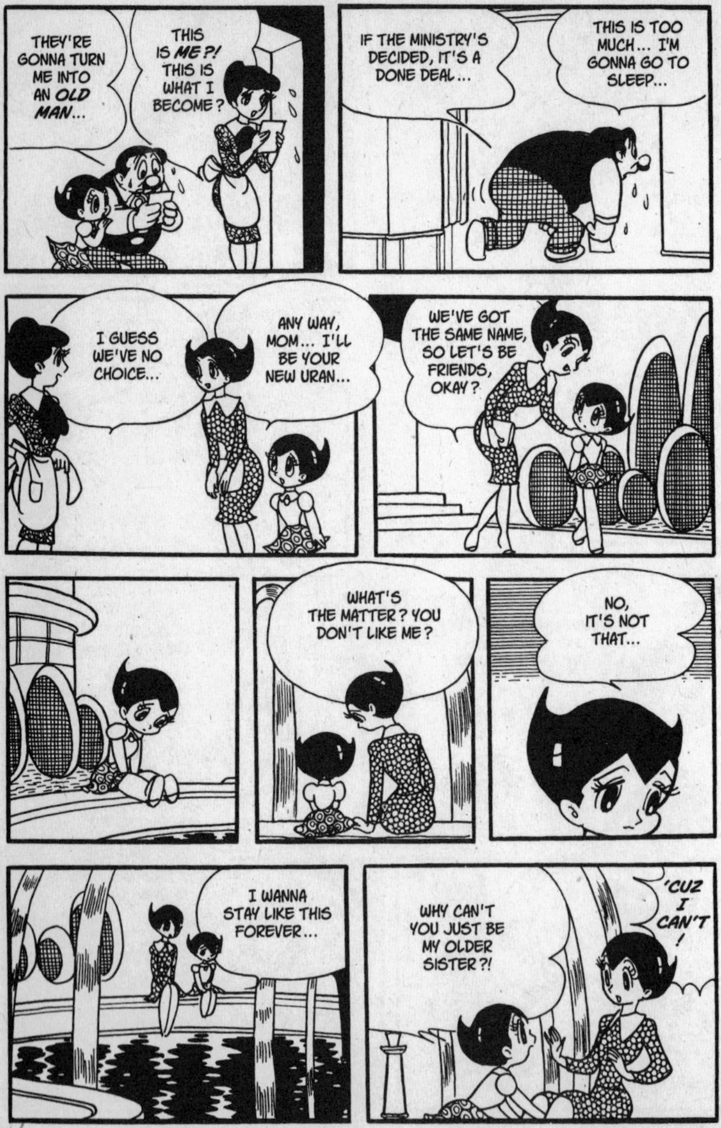
THEY'RE GONNA TURN ME INTO AN OLD MAN...
THIS IS ME?! THIS IS WHAT I BECOME?
IF THE MINISTRY'S DECIDED, IT'S A DONE DEAL...
THIS IS TOO MUCH... I'M GONNA GO TO SLEEP...
I GUESS WE'VE NO CHOICE...
ANY WAY, MOM... I'LL BE YOUR NEW URAN...
WE'VE GOT THE SAME NAME, SO LET'S BE FRIENDS, OKAY?
WHAT'S THE MATTER? YOU DON'T LIKE ME?
NO, IT'S NOT THAT...
I WANNA STAY LIKE THIS FOREVER...
WHY CAN'T YOU JUST BE MY OLDER SISTER?!
'CUZ I CAN'T!

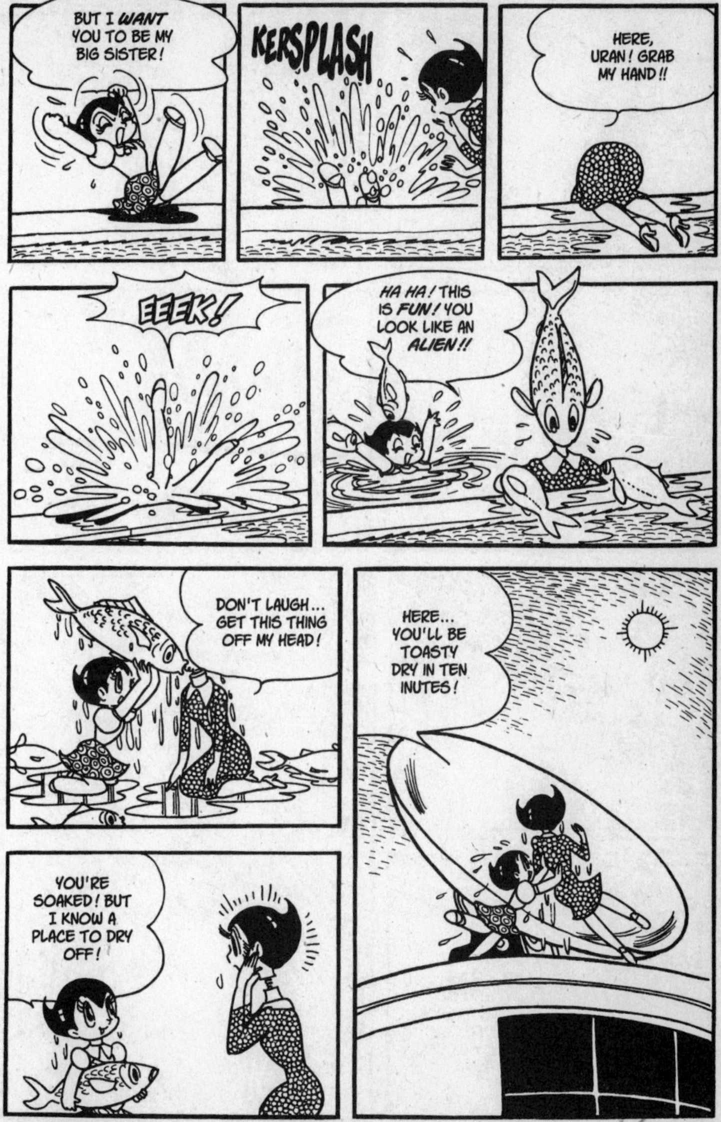
BUT I WANT YOU TO BE MY BIG SISTER!
KERSPLASH
HERE, URAN! GRAB MY HAND!!
EEEK!
HA HA! THIS IS FUN! YOU LOOK LIKE AN ALIEN!!
DON'T LAUGH... GET THIS THING OFF MY HEAD!
YOU'RE SOAKED! BUT I KNOW A PLACE TO DRY OFF!
HERE... YOU'LL BE TOASTY DRY IN TEN INUTES!

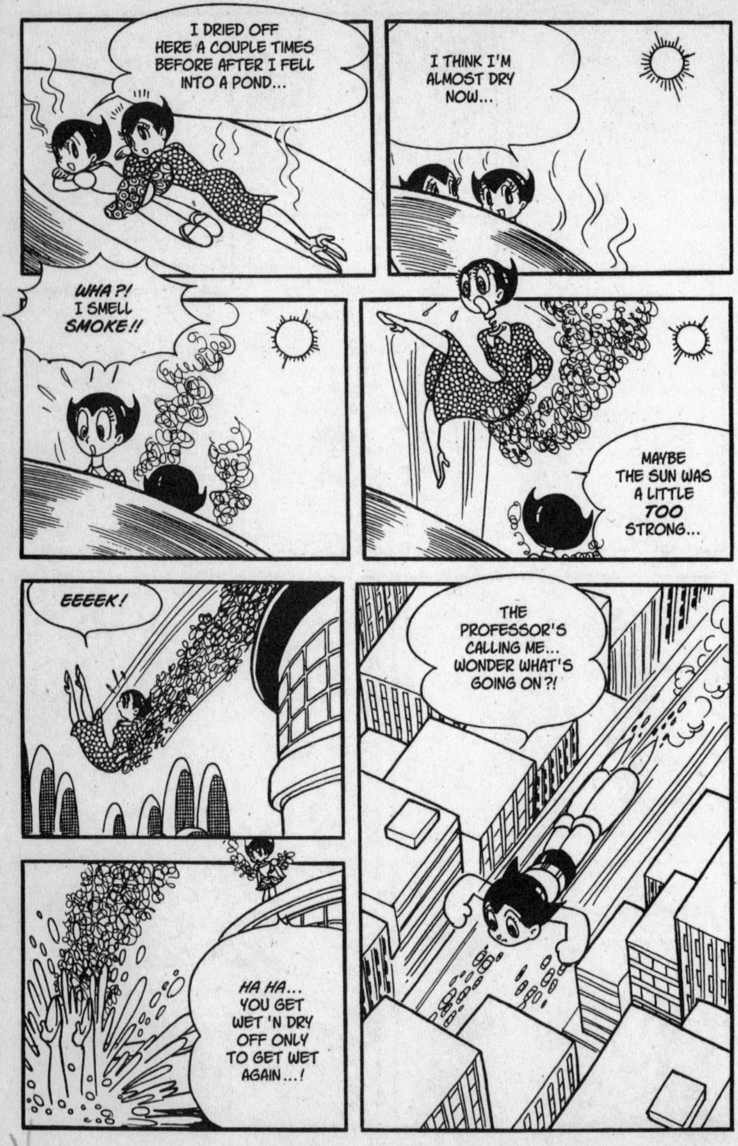

I DRIED OFF HERE A COUPLE TIMES BEFORE AFTER I FELL INTO A POND...
I THINK I'M ALMOST DRY NOW...
WHA?! I SMELL SMOKE!!
MAYBE THE SUN WAS A LITTLE TOO STRONG...
EEEEK!
THE PROFESSOR'S CALLING ME... WONDER WHAT'S GOING ON?!
HA HA... YOU GET WET 'N DRY OFF ONLY TO GET WET AGAIN...!

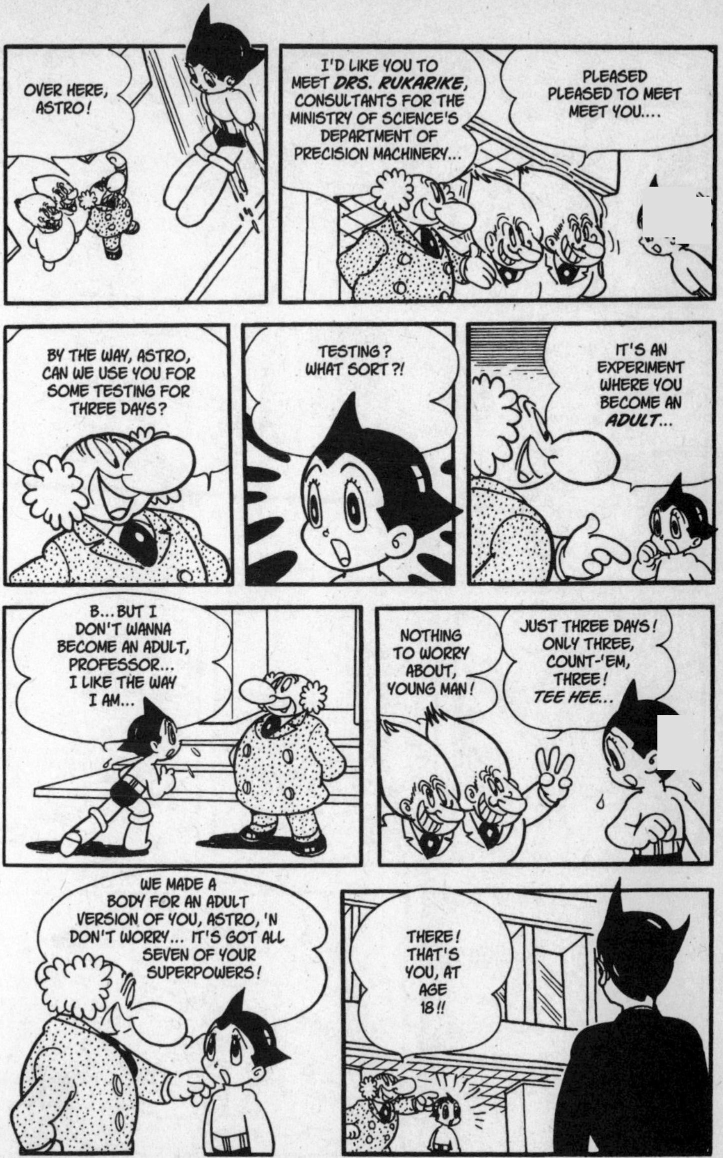
OVER HERE, ASTRO!
I'D LIKE YOU TO MEET DRS. RUKARIKE, CONSULTANTS FOR THE MINISTRY OF SCIENCE'S DEPARTMENT OF PRECISION MACHINERY...
PLEASED PLEASED TO MEET MEET YOU....
BY THE WAY, ASTRO, CAN WE USE YOU FOR SOME TESTING FOR THREE DAYS?
TESTING? WHAT SORT?!
IT'S AN EXPERIMENT WHERE YOU BECOME AN ADULT...
B...BUT I DON'T WANNA BECOME AN ADULT, PROFESSOR... I LIKE THE WAY I AM...
NOTHING TO WORRY ABOUT, YOUNG MAN!
JUST THREE DAYS! ONLY THREE, COUNT-'EM, THREE! TEE HEE...
WE MADE A BODY FOR AN ADULT VERSION OF YOU, ASTRO, 'N DON'T WORRY... IT'S GOT ALL SEVEN OF YOUR SUPERPOWERS!
THERE! THAT'S YOU, AT AGE 18!!

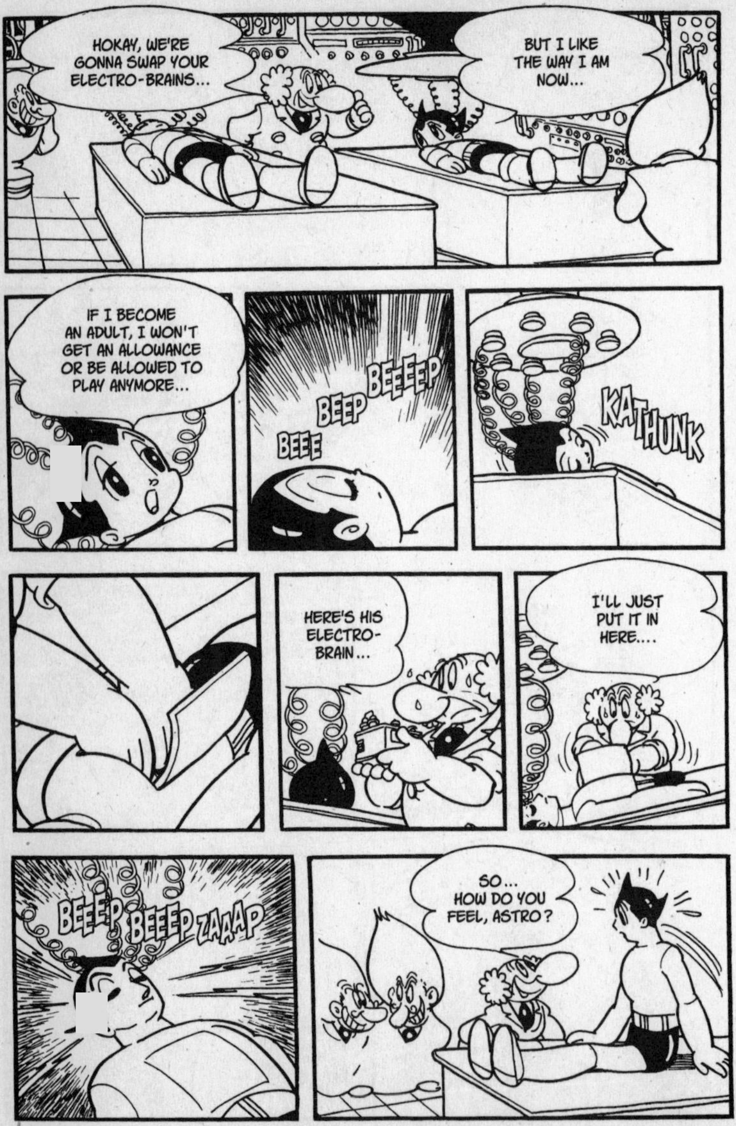
HOKAY, WE'RE GONNA SWAP YOUR ELECTRO-BRAINS...
BUT I LIKE THE WAY I AM NOW...
IF I BECOME AN ADULT, I WON'T GET AN ALLOWANCE OR BE ALLOWED TO PLAY ANYMORE...
BEEE
BEEP
BEEEEP
KATHUNK
HERE'S HIS ELECTRO-BRAIN...
I'LL JUST PUT IT IN HERE....
BEEEP
BEEEP
ZAAAP
SO... HOW DO YOU FEEL, ASTRO?

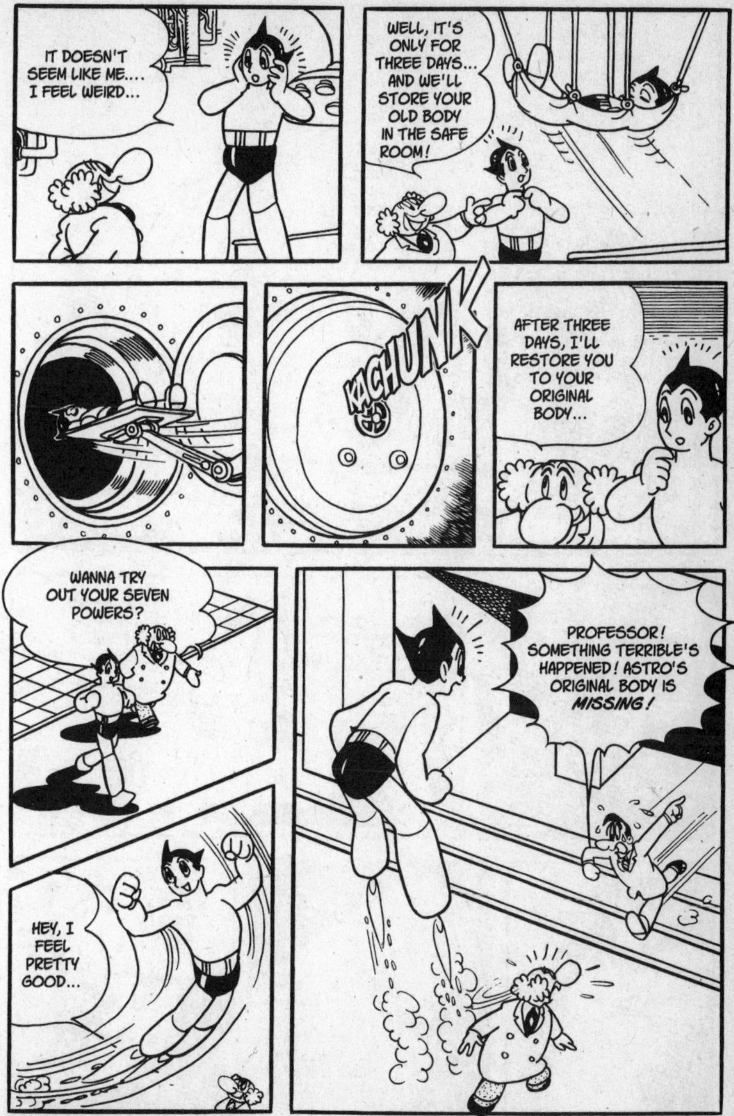
IT DOESN'T SEEM LIKE ME.... I FEEL WEIRD...
WELL, IT'S ONLY FOR THREE DAYS... AND WE'LL STORE YOUR OLD BODY IN THE SAFE ROOM!
KACHUNK
AFTER THREE DAYS, I'LL RESTORE YOU TO YOUR ORIGINAL BODY...
WANNA TRY OUT YOUR SEVEN POWERS?
HEY, I FEEL PRETTY GOOD...
PROFESSOR! SOMETHING TERRIBLE'S HAPPENED! ASTRO'S ORIGINAL BODY IS ***MISSING!***

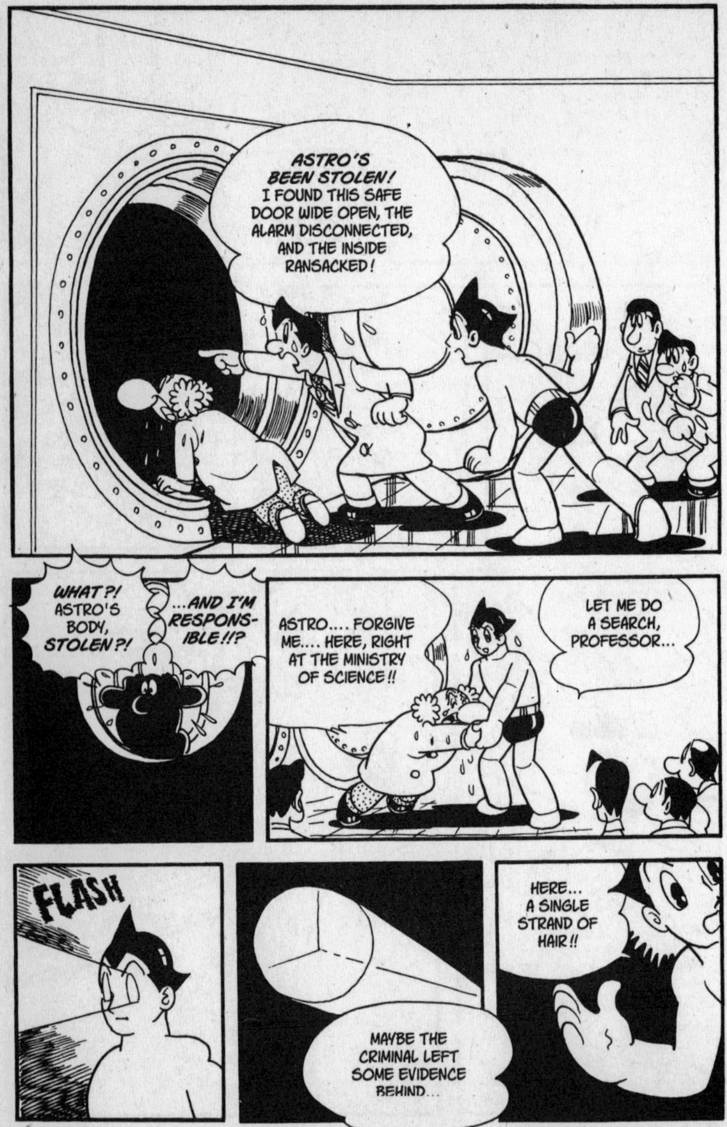
ASTRO'S BEEN STOLEN! I FOUND THIS SAFE DOOR WIDE OPEN, THE ALARM DISCONNECTED, AND THE INSIDE RANSACKED!
WHAT?! ASTRO'S BODY, STOLEN?!
...AND I'M RESPONSIBLE!!?
ASTRO.... FORGIVE ME.... HERE, RIGHT AT THE MINISTRY OF SCIENCE!!
LET ME DO A SEARCH, PROFESSOR...
FLASH
MAYBE THE CRIMINAL LEFT SOME EVIDENCE BEHIND...
HERE... A SINGLE STRAND OF HAIR!!

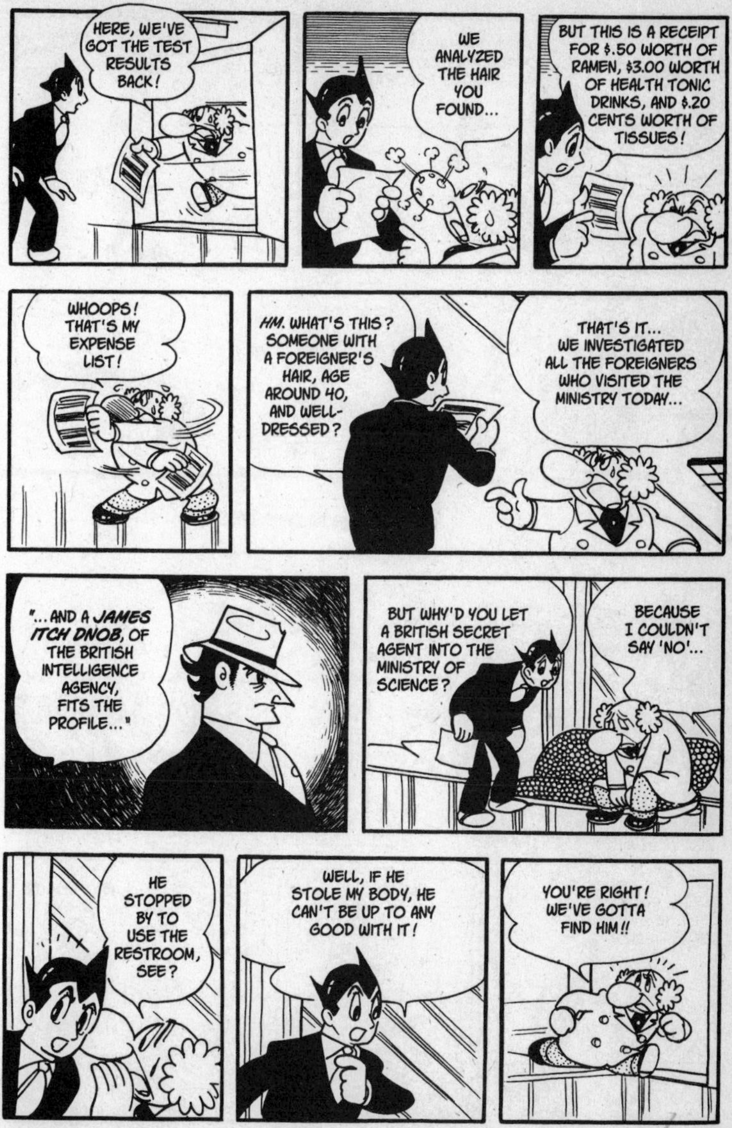
HERE, WE'VE GOT THE TEST RESULTS BACK!
WE ANALYZED THE HAIR YOU FOUND...
BUT THIS IS A RECEIPT FOR $.50 WORTH OF RAMEN, $3.00 WORTH OF HEALTH TONIC DRINKS, AND $.20 CENTS WORTH OF TISSUES!
WHOOPS! THAT'S MY EXPENSE LIST!
HM. WHAT'S THIS? SOMEONE WITH A FOREIGNER'S HAIR, AGE AROUND 40, AND WELL-DRESSED?
THAT'S IT... WE INVESTIGATED ALL THE FOREIGNERS WHO VISITED THE MINISTRY TODAY...
"...AND A *JAMES ITCH DNOB*, OF THE BRITISH INTELLIGENCE AGENCY, FITS THE PROFILE..."
BUT WHY'D YOU LET A BRITISH SECRET AGENT INTO THE MINISTRY OF SCIENCE?
BECAUSE I COULDN'T SAY 'NO'...
HE STOPPED BY TO USE THE RESTROOM, SEE?
WELL, IF HE STOLE MY BODY, HE CAN'T BE UP TO ANY GOOD WITH IT!
YOU'RE RIGHT! WE'VE GOTTA FIND HIM!!

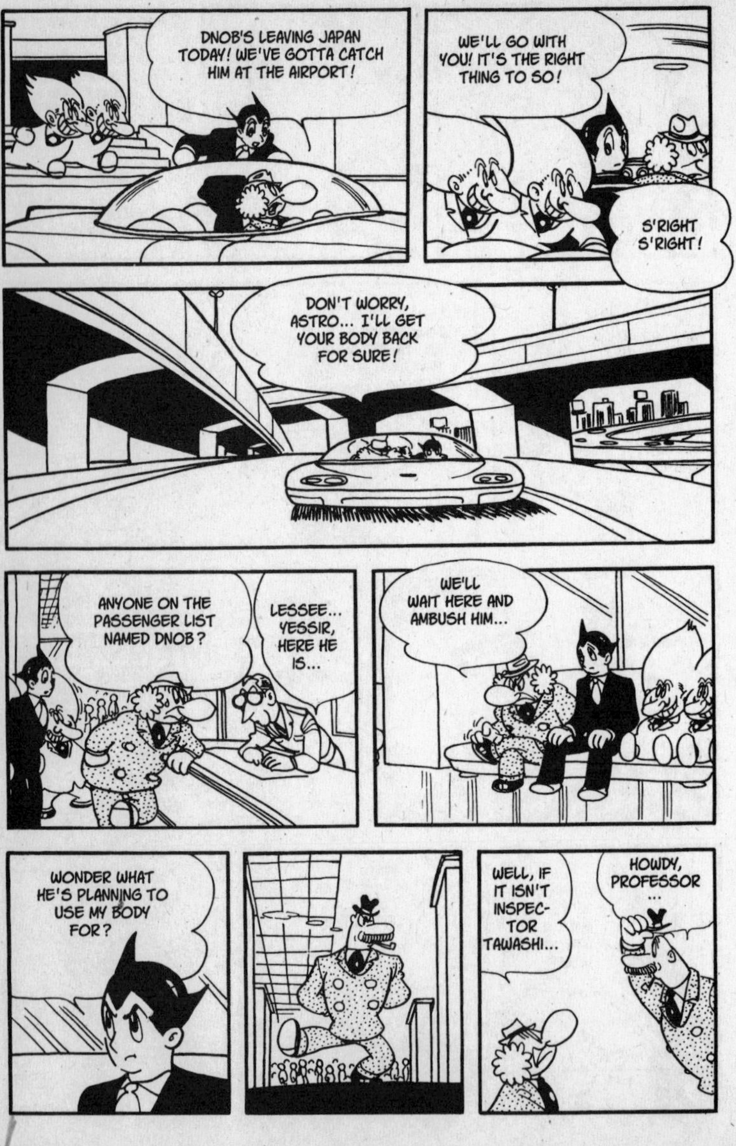
DNOB'S LEAVING JAPAN TODAY! WE'VE GOTTA CATCH HIM AT THE AIRPORT!
WE'LL GO WITH YOU! IT'S THE RIGHT THING TO SO!
S'RIGHT S'RIGHT!
DON'T WORRY, ASTRO... I'LL GET YOUR BODY BACK FOR SURE!
ANYONE ON THE PASSENGER LIST NAMED DNOB?
LESSEE... YESSIR, HERE HE IS...
WE'LL WAIT HERE AND AMBUSH HIM...
WONDER WHAT HE'S PLANNING TO USE MY BODY FOR?
WELL, IF IT ISN'T INSPEC-TOR TAWASHI...
HOWDY, PROFESSOR ...

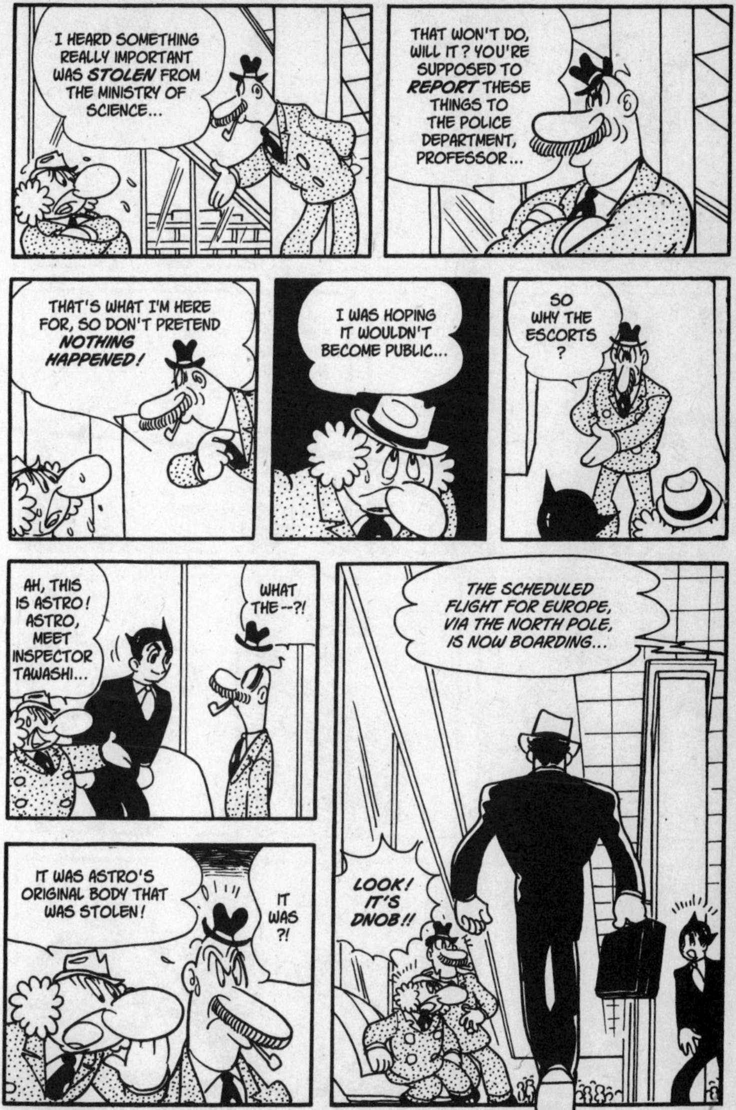
I HEARD SOMETHING REALLY IMPORTANT WAS STOLEN FROM THE MINISTRY OF SCIENCE...
THAT WON'T DO, WILL IT? YOU'RE SUPPOSED TO REPORT THESE THINGS TO THE POLICE DEPARTMENT, PROFESSOR...
THAT'S WHAT I'M HERE FOR, SO DON'T PRETEND NOTHING HAPPENED!
I WAS HOPING IT WOULDN'T BECOME PUBLIC...
SO WHY THE ESCORTS ?
AH, THIS IS ASTRO! ASTRO, MEET INSPECTOR TAWASHI...
WHAT THE--?!
IT WAS ASTRO'S ORIGINAL BODY THAT WAS STOLEN!
IT WAS ?!
THE SCHEDULED FLIGHT FOR EUROPE, VIA THE NORTH POLE, IS NOW BOARDING...
LOOK! IT'S DNOB!!

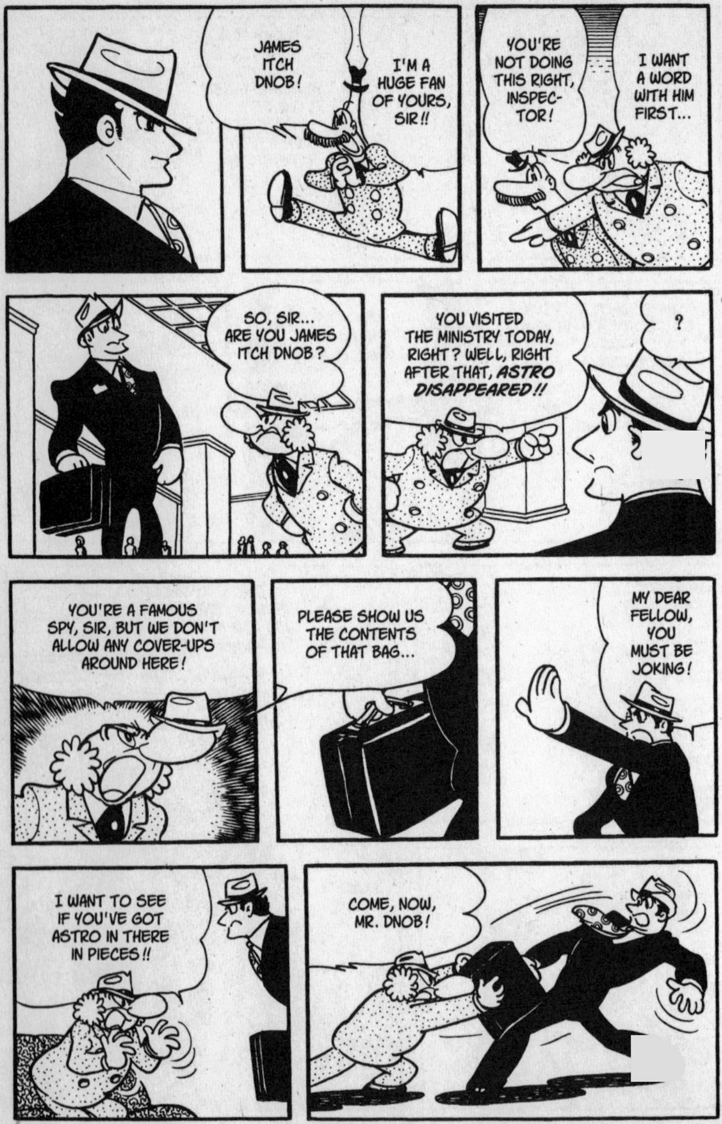
JAMES ITCH DNOB!
I'M A HUGE FAN OF YOURS, SIR!!
YOU'RE NOT DOING THIS RIGHT, INSPEC- TOR!
I WANT A WORD WITH HIM FIRST...
SO, SIR... ARE YOU JAMES ITCH DNOB?
YOU VISITED THE MINISTRY TODAY, RIGHT? WELL, RIGHT AFTER THAT, *ASTRO DISAPPEARED!!*
?
YOU'RE A FAMOUS SPY, SIR, BUT WE DON'T ALLOW ANY COVER-UPS AROUND HERE!
PLEASE SHOW US THE CONTENTS OF THAT BAG...
MY DEAR FELLOW, YOU MUST BE JOKING!
I WANT TO SEE IF YOU'VE GOT ASTRO IN THERE IN PIECES!!
COME, NOW, MR. DNOB!

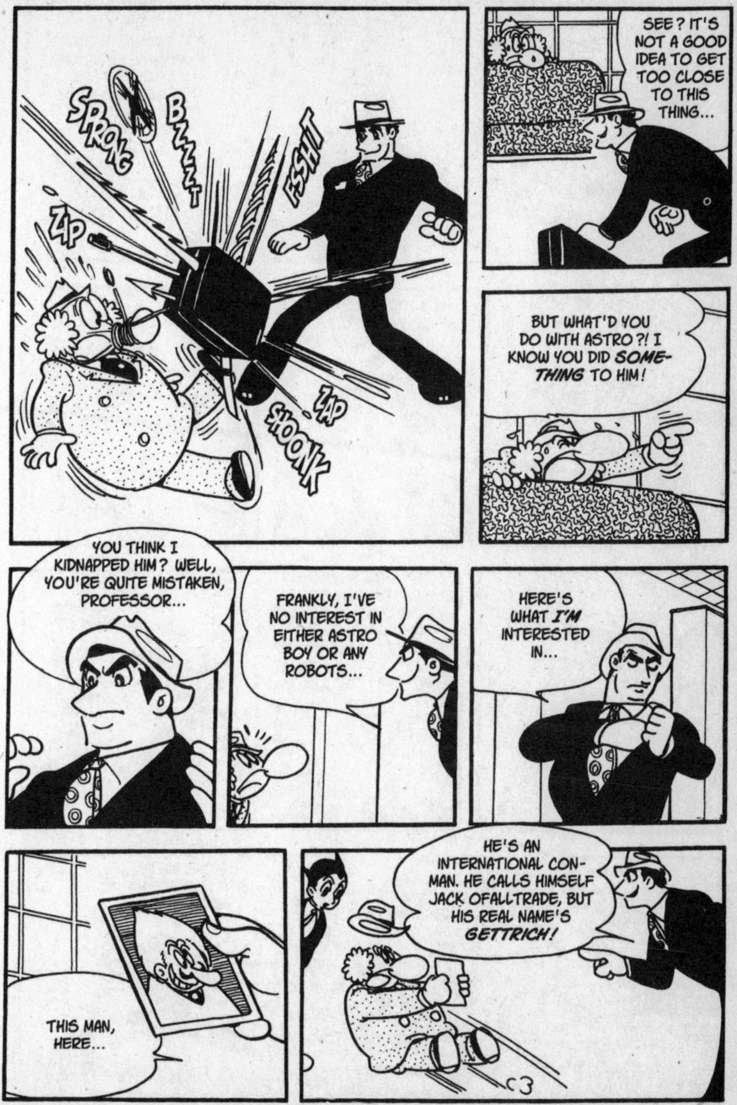
SPRONG
BZZZT
FSSHT
ZAP
ZAP
SHOONK
SEE? IT'S NOT A GOOD IDEA TO GET TOO CLOSE TO THIS THING...
BUT WHAT'D YOU DO WITH ASTRO?! I KNOW YOU DID SOMETHING TO HIM!
YOU THINK I KIDNAPPED HIM? WELL, YOU'RE QUITE MISTAKEN, PROFESSOR...
FRANKLY, I'VE NO INTEREST IN EITHER ASTRO BOY OR ANY ROBOTS...
HERE'S WHAT I'M INTERESTED IN...
THIS MAN, HERE...
HE'S AN INTERNATIONAL CON-MAN. HE CALLS HIMSELF JACK OFALLTRADE, BUT HIS REAL NAME'S GETTRICH!

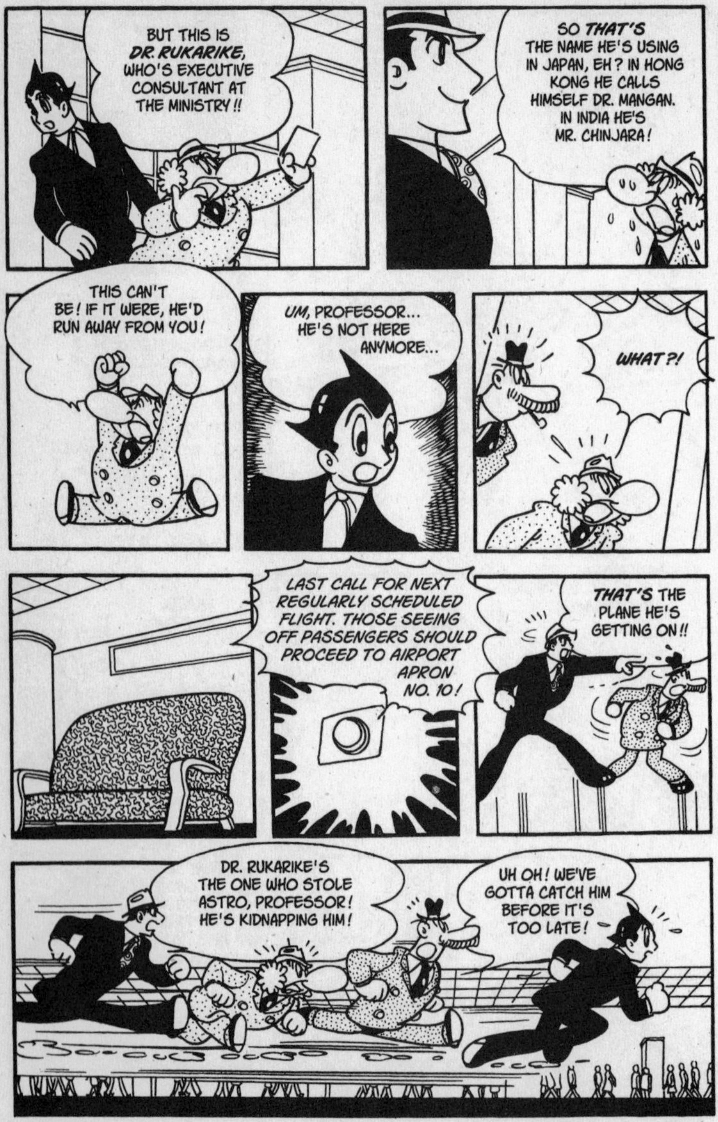
BUT THIS IS DR. RUKARIKE, WHO'S EXECUTIVE CONSULTANT AT THE MINISTRY!!
SO THAT'S THE NAME HE'S USING IN JAPAN, EH? IN HONG KONG HE CALLS HIMSELF DR. MANGAN. IN INDIA HE'S MR. CHINJARA!
THIS CAN'T BE! IF IT WERE, HE'D RUN AWAY FROM YOU!
UM, PROFESSOR... HE'S NOT HERE ANYMORE...
WHAT?!
LAST CALL FOR NEXT REGULARLY SCHEDULED FLIGHT. THOSE SEEING OFF PASSENGERS SHOULD PROCEED TO AIRPORT APRON NO. 10!
THAT'S THE PLANE HE'S GETTING ON!!
DR. RUKARIKE'S THE ONE WHO STOLE ASTRO, PROFESSOR! HE'S KIDNAPPING HIM!
UH OH! WE'VE GOTTA CATCH HIM BEFORE IT'S TOO LATE!

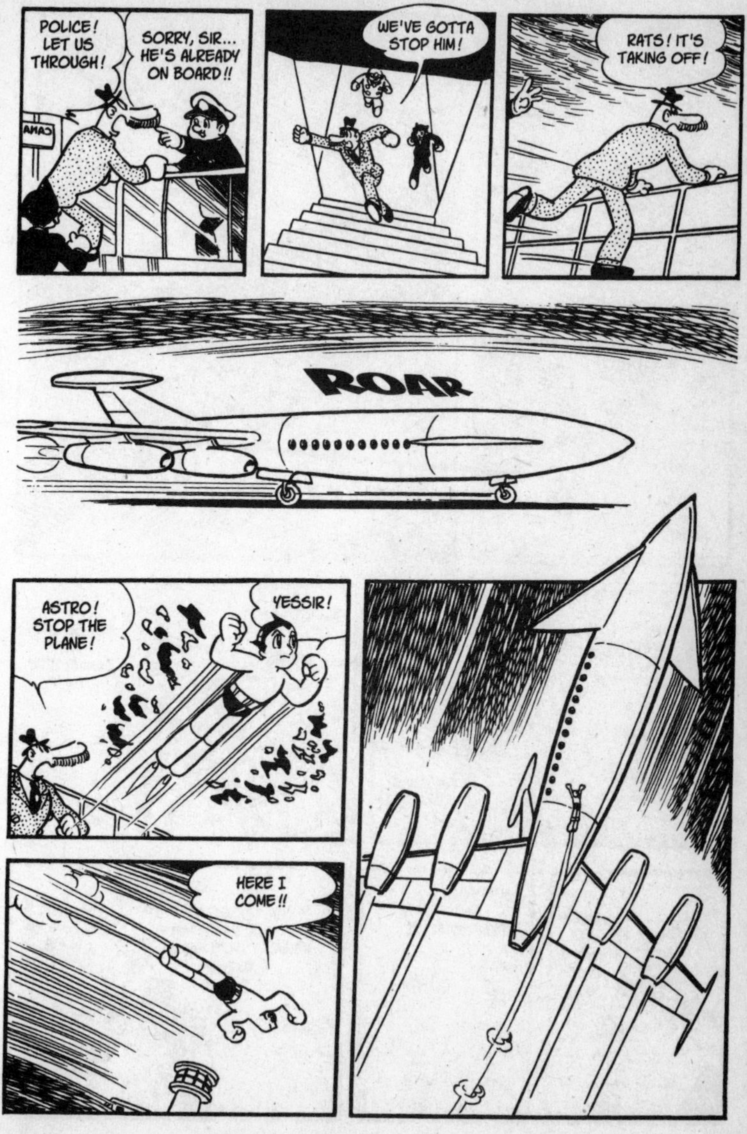
POLICE! LET US THROUGH!
SORRY, SIR... HE'S ALREADY ON BOARD!!
WE'VE GOTTA STOP HIM!
RATS! IT'S TAKING OFF!
ROAR
ASTRO! STOP THE PLANE!
YESSIR!
HERE I COME!!

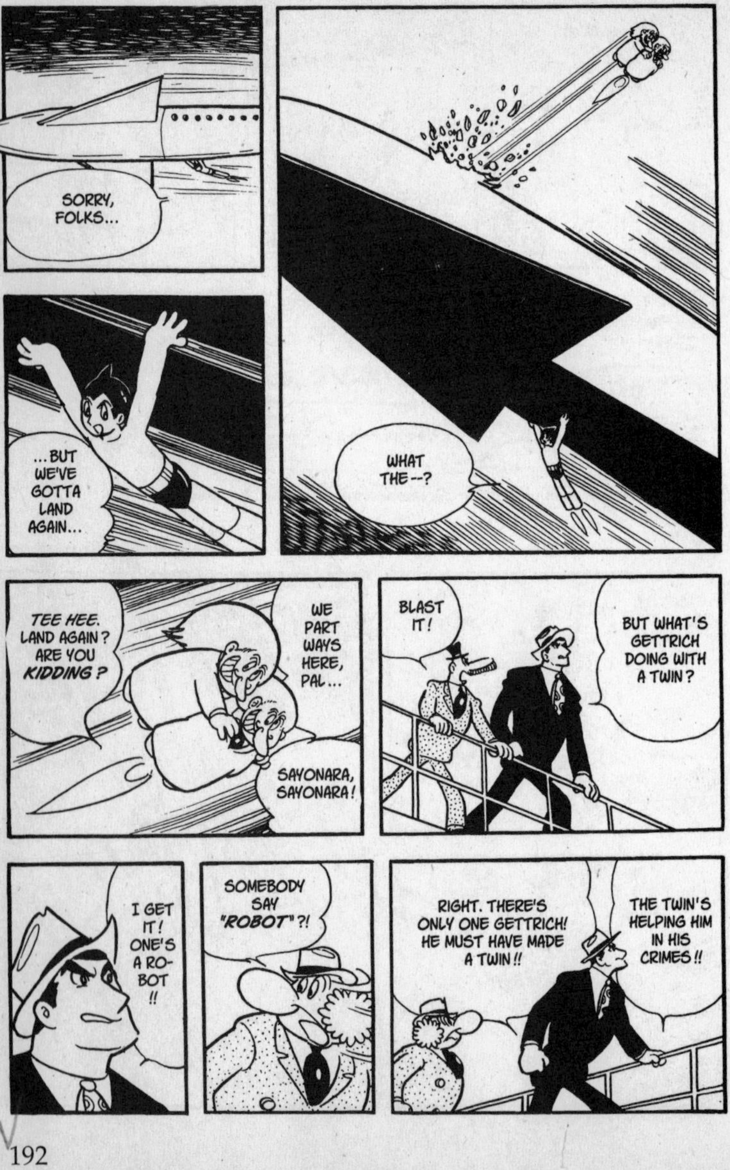
SORRY, FOLKS...
...BUT WE'VE GOTTA LAND AGAIN...
WHAT THE--?
TEE HEE. LAND AGAIN? ARE YOU KIDDING?
WE PART WAYS HERE, PAL...
SAYONARA, SAYONARA!
BLAST IT!
BUT WHAT'S GETTRICH DOING WITH A TWIN?
I GET IT! ONE'S A RO-BOT !!
SOMEBODY SAY "ROBOT"?!
RIGHT. THERE'S ONLY ONE GETTRICH! HE MUST HAVE MADE A TWIN!!
THE TWIN'S HELPING HIM IN HIS CRIMES!!

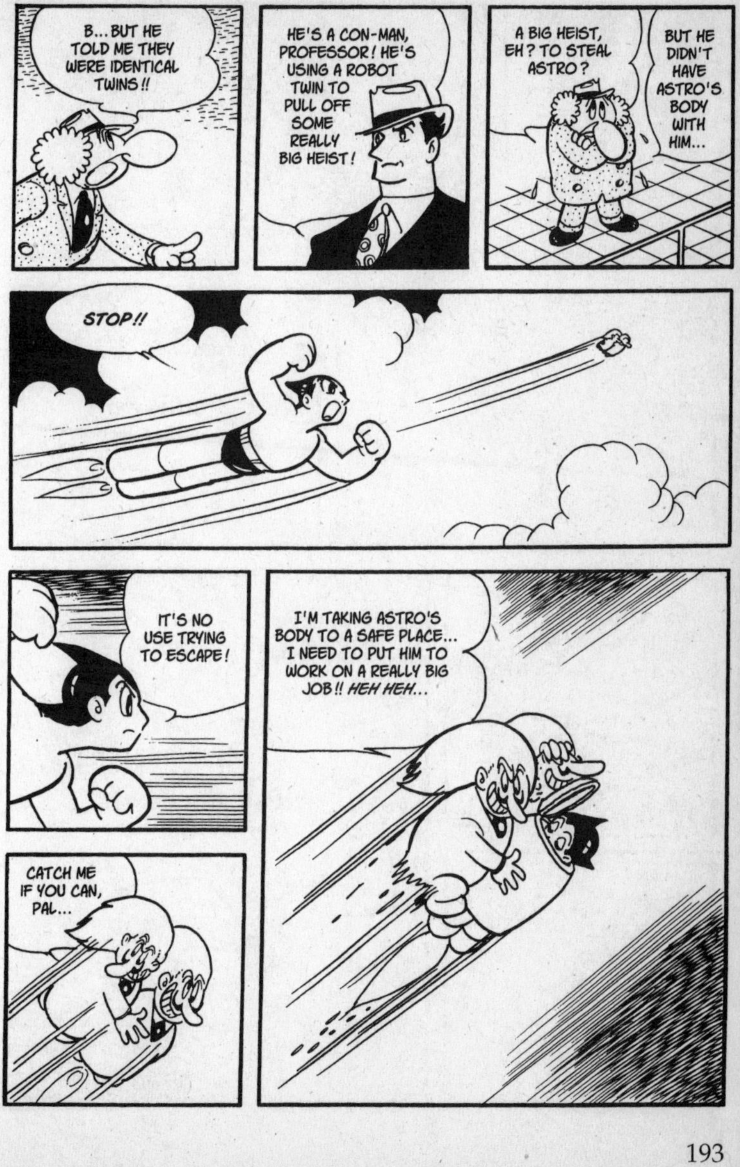
B... BUT HE TOLD ME THEY WERE IDENTICAL TWINS!!
HE'S A CON-MAN, PROFESSOR! HE'S USING A ROBOT TWIN TO PULL OFF SOME REALLY BIG HEIST!
A BIG HEIST, EH? TO STEAL ASTRO?
BUT HE DIDN'T HAVE ASTRO'S BODY WITH HIM...
STOP!!
IT'S NO USE TRYING TO ESCAPE!
CATCH ME IF YOU CAN, PAL...
I'M TAKING ASTRO'S BODY TO A SAFE PLACE... I NEED TO PUT HIM TO WORK ON A REALLY BIG JOB!! HEH HEH...

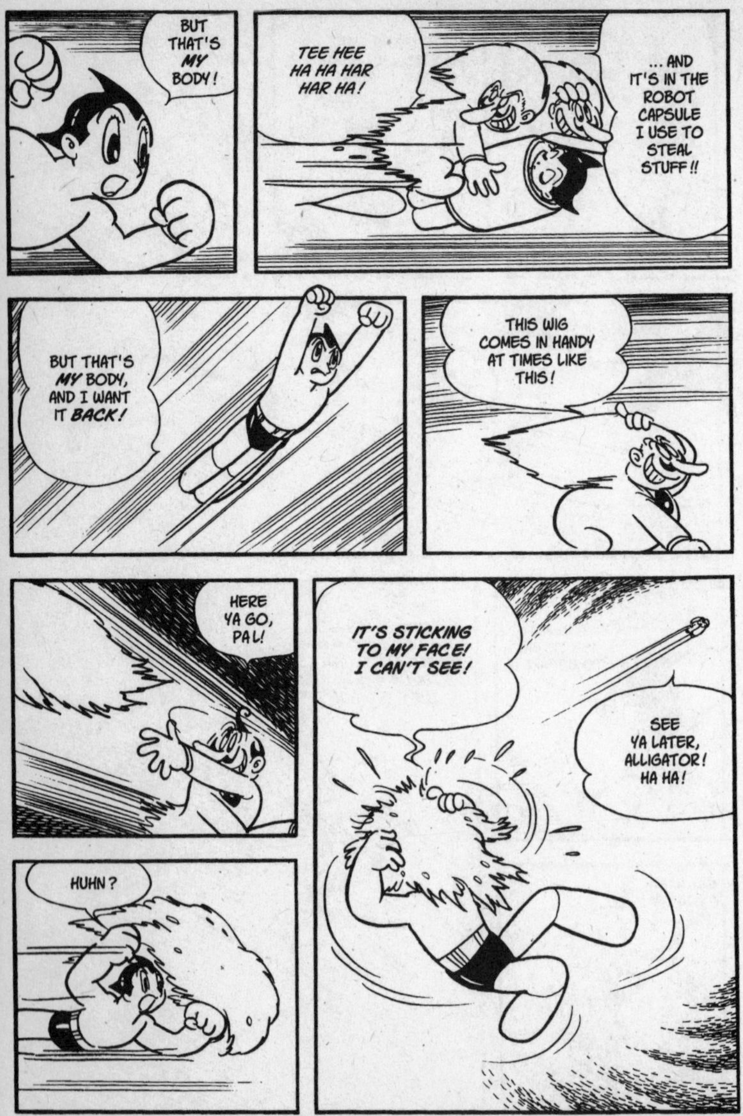
BUT THAT'S *MY* BODY!
TEE HEE HA HA HAR HAR HA!
... AND IT'S IN THE ROBOT CAPSULE I USE TO STEAL STUFF!!
BUT THAT'S *MY* BODY, AND I WANT IT *BACK!*
THIS WIG COMES IN HANDY AT TIMES LIKE THIS!
HERE YA GO, PAL!
HUHN?
IT'S STICKING TO MY FACE! I CAN'T SEE!
SEE YA LATER, ALLIGATOR! HA HA!

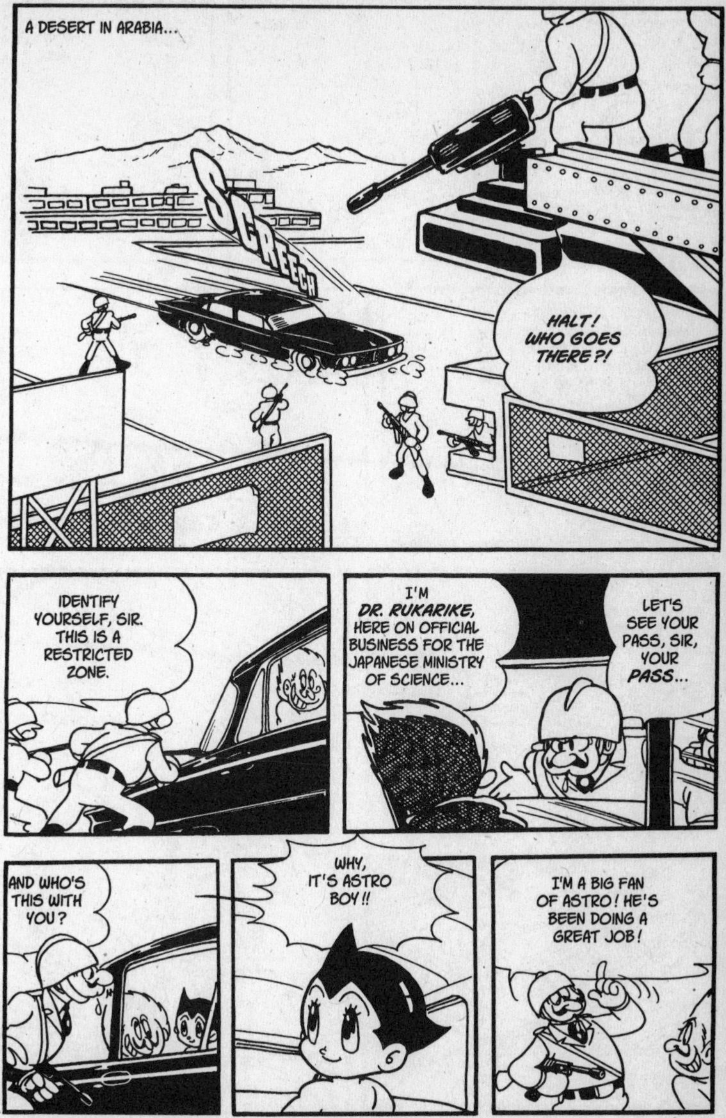
A DESERT IN ARABIA...
SCREECH
HALT! WHO GOES THERE?!
IDENTIFY YOURSELF, SIR. THIS IS A RESTRICTED ZONE.
I'M *DR. RUKARIKE,* HERE ON OFFICIAL BUSINESS FOR THE JAPANESE MINISTRY OF SCIENCE...
LET'S SEE YOUR PASS, SIR, YOUR *PASS*...
AND WHO'S THIS WITH YOU?
WHY, IT'S ASTRO BOY!!
I'M A BIG FAN OF ASTRO! HE'S BEEN DOING A GREAT JOB!

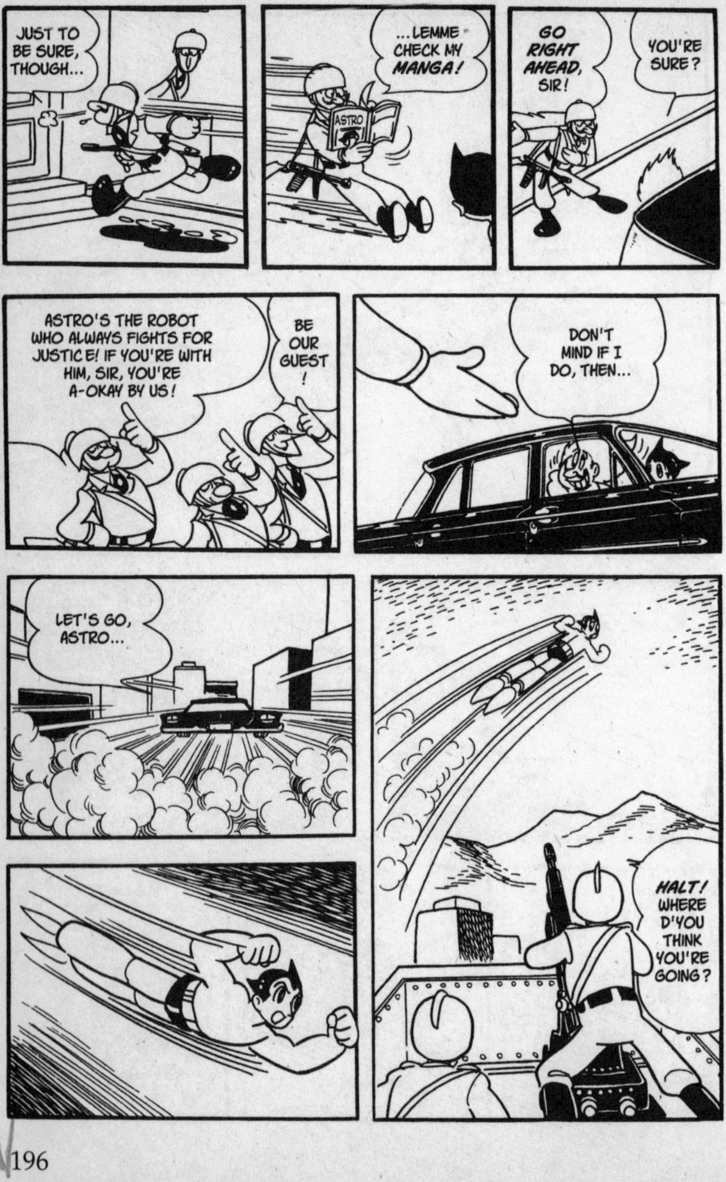
JUST TO BE SURE, THOUGH...
...LEMME CHECK MY MANGA!
ASTRO
GO RIGHT AHEAD, SIR!
YOU'RE SURE?
ASTRO'S THE ROBOT WHO ALWAYS FIGHTS FOR JUSTICE! IF YOU'RE WITH HIM, SIR, YOU'RE A-OKAY BY US!
BE OUR GUEST!
DON'T MIND IF I DO, THEN...
LET'S GO, ASTRO...
HALT! WHERE D'YOU THINK YOU'RE GOING?

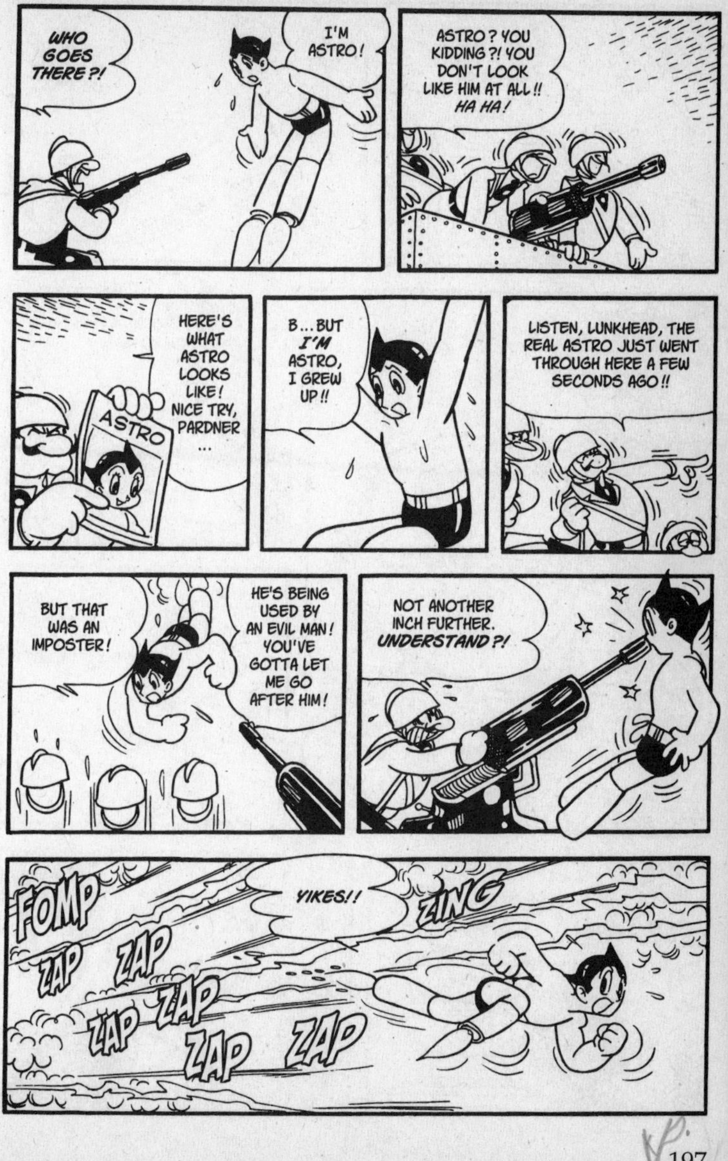
WHO GOES THERE?!
I'M ASTRO!
ASTRO? YOU KIDDING?! YOU DON'T LOOK LIKE HIM AT ALL!! HA HA!
HERE'S WHAT ASTRO LOOKS LIKE! NICE TRY, PARDNER ...
ASTRO
B... BUT I'M ASTRO, I GREW UP!!
LISTEN, LUNKHEAD, THE REAL ASTRO JUST WENT THROUGH HERE A FEW SECONDS AGO!!
BUT THAT WAS AN IMPOSTER!
HE'S BEING USED BY AN EVIL MAN! YOU'VE GOTTA LET ME GO AFTER HIM!
NOT ANOTHER INCH FURTHER. UNDERSTAND?!
FOMP
YIKES!!
ZING
ZAP
ZAP
ZAP
ZAP
ZAP
ZAP

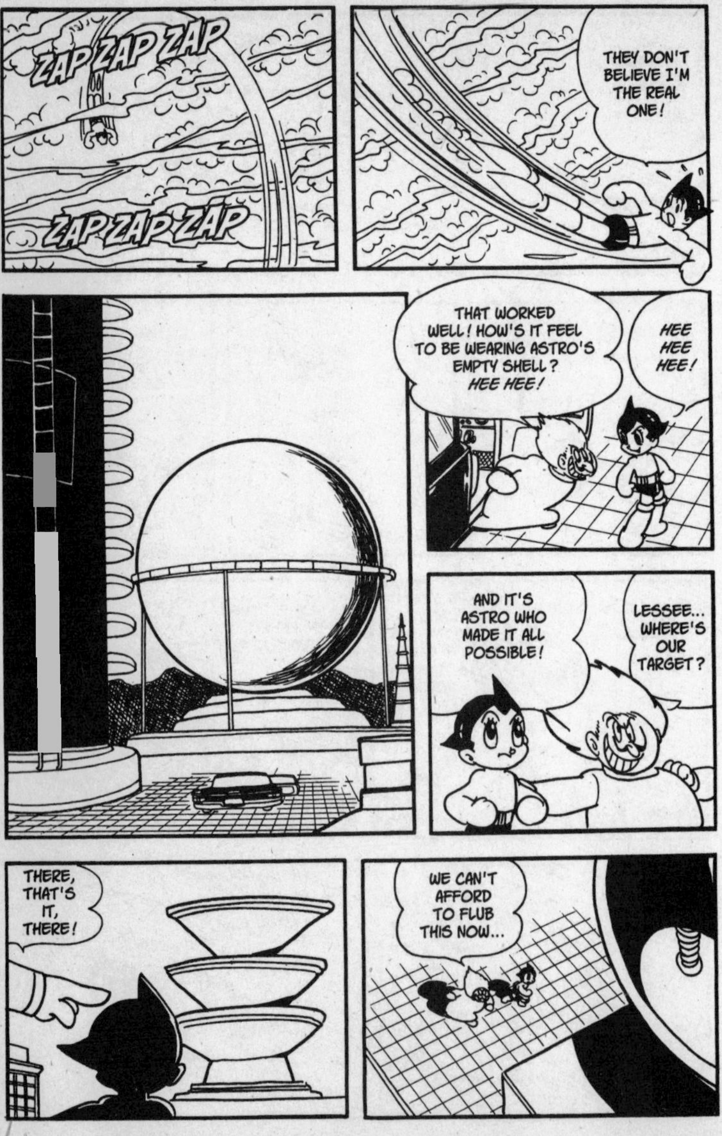
ZAP ZAP ZAP
ZAP ZAP ZAP
THEY DON'T BELIEVE I'M THE REAL ONE!
THAT WORKED WELL! HOW'S IT FEEL TO BE WEARING ASTRO'S EMPTY SHELL? *HEE HEE!*
HEE HEE HEE!
AND IT'S ASTRO WHO MADE IT ALL POSSIBLE!
LESSEE... WHERE'S OUR TARGET?
THERE, THAT'S IT, THERE!
WE CAN'T AFFORD TO FLUB THIS NOW...

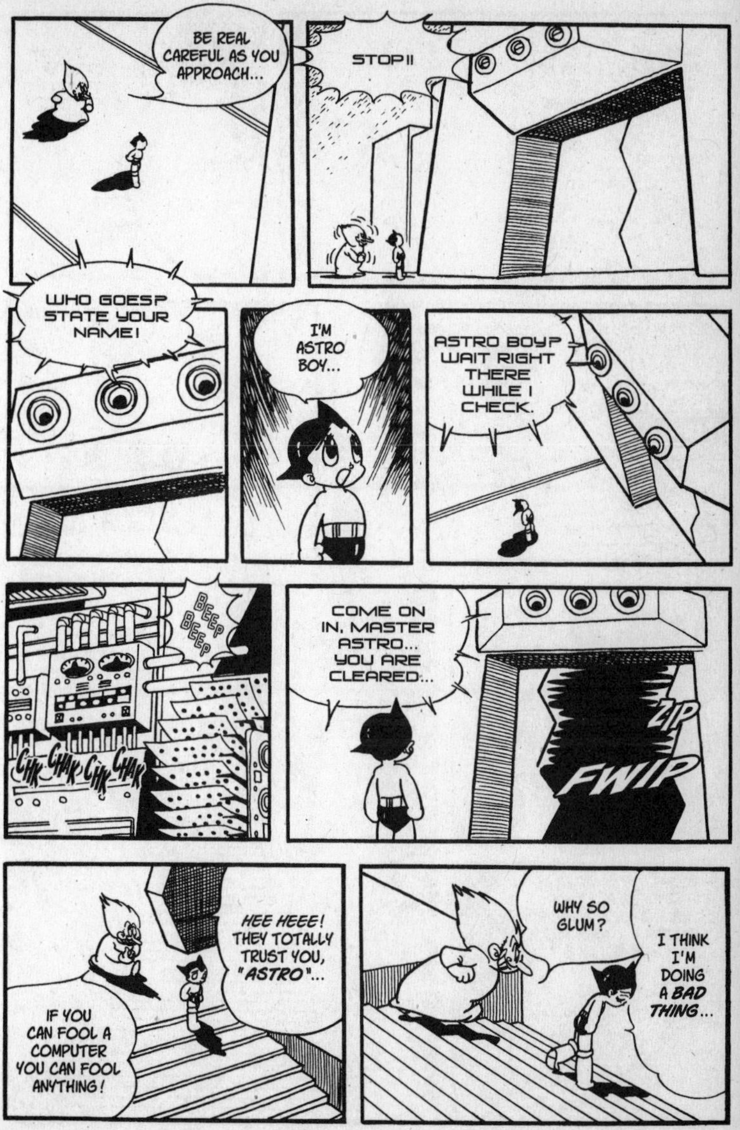
BE REAL CAREFUL AS YOU APPROACH...
STOP!!
WHO GOES? STATE YOUR NAME!
I'M ASTRO BOY...
ASTRO BOY? WAIT RIGHT THERE WHILE I CHECK.
BEEP BEEP
CHK CHAK CHK CHAK
COME ON IN, MASTER ASTRO... YOU ARE CLEARED...
ZIP
FWIP
HEE HEEE! THEY TOTALLY TRUST YOU, "ASTRO"...
IF YOU CAN FOOL A COMPUTER YOU CAN FOOL ANYTHING!
WHY SO GLUM?
I THINK I'M DOING A BAD THING...

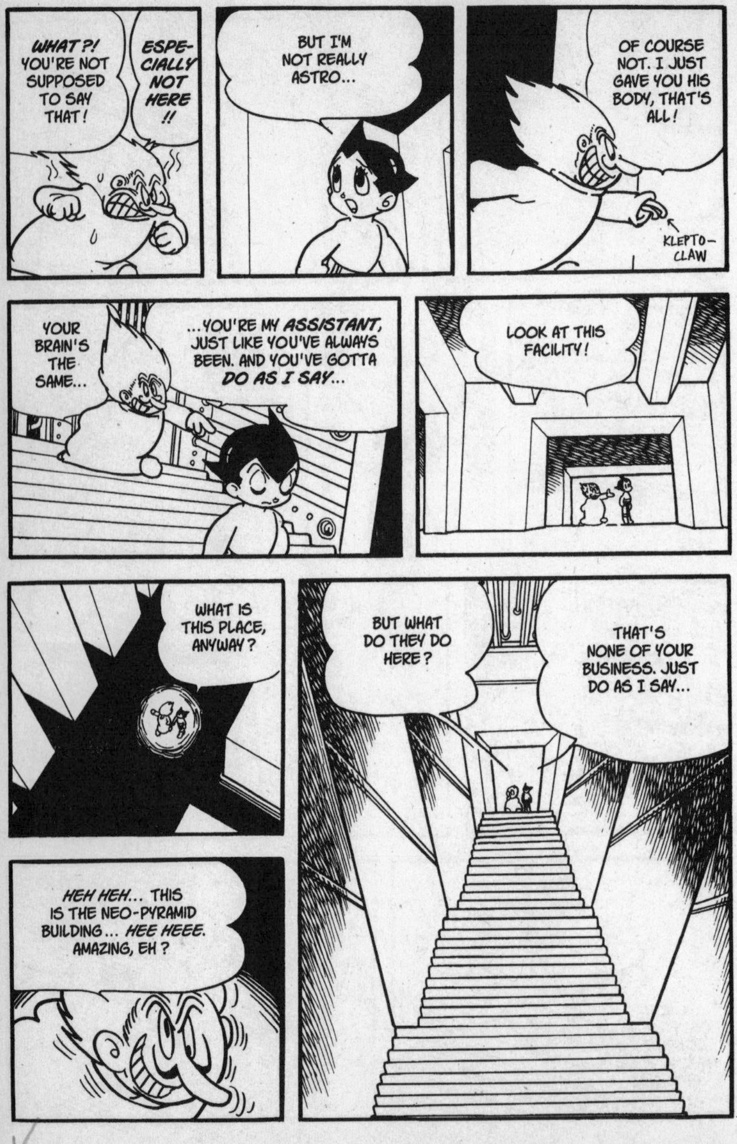
WHAT?! YOU'RE NOT SUPPOSED TO SAY THAT!
ESPE-CIALLY NOT HERE!!
BUT I'M NOT REALLY ASTRO...
OF COURSE NOT. I JUST GAVE YOU HIS BODY, THAT'S ALL!
KLEPTO-CLAW
YOUR BRAIN'S THE SAME...
...YOU'RE MY ASSISTANT, JUST LIKE YOU'VE ALWAYS BEEN. AND YOU'VE GOTTA DO AS I SAY...
LOOK AT THIS FACILITY!
WHAT IS THIS PLACE, ANYWAY?
HEH HEH... THIS IS THE NEO-PYRAMID BUILDING... HEE HEEE. AMAZING, EH?
BUT WHAT DO THEY DO HERE?
THAT'S NONE OF YOUR BUSINESS. JUST DO AS I SAY...

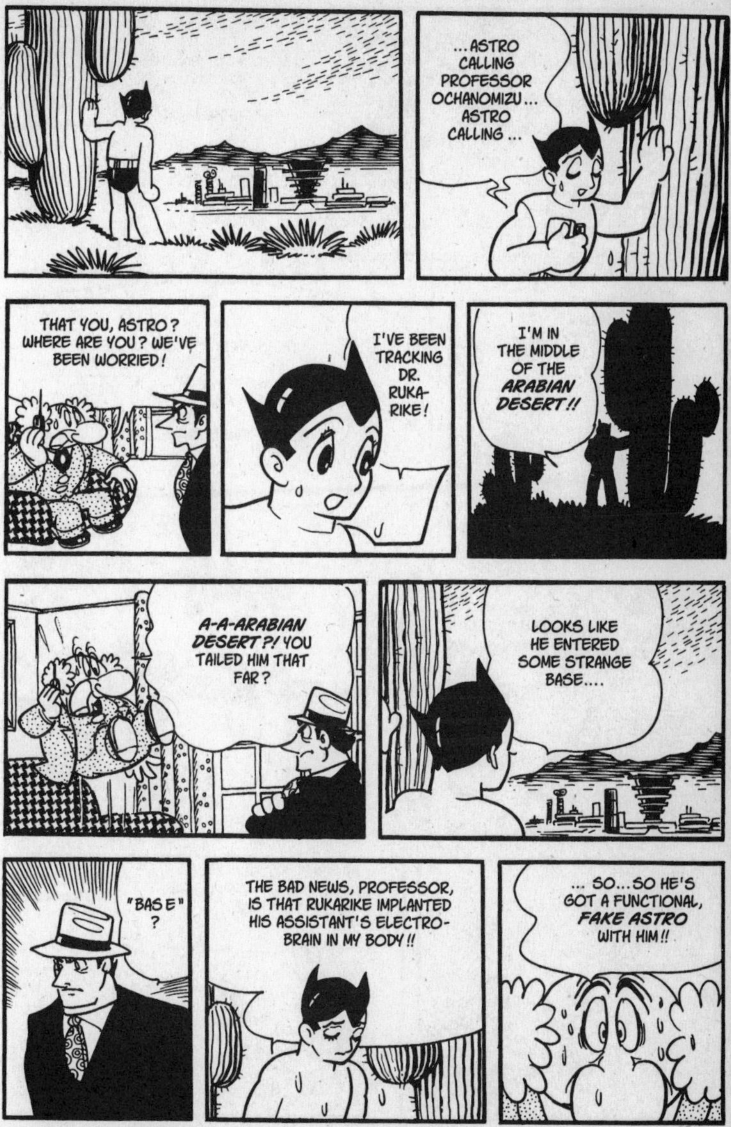
...ASTRO CALLING PROFESSOR OCHANOMIZU... ASTRO CALLING ...
THAT YOU, ASTRO? WHERE ARE YOU? WE'VE BEEN WORRIED!
I'VE BEEN TRACKING DR. RUKA-RIKE!
I'M IN THE MIDDLE OF THE ARABIAN DESERT!!
A-A-ARABIAN DESERT?! YOU TAILED HIM THAT FAR?
LOOKS LIKE HE ENTERED SOME STRANGE BASE....
"BASE"?
THE BAD NEWS, PROFESSOR, IS THAT RUKARIKE IMPLANTED HIS ASSISTANT'S ELECTRO-BRAIN IN MY BODY!!
... SO...SO HE'S GOT A FUNCTIONAL, FAKE ASTRO WITH HIM!!

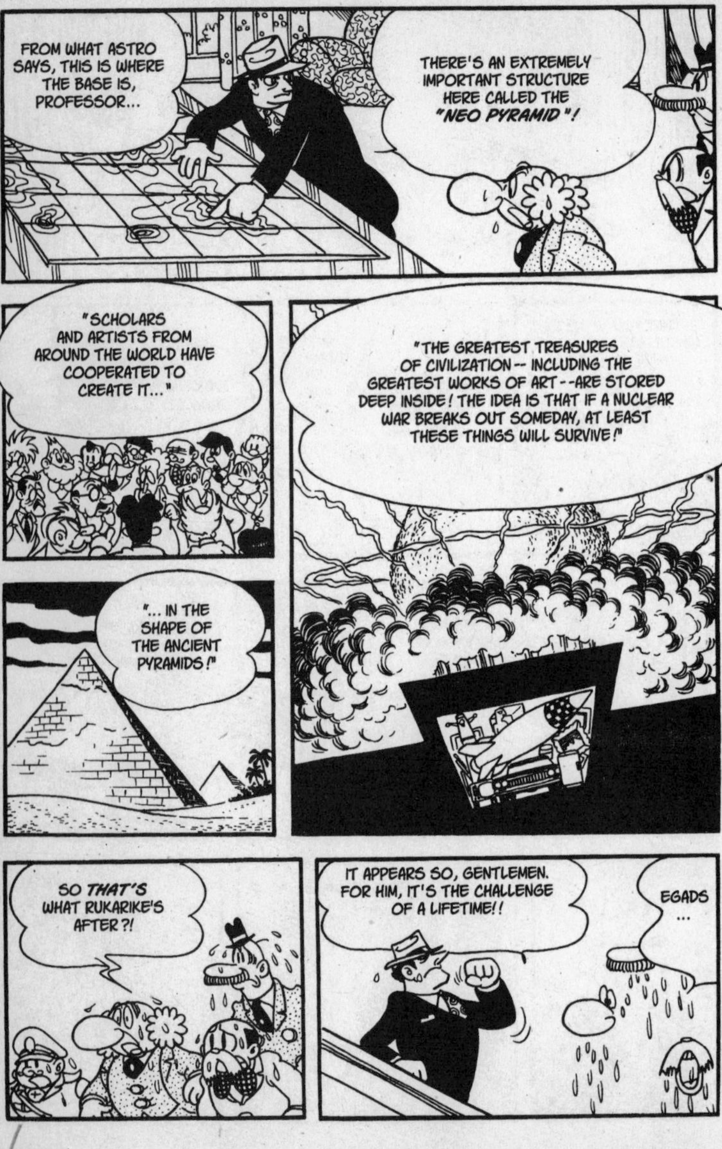
FROM WHAT ASTRO SAYS, THIS IS WHERE THE BASE IS, PROFESSOR...
THERE'S AN EXTREMELY IMPORTANT STRUCTURE HERE CALLED THE "NEO PYRAMID"!
"SCHOLARS AND ARTISTS FROM AROUND THE WORLD HAVE COOPERATED TO CREATE IT..."
"... IN THE SHAPE OF THE ANCIENT PYRAMIDS!"
"THE GREATEST TREASURES OF CIVILIZATION -- INCLUDING THE GREATEST WORKS OF ART --ARE STORED DEEP INSIDE! THE IDEA IS THAT IF A NUCLEAR WAR BREAKS OUT SOMEDAY, AT LEAST THESE THINGS WILL SURVIVE!"
SO THAT'S WHAT RUKARIKE'S AFTER?!
IT APPEARS SO, GENTLEMEN. FOR HIM, IT'S THE CHALLENGE OF A LIFETIME!!
EGADS ...

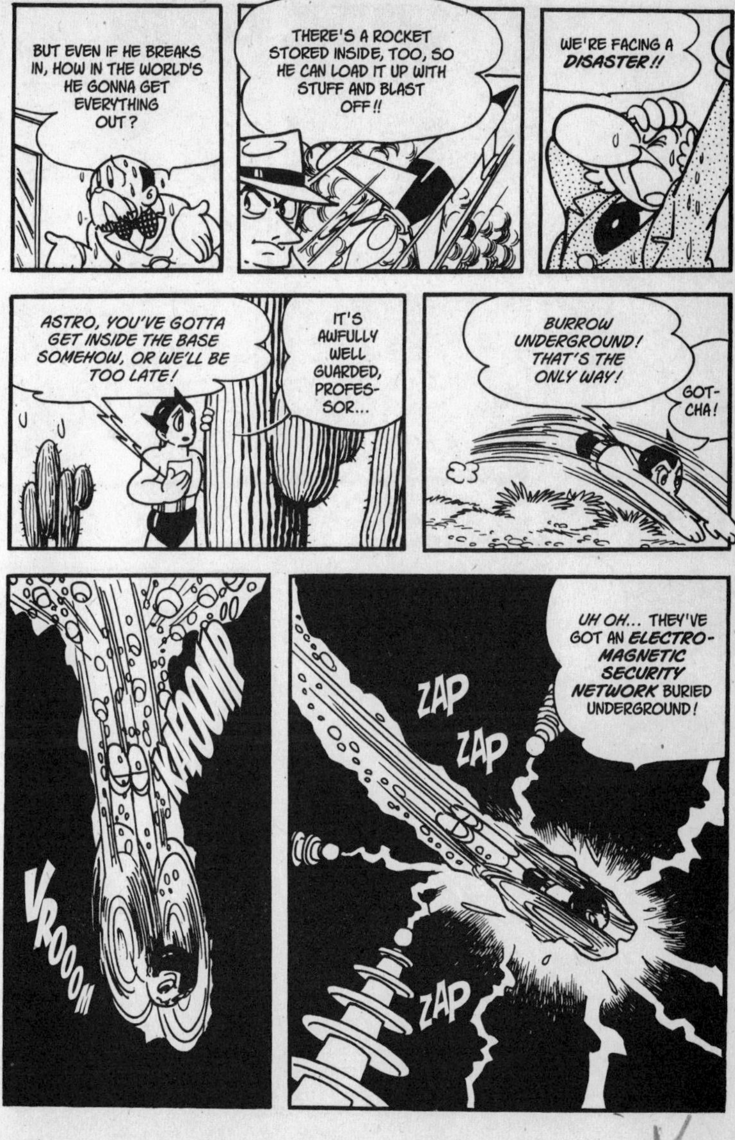
BUT EVEN IF HE BREAKS IN, HOW IN THE WORLD'S HE GONNA GET EVERYTHING OUT?
THERE'S A ROCKET STORED INSIDE, TOO, SO HE CAN LOAD IT UP WITH STUFF AND BLAST OFF!!
WE'RE FACING A *DISASTER!!*
ASTRO, YOU'VE GOTTA GET INSIDE THE BASE SOMEHOW, OR WE'LL BE TOO LATE!
IT'S AWFULLY WELL GUARDED, PROFES-SOR...
BURROW UNDERGROUND! THAT'S THE ONLY WAY!
GOT-CHA!
KAFOOMP
VROOOM
ZAP
ZAP
UH OH... THEY'VE GOT AN ***ELECTRO-MAGNETIC SECURITY NETWORK*** BURIED UNDERGROUND!
ZAP

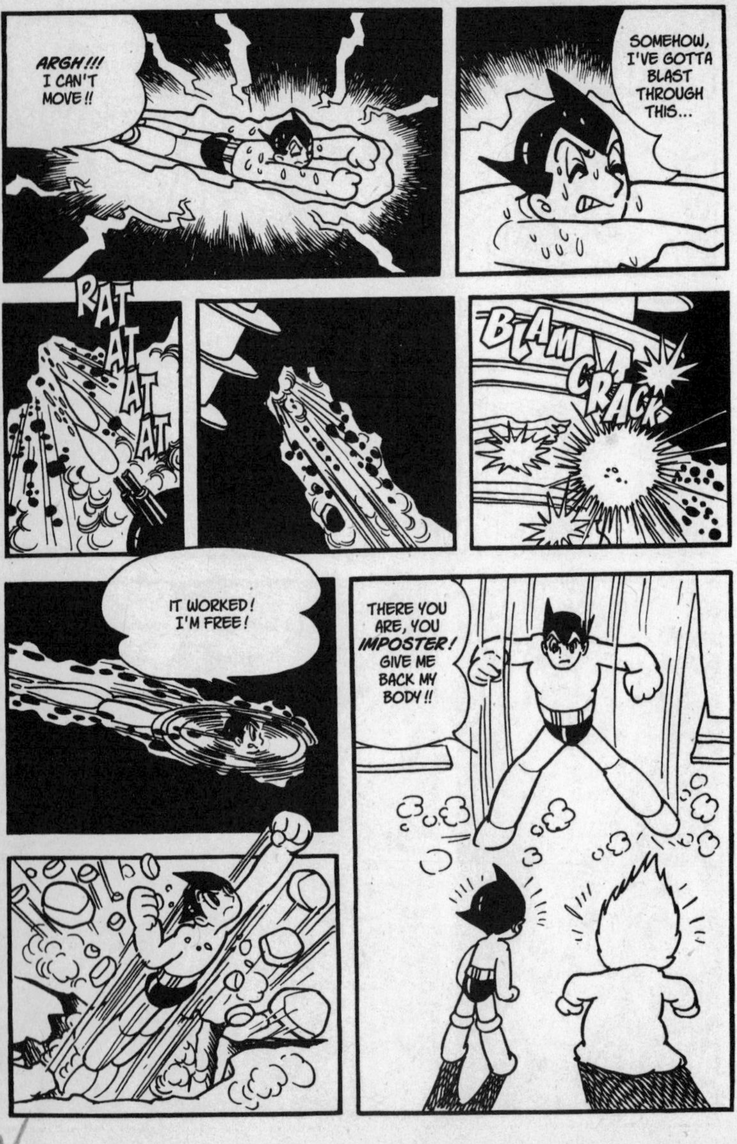
ARGH!!! I CAN'T MOVE!!
SOMEHOW, I'VE GOTTA BLAST THROUGH THIS...
RATATATAT
BLAM
CRACK
IT WORKED! I'M FREE!
THERE YOU ARE, YOU IMPOSTER! GIVE ME BACK MY BODY!!

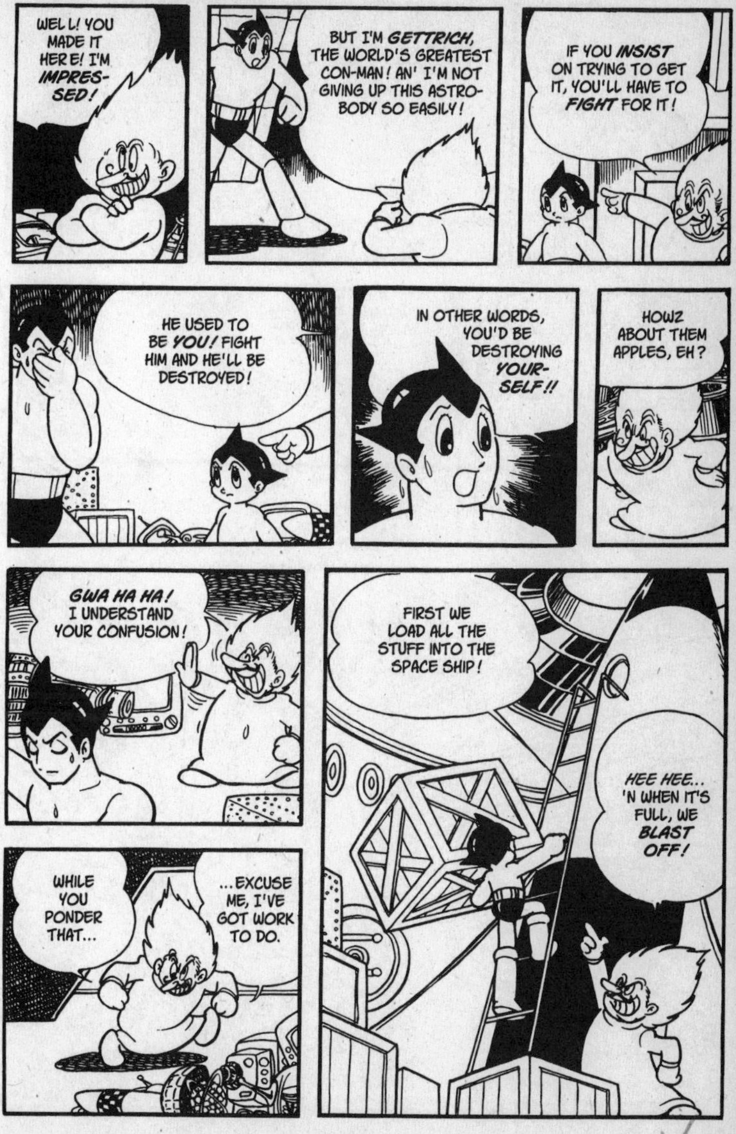
WELL! YOU MADE IT HERE! I'M IMPRES-SED!
BUT I'M GETTRICH, THE WORLD'S GREATEST CON-MAN! AN' I'M NOT GIVING UP THIS ASTRO-BODY SO EASILY!
IF YOU INSIST ON TRYING TO GET IT, YOU'LL HAVE TO FIGHT FOR IT!
HE USED TO BE YOU! FIGHT HIM AND HE'LL BE DESTROYED!
IN OTHER WORDS, YOU'D BE DESTROYING YOUR-SELF!!
HOWZ ABOUT THEM APPLES, EH?
GWA HA HA! I UNDERSTAND YOUR CONFUSION!
WHILE YOU PONDER THAT...
...EXCUSE ME, I'VE GOT WORK TO DO.
FIRST WE LOAD ALL THE STUFF INTO THE SPACE SHIP!
HEE HEE... 'N WHEN IT'S FULL, WE BLAST OFF!

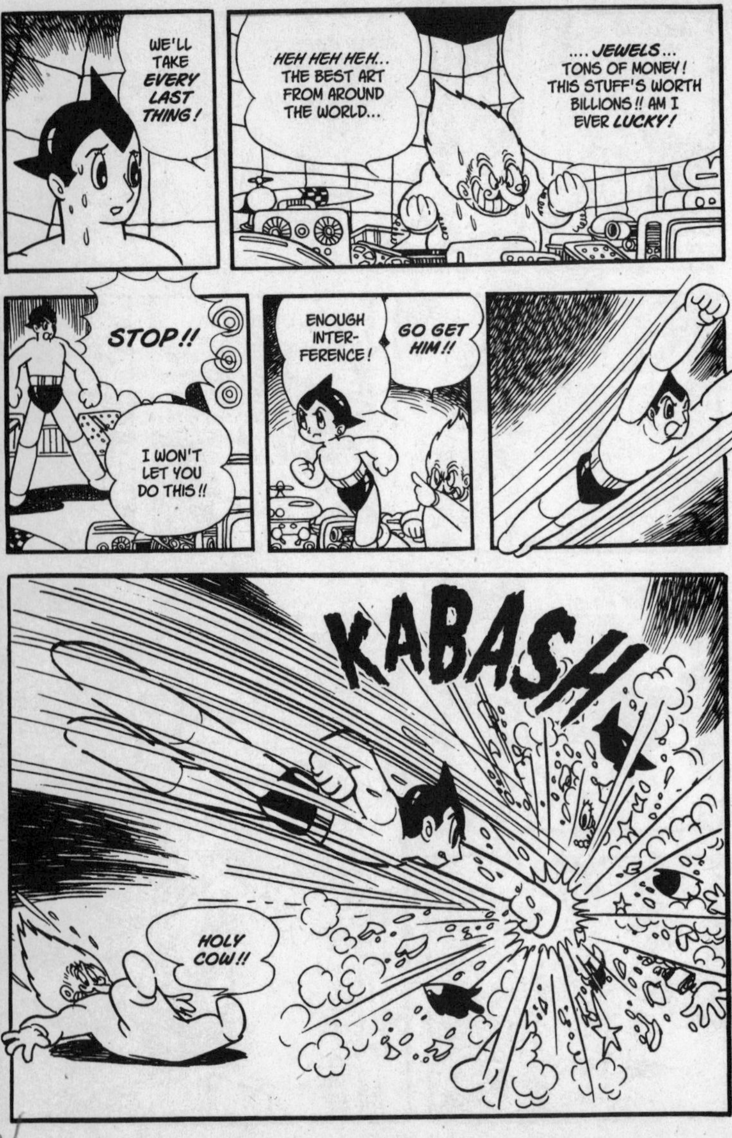
WE'LL TAKE EVERY LAST THING!
HEH HEH HEH... THE BEST ART FROM AROUND THE WORLD...
.... JEWELS... TONS OF MONEY! THIS STUFF'S WORTH BILLIONS!! AM I EVER LUCKY!
STOP!!
I WON'T LET YOU DO THIS!!
ENOUGH INTER-FERENCE!
GO GET HIM!!
KABASH
HOLY COW!!

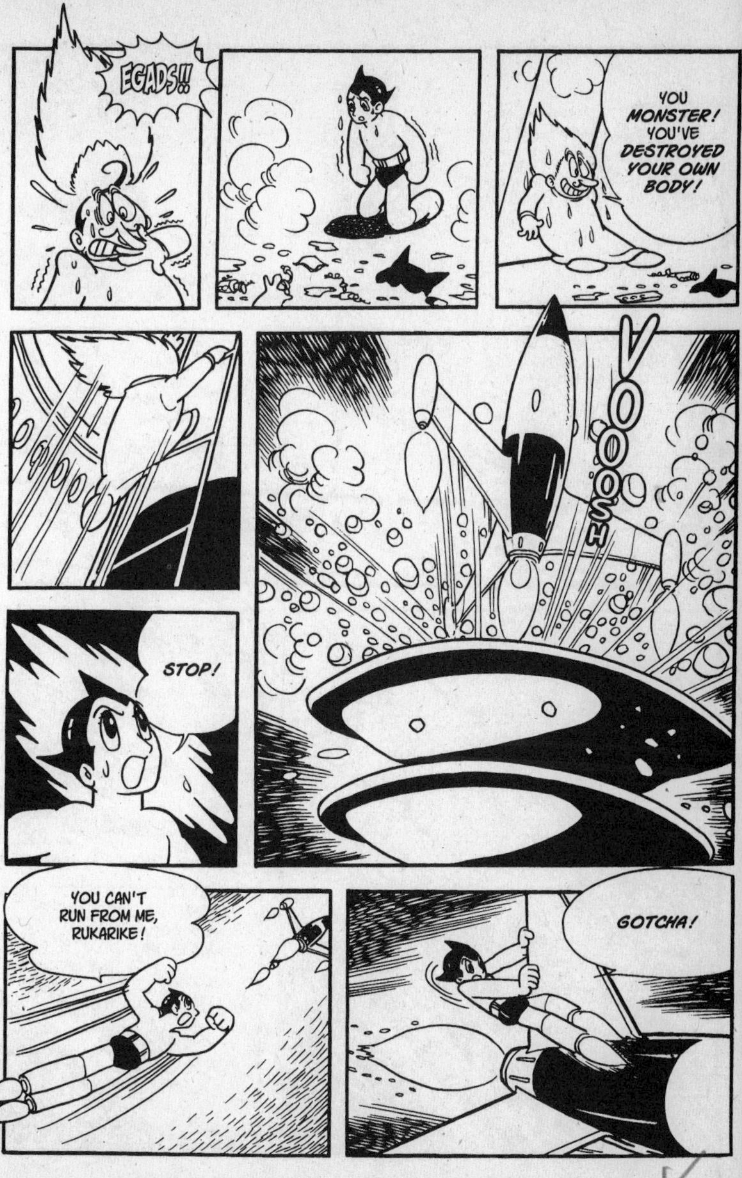
EGADS!!
YOU MONSTER! YOU'VE DESTROYED YOUR OWN BODY!
STOP!
VOOOOSH
YOU CAN'T RUN FROM ME, RUKARIKE!
GOTCHA!

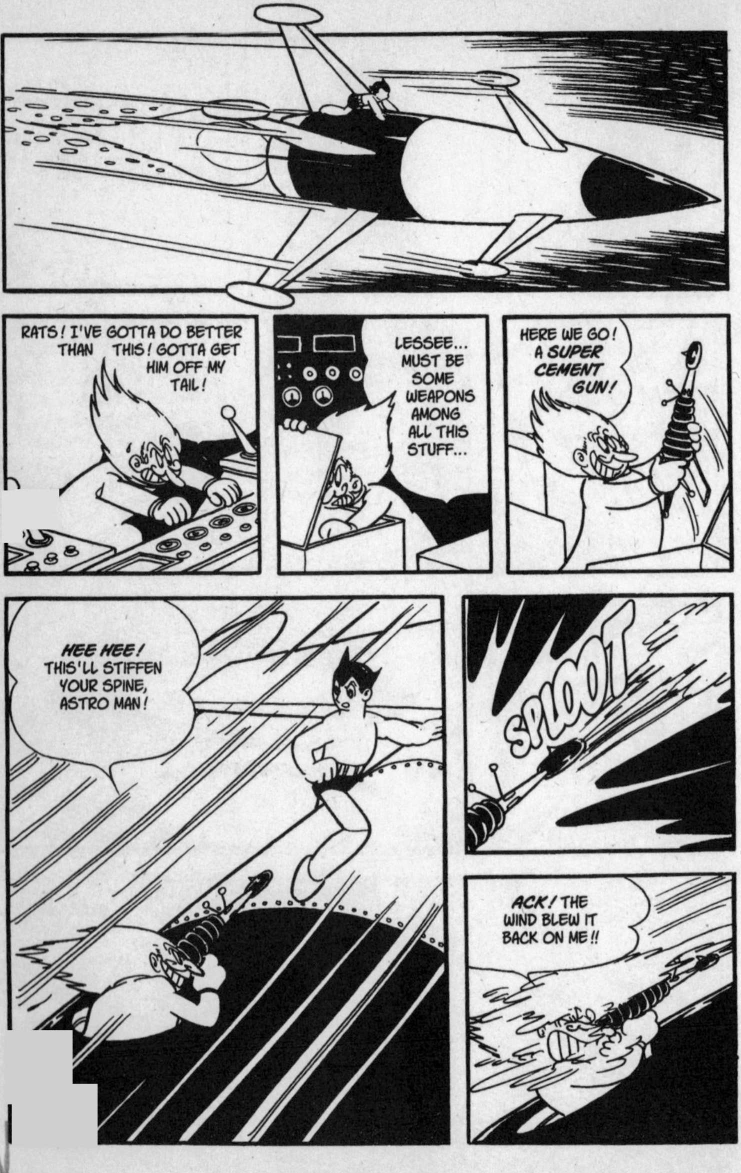
RATS! I'VE GOTTA DO BETTER THAN THIS! GOTTA GET HIM OFF MY TAIL!
LESSEE... MUST BE SOME WEAPONS AMONG ALL THIS STUFF...
HERE WE GO! A SUPER CEMENT GUN!
HEE HEE! THIS'LL STIFFEN YOUR SPINE, ASTRO MAN!
SPLOOT
ACK! THE WIND BLEW IT BACK ON ME!!

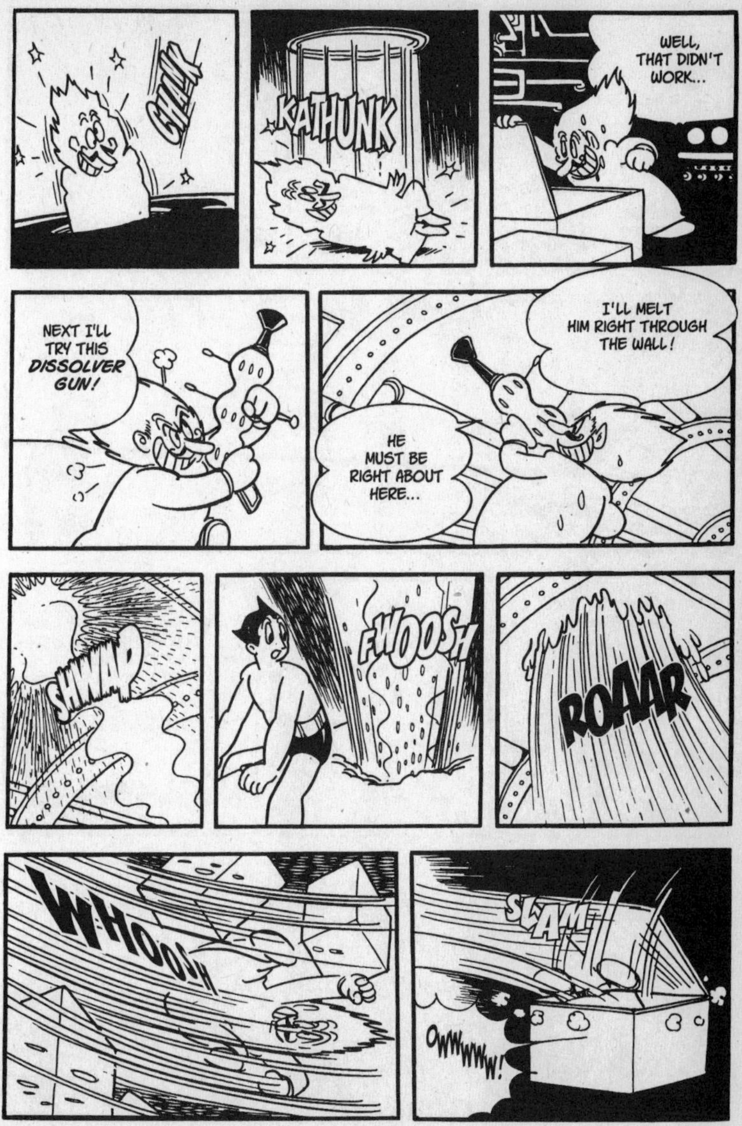
CHAK
KATHUNK
WELL, THAT DIDN'T WORK...
NEXT I'LL TRY THIS *DISSOLVER GUN!*
I'LL MELT HIM RIGHT THROUGH THE WALL!
HE MUST BE RIGHT ABOUT HERE...
SHWAP
FWOOSH
ROAAR
WHOOSH
SLAM
OWWWWW!

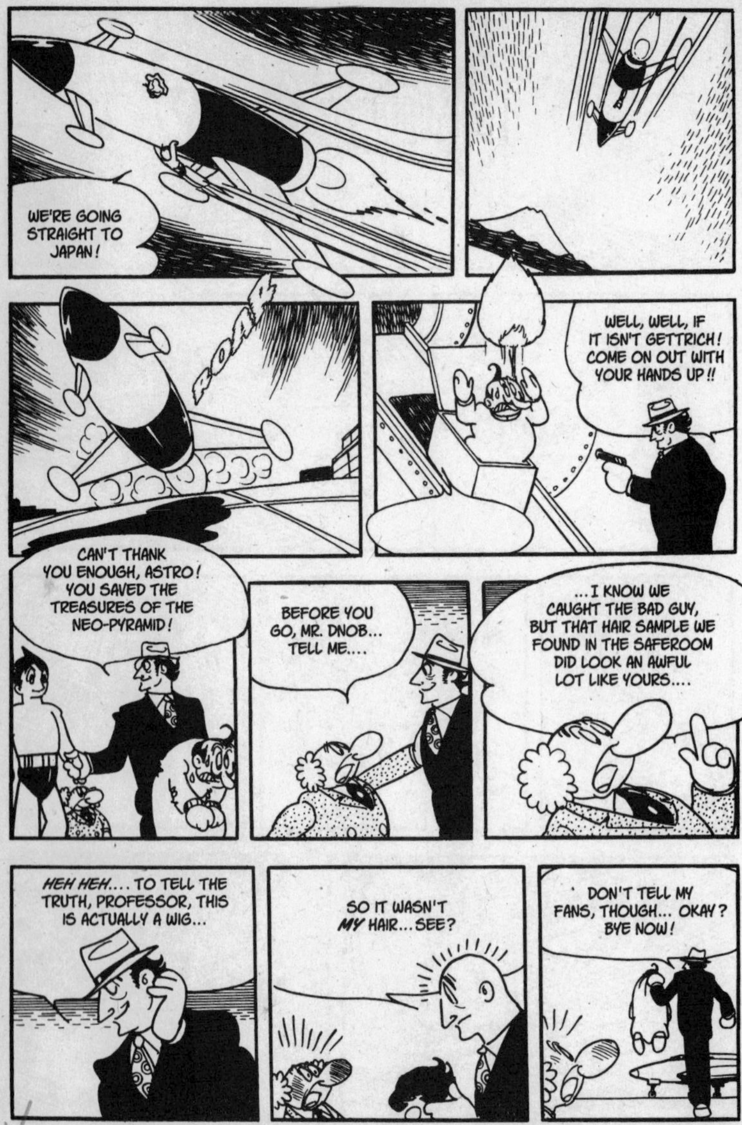
WE'RE GOING STRAIGHT TO JAPAN!
ROAR
WELL, WELL, IF IT ISN'T GETTRICH! COME ON OUT WITH YOUR HANDS UP!!
CAN'T THANK YOU ENOUGH, ASTRO! YOU SAVED THE TREASURES OF THE NEO-PYRAMID!
BEFORE YOU GO, MR. DNOB... TELL ME....
...I KNOW WE CAUGHT THE BAD GUY, BUT THAT HAIR SAMPLE WE FOUND IN THE SAFEROOM DID LOOK AN AWFUL LOT LIKE YOURS....
HEH HEH.... TO TELL THE TRUTH, PROFESSOR, THIS IS ACTUALLY A WIG...
SO IT WASN'T *MY* HAIR... SEE?
DON'T TELL MY FANS, THOUGH... OKAY? BYE NOW!

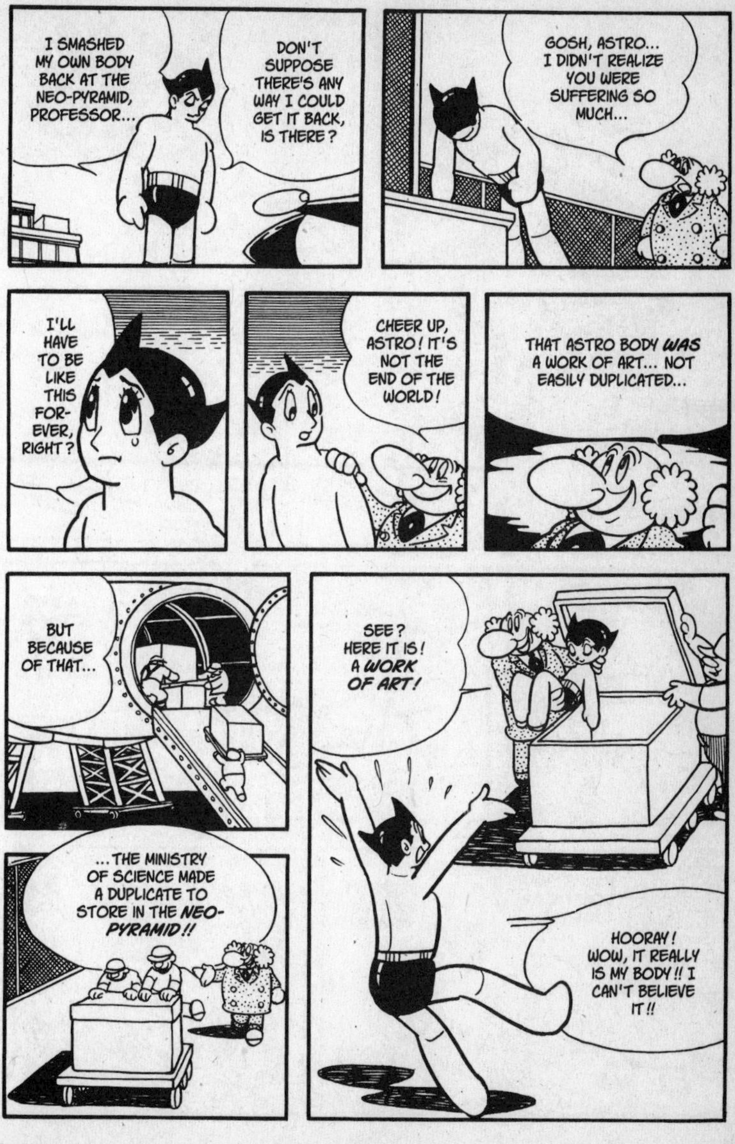
I SMASHED MY OWN BODY BACK AT THE NEO-PYRAMID, PROFESSOR...
DON'T SUPPOSE THERE'S ANY WAY I COULD GET IT BACK, IS THERE?
GOSH, ASTRO... I DIDN'T REALIZE YOU WERE SUFFERING SO MUCH...
I'LL HAVE TO BE LIKE THIS FOREVER, RIGHT?
CHEER UP, ASTRO! IT'S NOT THE END OF THE WORLD!
THAT ASTRO BODY WAS A WORK OF ART... NOT EASILY DUPLICATED...
BUT BECAUSE OF THAT...
... THE MINISTRY OF SCIENCE MADE A DUPLICATE TO STORE IN THE NEO-PYRAMID!!
SEE? HERE IT IS! A WORK OF ART!
HOORAY! WOW, IT REALLY IS MY BODY!! I CAN'T BELIEVE IT!!

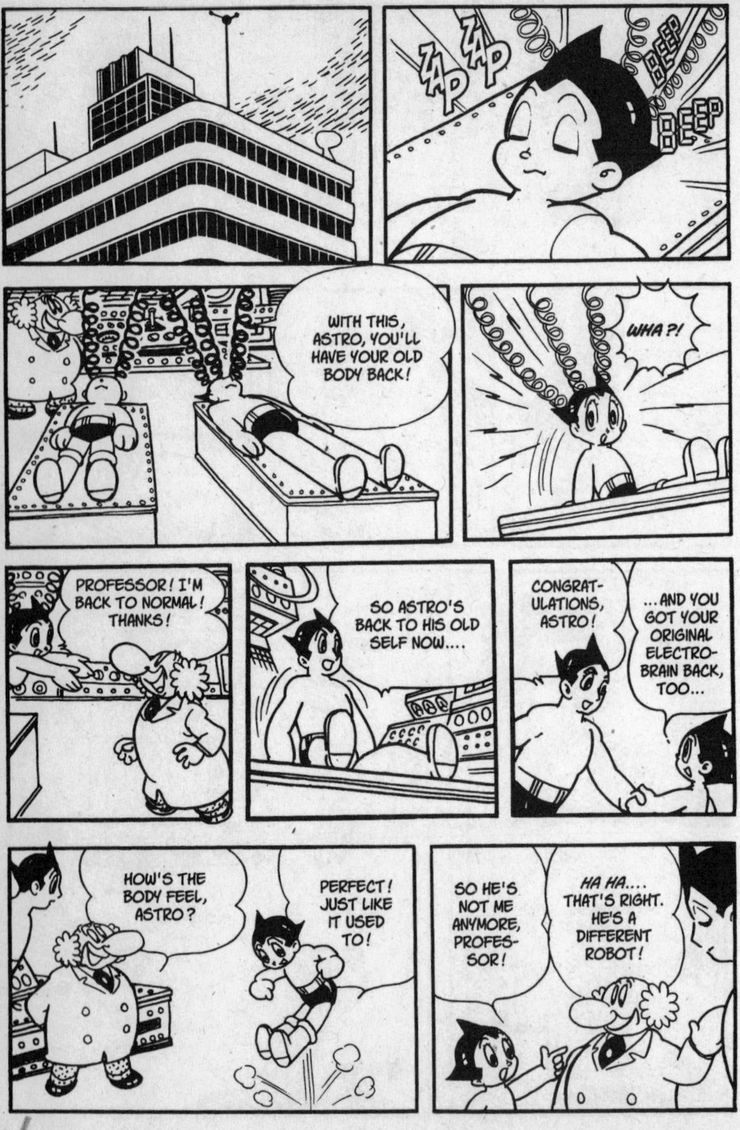
ZAP
ZAP
BEEP
BEEP
WITH THIS, ASTRO, YOU'LL HAVE YOUR OLD BODY BACK!
WHA?!
PROFESSOR! I'M BACK TO NORMAL! THANKS!
SO ASTRO'S BACK TO HIS OLD SELF NOW....
CONGRAT-ULATIONS, ASTRO!
...AND YOU GOT YOUR ORIGINAL ELECTRO-BRAIN BACK, TOO...
HOW'S THE BODY FEEL, ASTRO?
PERFECT! JUST LIKE IT USED TO!
SO HE'S NOT ME ANYMORE, PROFES-SOR!
HA HA.... THAT'S RIGHT. HE'S A DIFFERENT ROBOT!

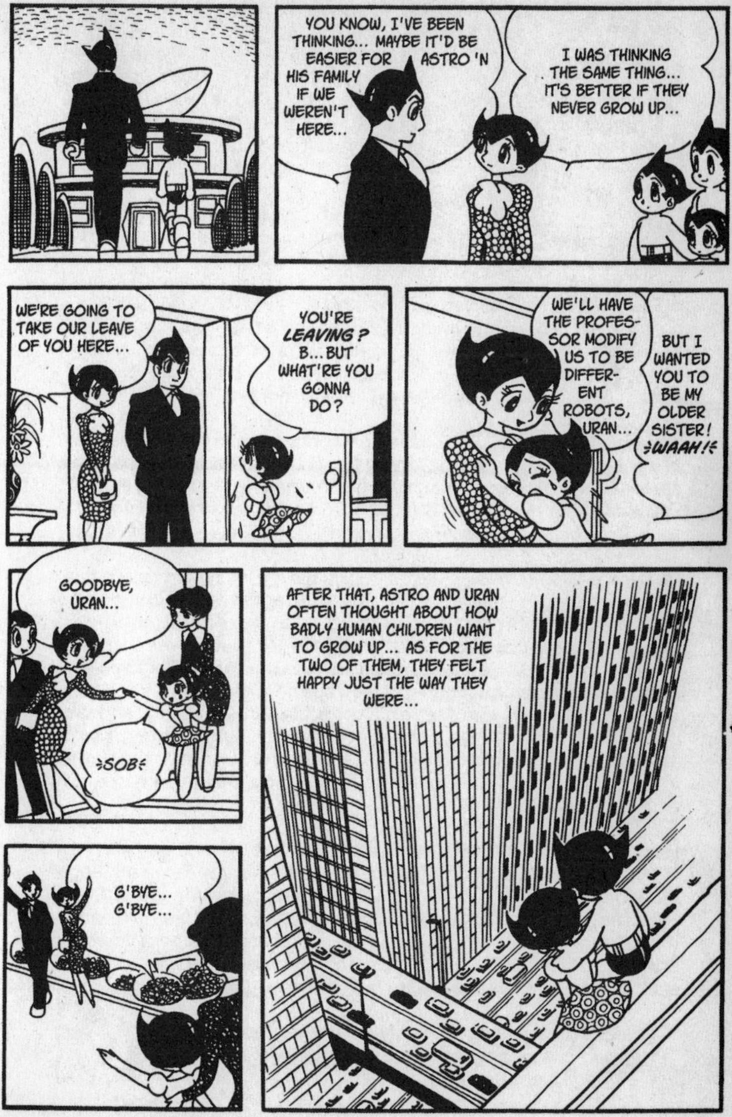
YOU KNOW, I'VE BEEN THINKING... MAYBE IT'D BE EASIER FOR ASTRO 'N HIS FAMILY IF WE WEREN'T HERE...
I WAS THINKING THE SAME THING... IT'S BETTER IF THEY NEVER GROW UP...
WE'RE GOING TO TAKE OUR LEAVE OF YOU HERE...
YOU'RE LEAVING? B... BUT WHAT'RE YOU GONNA DO?
WE'LL HAVE THE PROFESSOR MODIFY US TO BE DIFFERENT ROBOTS, URAN...
BUT I WANTED YOU TO BE MY OLDER SISTER! WAAH!
GOODBYE, URAN...
SOB
G'BYE... G'BYE...
AFTER THAT, ASTRO AND URAN OFTEN THOUGHT ABOUT HOW BADLY HUMAN CHILDREN WANT TO GROW UP... AS FOR THE TWO OF THEM, THEY FELT HAPPY JUST THE WAY THEY WERE...

THE END

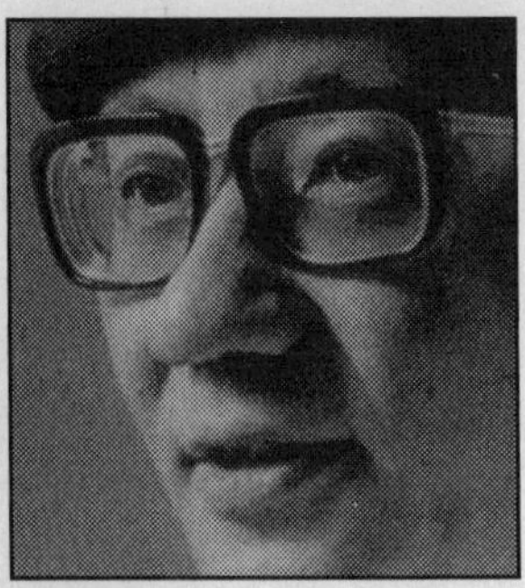

Osamu Tezuka was born in the city of Toyonaka, in Osaka, Japan, on November 3, 1928, and raised in Takarazuka, in Hyogo prefecture. He graduated from the Medical Department of Osaka University and was later awarded a Doctorate of Medicine.

In 1946 Tezuka made his debut as a manga artist with the work *Ma-chan's Diary*, and in 1947 he had his first big hit with *New Treasure Island*. In over forty years as a cartoonist, Tezuka produced in excess of an astounding 150,000 pages of manga, including the creation of *Metropolis*, *Mighty Atom* (a.k.a. *Astro Boy*), *Jungle Emperor* (a.k.a. *Kimba the White Lion*), *Black Jack*, *Phoenix*, *Buddha*, and many more.

Tezuka's fascination with Disney cartoons led him to begin his own animation studio, creating the first serialized Japanese cartoon series, which was later exported to America as *Astro Boy* in 1963. Tezuka Productions went on to create animated versions of *Kimba the White Lion* (*Jungle Emperor*) and *Phoenix*, among others.

He received numerous awards during his life, including the Bungei Shunju Manga Award, the Kodansha Manga Award, the Shogakukan Manga Award, and the Japan Cartoonists' Association Special Award for Excellence. He also served a variety of organizations. He was a director of the Japan Cartoonists' Association, the chairman of the Japan Animation Association, and a member of the Manga Group, Japan Pen Club, and the Japan SF Authors' Club, among others. Tezuka became Japan's "comics ambassador," taking Japan's comics culture to the world. In 1980, he toured and lectured in America, including a speech at the United Nations.

Regarded as a national treasure, Osamu Tezuka died on February 9, 1989 at the age of 60. In April 1994, the Osamu Tezuka Manga Museum opened in the city of Takarazuka, where he was raised. His creations remain hugely popular in Japan and are printed in many languages throughout the world, where he is acclaimed as one of the true giants of comics and animation, his work as vital and influential today as it was half a century ago.

"Comics are an international language," Tezuka said. "They can cross boundaries and generations. Comics are a bridge between all cultures."

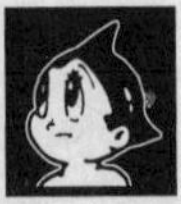